Invasion to Embassy

Land in Aboriginal Politics in New South Wales, 1770–1972

Heather Goodall

ALLEN & UNWIN
in association with
BLACK BOOKS

Publication of this title was assisted by The Australia Council, the Federal Government's arts funding and advisory body.

Australia Council
for the Arts

The assistance of Black Books, the Australian Academy of the Humanities and the Rona-Tranby Foundation for Oral History is gratefully acknowledged.

First published 1996
Allen & Unwin Pty Ltd
9 Atchison Street, St Leonards, NSW 2065 Australia
Phone: (61 2) 9901 4088
Fax: (61 2) 9906 2218
E-mail: 100252.103@compuserve.com

National Library of Australia
Cataloguing-in-Publication entry:

Goodall, Heather.
 Invasion to embassy: land in Aboriginal politics in New
 South Wales, 1770–1972.

 Bibliography.
 Includes index.
 ISBN 1 86448 149 8.

 1. Native title (Australia). 2. Aborigines, Australian—
 New South Wales—Government relations. 3. Aborigines,
 Australian—New South Wales—Land tenure. 4. Aborigines,
 Australian—New South Wales—Politics and government.
 I. Title.

333.208999150944

Set in 9.5/12 pt Arrus by DOCUPRO, Sydney
Printed by South Wind Productions, Singapore

10 9 8 7 6 5 4 3 2 1

Return to us this small portion of a vast territory which is ours by Divine Right.

—William Cooper, 1887, Cumeragunja

They'd only be spruikin' on land rights, that's all, on land rights . . . y'know. 'Why hasn't the Aboriginal people got land rights?', they said. 'The Aboriginal's cryin' out for land rights!'

—Jack Campbell, on the 1920s Land movement in NSW, Sydney, 1980

They gave us rations, a little bit of rations when the manager was here, but we still want this ground. We are hungry for our own ground.

We should have land, this is our land. We are hungry for our land.

—Milli Boyd, Woodenbong, 1972

Mutawintji: Closed by the owners

—Blockade notice written by Paakantji landowners, 'Mootawingee', 1983

Contents

Maps

Acknowledgments

There are many people whose assistance has been important in the work for this book, but my enduring gratitude goes to the Aboriginal and non-Aboriginal people who shared their memories and analyses with me over the years. They cannot be held responsible for its shortcomings, but each in their own way has shaped the content or the directions of this book.

I have been given great assistance by the Mitchell and State Libraries of NSW, the Australian Institute for Aboriginal and Torres Strait Islander Studies, the NSW Department of Aboriginal Affairs and the NSW State Archives. Permission to reproduce her diagram and valuable comments on a portion of the text were given by Nancy Williams. The maps for the book have been created with exemplary cartographic professionalism by Flexigraphics. Generous access to family albums, scrapbooks and personal memories was made available by the late Pearl Gibbs during 1981; by John Maynard and Cheryl Oakenful from Fred Maynard's family and by Rhoda Roberts, the daughter of Frank Roberts, Jnr.

The publication of this book has been supported by the Rona-Tranby Foundation for Oral History and the Australian Academy of the Humanities; this has contributed towards keeping costs low enough to ensure wide availability of the book to the Aboriginal communities who contributed time and support to its research.

I am deeply grateful to have been offered inspiration, endless patient teaching and warmly open family homes by many members of the Flick family but most constantly by Isabel Flick, and Joe and Isabel Flick and their families. I have been taught and supported with the same generous care by Jacko and Nan Campbell, Tombo Winters, Noeline and Jack Walford, Julie Whitton, Mavis and George Rose, Esse and Doc Coffee, Felix and Edna Hooper, Roy and June Barker, Margie-Ann Whyman, Dorie Hunter and her family, Ted and Ann Thomas, Milli Boyd, Jesse Williams, Phoebe Mumbler, Pat and Bill Cameron and Esther Alvares and Ian Cameron.

I have been stimulated and challenged over many years in shared projects with Karen Flick, Kevin Cook, Judy Chester, Terry Widders,

Acknowledgments

Brian Doolan, Gary Williams, Greg Davis, Marcia Langton, Delia Lowe, William Bates, Pat O'Shane, Phil Eyre and Lizzie Williams, Eric Wilson and Roslyn Barker, Greg Murphy, Jackie Huggins, Lester Bostock, Dick Buchhorn, Lilla Watson, Terry Fox, Jack Waterford, Fred Hollows, my colleagues Paula Hamilton and Ann Curthoys, Lyndall Ryan, Diane Barwick, Henry Reynolds, Carolyn Allport, Peter Read and Heather Radi. I am even more indebted to those who spent time in painstaking reading and offered important and enriching comments on drafts of this book: my heartfelt thanks go to Peter Thompson, Barbara Flick, Meredith Burgmann, Judy Torzillo, Kaye and Bob Bellear, David Hollinsworth, Jeremy Beckett, Faith Bandler and Jack Horner. The final shaping of the manuscript was undertaken by Venetia Somerset, whose sensitive editing was invaluable.

This work was nurtured by close friends who have now each been lost to tragic premature deaths: Peter Tobin, Lyn Thompson, Stephen Fitzpatrick and John Terry. There is a strong part of each of them in this book.

My family have all encouraged this work, but it would have been impossible without the deeply sustaining emotional and practical support of my parents-in-law, Judy and Jack Torzillo. My children have been loving and patient at the demands my work has made on my time with them, and they have constantly posed exciting questions about researching and writing the past. Above all, I am grateful to my husband Paul Torzillo, who has been my steady source of sensitive questions, penetrating insights, great jokes and warm support.

Heather Goodall
1996

A Note on Usage

When I am referring to indigenous people across New South Wales or Australia, I will use the words Aborigines or Aboriginal people as nouns and Aboriginal as an adjective, following Professor Eve Mumewa Fesl, 1995. When I am referring to the indigenous people of particular regions, however, I will refer to them by the words they currently use to name themselves. These derive from the local language words for 'person' or 'human being', but since the invasion they have come to mean 'one of us' or 'one of our people', that is, 'an Aboriginal person from our area'. They may also be used inclusively to refer to all Aboriginal people. These words are Koori, Murri and Wiimpatja in New South Wales, and I have chosen spellings which are recognisable to contemporary Aboriginal users, although a diversity of spellings exist. The areas in which these words are used, their pronunciation and the variations in their spelling are shown on Map 1, p. xii.

Pronunciation of Aboriginal words

The Aboriginal language groups referred to in the text are shown on Map 2, p. xiii. There are some useful guidelines to pronunciation which hold for most indigenous languages in Australia:

1) Stress for all words is on the first syllable
2) Vowels are short and are pronounced as in the following English words:
   a as in *cut*
   u as in *put*
   i as in *sit*.
   Long vowels are spelt by doubling the letter, as in Wiimpatja or Ngiyampaa.
3) The consonant pair *ng* represents one sound, and at the beginning of a word is pronounced exactly like the 'ng' in 'sing'.
4) Aboriginal language speakers do not distinguish between the voiced and unvoiced consonant pairs: *t* and *d*; *p* and *b*; *k* and *g*. They are therefore alternatives in the spelling of Aboriginal words. The same

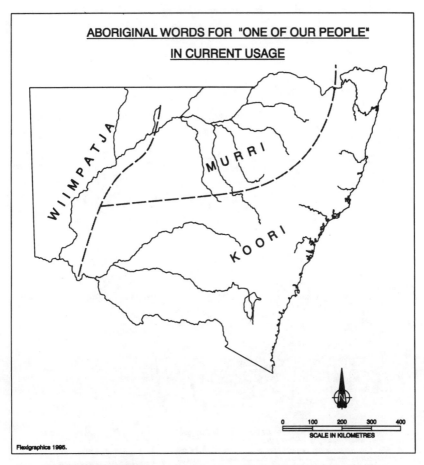

ABORIGINAL WORDS FOR "ONE OF OUR PEOPLE" IN CURRENT USAGE

Flexdgraphics 1995.

PRONUNCIATION

Murri: pronounced like the English word "Murray". It can be written as "Murrie" or as "Mari".

Koori: There are two regional variations in pronunciation. In the south coast and inland southern areas, as well as in Victoria, the first consonant sounds like an English "k". On the North Coast of NSW, the word is pronounced with the first consonant sounding like a hard "g". The word can be written as "Koorie", "Goori", "Goorie", "Kuri" or "Guri".

Wiimpatja: this word is pronounced with the stress on the first syllable, and the double "i" indicates a lengthened vowel.

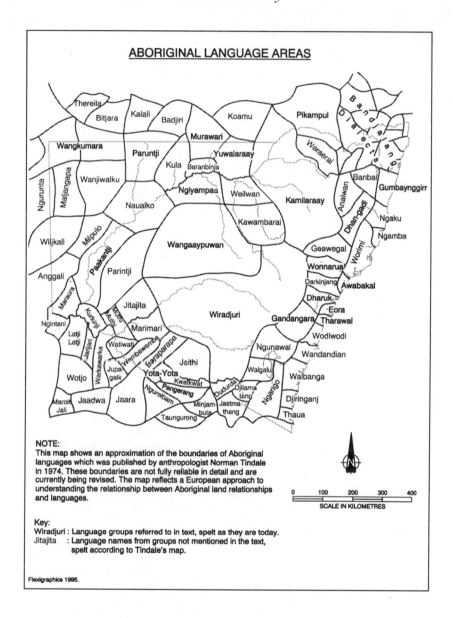

ABORIGINAL LANGUAGE AREAS

NOTE:
This map shows an approximation of the boundaries of Aboriginal languages which was published by anthropologist Norman Tindale in 1974. These boundaries are not fully reliable in detail and are currently being revised. The map reflects a European approach to understanding the relationship between Aboriginal land relationships and languages.

Key:
Wiradjuri : Language groups referred to in text, spelt as they are today.
Jitajita : Language names from groups not mentioned in the text, spelt according to Tindale's map.

Flexigraphics 1995.

word may be spelt either as Kamilaraay or as Gamilaraay; Paakantji or Baagandji; Yota-Yota or Yoda-Yoda. Communities developing consistent spelling systems generally choose to use either the unvoiced set (*t*, *p* and *k*) or the voiced set (*d*, *b* and *g*). Actual pronunciation may differ between individual speakers and may be influenced by original dialect differences.

Land terms

I have used the words 'country' and 'lands' interchangeably to refer to the area(s) for which Aboriginal people were the owners and custodians.

An area set aside as a 'reserve' for Aborigines was and is technically 'Crown Land Reserved for the Use of Aborigines'. The term 'reserve' was used by NSW administrations to refer to such land if it did not have a supervisory manager resident on it. Aborigines usually called such a place a 'reserve' but occasionally they called it a 'camp'.

The term 'camp' was more usually used by all parties to refer to an Aboriginal living area on land not reserved for Aborigines, which might sometimes be town common, sometimes vacant Crown land, sometimes land 'owned' privately by non-Aborigines, or land reserved for other purposes such as a travelling stock route or water reserve.

When the Protection or Welfare Board appointed a manager to live on a reserve and supervise the Aboriginal residents, the reserve became known as a 'station' in all official references. In most cases managed reserves ('stations') were known by both Aborigines and local whites as 'the Mission', despite the fact that the NSW government removed any church control over any reserved land in 1893, and from that time onwards missionaries came onto reserve and station land only at the invitation of the Board to conduct religious services. I have chosen to use the Board term 'station' to indicate clearly the secular authority and aims with which the Board managers and matrons implemented.

To avoid confusion, I refer to the pastoral concerns which are often called sheep or cattle 'stations' as 'pastoral properties' or 'properties'. The term 'stations' refers only to Board reserves with resident managers.

Abbreviations

AAF	Aboriginal–Australian Fellowship
AAL	Australian Aboriginal League
AAPA	Australian Aboriginal Progressive Association
ABC	Australian Broadcasting Corporation
ALP	Australian Labor Party
ANA	Australian Natives Association
APA	Aborigines Progressive Association
APB	Aboriginal Protection Board
APNR	Association for the Protection of Native Races
ASP	Australian Society of Patriots
AWU	Australian Workers' Union
CPA	Communist Party of Australia
DWO	district welfare officer
FAA	Foundation for Aboriginal Affairs
FCAA	Federal Council for Aboriginal Advancement
FCAATSI	Federal Council for the Advancement of Aborigines and Torres Strait Islanders
MLA	Member of the Legislative Assembly
P & C	Parents' and Citizens'
PWIU	Pastoral Workers' Industrial Union
SAFA	Student Action For Aborigines
TLC	Trades and Labor Council
VAAL	Victorian Aborigines Advancement League

Introduction

This book arises from research aimed initially at investigating Aboriginal politics in the public arena in New South Wales from the 1880s to the 1940s. As I carried out that work, I was struck by the continuity in Aboriginal statements of a strong interest in land and place. This contradicted the conventional wisdom, which is that after the initial defence of land during the early stages of the invasion, Aboriginal people in the south-east were politically dormant until the 1930s. Then, it is now acknowledged, they launched a campaign for equal civil rights, and in the process became involved in a series of alliances with white Christians and trade unionists. This south-eastern concern with the politics of equality continued into the 1950s and 1960s, with the campaign to change the Federal Constitution culminating in the referendum in 1967 and with the Freedom Ride in 1965. Only, we have been told, after the Northern Territory campaigns of the Yolngu people at Yirrkala in 1963 and the Gurindji in 1966, when the issue of land rights based on traditional ownership was introduced, did south-eastern Aboriginal people take up the call for land rights in their own areas.

In fact, as the archival records show, there have been frequent south-eastern Aboriginal expressions of their rights to and need for land, beginning at least as early as the mid-nineteenth century. These demands have been based on assertions of both traditional rights and the right to compensation for dispossession. Not only have there been formal written petitions or deputations to white officials, and later organised political bodies which made land a central platform, but there have also been many individual and community actions, some planned and some spontaneous, ranging from brief sit-ins and long-term squats to tenacious legal and physical battles. These actions confirm a persistent demand for land among Aboriginal people from the time the invasion violence eased.

In this book I trace some dimensions of those land issues in Aboriginal politics in New South Wales. I discuss many different political movements, from formal organisations to spontaneous grassroots actions. In some, land has been the principal issue, but for many others land

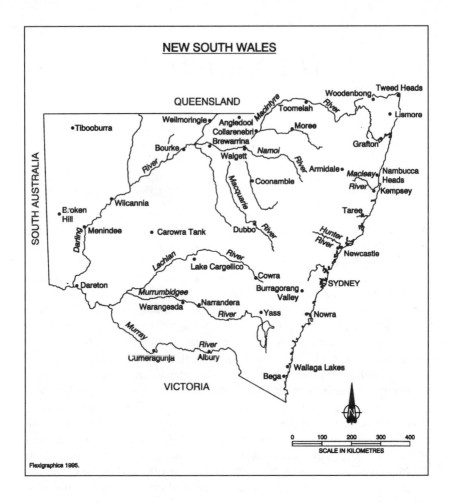

NEW SOUTH WALES

QUEENSLAND

SOUTH AUSTRALIA

VICTORIA

Tweed Heads
Woodenbong
Lismore
Toomelah
Moree
Weilmoringle
Angledool
Collarenebri
Brewarrina
Grafton
Tibooburra
Bourke
Walgett
Namoi
Armidale
Macleay
Nambucca Heads
Coonamble
Kempsey
Wilcannia
Taree
Broken Hill
Menindee
Carowra Tank
Dubbo
Hunter River
Newcastle
Lake Cargellico
Cowra
Dareton
Murrumbidgee
Narrandera
Burragorang Valley
SYDNEY
Warangesda
Yass
Nowra
Murray
River
Cumeragunja
Albury
Wallaga Lakes
Bega

Macintyre River
River
Macquarie River
Lachlan River
Darling River

0   100   200   300   400
SCALE IN KILOMETRES

Flexigraphics 1995.

has been one element in a platform of goals. My analysis considers the reasons for the changing balances between the various demands in Aboriginal political platforms, as well as the effect both allies and opponents have had in Aboriginal decisions about how to present their often complex goals.

These broad platforms of political aims have often reflected Aboriginal interests in issues of civil rights and equality of access to resources and services, at the same time as asserting Aboriginal prior rights in land. Aboriginal activists have not felt any contradiction between the two types of demands. They have usually presented their civil political standing and authority as arising from their prior custodianship of their lands.

I do not expect to be able to record here all that land means and has meant for Aboriginal people. As a historian I deal with scattered sources and distant periods, so the glimpses I gain about the past are always fragmentary and usually represent only the most public aspects of any debate. As a Celtic Australian, I have been brought up with different cultural experiences from those of Aboriginal Australians, and so I am far from being able to interpret cultural or political meanings on behalf of Aboriginal landholders. What I do hope to do is to record and analyse what Aboriginal people have said publicly about their goals and what they have done to achieve them.

Even within these limitations, the exploration of the way the land issue has threaded its way through Aboriginal politics since the invasion raises many fruitful questions. These illuminate both Aboriginal and non-Aboriginal history in south-eastern Australia. This book sets out to explore some of those questions.

First, while land is a constant presence in Aboriginal political demands, the *ideas* of land expressed in these public debates have been varied and complex. Sometimes land has been demanded as a concrete goal, with particular areas in mind; at the same time land might be also an ideal and a rallying call, a symbol of both rightful possession and unjust dispossession, and as well a focal point for identification. At times the demand has been urgent, an insistence that land is the immediate goal of the movement. At other times it has become a longer-term goal, while other demands, such as equality of wages and political rights, have been seen as urgent. A central question is why such shifts in public priority have occurred. Do they reflect changing interests in land among Aboriginal people? Or do they reflect changes in the context in which Aboriginal demands were being made?

Second, the demand for land has not always been put forward with equal force across the State. Often it has been a regional Aboriginal movement which has raised the land issue with most urgency or persistence, a call which may or may not have been taken up by organisations representing Aboriginal people in other regions. Decades later, a very different regional pattern of demand for land rights had often emerged, with Aboriginal spokespeople from another area of the State being the ones to raise and press the land issue. What caused these differences? Did they arise from different traditional relations to land? Or from changing pressures on Aboriginal people in different regions of the State? Or again from differing strategic decisions about how to express Aboriginal interests?

Third, there have been shifts in the composition of the allies Aboriginal movements have found among white Australians. Some groups have endorsed Aboriginal land demands in one period and opposed them in others. Why have these changes occurred? What has led these different white interest groups and organisations to favour or condemn Aboriginal land aspirations?

These questions demand a consideration of Aboriginal land interests which recognises their historicity, the ways they arise from particular historical contexts. Aboriginal people have been engaged in the changing conditions of life under colonialism, developing new strategies and imagining new futures for themselves at the same time as sustaining fundamental elements of their aspirations. So the expression of Aboriginal land demands reflects such changes as well as continuity.

Considering these questions about Aboriginal political demands for land leads inevitably to reflecting on the importance of land as an idea as well as a commodity for white Australians. Land has been a central element of political debate and desire for different groups of white Australians too over many years of colonial experience.

The Aboriginal demands for land were never expressed in a vacuum. Instead, they were interventions into that mainstream discourse about land, its values, its rightful or desirable possessors and its meanings. The nineteenth-century debates over squatting and free selection, with their implications for social formations and the changing face of political and economic life, influenced the ways Aboriginal spokespeople chose to frame their demands for land. Later, the shifts in rural technology and the dreams of massive irrigation schemes to increase the productivity of the land were the context for Aboriginal decisions about strategies for making their claims. Throughout the twentieth century, the wilderness and environmental movements, with all their contradictions and shifts in meaning, have been a fertile field of engagement for Aboriginal land interests.

This exploration has involved a reflection on my own interests and motives in supporting south-eastern Aboriginal land aspirations during the 1970s and 1980s. What was it that white Australians like myself found attractive, even compelling, in the Aboriginal land movements of the time? Acknowledging the needs for Aboriginal people to be formulating their own demands, we supported their strong push for land. This left us needing to reconcile our own liberal egalitarian positions with Aboriginal arguments for access to land which rest on prior and overriding traditional rights for indigenous custodians as well as on grounds of historical disadvantage. Were we seeking to cement our own relationships with Aboriginal people by endorsing unquestioningly their priorities for the land? Or were we seeking through them to clarify and perhaps strengthen our own tenuous, often imaginary, relationship to the land? How far did our needs and interests influence the expression of Aboriginal demands? And if our starting points have been complex, what has been the effect on us of our involvement? Are there fruitful syntheses to be found between these divergent political positions? What have we learnt from this engagement with Aboriginal people and the land?

Such questions provide the threads which run through the book, linking each segment. This is not quite a continuous narrative, although all my training and impulses are to try to make it one. I have chosen successive periods of high Aboriginal political activity to explore the nature of the land issues present. A number of these periods are separated by times of lesser activity, or at least less surviving evidence, and so the continuities in personnel and direct organisational links are often impossible to trace even if they were there. In any case, as I have sought to follow Aboriginal land politics over close to two centuries, each of these periods has had to be researched in different ways. The 1860s and 1870s, for example, are accessible only by documentary sources. Many of these were written by non-Aborigines whose relationship to Aboriginal people was at best ambivalent and at worst repressive. Even the interestingly high number written by Aboriginal people themselves were usually petitions written for an official audience, which is reflected in their language and structure. In contrast, the 1920s has a greater diversity of Aboriginal-authored material, as well as illuminations from memory, with some Aboriginal people alive in the early 1980s who could recall a few of the 1920s activists and the campaigns they fought over their lands. The 1950s are different again. There are still many people living who have memories of involvement in those complex times. Their reflections can be considered in relation to the material created in the process of surveillance by the NSW Welfare Board or ASIO.

The parts of the book are therefore more like a series of 'moments' in Aboriginal politics than a continuous story. Each period has different sets of sources, with their own range of information and their own silences. So each 'moment' has a different perspective, but in each I concentrate on tracing Aboriginal political expressions and actions, on asking how land issues emerge and why. In each I also suggest the contemporary white debates and concepts about land and the ways the Aboriginal and non-Aboriginal debates interacted, exploring alliances and oppositions.

It is necessary first, however, to establish the basis on which the dynamic interactions between Aboriginal people and their colonisers have occurred. Chapter 1 draws on recent work in many parts of Australia to suggest the complex roles land has played in Aboriginal religious, social, cultural and political life in New South Wales. Arising from this, I suggest possible directions in which Aboriginal people might have sought to use land economically, socially, culturally and politically to establish meaningful continuities in the very changed circumstances of colonisation. I use the words 'owners' and 'custodians' interchange-ably to indicate Aboriginal holders of traditional 'native title'. The concept of 'custodians' carries the sense of obligation which is so heavily engaged with Aboriginal concepts of landholding (see Chapter 1), while the word 'owners' implies the full and righful possession which is also undoubtedly central to the Aboriginal concepts. Where I am discussing the colonising society's concept of landholding, which is that land is a commodity to be bought and sold with the agreement of the state, and whose ownership confers no obligations, I indicate that it is Europeans' or white peoples' ownership to which I refer.

In the first of the historical moments, Part I, I discuss the often violent processes of invasion and resistance and the very different ways they occurred in different regions. But I want to look beyond the ruptures caused by the brutality, to see the continuities possible despite the massive impact of the invasion on Aboriginal life. By exploring a number of case studies, I suggest those continuities which were demon-strated when Aboriginal people began to re-establish themselves after the worst violence of the invasion had eased.

The second moment, Part II, traces the impact of intensifying agriculture on Aboriginal communities in the east and south-west of the State, and their resulting campaigns to restore and protect their contin-ued access to some of their own country. From the 1860s to the 1890s, they adopted many strategies, from petitions to government to the direct action of squatting on their lands. They began building and farming, creating a modest base from within their own cultural framework from which to engage with the emerging white Australian society and econ-omy. These were Aboriginal victories, however completely they were later to be erased from the memory of the non-Aboriginal public. The traces these victories left in documents and on various official maps allow us to see a widespread movement by Aboriginal people to regain their land.

The third moment, Part III, traces the increasingly desperate Aborig-inal defence of those regained lands from the 1910s to the late 1920s. A rising white population, Federation zeal and closer-settlement rhetoric had intensified pressure on the pockets of Aboriginal farming land. Their responses varied widely, from individual resistance and refusal to be evicted, to legal battles, through to attempts to negotiate concessions with the State government bureaucracies which implemented the evic-tions. Yet inexorably, these bitterly defended patches of land were taken into white possession. The Aboriginal farmers of the coastal areas moved beyond individual resistance and formed a political organisation, with a membership network spread along the seaboard. Their demands are recorded in archives and in press reports, and, for the first time, there are fragments of correspondence between Aboriginal people suggesting how they expressed their goals internally.

Part IV explores the 1930s, a very different time when the lands defended in the previous decade had all but gone in a second dispossession, and the Depression had totally altered the conditions faced by Aboriginal people all over the State. This turbulent period saw not only a new set of regional political organisations representing Aboriginal people, but a wave of political actions at community level, many of them in the western areas of the pastoral industry. In the 1930s, however, changes in the pastoral industry saw these people faced with intense pressure to leave their land, some forced into cattle trucks and shipped hundreds of miles away from their own country. Their resistance took many forms, but often it was the most direct, grassroots response of escape and return, demonstrating the tenacity with which they were intent on defending their contacts with their land.

Part V traces the issue of land through a set of struggles more usually seen as being about civil rights and equality: the segregation of rural towns, and particularly residential segregation. The marks of both the defeats and the victories of the prewar decades can be seen in the demands and tactics of the Aboriginal political movements of the 1950s and 1960s. Press reports, Aboriginal correspondence and activists' memories reveal a diverse and shifting situation. The period was one in which many Aboriginal people tried to manoeuvre so that they could retain access to their land. Yet it was also a time when many reluctantly made the decision to move away from their home country, often for ever. This diaspora did not, however, sever their connections with their land: some Aboriginal people continued to nurture their relationship with both land and kin back home, while others sought to locate themselves socially and morally by negotiating a land relationship in their new homes.

Despite the public representations of Aboriginal political interests as being equality of civil rights, the resurgence of land as an issue among Aboriginal people in the south-east was quite obvious by the mid-1950s, arising from the particular changing pressures in this intensely colonised part of Australia. The attention of many whites and some Aboriginal activists was focused on campaigns such as the Freedom Ride in 1965, and then the referendum in 1967, both campaigns to win acknowledgment as citizens. Yet on Australia Day 1972, Aboriginal people from New South Wales set up the Tent Embassy, that most powerful symbol of their sense of exclusion from the nation and from their own land. Part VI explores the way Aboriginal activists chose to demonstrate the authority for the Tent Embassy by making a journey through eastern New South Wales to record the cherished desires for traditional lands held by their elders and fellow community members. These testimonies in 1972 open up the range of meanings land held for Aboriginal people 200 years after Cook's landing began the British invasion. These meanings, some conserved unchanged and others emergent from the tragedies and victories of those years of colonisation, were the ground on which the Aboriginal communities of New South Wales went on to re-establish, yet again, their Land Rights movement.

1
Land and Meanings

The invasion of Australia by Britain in 1788 is usually seen as either the beginning of the story of settler progress or the end of the story of Aboriginal civilisation. Yet while the invasion forced great changes onto Aboriginal societies, Aboriginal people were not wiped out, and they drew on their cultural, social and economic knowledge to negotiate the directions for their varied futures. This chapter explores the ways in which land holds and makes meaning for Aboriginal societies. The many-faceted role of land in Aboriginal culture meant that there were possibilities for continuity as well as the discontinuities which the invasion caused in south-eastern Australia.

THE INSCRIPTION OF CULTURE ONTO LAND

The significance of land to Aboriginal people is often expressed in ways which focus on its religious meanings, the power of the spiritual values it holds. While this spiritual dimension is central, there are additional, complementary dimensions to Aboriginal relations to land. These include the role land plays in social relations, political relations, and in the cultural construction and transmission of knowledge. Such categories reflect the Western distinction between the secular and the religious, and from within Aboriginal cultures this distinction may mean very little. A close look at the secular dimensions of the role of land does become important, however, in understanding how Aboriginal societies have responded to the massive disruptions caused by the invasion.

There are few sources to reveal the complex relations of Aboriginal people with their lands in the south-east before 1778. Those which do exist are fragments, localised and heavily shaped by the limitations of their authors' knowledge. Early observers were increasingly caught up in the bitterness of border wars or the debates surrounding them, while later ethnographers were intent on 'salvage' and often failed to account for dynamic change over a century of colonisation. All of them were asking very different questions from those we might ask today.

These works are only useful if they are read in relation to the large body of recent work which has arisen in northern and central Australia. Some has been prompted by changing debates in Western politics and philosophy, such as the inquiry into the rights and status of women. Far more has been the result of the political and legal demands of the land rights courts in the Northern Territory, which have required a clarified European understanding of Aboriginal landholding. Aboriginal people now have a very direct motivation to explain how they see their relations with the land. This has led them to participate as never before in teaching white commentators. The result has been massive changes in the paradigms of Aboriginal landholding, inheritance, boundaries, the rights and obligations of owners, as well as a better appreciation of the role of Aboriginal women in ceremony and land custodianship.

Some insights into Aboriginal landholding arising from this recent work can be widely generalised and are consistent with the fragments of knowledge available about south-eastern land relations.

Land as an economic resource

An obvious point is that the land and its products were the basic economic resource of its Aboriginal owners before the invasion. No Aboriginal society, however, was passive in harvesting this resource; there were many techniques used to regularise and increase the numbers and growth of game and plants. These were allocated in particular ways according to religious and kinship practices, and harvesting them enabled the economic independence and autonomy of the land's custodians. The productivity of the land and the health of its owners were not assumed; they were believed to depend on the custodians fulfilling their obligations to care for the land by performing the proper ceremonies and ensuring that the land was used in proper ways. Central Australian Aboriginal perceptions of well-cared-for land are described in Aboriginal English terms such as 'quiet', indicating land which is actively used and managed by its Aboriginal owners, tended in ceremonies, hunted and harvested appropriately, with flourishing native flora and game, and regularly burnt out to 'clean' it.[1]

Religious knowledge embodied in and inscribed onto land

A fundamental principle of the Aboriginal worldview is that land is seen to embody profound religious and philosophical knowledge. The 'Dreaming' is a widely used Aboriginal English term for this knowledge, but each Aboriginal language has a word which expresses the concept more accurately. In Western Desert languages, for example, the word *Tjukurpa* is usually translated as 'Law', and conveys a sense of the profound authority as well as sacredness which the Dreaming knowledge holds. It is composed of a body of oral tradition held in memory and taught in performance as the words and music of songs, as painting and dance. All of these performed works are celebrations of and communications with the continuously existing Dreamings about which they speak. Dreaming events are set in a period long past, far beyond everyday experiences of time, but this 'dreaming time' also continues, separate from everyday time but parallel to it.

Some songs and performances in any Aboriginal society's canon of oral tradition are learned from and exchanged with other people, often rapidly and across great distances.[2] A greater proportion of such a society's body of law and oral tradition, however, is tied very directly to the land which that group owns. The stories and songs are occasionally about events associated with a single site, but far more often they celebrate journeys across country. These are travels made by ancestral figures, in human and non-human form or both, during which they are engaged in epic struggles of competition, love and conflict, sometimes creating landforms as they go. Some sense of these Dreaming figures is embodied within the sites at which each episode of their journey occurred, but they often come to rest at some final point, where they and much of the power associated with them continue to exist. Dreaming journeys have been called tracks, strings, pathways by Aboriginal people, and they can all be mapped out onto the countries they cross. The knowledge then is both embodied in and inscribed onto the land.

Sometimes Aboriginal people will travel along these Dreaming tracks, following the journey, stopping at the focal site of each episode, recounting what knowledge is permissible to speak to those around, tending the places that need attention. This may be a deliberate tracing of the Dreaming, or it may occur in the process of using the lands for harvesting food and teaching young people about their country. Often the Dreaming stories are told in ceremonies in which the songs of long travels are performed by those who have the responsibility for singing and teaching them. The events associated with each site will be clustered into adjacent stanzas. Even when the performance occurs far from any of the places it names, its audience will follow the story's path across the land in their imagination as well as following the narrative thread of the song and drawing out its meanings for themselves.

These Law journeys are powerful dramas of ethical and emotional struggles, as well as physical conflicts, between the great protagonists of the creation stories. They teach Aboriginal people to see an animate and enlivened landscape where landforms, watercourses and trees convey not just their outward shapes but the excitement and power of the ancestral figures whose essence they embody. As Aboriginal people grow

3

in learning, progressing through the stages of initiation and induction into the deepest meanings of their oral tradition, there is a strengthening sense of the immanence of these great dramas, and their constant dynamic presence in the land. During ceremonial re-enactments, elderly men and women of high knowledge at times seem totally immersed in the pleasure as well as the power of these great narratives as they teach younger people the songs and meanings they have learnt.

Environmental knowledge

The knowledge in Dreaming journey stories is intimately related to the particular lands which form its framework. It has long been known that this oral tradition carried information about the environment, the climate and the habits of game and edible plants. A song may have many references to ecological relationships between species, indicating seasonal times for harvesting, or recording correspondences between the activity of one species which provides a signal that another unrelated species is ready for harvest. Only now, however, as more detailed ecological studies are done, is it becoming apparent just how precise some of this information may be. A. E. Newsome, a zoologist working in central Australia, has recorded minute details of the red kangaroo habitat in the MacDonnell Ranges, and compared his findings with the oral traditions of the Arrernte landowners concerning the journeys of their Red Kangaroo ancestral figures. Newsome found that

> a map of the ancestors' overland trek, breathing life and form into the
> landscape as they went, corresponded with uncanny precision to maps of
> the preferred habitats of red kangaroo . . . Conversely, a map of the
> subterranean portions of the ancestors' Dreamtime journeys, during
> which their radiant powers diminished, corresponded neatly with
> expanses of desert lands largely inhospitable to red kangaroo populations.[3]

The Arrernte oral tradition incorporated an effective conservation mechanism. The hunting of the red kangaroo was forbidden in the vicinity of the sacred site associated with the ancestral Red Kangaroo's emergence from the underground part of its journey. This site was in fact located within the most favourable habitat for the species, and so the controls over human harvesting ensured the red kangaroo was protected near its best habitat.

Such detailed knowledge may not be consciously presented by its holders as 'custodial' or 'environmental' information. Nevertheless it has provided a huge body of management guidance for Aboriginal landowners who are both informed and motivated to care for their land by their most respected philosophical texts.

Historical knowledge and interpretation inscribed onto land

The view of Dreaming knowledge from within Aboriginal cultures is that it is received knowledge from the distant past, and cannot be changed in the everyday experience of the 'present' time that recent generations know. A relation between events witnessed by humans and the Dreaming knowledge is demonstrated by the presence of stories about ancient and large-scale events such as rising sea levels and changing river courses, but these events occurred so long ago that they are easily reconciled with a belief in the immutability of the Dreaming.

Yet recent events too are able to be drawn into Dreamings, under conditions which involve wide agreement that such knowledge is significant.[4] The memories of individuals and the shared recollections of communities do not hold fragmented scraps of observed data about events. Instead, as people share and discuss their memories together, they interpret events, from their cultural knowledge and previous experiences, to give them meaning and coherence.[5] These interpretations may then go on to shape their later actions and interpretations, feeding back into and ultimately changing the cultural knowledge which shaped them in the first place.[6] The knowledge which may enter into the Dreaming oral tradition will then be a complex of observed data and the interpretations woven from them, already a creation of the interaction of culture and event.

An example of the process of incorporating interpretive accounts of recent events into Dreamings may be found by comparing the numerous Aboriginal analytical accounts of the invasion which use the central figure of Captain Cook to represent white power and authority. Many come from northern Australia, despite the fact that Cook did not travel to that area. Yet Aboriginal historians have seized on the enormous significance attached to the Cook figure in the white Australian historical dogma of courageous exploration and peaceful settlement and, inverting the image, have made him the central figure in their very different account of invasion and repression.[7]

The particular ways such newly developed interpretations are drawn into Dreaming stories are complex and vary from society to society, but some fundamentals seem to be widespread. First, whether the initial expression of a new interpretation or story is one of individual or group creation, it will only become a part of the body of Dreaming oral tradition by a process of community endorsement. This may be a very slow process, perhaps across generations, of reaching consensus on whether events and the meanings they embody are significant enough to be drawn into the existing weave of Dreamings.

Second, the place of such new material in the body of knowledge will be determined partly by its content and meaning. Accounts of

5

events or new interpretations may be incorporated into existing Dreaming stories as new episodes or stanzas, because they are seen as consistent with its themes.[8] This process troubles Western-trained historians, who try to interpret oral traditions but who depend on dates and chronologies to order their material and to explain causation. Incorporating events into Dreaming will strip the story of its markers in 'real', datable time, and locate it instead as an episode within the narrative sequence of the existing song cycle, making it usually impossible to link such accounts to any Western form of 'history'.

Third, while content may determine which Dreaming story will be the home for new knowledge, the organising framework for the re-arrangement of the story will continue to be the land itself. Dissociated from the chronological sequence of 'real' time, new material becomes organised instead according to where events occurred, and enters the Dreaming song in the stanzas which relate to the site of the incident. The Dreaming journey's path across the land becomes the organising principle for the placement of new information into that song.

This organisation of new historical knowledge by its relation to place as well as theme has been described now by a number of authors.[9] Perhaps the most graphic account has been given by Marcia Langton, who has described two events, one in the 1930s and another in the 1980s, in which Kimberley Aboriginal men suffered severe government punishment when they tried to defend Aboriginal Law against white transgression. Song stanzas about these two events have been incorporated into a far older song cycle which told the story of the epic journey of two ancestral Law men from the east to the west Kimberley as they brought traditional Law to these lands. The stanzas about the recent events were incorporated into this story because they addressed the same deep and difficult questions about Law and right behaviour in hard, challenging times. Each of the recent stories was drawn in at the point in the traditional narrative where the ancestral figures reached the place where the historical events had happened, because this was the Dreaming about the Law in relation to that specific country. In this way, the analysis of historical event was being inscribed onto the land.[10]

Kin relations inscribed onto land

In Aboriginal societies, people are closely identified with their lands and the animal and plant species on them. Aboriginal philosophies do not have a deep dichotomy between 'man' and 'nature' or 'culture' and 'nature' as European traditions do. Association with land must therefore mean associations with other people and with other, non-human, living species. Relations with non-humans may arise from a person's birth site being near a place associated with a particular animal or plant, or it may arise from the inherited 'totem' or 'meat' which defines one's relation to an ancestral figure who was transformed between human and animal form during their mythic journeys which in turn created the landforms. 'Within each clan, human and animal are bound together by common descent, mutual concern and shared destiny.'[11] These associations between human and non-human tie Aboriginal people inextricably within the network of other living species, the ecosystem which is adapted to its particular habitat, its lands. The structure of relationships within which an Aboriginal person identifies themselves is not then a solely human-focused one.

An Aboriginal person will have a number of different ways to gain their relationship to land. There are vertical relationships, which arise because an Aboriginal man or woman receives some of their rights to country by inheritance through their father's or mother's side, and in some societies, in ambilineal inheritance from both. There are also relationships which occur horizontally, within generations. These are not random, but arise from the ongoing social processes of marriage and birth. They may be built up with a high degree of attention and care, as Rose has observed in central Australia: 'Usually people arrange marriages to maximise their ties to different countries, creating overlapping networks of rights and responsibilities'.[12] So it is reasonably predictable that the owner of one country will fall into a particular kin relationship with the owners of nearby lands. Another important way in which rights in land are acquired are from one's conception or birth site. Further, minor sources of interest in land arise from the conception and birth sites of one's children, and from the burial sites of parents and close relatives.

These will all bring a person into association with the owners of adjacent countries. Then the performance of ceremonies, and the teaching of the young people who will succeed to the custodianship of both songs and the country they celebrate, requires mutual co-operation and collaboration, for most songs traverse many people's countries and involve custodians for each of the stretches of country and its associated stanzas. Owners will know well not only the sections of songs for the country with which they are most closely associated, but also the preceding and following stanzas for adjacent countries.

Many authors have written about this carefully negotiated congruence of land relations and the custodianship of ceremonial story. Ken Maddock has generalised to say that 'Australia is covered with cultural compositions, in each of which a named portion of earth [a place], a named portion of life [a species] and a named portion of society [a group] are together indissolubly'.[13]

In her description of Yolngu society in north-east Arnhem Land,

Nancy Williams has been able to represent graphically the relationship between land estates and kin groups.[14] It is possible that this relationship can be most readily visualised in the fertile coastal regions where high productivity may allow people to be related to relatively small, tightly defined areas of land. The central Australian savannah lands of the Walpiri are less fertile, but similar graphic representations of their land–kin relationship have been made by Meggitt, who represents it as a vertical sequence of superimposed grids.[15] Rose, who is also describing grasslands people, gives a similar account: 'Country is the nexus of individuals, social groups, Dreamings, nourishing relationships, birth and death. Conversely, an individual is a nexus of countries'.[16] In the Yarralin community, people use land to explain social relationships, equating not only individuals but social, classificatory groups with the land itself. Rose describes how Dora Jilpngarri explained the relations between kin and place in a discussion about possible marriage partners: 'Your relations, that's one country. You can't marry'.[17]

The situation in desert areas needs to be more flexible, to cope with the extreme conditions and consequently variable productivity of the land. The lands with which any one person may be associated are more extensive in such areas, and the system may allow for active rights over a number of lands at a time. Fred Myers, describing the arid Western Desert, argues that individual autonomy as well as group relatedness is an essential aspect of all social and political interactions in Pintupi life, yet he also describes both of these as being inscribed onto the land:

> In the end, ownership of country—denoting close association among a set of individuals—projects into transhistorical time the valued social relations of the present . . . Ultimately, landownership is tied to a politics that emphasises both the claims of relatedness and those of personal autonomy.

Among the Pintupi, people view *country* as an objectification of kin networks and as a record of social ties.[18] Myers explains that the Pintupi refer to places and their stories by the 'subsection' or 'skin' name of the owner of that place.[19] This means that not only are the journeys of the Dreaming figures and their stories mapped onto the land, as well as being embodied in it, but so too is the complex kin structure of Aboriginal societies.

Land then is central to Aboriginal self-identification on many levels because it forms the physical and symbolic basis on which one is *related*: related to religious knowledge and practice, related to one's kin and wider society, related to one's history and to the economic resources to which one is entitled by right.

8

The nature of landholding: obligations and rights

It seems clear that Aboriginal societies developed a precise, although complex, concept of landholding. It was very different from the European concept of land as individually owned private property, a commodity to be bought, sold, and used to generate capital. This Western concept of land as private possession is itself very recent, only developing in the same century that saw the white invasion of Australia. Creating private property in land in England was a slow process of usurping older and long-established notions in which multiple rights in land were recognised, including those of common usage.[20]

In Aboriginal societies, individual men and women hold particular relationships to land, inherited from parents and arising from their own conception and birth sites. The implications of that landholding may differ for men and women, in that the consequent responsibilities for ceremonial performance and teaching may lie in parallel, sex-segregated ceremonial cycles, as happens in Western Desert societies, or may involve subsidiary roles for women within a unified ceremonial system, as is more often the case in Arnhem Land.[21] Nevertheless, women's rights in land are substantial, and in central Australia include custodianship of particular sites associated with the social and health interests of women.[22]

Yet despite the specificity of these relationships, they do not allow automatic rights. Instead they confer obligations and responsibilities. Owners must care for the land and the living beings, including the people, associated with it. 'Holding' or 'caring for' the land implies many things, but usually means that custodians will learn, perform and teach the ceremonies belonging to the Dreamings for that land; they will protect the land, its species and people from damage and unauthorised use; and they will husband the land, use it, harvest it and do the things it needs, such as burning, to maintain its productivity.[23]

These responsibilities may not always be taken up. A person may hold rights to a number of countries, inherited from both parents, but live mainly on one. This means they can only fulfil their obligations as custodians fully in one area, allowing their rights in other lands to remain secondary to those of the people who both hold rights in that land and are able to fulfil its demands. The process of becoming a full custodian is one which takes time. Myers concludes: 'Landowning in the Western Desert . . . is not a given, but an accomplishment'.[24] Rose makes the same point: 'Such a relationship is built up over time through knowledge and the assumption of responsibility . . . A person is born with rights, but each must choose further to develop their own relationships with country'.[25]

It is the fulfilment of one's obligations, the active embracing of

9

responsibility, which allows a custodian to be accorded the fullest benefits of their landholding role: political authority for that land, which involves an increasing ceremonial seniority and standing, and political autonomy and personal sovereignty. The custodian decides who may have permission for the economic use of his or her country, and has the right to be consulted over social and political issues which affect it.[26] Such high political authority gained over one area could not be transferred to another. Landholding confers wide rights and powers but only as an outcome of the active fulfilment of one's responsibilities and only in relation to one's own country.

All Aboriginal societies had to face the possibility that the normal processes of succession to ownership would fail, whether because of infertility, deaths by disease, or by incapacity to fulfil obligations. As we could expect in a culture which has flourished for so long, there was normally enough flexibility to cope with this: people with secondary rights to an area could assume full responsibility. Neither would the complex ceremonial knowledge of an area suffer if an owner could not fulfil obligations: close relatives who were well versed in the songs of a site, and adjacent landowners who would have participated in the ceremonies, could step in.[27] Both Myers and Payne, writing on Western Desert men's and women's rites and land respectively, observed that the death of a significant song-owner could lead to vigorous contestation for succession among a number of people with substantial claims.[28]

There is evidence now from post-invasion times that if an owner fails to carry out responsibilities, they may be challenged to forfeit their rights by others who feel they hold entitlements for that country and are better able to fulfil the obligations of custodianship. While it seems that competitive acquisition of territory was not normal, there was and is the potential for strong negotiation over ownership, which ensures that fulfilment of obligations will be maximised.[29]

In more traditional communities, political standing and authority seem expected to be manifested in landholding, to flow from successful fulfilment of obligations and ceremonial responsibilities. Invasion has created many situations where Aboriginal people have been forced onto other people's lands, and in some there have been negotiated settlements around custodianship. At Warabri, in the Northern Territory, Walpiri visitors continued to assert their ownership of their own distant lands and did not assume an owner's role for local areas, but instead developed a type of political power by becoming brokers between the European invaders and the Anmatye-Kaytitj landowners. In the Pilbara, however, migrants from the inland desert areas gradually came to assume direct relations to the local lands, either by incorporation into local kin networks by marriage and engagement in ceremony, or by more direct negotiation with landholders to take on some of their responsibilities and so, eventually, some of their political authority.[30]

LAND AND ABORIGINAL PEOPLE IN THE SOUTH-EAST

We can now ask how the insights from the recent work allow us to read the fragments of evidence available about land relationships and their meanings in the south-east. Are the patterns from the northern and central areas of the continent always relevant to the south-east at the time of invasion? And if so, how did they then change or develop under the impact of invasion?

The main sources for answering the first question are the objects and material left by Aboriginal people of the time, which we can analyse archaeologically, and the writings and drawings of the early Europeans in the south-east. Both these sources are limited. Objects can tell us only so much about activities in the past, and we must then speculate about the beliefs which lay behind them. The writings of white colonisers were strongly shaped by their assumptions about 'nomadic' 'savages' and 'hunters and gatherers'. These ideas always told more about European thought than the realities of any colonised peoples' lives, and once in Australia, colonists' impressions were further distorted by ignorance of Aboriginal languages, misinterpretation of customary practices and, as invasion warfare intensified, by hostility and fear. Yet both types of evidence offer at least broad suggestions about Aboriginal relations to their lands.

Archaeological studies suggest some significant differences in relations between land and society in the Aboriginal south-east when compared to the European colony, which developed by clinging to the coastal fringe and looking backwards along maritime networks to a distant metropolis. For Aboriginal people, the south-east coast was certainly well populated, but it was the inland rivers which carried the largest communities and which were the homes of technologically innovative societies as well as the most active traders of material goods and intellectual property.

No Aboriginal societies were wholly dependent on 'nature', and each had developed its own strategies and technologies for increasing the carrying capacity of its lands. These led to marked differences in Aboriginal lifestyle between regions. The grasslands people of the central areas, such as the Kamilaraay, Wiradjuri, Ngiyampaa and Paakantji, used firestick farming extensively to enhance the grass-seed crop, thereby increasing both the game which fed on the grass shoots and the grain which was harvested and stored for later use.[31] Where their lands encompassed the Darling River system, engineering works like the

11

extensive Brewarrina fisheries were constructed to maintain a consistent yield of fish no matter how dry or flooded the rivers might be.[32] Such grasslands people moved substantial distances over their broad countries, their patterns of movement planned according to the economic and cultural knowledge stored in their oral traditions. They were engaged in active trading networks, supplementing their tools and other goods from far distant quarries and coastal regions. Mulvaney has pointed out that the Darling River and adjacent Flinders Ranges area, where seed harvesting and storage was so sophisticated, 'combined the greatest population mobility with the greatest opportunity for meeting people or receiving goods from distant regions, funnelling along the great waterways'.[33]

The lands surrounding the Murray River were used even more intensively. Aboriginal people of the Yota-Yota and other language groups had developed such sustained harvesting of the rich fish, game and plants there that they lived virtually sedentary lives in villages which were observed by the earliest white explorers. Their strategies were successful enough to have developed a dense population, although the sedentary nature of their lifestyle made them vulnerable to the diseases of scarcity found more often in early agricultural societies than in harvesting populations like grasslands Aboriginal people.[34]

Archaeological analyses also suggest the interest in both exchange and innovation which had been present before the European invasion. Rapid and widespread exchange of goods and ideas—in, for example, the form of elaborate, newly created song performances—over well-established trading networks are demonstrated in the archaeological record and were witnessed by Europeans to be continuing over the first century of colonisation.[35] This is suggested by Lourandos to have been one of the social pressures generating *intensification*,[36] the changes evident over the past 5000 years in Aboriginal techniques of regularising and harvesting resources. Such changes allowed larger communities to develop and be supported, linked by ever wider exchange and competitive gift-giving networks. These growing populations were able to expand still further, even against climatic conditions, into more arid lands, thus extending the area which had active custodianship until even the most hostile environments had owners before the invasion began.[37]

For evidence about how south-eastern Aboriginal people thought about their relationship to their lands at the time of the invasion, we have to turn to the written records of the colonisers. Heavily influenced as they are by the expectations the Europeans brought with them, these are nevertheless able to show something of the way Aboriginal people organised themselves and how they acted towards their lands.

Both archaeological and written evidence demonstrate the diversity

12

of south-eastern Aboriginal social and cultural patterns. The fertile coastal and riverine areas offered a greater range of plant and animal food, and so they supported a heavier population than did the savannah and arid areas in the north-west and far western regions of New South Wales and Victoria. The interactions of culture and environment generated patterns of land relations in the south-east in which wider land areas were associated with each language group in more arid inland regions, and smaller areas in more fertile or rugged areas, such as the major rivers or coastal lands.

There were significant differences too in the formal structure of social organisation between broad geographic regions, with central and northern grasslands people using a fourfold section system in which kinsfolk were identified by generation as well as descent (the Kamilaraay groups), while the southern coastal and inland people used a twofold moiety division (the Kurnai groups), and the eastern coastal people used only the biologically derived kinship terms to order social relations.[38] Further significant cultural differences separated inland from coastal people, such as whether their Law focused on the journeys of a number of ancestral Dreaming heroes and creatures or concentrated on the journeys of a central, pre-eminent mythological creator figure, often in creative conflict with an antagonist who took on varying forms. A large number of language groups were linked by such sharing of mythic or organisational structures, suggesting that the limitations of personal authority by country did not cause social or cultural isolation. On the contrary, the performance of great ceremony cycles, celebrating the journeys and creative powers of the mythic ancestors, continued to bring together participants from all the surviving language groups within these broad culture areas for more than a century after the invasion began.

This did not mean that relationships between Aboriginal groups were always warm and open. Travel across other people's land could only be made with many appropriate courtesies and rituals for seeking permission and paying respect. Even with such conventions, there are many records demonstrating Aboriginal fear and distrust of people whose country was at some distance. Fighting occurred, under highly ritualised conditions, in disputes which may have focused on the use of particular resources or crops, such as the native tobacco which was so prized in Pitjantjatjara lands.[39] Nevertheless, major ceremonial and cultural gatherings were held regularly, and goods and ideas were traded over far wider areas, indicating the successful negotiation of social tensions to maintain a rich network of cultural interactions.

The south-eastern diversity coexists with similarities in the fundamental principles of land relations. Central to the first colonisers' thinking was the assumption that Aboriginal people had developed no attachment to any particular land, whether by ownership or habit, because as 'nomads' they were subject to the whims of nature, and were forced to wander wherever their endless search for food might take them. It became clear to the earliest white observers that these assumptions were wrong. These early writings, as Henry Reynolds has documented, repeatedly comment that Aboriginal people were linked to quite specific areas of land, both economically in their harvesting rights, and emotionally in their sense of security within their own boundaries and their desire to maintain contact with their own country.[40]

The strong south-eastern Aboriginal sense of ownership of particular areas of land became even more obvious over time. By 1849, two decades of deepening conflict had caused great disruption and cost many Aboriginal lives in New South Wales and Victoria. Yet the Commissioners for Crown Lands consistently reported that across the whole of the area in which Europeans were then present, Aboriginal people were identified with, and claimed as their own, particular areas of land. Commissioner Fry's description for the Clarence River was typical: 'The country is divided amongst them into various partitions, each tribe occupying its own peculiar canton over which it roves at pleasure and regards as the source of maintenance and support'.[41]

The Commissioners were most aware, as would be expected of English officials, of the boundaries of each Aboriginal group's lands, but this aspect of their reports may obscure an actual Aboriginal focus in some areas on sites rather than boundaries. Nevertheless, while Reynolds has suggested that customary Aboriginal interest in sites rather than boundaries may have delayed recognition of the nature of the European invasion, this was no longer the case by 1849, when Commissioner Bingham from the Murrumbidgee District could report, as others were doing, that the Aboriginal people there 'feel deeply the alien occupation of their country'.[42]

It rapidly became apparent as well that social organisation and political authority were closely defined and bounded by land relationships, just as in northern and central Australia. This was soon observed around Sydney, and then as the warfare of the invasion intensified, whites found themselves challenged and resisted whenever they entered the territory of a new group of landowners. The military defeat of the eastern landholding groups of Wiradjuri-speakers around Bathurst in 1824, for example, was not enough to subdue the western Wiradjuri groups, who continued to fight the expansion of pastoralism into the 1840s. Yet the limitation of authority to one's own country meant that Aboriginal leaders in military resistance to invasion, such as Wyndradine in the east, were not able to co-ordinate all the Wiradjuri groups, who instead fought the invasion country by country. Whatever its problems for military strategy, this suggests that political and social authority in the south-east arose from the same land-based ceremonial obligations and relations as it continues to do in the centre and north.[43]

The close identification of people, land and language is also apparent in the south-east, although it has taken longer for European analysts to piece together the early notes taken on Aboriginal languages. Barwick, in her painstaking reinterpretation and mapping of the land relations of Victorian clans at the time of the invasion, has indicated the close identification of individuals and clans with their dialect name and their district of customary ownership and origin: they refer to themselves both geographically and socially by using their language name, indicated by its suffix *-(w)urrung* meaning 'mouth' or 'speech'.[44] Donaldson has discussed the different ways in which western New South Wales people named themselves and their languages, either by vocabulary differences or by land association. Some languages used land association directly. *Paakantji*, the name of the people and their language spoken on the western Darling, means 'belonging to' the river named *paaka* (Darling), while the language name of the neighbouring *Paarruntji* means 'belonging to' the river named *paarru* (Paroo); similarly *Parrintji* is the language 'belonging to' the scrub country or *parri*. Other languages, such as Ngiyampaa, Yuwalaraay and Kamilaraay, used vocabulary differences for identification, naming the language by a dialect group's choice for a word with a common meaning, such as 'no'.

Yet the languages named by vocabulary choices had another way of naming the groups *within* a dialect, and this naming system was directly associated with the country where they usually lived and for which that group owned the customary rights. So some Ngiyampaa-speaking people were identified as *pilaarrkiyalu*, 'the belar tree mob' or 'the people who lived where the belar trees grow', while others were called *nhiilyikiyalu*, 'the nilyah tree people'. This Ngiyampaa practice was based on identifying people and their dialects 'by social association with place'.[45] So too are the languages of the Kulin group from central Victoria, recorded in the mid-nineteenth century, which named dialects by using suffixes such as *-(w)illam* indicating dwelling place in association with a group of people, or as Curr translated it in 1886, 'the people who dwelt in any land'. So the name of the *Ngaruk-willam*, for example, who were the owners of land now in eastern Melbourne, means 'the people who owned the *ngaruk* (stones or rocky place)'.[46] Langloh Parker's study of the Yuwalaraay showed a pattern of naming individuals according to the place of their birth, which had been chosen by their mothers to fit their own land affiliation. This name, and the social group to which it signalled membership, was as important as the better-known 'section' or 'skin' names in determining social roles.[47]

15

Another widespread demonstration of the fundamental nature of traditional identification of people with land is found in the accounts of ceremonies which continued to take place long after the first wave of invasion. R. H. Mathews, recording initiation ceremonies from a wide range of locations late in the nineteenth century, spoke of the '*tauri* or country' of the Kamilaraay, Yuwalaraay and Ngiyampaa people who assembled at Gundabloui station for this reason during 1894. At significant times throughout the long ceremony, members of each language group placed themselves on the part of the ceremonial ground which was closest to their own lands, their *tauri*. Their camps were also oriented in this way, with each aligned so as to be closest to their own lands. And the initiates were instructed to sit in the ceremonial circles in such a way that they each faced their own *tauri*.[48] This process had been observed also in the southern districts which became Victoria. The relationships between countries were mirrored by the relative positions of the camps of each group which came to the large ceremonial gathering at Port Phillip Bay during 1838, so the land relations of the people determined their interactions with others and indeed their very physical use of space even when they were far from the country which gave them their identity.[49]

Describing the initiation gathering of the Wiradjuri and related peoples in 1893, Mathews recorded that the dramatic opening involved each of the participants entering the ceremony ring and announcing themselves by calling out the names of important sites, camping grounds and waterholes within their own lands.[50] Yet again, in a ceremony Mathews recorded among Kamilaraay and Pikampul people in 1896, the participants all, at crucial points in the ceremony, called out 'the names of places in their country'.[51] In the western areas, Aboriginal people remember this ritual identification. They recount how in the Ngiyampaa initiation ceremony, last held in 1914, each man announced himself to the assembled group by stepping forward and calling out not his own name but the name of the place of which he was owner.[52]

In at least some areas, it was not only the familiarity of day-to-day living and the knowledge it brought, nor only the learning of ceremonial oral tradition which fostered the sense of identification with land. This unity between person and place was intensified because it was central to the trials of endurance in initiation ceremonies. On the south-east coast, for example, the places for which the initiate was becoming custodian were named one by one while he underwent the painful test of tooth evulsion.[53]

The vast body of cultural knowledge on which Aboriginal people in New South Wales drew during these ceremonial gatherings, as well as in their daily lives, was linked to and inscribed onto the land, just as in central and northern Australia today. There are not many detailed accounts of oral tradition in the south-east, and some fragments which have been recorded have been decontextualised so that we no longer know who first told the story or which country it was about. Some observers, however, were sensitive enough to maintain language and land contexts for the stories they collected, and even to record the storytellers by whom they were taught. The Yuwalaraay people on the Narran River, for example, told many of their traditions to Katherine Langloh Parker during the later decades of the nineteenth century.[54] Her collections of these 'legends' are retold rather simply, with no suggestion that, like similar stories in other areas, these must have held complex and subtle meanings which either would not have been revealed to an outsider or would have been invisible to anyone who was not totally immersed in the society which created them.[55]

Langloh Parker does, however, remain faithful to the context of these stories on the land and rivers of the north-west. It is clear that these dramas were not played out only on an imaginary landscape but were embedded in the landforms of Yuwalaraay people's country. Story after story tells of ancestral journeys from named place to named place along the Narran and Barwon rivers, explaining why and how each watercourse and its surrounding landforms were created, and the powers each place continues to embody. These stories also explain the connections between kin groups of people, other species and the land, linking them all inextricably. Even in Langloh Parker's austere prose, these stories throb with passion and drama, and suggest the excitement which ceremonial re-enactments could hold, and the emotion which would accompany retellings of the stories at the places where each episode happened. They give us a faint glimpse of the enlivened land, the 'speaking land' that south-eastern Aboriginal people saw when they looked around their country before the invasion began. Such a glimpse allows us to see how the experiences of the invasion would be drawn into this web of meaning around place.

LAND AND MEANINGS AFTER THE INVASION

There are strong grounds then for arguing that for Aboriginal people in south-eastern Australia before the invasion, land was the physical and symbolic basis for almost every aspect of life. Social relations were expressed, managed and negotiated through relations to land; political standing was legitimated and authority grounded in landholding. Knowledge was structured by its relation to place, and it was taught, held in memory and performed according to this organisational framework. New experiences were analysed by and incorporated into that oral tradition and so they too became organised within it by place.

When we consider how Aboriginal societies in the south-east survived the invasion, these social, political and cultural meanings of land are crucial. The onslaught took a terrible toll of the lives of countless senior, authoritative and knowledgeable men and women who died because of introduced disease, violence and then the illnesses arising from poverty and repression. Much detailed specific knowledge about the Dreamings and ceremonies was lost in this way, and in some areas this was far beyond the restorative ability of the normal processes for ensuring proper succession to many of the lands of the south-east. Yet the Aboriginal people who survived carried with them a cultural experience of seeing land as the central organising principle of their society. They knew to which lands they belonged, even if they did not any longer have access to all the details of its stories. They expected to identify themselves by and with the land, to continue to be responsible for it, and to authorise their political standing with reference to it. The changed circumstances of their invaded lands made much of what they wanted to do impossible: they did not have unfettered access for harvesting or for ceremonies; they did not have all the ceremonial knowledge in some areas, nor the numbers they needed for some rituals. This may not have stopped people, however, from doing what they could, or from trying to do more. It may not have stopped them from negotiating and organising their lives and those of their families so that land continued to be a central goal and desire.

There are questions then which can be followed through any exploration of the history of colonised Australia, which would allow insights into the way Aboriginal people may have tried to look beyond the invasion to make meaning out of their changed lives.

One cluster of questions is about the way the rapidly changing history of invasion was understood and about how it was seen to be related to land. The events Aboriginal people faced after the invasion began were momentous, unprecedented and often bitterly painful. How did they analyse these events? Did they still seek to embed them into the stories of the lands on which they occurred? Did they still remember and teach about those happenings by reference to places?

Other questions ask how social relations were organised. Did Aboriginal people continue to negotiate their social lives and relationships through their land relations? Could this continue under the impact of major depopulation and disruption? Did new social practices and cultural forms emerge? Did these new ways of doing things, these new goals, still use land as the means to achieve social relatedness and gain political authority?

A related group of questions is about how Aboriginal individuals and communities have identified themselves under the pressure of colonisation. Have they continued customary ways of naming and perceiving themselves? Have they developed new ways of doing these things? Is land still so central a part of achieving identity? Does it fulfil this role in the same ways as before or are there new forms for old aspirations to gain identity?

While there are no single answers to such questions, the following chapters explore their implications in what we can learn about the history of colonised Australia.

Part I

Beyond the Invasion, 1788 to 1850s

2

Invasion and Land: 'a system of terrorism'

The invasion brought a period of intense conflict to south-eastern Australia, but it was also the beginning of a far longer engagement between Aboriginal Australians and their invaders. Beyond the invasion violence, land continued to be deeply important for Aboriginal people, just as it had been beforehand.

Yet land was also crucial, for very different reasons, to the British invaders. Land was at the centre of social relations and conflicts in industrialising Britain, as 'common' lands were enclosed for private production; villagers were hanged as poachers or forced to move to the new city slums and factories; and industrialists bought into the landed gentry. When they arrived in Australia, the different groups of British settlers carried expectations about land which shaped the way they understood what they saw and how they valued it. The administration expected social stability to flow from orderly and well-planned land distribution, and saw land as a major tool to implement social control and to shape future social relations. Although some convicts may have arrived with experience or memories of villagers' use of 'commons', most colonisers saw land as a prize to be fought over among themselves and won as private property. And all saw land as both a private possession and as a powerful symbol of personal and class power.

Aboriginal and European concepts of land were thus very different, spiritually, socially, economically and symbolically. But the invasion did not see a rapid supplanting of one set of ideas with another. Rather, these differing systems of ideas about land came to operate simultaneously, in ignorance of each other or in open conflict, and sometimes in uneasy tension and fragile co-existence.

'A SYSTEM OF TERRORISM'

The invasion was not a single event, but instead took place region by region, in a series of uneven steps, over more than a hundred years. The complex and often tragic course of these south-eastern invasions

23

cannot be explored here in detail, but we need to understand enough of the processes to ask what the invasion did to land relations for Aboriginal landowners.

The answer may seem self-evident, so familiar are we with the easy clichés of popular accounts. Did not the invasion push Aborigines off their land? Were they not all dispossessed in the south-eastern States and dispersed to live as beggars and fringe dwellers? The answers cannot be so simple. When we look at the evidence from the later nineteenth century, or even the early twentieth, we find extensive Aboriginal knowledge of association with land and strong sentiments of determination by many Aboriginal people to resist enforced movements. So the scattered evidence for the early invasion must be re-examined, to ask just how the invasion actually affected Aboriginal people's associations with their lands.

Disease

Only the Kooris of Port Jackson met the British at the same time as they met their ideas and their diseases. For Aboriginal people elsewhere these different kinds of impact arrived separately. News spread rapidly that there were unfamiliar types of human beings present on the coast. New objects such as axes and guns began to circulate well before most inland Aboriginal people saw a white person. Most fearfully, the Europeans carried illnesses to which Aboriginal Australians had no immunity. The most easily recognisable was smallpox, but viral infections such as measles and even influenza, regarded as less threatening by Europeans, caused severe systemic illness because Aboriginal people had no acquired immunity. These diseases rapidly attacked the dense populations of the coastal and inland river systems, far in advance of any invasion by people or stock.[1]

Smallpox first hit Kooris near Sydney in 1789, barely twelve months after the First Fleet landed. The catastrophe was so intense there that survivors were too ill to bury their loved ones, and were forced to leave their bodies on the beaches and in the camps where they had died. Estimates are that many of the coastal family groups were wiped out entirely, or were left with very few survivors. From Port Jackson the disease spread over the mountains and along the networks of people living along the Murray and Darling river valleys. The impact on groups further away seems to have been less severe, and the presence of mountainous barriers between groups of people may have slowed the progress of infection.

A single disaster like this would have led to major problems of reorganisation and regrouping, but the Kooris of Sydney then had to face the impact of influenza, measles and other diseases. There was a second smallpox epidemic in 1830, which may have spread further among Aboriginal groups than the first one because the European population had expanded widely into the inland by that time. This severely disorganised inland Aboriginal societies just as they were confronted with the beginning of the actual, physical invasion, when a great flood of whites and their herds poured into the grasslands which had been created by firestick farming.

The Yuwalaraay people on the Narran River, in north-west New South Wales, remembered the plagues in oral tradition. They retold the story to Langloh Parker in the 1880s and revealed the terrible guilt which so unjustly haunted the survivors.

> Ghastly traditions the blacks have of the time when Dunnerh-Dunnerh, the smallpox, decimated their ancestors. Enemies sent it in the winds, which hung it on the trees, over the camps, whence it dropped on its victims. So terror-stricken were the tribes that, with few exceptions, they did not stay to bury their dead and because they did not do so, flying even from the dying, a curse was laid on them that someday the plague would return, brought back by the Wundah or white devils; and the blacks shudder still, though it was generations before them, at the thought that such a horror may come again.[2]

The effects of disease must have been severe. People of all generations were lost, which would have disrupted the traditional social rules of a kin-based society which allowed marriage only to a limited number of potential partners. The losses within the middle-aged range would have taken people whose knowledge and authority was at its greatest, leaving the survivors depleted in the highest levels of ceremonial and oral tradition, and in leadership.

Yet the accounts of first contact by Europeans suggest that many Aboriginal survivors were still on their own country, despite the fact that the groups which explorers and overlanders met must have been the result of reorganisation after population loss. Only in the hardest-hit area, around Botany Bay and the southern shores of Port Jackson itself, was the loss of life so high from disease and violence in the first 50 years of the colony that large-scale immigration occurred. Mahroot, a Koori who belonged to the land around Botany Bay, told a Select Committee in 1845 that only four adults from his community of over 400 remained alive. He explained that because of the loss of so many of his own people, Kooris speaking a separate language, from around Liverpool (either western Dharuk or Gandangara people) had moved into his country, some of them living in relationships with the three remaining women from the Cook's River group. There is no other testimony to indicate what the western people saw themselves as doing, and Mahroot's account suggests there may have been some resentment between the surviving landowners and the newcomers, but he also indicated that this arrangement was stable and non-violent.[3]

A further instance of immigration into this Botany Bay area occurred only a little later in the century, with Tharawal and other people from further south on the Illawarra coast moving north to establish homes at La Perouse. The movement seems to have been motivated by an interest in the activities of the Sydney settlement, and reflected the disruption which early agriculture was causing to their southern homes. The migrants rapidly took up a strong sense of association with the land at La Perouse, legitimating their presence by traditional kinship and ceremonial links with the earlier owners. After several generations had been born there, the Aboriginal residents of La Perouse had taken on a role, sanctioned in their own body of knowledge, of fulfilling the obligations of the rightful owners and custodians of that place.[4]

These examples of migration seem to have been confined to those few areas where the original population had been greatly reduced by disease. In other areas, such as the Macleay River on the north coast and the Macintyre River in the north-west, where the surviving adult population was greater, there appears to have been very little movement onto other people's land. Aboriginal people there in the late 1840s expressed a very strong sense of ownership and association with particular areas of land in these two regions, despite illness and the stress which resulted from violence between them and whites. They gave no indication that they or their neighbours regarded it as acceptable to move onto and establish claims to their neighbours' lands. Observers' accounts confirm that such movements were not occurring on any large scale.[5]

The diseases which struck Aboriginal people before the actual incursion of whites therefore caused major depopulation and disorganisation, but not necessarily loss of association with land. In cases of near total loss of life there were neighbours who could move onto the land to restore human custodianship.

Invasion and violence

After disease came the physical invasion, when Europeans took over land for agriculture and brought their sheep and cattle for grazing. In many regions this was accomplished by violence, which ranged from small clashes to calculated and systematic genocide. In most areas disease made a greater impact on population numbers than violence. Yet the violence left such deep scars on the memories and imaginations of Aboriginal victims and of European perpetrators, and on the following generations of each group, that it must be regarded as the major weapon of dispossession by terror.

There was a general pattern to the invasion. The initial Aboriginal response to the presence of whites on their land was not to take flight. As Europeans moved into each new area, Aboriginal owners usually tried, despite increasing suspicion, to establish proper social relations with the invaders, by incorporating the strangers into local hierarchies through reciprocal trade and sexual relations. These attempts were often met by the failure of whites to appreciate the reciprocity expected, but just as often by callous disregard and contempt. Aboriginal demands for respect for local laws then became more assertive and harder to ignore. This escalation in Aboriginal demands was met by the invading settlers with more and more ruthless attempts to take total possession of the land by destroying the Aboriginal landowners themselves.

But such a general pattern does not hold for each area in detail, and if we are to trace events beyond the violence of the invasion, we need to explore the differences in each regional history as well as the commonalities. Both the type of activity Europeans wanted to undertake and the pressures they were under themselves made a great difference to the way they interacted with Aboriginal landowners. The condition of the surviving Aboriginal owners and their strategic approach to the invasion provided the other set of variables in the invasion engagement. The histories of each of these regions will be followed through later chapters, tracing how these different experiences of invasion shaped the interactions between Aborigines and their invaders.

Invasion around Sydney: Dharuk and Gandangara lands

The Hawkesbury riverbank land was already productive in the way that Europeans wished to use it. The Dharuk landowners cultivated yams in its rich soils, and it formed an essential element of their economy. The invasion of their land occurred because Europeans wanted to use it in precisely the same way, in direct competition with its owners. The style of this invasion was so brutal because it was conducted by desperate men. The white farmers penetrating Dharuk land during the 1790s had lost their earlier crops in the poor sandstone soils of the coast. The colony was facing famine and its administrators were urgently looking for fertile land to feed the starving white colonists. The seizure of the Dharuk yam farming lands was therefore ruthless and absolute, forcing the Dharuk people into armed resistance as they saw their basic resources totally removed from their control.[6]

Violence was intense along the Hawkesbury in the 1790s. Settlers repeatedly attacked Aborigines trying to harvest the new crops which had been planted in their old yam beds, and the brutal methods which settlers used to murder Dharuk people, often children, incensed their families and exacerbated violence. The fighting was called a war by white observers, and the death toll was high. At least 26 whites were killed along the banks of the Hawkesbury from 1794 to 1800, but there were many more Aboriginal deaths. At one stage 60 soldiers were sent out 'to destroy all [Aboriginal people] they could meet and drive them utterly from the Hawkesbury'.[7] The Aboriginal dead at one campsite were left hanging on gibbets, to terrorise their kinsfolk. A new governor, Philip King, in 1801 endorsed this violence by ordering settlers to fire on Aborigines at will to force them away from white farms. The conflict on Dharuk land continued, with the Kooris, particularly around Parramatta, forming well co-ordinated fighting bands under a skilled strategist, Pemulwye. Only with his death at the hands of the British in 1802 did the armed resistance diminish. This has been regarded as a decisive victory for the British, leading to the eventual disappearance of the Dharuk as an identifiable group. Yet there is evidence of continuing presence of the Dharuk, as Mahroot testified, dispersed among surviving neighbours and also in relationships with whites. Most of these Dharuk survivors, as Brook and Kohen have exhaustively documented, continued to live on their own land.[8]

The Gandangara lands were adjacent to Dharuk country, but were sheltered from this early violence because the Nepean's poor sandstone soils were less attractive to white farmers. These Kooris attempted negotiations about land with Governor King in 1804, and seemed to have succeeded. They argued that they were being blocked from their lands, particularly their fertile riverbank yam beds, and that they were shot at if they were seen on white men's farms. They asked for land, 'to retain some places on the lower part of the river'. King assured the Gandangara that there would be no further white penetration.[9]

This promise was dishonoured after King's departure in 1807, and there were renewed white incursions. Then drought hit in 1814, increasing difficulties for both Aboriginal and white groups. Inland clans of Gandangara people congregated more frequently near the better-watered Cowpastures, and heightened tensions led to a series of killings, some by Kooris, many more by whites. Anxieties intensified among whites, who feared a 'coalescence' of Aboriginal people from other areas, notably the Jervis Bay groups (Tharawal) with the mountain tribes (Gandangara) to kill all whites. The escalating tensions worsened in March 1816, when some whites who had employed Kooris not only refused to pay them but then violently drove them away. This led to retaliatory violence by Kooris. Governor Macquarie had been eager to portray himself as fostering good relations between Aborigines and whites, but in April 1816 he announced he had come to the 'painful resolution of chastening these hostile tribes, and [of inflicting] terrible and exemplary punishment upon them'. He ordered military punitive squads into the

Gandangara lands, with instructions to hang the bodies of the 'guilty' Aboriginal victims in trees 'in order to strike the great terror into the survivors'.[10]

The Dharuk men who guided these expeditions appear to have led the soldiers away from the Gandangara, but the soldiers without guides found and killed about sixteen people, and there were more than twenty arrests. These included a number of people from the 'Burra Burra' band, the custodians for the Burragorang Valley. Some were transported to other colonies, and the Governor claimed to have succeeded in dispersing the Gandangara. But their rugged country had protected them, and allowed them a substantial adult survival rate compared to the Dharuk; particularly in the more difficult areas such as the Burragorang, this ensured the survival of the Gandangara as a fairly organised social group. Although apparently defeated, the Gandangara were to re-emerge rapidly, demanding their land back before the 1860s were over.[11]

Another coastal invasion: Dhan-gadi lands

Not all coastal invasions were like Sydney. In the Macleay Valley during the 1840s and 1850s, very different patterns of interaction arose from different European land uses. Dense Aboriginal populations lived in these warm coastal river valleys, whose affluent economies were based on a wide range of food available from woodlands, rivers and estuaries as well as the sea. The first European invaders were cedar-cutters, seeking individual trees, and their goals were initially in little conflict with Koori land use.

Few outbreaks of violence occurred there until the penetration of squatters with sheep and cattle in the 1840s. Even this more intensive land use, however, was in less conflict with Koori uses than on the western plains. The rugged landscape of the coast and its humid climate limited the areas which were suitable for sheep, and so lower-stocked cattle farms were more favoured. Probably a more important factor was that the international market, which exerted an overwhelming influence on the economy of this small colony, had moved from a boom in wool prices during the 1830s to a severe slump in the 1840s. The effect for the Macleay area was to slow down the pace and ferocity of the invasion. While isolated clashes did continue in the rugged inland areas until far later than was the case on the western plains, the general level of violence was lower. This allowed more people to survive, which meant a strong continuity in the coastal communities' detailed cultural knowledge.[12]

The grasslands invasion

It was the Aboriginal owners of the grasslands west of the mountains who faced the most rapid and consistently violent invasion. From the 1820s to early in the 1840s, there was a massive flood of people and stock over the mountains west from Sydney, north-west up the Hunter Valley, south from Moreton Bay and north from Port Phillip, to take advantage of the fine Aboriginal-created grazing lands.

The first open warfare broke out around Bathurst. There were eight years of calm after the first European penetration, because the numbers of settlers and stock remained low and the area of their land use was strictly limited. This ended when restrictions on pastoral expansion were lifted in 1821. The white population rose from 114 in 1820 to 1267 in 1824, the combined sheep and cattle numbers increased from 33 733 in 1821 to 113 973 in 1825, and the land alienated to Europeans increased from 2520 acres in 1821 to 91 636 acres in 1825. This rapid increase intensified pressure on the Aboriginal landowners, the eastern clans of Wiradjuri-speakers, who were being pushed away from key economic resources at the same time as they were suffering the effects of a severe drought from 1822 to 1824. Conflict broke out in this tense atmosphere and led to the declaration of martial law in 1824.[13]

The conflict on the eastern Wiradjuri country was followed by a few years of less open hostilities as the grasslands' owners reeled under the onslaught of the men and stock pouring across the plains, taking up prime land and changing forever the ecosystem of the plains. By the early 1830s, however, Aboriginal groups on all the major inland rivers were in crisis as they rapidly lost access to their fertile land, game and sacred sites. There was generalised warfare along the frontier from Port Phillip to the Darling Downs and beyond into Queensland from 1835 to 1842, although there was no formal strategic co-operation between the Aboriginal groups as each defended their own lands.[14] Aboriginal people retaliated against settler attacks on people or trespasses onto land or sacred sites. The administration's consequent military 'punitive' expeditions invariably took Aboriginal people as their only targets.

Along the Murray

Like the north coast populations, the Murray Valley Aboriginal populations were dense and sedentary.[15] They were more vulnerable to introduced diseases because they lived on one long river system rather than in separate valleys protected by rugged mountains. This may have meant that they suffered heavy loss of life in both the 1789 and the 1830 smallpox epidemics, as well as in the other viral attacks which must have raged in between. Their geography also made them more vulnerable to the physical invasion: their open, wooded, well-watered country was initially more attractive to squatters than the treeless blacksoil northern plains. So the Murray Valley people suffered the most rapid overrunning of their land by stock from two directions, Port Phillip in the south and Sydney in the north-east. Violence was widespread and intense, taking the lives of many Kooris as well as whites. The outcome was one of the most severe depopulations of any south-eastern area outside Sydney.[16]

Assassination and terrorism in the north-west

The fierce struggles over the grasslands are best revealed for the northern slopes and plains. There is much surviving evidence of the conflict there, which allows us to explore more fully than in some other areas the details of Aboriginal relations to their land under the pressure of violent invasion.

The Kamilaraay and their closely related neighbours responded rapidly and vigorously to early white incursions and so gained a reputation among whites as warlike and hostile. This, combined with the less attractive nature of the blacksoil plains or more remote scrub country, allowed a brief early respite from pressure. But the booming international market in the 1830s fanned the squatters' desires for land, and the Kamilaraay faced a ruthless campaign by both military and private vigilante forces. The extensive 'pacification' expedition of Major Nunn in 1838 left masses of documentation attesting to its determination to hunt down Aboriginal landowners. It cost between 70 and 300 Kamilaraay lives.[17]

The process continued after Nunn withdrew, with private hunters pursuing Murris. Around Myall Creek later in 1838, massacres left well over 30 Murris dead, most of them decapitated with cutlasses, others left hacked and bleeding then thrown alive onto a fire. Some of the killers were themselves hunted and caught. Twelve of the stockmen who had committed the murders at Myall Creek were arrested by the newly arrived Governor Gipps, although their employer, John Fleming, who appears to have orchestrated as well as participated in the massacre, escaped to freedom at Wilberforce. The twelve men were tried and convicted of murder, but colonists rallied to their defence. Gipps succeeded in putting seven of the death sentences into effect, but five escaped hanging when the administration lost its nerve in the face of massed public pressure. These murders had an impact on English public opinion, but in the colony the main effect was to cloak public discussion of any conflict. Whites were now far more careful to maintain silence about any violence they were aware of, in order to shield the white perpetrators from the gallows.

Yet the killing did not stop. The extent of continuing violence, its impact on Murri landowners, and its poisonous corrosion of the morality of settler society were all suggested in the correspondence of Richard Bligh, a Commissioner for Crown Lands. Newly stationed at Warialda to cover the Gwydir District in 1847, Bligh was overwhelmed by white complaints about the savagery of the local Aboriginal groups. Those accused were now more often the Pikampul on the Macintyre, rather than the Kamilaraay on the Namoi and Gwydir rivers. Bligh wrote his first annual report in January, 1848, angrily accusing Murris of 'savage and murderous outrages'.[18] Over the next twelve months, however, Bligh began to investigate these 'outrages' more carefully, and in his report of January 1849 he admitted he had been misled by settlers' accounts. He now believed that the Murri actions had all been carried out in retaliation after white attacks, and that the blame for 'injury and crime' had to be laid 'fearfully against the white population'.[19]

The Gwydir Crown Lands District was a mixture of sheep and cattle runs, which were managed very differently in relation to Aboriginal landowners. The sheep runs had long employed Murris as shepherds, a practice occurring as early as 1838 at the time of the Myall Creek massacre, and by 1848 Murri women were also being employed as domestic servants and in the trusted position of nanny to white children. There were also continuing sexual relationships with Murris. Some white owners or managers would offer shelter to Aboriginal people, beyond those employed on the sheep run. Yet on adjacent cattle runs, a very different regime existed. Run-holders insisted that cattle were dangerously disturbed by the presence of Aboriginal people, and maintained that any Aborigine sighted within the boundaries of a run would be shot. These men or their employees were involved, Bligh found, in systematic raids to hunt down and murder Murris sheltering on their neighbours' sheep runs.

Bligh reported that his investigations in the Gwydir area had shown him that 'a system of assassination has been pursued by the whites'. He gave details of a series of massacres. The testimony of one or two remorseful accomplices had given him adequate evidence for his own conclusions, but not enough to mount prosecutions, a bitter lesson he had learnt over the year. He believed that this murderous violence had caused a moral corruption among whites in the area, describing such a 'state of combination and system of terrorism' that these murders were 'known by everyone by the common fame of the country', yet even 'respectable' settlers refused to testify against the murderers.

The report ended by giving a glimpse of the actions and perceptions of the Pikampul Murris:

> To turn to the other side of the question there can be no doubt that the
> natives or more properly speaking a small number of the worst disposed

amongst them have during the past year committed considerable aggressions on the cattle of the settlers in this quarter, but when I consider they are forbidden on pain of death to show themselves upon most of the cattle runs because their presence disturbs these animals and that they are followed and attacked when they take refuge on the sheep stations it can hardly excite surprise that they should avail themselves of any safe opportunities for revenge. I do not know that their wretched state can be more clearly described than in the words of one of themselves, when told to go away from a sheep station at which so large a number of these creatures had congregated as to make it impossible for the well disposed owner to supply them all with food:

'Which way blackfellow yan [i.e. go]? Supposing this way you shootem. Supposing that way you shootem. All about shootem.'[20]

The pattern which emerges from Bligh's voluminous correspondence is of Murris moving to seek shelter wherever possible, and retaliating whenever possible. But, he reported, they did not wish to flee from their traditional lands, and did not try to do so. He made it clear that despite the bewildering violence, the Aboriginal language groups in his district kept closely to their own countries, and that all their increasingly desperate efforts were turned towards remaining within the boundaries of that meaningful area.[21]

The impact of violent invasion then was unquestionably massive disruption to social life, and to future social reproduction, but at first it did not force people off their lands. Instead, Aborigines moved around to safe places within their own country. In the turmoil of terror and challenge, the significance of traditional relations to land did not decrease, but may have become even more important as one of the few remaining sources of stability and certainty.

REMEMBERING THE VIOLENCE THROUGH THE LAND

Traditional country was the setting for the pain Murris bore from the invasion violence; it was their own country on which they resisted, bled, and died. But because some also survived on their land, it became their witness. Aboriginal people continued to build new knowledge into the existing web of stories which linked their significant places. Even in the disrupted situation of the south-eastern communities, where details and meanings of many stories must have been lost to disease and assault, there continued to be a desire to teach by recounting the stories from the land. The memories of pursuits and massacres were denied by whites, hidden and covered over, to fester far into the future. Aboriginal people laid these stories out onto their land. They told and retold them to their children as part of the body of knowledge which could be read from the land. The history of violent invasion was transmuted by the forms and conventions of oral traditions, but nevertheless conserved to become part of the learnt heritage of their children.

Well over a century later, such stories were still known. Ivy Green, a Murri woman from Dungalear, north-east of Walgett, recounted in 1980 the stories her grandmother had told her as a young child, in the process of teaching her about the country on which she was growing up.

> Old Granny was tellin' us, they were livin' down here at a place called
> Bundabreena, on the river. Mob of white people came here one day,
> when there were a lot of blackfellas there. This old woman was carryin'
> little kids, poor bugger, two twins she had in a thing they had, *gulay*
> they called it, bag like the Chinamens carry. He shot the old woman,
> and he shot the father, and he got the two little kids and put a handful
> of dirt in their mouth and choked 'em, but they [Murris] couldn't catch
> 'em, they [whites] was killin' 'em. They was killin' 'em, fast.[22]

R. H. W. Reece searched for oral traditions of the Myall Creek massacres among Murris at Moree, and found a narrative which had indeed recorded many of the elements of the massacres, told with close attention to the sites of each episode, but with an interpretation which arose from Kamilaraay traditions rather than English expectations.[23]

The teaching of stories about the invasion was woven into the fabric of everyday life in the later, very changed circumstances of life under colonialism. Wilpi was a Wangkumara man living in Bourke during the 1970s, known by the English name of George Harrison. He explained how he learnt the invasion history as part of the whole range of traditional knowledge about his land, while being taught stockwork on a cattle property during the early years of the twentieth century.

> Old fellas used to tell us, 'you want to come out, learn to work' and we
> was pleased to too, didn't know what horses was like. So we went down
> onto the Cooper then, onto the floodwater country then, they took us
> out there.
>
> And the old fellas used to show us sandhills here and sandhills there,
> all different islands, y'see, and they had names for these waterholes, see
> where all the Abos got shot down there when the troopers came in to
> shoot them, see. They was killin' cattle, see, at the waterhole. So anyway,
> they told us all these names, showin' us where they were shot and all . . .
>
> So we went out, we were workin' with 'em there, oh for a good
> while, riding' about with 'em, musterin' cattle, and they used to say,
> 'well, you go to a waterhole', you know they name 'em there. Like they
> call 'im *Watuwara*, that's 'water where the birds live', then next, where
> they shot the Murris, they call that *Thuliula*, that's a mussel see, *Thuliu*,
> and the next one, about a mile away, they call that 'little *Thuliula*'.[24]

Aboriginal people did not just retain these stories within their own communities. They communicated their anger over land very clearly to their white invaders. Alongside their protests over the violent assaults on their people, Aboriginal spokespeople and negotiators made it clear that loss of land for economic as well as social and cultural purposes was an overwhelming grievance. In the very earliest days of the British presence, Kooris around Port Jackson expressed anger and concern when whites began clearing their land. Lieutenant William Bradley was among a number who recorded such Aboriginal statements: 'The natives were well pleas'd with our People until they began clearing the Ground at which they were displeased and wanted them gone'.[25]

In the decades which followed there were many white observers who were told by Aborigines of their sense of bitterness and loss over the invasion of their lands. Those Europeans in particular who learnt some of the local language recorded translated statements which demonstrated that this loss of land for social and economic purposes was a burning cause for dissatisfaction. Reynolds has gathered many of these reported statements, such as that from Tasmania in which Aborigines stated through an interpreter that they regarded themselves as 'engaged in a justifiable war against the invaders of their Country'. In another example from South Australia, an Aboriginal man confronted a settler and said 'damn you eyes, go to England, this my land'. In Victoria, many of the protectors in the early 1840s quoted Aborigines saying words such as 'no good white man take away country'.

The NSW Crown Lands Commissioners all reported similar sentiments from Aborigines in their areas, the most direct being the Commissioner for the Murrumbidgee District who reported in 1848, 'They feel deeply the alien occupation of their country'.[26]

Land was seen by its Aboriginal owners as a central factor in their experience of colonialism. Their sense of invasion, of loss and deprivation of land was expressed clearly and unarguably. It was expressed to whites alongside Aboriginal pain at the deaths of their loved ones and offence at transgressions of their laws. It is no surprise then that their goals in reorganising their communities beyond the invasion were to have land as a central and pervasive theme.

3

Land and White Desire: Nostalgia and Imagination

When the British landed in Australia in 1788, they brought with them well-established although often contradictory ideas about the land and the people who lived there.[1] They assumed that the land was 'in a state of nature', unshaped by human activity or intention. They believed that Aboriginal people wandered the earth randomly, in response to the vagaries of nature, and did not change the earth in any way. They assumed further that European knowledge and tools could be applied directly and successfully, making the new land immediately productive and, in appearance and in crops, just like the old.

PERCEPTIONS

As the colony became established, there was often conflict between expectations and experience. The British characterisations of the land in letters and journals as well as in more formal documents varied widely, but it seems that almost all the English were surprised and impressed at how much land there was in the new colony. 'Spacious' and 'expansive' were recurring adjectives in the newcomers' writings, with this unfamiliar space sometimes seeming attractive and at others threatening and oppressive.

The early writings about the land in New South Wales frequently used the terms 'wild' and 'waste'. The prevailing metaphors opposed 'civilisation' to 'savagery', echoing the desire of Enlightenment thought to impose a particular form of order. Governor Phillip wrote about Port Jackson as a place where 'a settlement of civilised people is fixing itself upon a newly discovered or savage coast'. The Eora landowners would have looked on Port Jackson in early 1788 and seen a land which was clean and ordered because it had owners to manage, use and care for it. Phillip saw only disturbing 'tumult and confusion' and an almost sexually offensive 'promiscuous' abundance which he desired to control by ordering it in regular, geometric patterns.[2]

The term 'waste' land evoked a land barren and sterile, threatening to the struggling white farmers in its disorder and infertility. A more benign meaning was that it was potentially productive land which was only temporarily lying idle, waiting for the active management of European farming. There was clear criticism of the native inhabitants here, for they had 'wasted' it by their profligate 'hunting and gathering', which did nothing to enhance nature by carrying out God's command in Genesis to make the land fruitful and productive.

A still more positive perception of the Australian land called 'waste' arose when settlers saw the inland grassed plains of western Sydney. These grasslands had been created by active Aboriginal managers fire-stick-farming their lands. Although their work was not recognised by the British, the value of their open wooded plains and grassy pastures certainly was. The Macarthurs, for example, described the Gandangara lands they took up around Camden as 'parkland', a landscape which in English eyes was the goal of one form of land management, and in aesthetic terms was referred to as a rural arcady.

In all of these early perceptions, there were no meanings for the British in the land other than those given by settler activity. No human role in creating the parklands was acknowledged, and in the white interpretation they were a gift from God, but still required settler labour and ownership to make them productive. The invaders believed they had nothing to learn from the land itself, as they intended to change it to suit themselves, and they certainly did not expect to learn anything from the land's Aboriginal owners.

DESIRES FOR THE FUTURE

Even though the invading English were a tiny population initially and remained a minority on the continent until the 1840s, they cannot be seen as a homogeneous group with common interests. Their goals and aspirations were shot through with contradictions and tensions even in the first decades of the colony's existence. One thing common to all of them was that land was at the centre of each group's goals, and also therefore at the centre of each major social conflict. For more than a century, land and the method of disposing of it was the issue which aroused stronger feelings than any other matter among white Australians, because each group saw land as having intense symbolic value as well as high material value. Land was 'the vital and living issue in public affairs'.[3]

The government

Governor Phillip's writings about the land showed the very strong desire of successive administrators of the new colony to impose control over the land and the people in it by ordering the way space was used and owned. The French Revolution occurred shortly after the invasion of Australia began, and the vision of urban industrial cities generating miserable slums and uncontrolled mobs haunted the governments of Europe. The view of the future of the Australian colonies was therefore modelled not on contemporary England but on a nostalgic view which looked back to a largely imaginary pre-industrial Britain, in which independent freeholding farmers were claimed to have provided the basis of British social, cultural and economic freedoms.[4] These 'yeoman' farmers were mythologised as quintessentially 'British', belligerent but loyal and orderly. The Australian colony was seen as a new breeding ground for these 'sinewy, plucky, pushing, predominating Englishmen'.[5] The key to ensuring the development of the desired type of settler was seen to be control over the size of land on which farmers could settle, and the goal of creating a myriad small, interlocked freehold cultivated farms, all embedded within a network of church and administrative structures, remained at the heart of government policy for over a century.

There was an extra relevance to this desire in the Australian context. This was the belief in the moral power of hard agricultural labour to redeem those who worked the land.[6] The Botany Bay convict colony was represented in some British writings as a cesspool of crime and depravity, but for those people who wanted to rehabilitate its citizens, the tool seemed to be productive labour, with the goal of a small independent freehold farm as its prize. The yeoman farmer myth was well suited to such a redemptive view, offering a rehabilitation which would produce not only a free and independent colonial population but also an orderly and law-abiding one.

Land and its distribution was therefore seen as a central means of controlling future social development in the colony. From individual grants of land as rewards for loyal soldiers and well-behaved, freed convicts to large estates given out to establish a landed gentry, the Crown held great powers to distribute wealth and to shape all aspects of social relations.

For this reason the British administration wanted no doubt over its right to distribute or withhold land. The general assumption, though untested until the 1880s, was that Cook's declaration of English possession of the east coast in 1770 had delivered both political sovereignty and real property to the British Crown. If this were true, it would have given the governor of the colony the absolute right to decide on every land alienation. The intense Aboriginal resistance to this proposition was not heard in any English court during the nineteenth century. There was no serious British legal challenge to the Crown's rights until Batman tried to pre-empt the Crown's right to be the only body to acquire land from the indigenous people when he claimed to have purchased grazing land from the Aboriginal owners of Port Phillip Bay in 1835. The British government responded rapidly and unequivocally to assert its standing. The resulting legal finding did not deny the Aboriginal right to own the land or to sell it, but it did emphatically deny that Batman had any rights to buy Aboriginal land. Only the Crown could acquire land, and therefore only the Crown could control its distribution.[7]

The squatters

Squatters were not the only powerful group in the colony, but they came to dominate its politics and the terms of its dealings with land. There were many men who benefited from government generosity in granting land in the early years of settlement, or who purchased freehold in the settled districts of the new colony as it began to prosper. These landed gentlemen held their property in freehold, by then the conventional form of landed private property in Britain, and the one which the British administration looked on as most beneficial to the development in the colony of a responsible, productive citizenry.

The squatters who pushed their stock out into the vast unsurveyed plains of New South Wales had no freehold, and they held their runs without even official sanction in the early 1820s. As the rich returns of the international market became apparent, the squatters could argue convincingly that they held the key to the future success of the colony. In return, they believed they deserved secure long-term tenure over the land on which their stock grazed. The various schemes for the regulation of squatting proposed during the 1830s were seen by graziers as a threat to their livelihood, and they mobilised to defend their claims. In the process, they constructed a public record of their view of land and their relation to it.

The writing and polemics of squatters took up the concept of Australian land as 'wasted' land, to which only their efforts brought value or meaning. They argued that their activities were of a higher order than that of the indigenous inhabitants, and that they therefore had a right of unfettered access. Their risk-taking and commitment to development of the unknown inner plains was then said to entitle them to a more permanent form of tenure. Squatters repeatedly argued that they should have the rights to acquire as freehold all their extensive runs, the implication being that the freehold purchase price should be based on a far lower sum than that for land in the settled districts. The publicist who expressed the squatting interest most clearly was W. C. Wentworth. When speaking about 'these spacious domains' in 1844,

Wentworth touched on each of these points: 'All the value of this country has been imparted to it by its [white] population and consequently the country itself is our rightful and first inheritance . . . These wilds belong to us and not to the British Government'.[8]

There was no sympathy in this interpretation for Aboriginal rights to land, because the squatters wanted maximum control and security over their runs and any suggestion of unextinguished Aboriginal rights challenged this. The squatters had no interest in Aboriginal knowledge about land because while the violent confrontations of the frontier continued, all that meant was a threat to the security of flocks and herds as Aboriginal people either hid themselves or hid stolen stock. Nor did the squatters have any interest in conserving the people themselves, as long as an abundance of convict labour meant that there was no need for Aboriginal workers on the runs.

The superiority of agriculture

Although government and other colonists were reluctant to impede the profitable expansion of squatting, a deep ambivalence about pastoralism became apparent. The immense distances of the land meant that the squatters soon outran any infrastructure of moral and social control such as the churches or the magistracy. In the early nineteenth century Europeans still believed that societies could degenerate into disorder and atheism if the conventions and practices of civilisation were not policed by church and state. This concern was exacerbated by anxieties about the particular *nomadic* nature of pastoralism, with one squatter describing his fellows as being like 'Bedouin tribes'.[9]

The squatters' claim to permanent tenure over land was disputed. The government and many other colonists saw the squatters as opportunists whose transient presence offered no lasting benefits for the colony. Freeholders in the settled districts were angered that squatters might gain vast areas in secure title at a far lower price than they had had to pay. Squatters were seen to be greedily demanding too big a share of this expansive country and wanting to 'lock up the land'. The government feared the unrest that such a land grab would generate, while other colonists feared they would miss out.

The strongest element in the arguments against the squatters was the widely held conviction that the absolute foundation of European civilisation and British greatness rested on agriculture. The idea of a hierarchical array of societies, ranked from the lowest 'hunters and gatherers' through 'nomadic herders' to 'civilised' farmers and then the highest rank of urban city dwellers arose from Greek thought, and was used to good effect in the days of Roman imperial expansion. Christian theorists, still accepted in the early nineteenth century, had argued that this was part of the 'great chain of being' culminating in God. Societies were either on fixed positions in the hierarchy or they could regress if they failed to nurture and police their moral development. The later nineteenth century was to change the direction in which peoples were thought to have moved, their progress upward or stasis on a lower level being determined genetically. Whatever the motor for change, the relative positions of 'hunting and gathering', pastoralism and agriculture were identical and unchallenged: agriculture was unquestionably the most civilised.

This assumption of the moral and social superiority of agriculture permeates all early colonial writing, and the squatters themselves were constantly acknowledging its power. The way in which the early nine-teenth-century Europeans believed these social and economic practices transcended racial, biological considerations is exemplified in the writings of Crown Lands Commissioner Fry, from the Clarence River, in 1848.

> Like the Native, the European [squatter] occupies without possessing the
> soil. He has never appropriated it by agriculture, his pursuits are
> pastoral, of all others the least likely to generate industrial habits.
>
> A knowledge of agriculture is an indispensible preliminary to
> civilisation . . . As it is from agriculture that the elements of all art are
> derived, so in the order of instruction it must precede every branch of
> human attainment.[10]

So squatters were seen as impermanent, a temporary stage even though profitable, and needing to make way for the 'real', 'permanent' settlers who would conduct agriculture and so build 'civilisation'. The widely shared assumption was that the goal of colonial development was intensive agriculture, a dense population and the growth of towns spread out across the countryside.

The government was seen as having an obligation to foster such progressive intensification of population and land use. Governor Gipps was one of many senior administrators who expressed the view that the government should arbitrate between the contending interest groups, acting as a trustee of the Crown lands for the benefit of all settlers, rather than as a landlord interested only in gaining the highest profit from the rent or alienation of land.[11] Some officials went further, arguing that squatters should be compelled to retire from the land whenever permanent settlers were ready to take up smaller farming lots.[12] The goal, as John Dunmore Lang expressed it in 1833, was to achieve 'a numerous, industrious and virtuous agricultural population' on farm blocks of 20–50 acres, suggesting the common assumptions about the relationship between morality, industry and land distribution, as well as the expectation that administrative policy could achieve this outcome.[13]

So although squatters were powerful in the 1830s and 1840s in New South Wales, they did not have the unambiguous endorsement of government or of other affluent interest groups. There was a desire to demonstrate firmly to the squatters that whatever tenure they achieved over their runs, they did not possess them in freehold, but had little more than a form of agistment rights. This meant there was at least the potential for these groups to hold some sympathy for the interests of Aboriginal landowners if these were in opposition to squatters' claims over land.

Convicts and workers

Many members of the working class, the soldiers and the poor also saw themselves as having a potential interest in the land of the new colony. Perhaps they too had nostalgia for a previous order. Some may have carried memories of enclosure and dispossession in England, and certainly Welsh peasants were being forced off their commons by enclosure at just this time. The Irish too, as convicts or later immigrants, were intensely aware of their dispossession from their lands by the colonising British. For each of these groups there may have been a desire to restore a link to the soil, a security expressed in association with a particular area of land, even if it was in a distant and at first alien land.[14]

Beyond memories of the usage rights of peasants or tenant farmers, there was the widespread popular myth of the yeoman freeholder, on whom so many of the past glories of Britain were said to have rested. M. Williams has reviewed the representation of the land issue in the contemporary press and writings of white Australians in the early nineteenth century:

> The Old Testament image of every man ending his day sitting at the door of his house 'under his vine and under his fig tree' was repeated monotonously, becoming an allegorical symbol expressing the assumptions and aspirations of a whole section of English society for a simpler, more natural way of life, not as a peasant or a tenant farmer, but as a yeoman—independent, 'sturdy' and imbued with democratic ideals.[15]

This was a goal, looking towards both past and future, which could be as attractive to working people as to governments eager to recreate an orderly past which had long been lost in England. Even when the land hunger of working people was built on a nostalgia for what had been the collective rights of use of the commons, the vision they embraced for the future was the individual rights of the yeoman freeholder.

There were also forward-looking desires among workers and the poor in England. These can be glimpsed in the eagerness with which spouses of convicts tried to migrate to join them, and they were fostered by rosy accounts such as those of Alexander Harris's *Settlers and Convicts* in the 1830s. One source of such ideas flowed from the American revolution, in which Jeffersonian ruralists argued that there was a strong link between individual freedom and access to land for farming.[16]

Other forms of more explicitly forward-looking desires were the political utopias being generated in England, particularly by Chartists. These were different from the individual ideals of yeoman freeholders, and at least referred to the possibility of alternative, collective interests in land. Rather than seeing land in Australia as a means for working men to join the number of the capitalists, they argued that to settle poor men on the new land was an opportunity to overturn the existing class order, where only men of wealth could acquire land as private property.[17]

The immense scale of the new colony seemed to offer the opportunity for anyone to gain land, relatively cheaply. The convicts and then working-class people in New South Wales may have shared with Aboriginal people a history of dispossession at the hands of English capitalists, but they had nothing to gain by aligning themselves with the colonised in this new land. Instead, working people had a strong interest in the establishment of uncontested British rights to the land in Australia, as only then would they be in the most advantageous position to gain pieces of that land themselves. In some situations, they could by the later nineteenth century be seen to be in direct competition with Aboriginal people for the remaining scraps of land which the squatters had not taken up.[18]

4

Recognising Native Title, 1838–52

Given the strongly held expectation among all British colonisers that land and its distribution would be used as a tool for social control and management, it is not surprising that initial attempts to negotiate and manage Port Jackson Aborigines should involve land. The British administration asserted that all land was now vested in the Crown, to distribute as it saw fit. Beyond the urgent need for success in farming, the granting of land rapidly became a way of rewarding good conduct or loyalty in convicts and soldiers.

The administration tried to manage Aborigines in similar ways. There were some substantial grants to missionaries to establish schools and mission stations, at Parramatta, Black Town and later at Port Macquarie and Wellington. There were also early attempts to use land grants to individual Aborigines as rewards for co-operation or collaboration with the military pacification of surrounding groups, as with the grants to Nurragingy and Colebee near Black Town. Land was used in an attempt to bribe Aborigines into cultural co-operation, with expectations of the educative and redemptive effects of agriculture. In 1816 Governor Macquarie ordered grants of land and seed for 'wheat, maize, potatoes' to be made to such Aborigines 'as are inclined to become regular settlers'. It seems probable that the grant would have been explained to Aboriginal people in these terms: a portion of their own land would be available to them, forever, if they decided to live on it exclusively.[1]

These early grants were seen at the time as failures because Aborigines did not take up either cultivation or a sedentary lifestyle. The missionary-controlled grants were usually rejected by Aborigines as soon as it became apparent that to live on them would mean that they would lose control over their children and be denied access to other areas of their country. The individual grants have been seen in the same way; some authors suggest that they were abandoned by Aborigines because they lacked interest in both cultivation and preserving some tenure over their own land.[2] There is very little evidence which can be used to explore the Aboriginal perception of these grants. The assumption that Aborigines did not value these small patches of land has certainly been oversimplified. Recent research in the Blacktown area, for example, shows that the descendants of Colebee and other Aboriginal grantees remained on the actual grants or in close proximity to them until well into the twentieth century.[3]

There is one contemporary account of Aboriginal views of these early grants of land. Mahroot, an Eora man of Botany Bay, was determined to remain on the small grant within his traditional country at Botany Bay given to him by Governor Bourke (1833–37). He spent a great deal of his testimony before the NSW Legislative Council Select Committee in 1845 speaking about his knowledge of his traditional country and his language group, then told how he had built a house on the land, and made a living fishing and leasing out a section of the land for rent. An insight into the way whites viewed these grants was suggested by the questioning of the chairman, barrister Richard Windeyer, who opposed Aboriginal land rights and was an active defender of the Myall Creek murderers. Yet he endorsed the idea that Aboriginal people should accept small patches of land in what appeared to be an adherence to European conventions, no doubt to end any further pressure to acknowledge their rights to wider areas. Windeyer assured Mahroot that 'the land is yours and your children's forever and no-one can take it away from you'.[4]

THE RECOGNITION OF ABORIGINAL LAND RIGHTS

The 1830s marked a shift in British interests in the colonising process. With the ending of slavery in British colonies in 1833, the Anti-Slavery Society, the Exeter Hall humanitarians and other reformers turned their vast energies and attention to the condition of the indigenous people in the various British colonies. Maoris in New Zealand, Indians in Canada and Aborigines in Australia all now became the subjects of great investigation and advocacy.

The reforming groups held considerable political power in the English government during the 1830s and 1840s. Their desire to improve the conditions of native colonised peoples therefore had real effects in altering the approach of the British state to its colonial administrations. Reports of the Tasmanian massacres of Aboriginal people reached London in 1831 and 1834, fuelling humanitarian distress at the consequences of violent invasion, but also convincing them that the financial cost of continuing this method of colonisation was too high. In their view, it was both more just and more economically sound to recognise the grievances of indigenous people over land, and then negotiate a fair price as compensation.

During the mid-1830s, most humanitarian attention was focused on intervening in the plans for the new colony of South Australia, but their concern led also to the creation of a Protectorate in the southern areas of New South Wales in 1838. This was to be a different approach from the grants of land to missionary bodies for schools or ration stations. Instead, Aboriginal land and cultural interests were acknowledged for the first time. Protectors were to travel with Aboriginal people, acting as advocates to convey the Aboriginal position in disputes with whites over land and other conflicts. The implicit basis for the Protectorate was the recognition of the legitimacy of Aboriginal hunting practices. There was to be no attempt to change Aboriginal economic and social use of their lands. In practice, the Chief Protector, G. A. Robinson, in charge of the Port Phillip District, was the only protector to move around with Aboriginal people; other protectors with families rapidly chose to establish fixed ration stations, undermining the possibility of continued support for Aboriginal land use.

At the time the Protectorate came into being, the grasslands wars were at their height in south-eastern Australia, so these years saw a wide gap open up between the British Colonial Office and many Australian colonists. The British attempts to recognise some Aboriginal rights and ameliorate their increasingly impoverished conditions met with repeated evasion and obstruction.[5] Most white colonists were swept up in the emotion-drenched hostility and fear generated by the need to justify a ruthless and bloody frontier war. The news of the Nunn expedition and then the Myall Creek massacres in 1838 confirmed the fears of the British reformers. The conviction and execution of some of the Myall Creek murderers did little to assist Aborigines in Australia, for the resentment of colonists at what was regarded as British reformers meddling in colony business intensified. The humanitarians' attempts to institutionalise the recognition of native title in the South Australian colony foundered on the entrenched colonial determination to avoid acknowledging any substantial Aboriginal rights.[6]

The early 1840s saw a less optimistic reform movement, one more inclined to take practical steps to make small gains. An early casualty was the interest in supporting traditional Aboriginal hunting and gathering across the whole range of clan territory. The Land and Emigration commissioners concluded in 1840 that the policy throughout the whole Empire should involve the granting of 'moderate reserves'. 'By moderate reserves, we mean reserves of that extent which would enable them to live, not as hunters, in which case no good would be done, but as cultivators of the soil.'[7]

The pervasive and powerful agrarian ideal was now clearly at work. No longer were indigenous colonised people to be supported in maintaining their traditional economies and forms of land use. Instead they were to be submitted to the same material pressures to transform themselves into sturdy yeomen as were being applied to white immigrant workers and convicts in the rural colonial economies.

The continuing focus of attention for the British reformers in the 1840s was the recognition of native colonised peoples' property rights in land. Henry Reynolds has celebrated this English movement as the first 'land rights' movement, but the rights in land being advocated were limited to those recognisable by the law of the emerging bourgeois state. Rather than any recognition of Aboriginal values, spiritual or social meanings in land, the reformers wanted to extend to indigenous people in all colonies the protection offered by the English legal system. They believed that British colonisation could be just and fair, if only the fullest advantage were taken of the colonisers' law. As private property had become such a focal point of the emerging bourgeois legal and economic system, it was a correspondingly central issue for those reformers who wished to draw colonised peoples under the protection of the best of their 'advanced' society. Yet for all its cultural limitations, the humanitarian intention was nevertheless to transfer real resources, either land itself or financial benefit, to be paid as compensation to the colonised peoples of the Empire.

The context of this attempt at recognition, as we saw in the last chapter, was the broader attempt to control the distribution of land in the colony, to establish a system of social management to contain pastoralism and yet allow the Crown to profit from squatting. The Land Act of 1842, the sixth year of Queen Victoria's reign, began to regularise the sale of land in the colony, and at the same time reflected the rising British concern about Aborigines and about their access and rights to land.[8] The Act allowed for the first time for Crown land to be reserved for the use of Aborigines. It did not, however, address the main government concern about squatting, which had expanded across such vast expanses that survey for sale would not catch up in the foreseeable future.

Governor Gipps had attempted in 1843 to devise a workable means of the Crown controlling and profiting from pastoralism, without either impeding its growth or giving the squatters permanency of tenure. The squatters had responded by mobilising intense pressure to avoid any weakening of their hold over the land. The bitterness of the struggles of the early 1840s was revealed in Gipps's belief that the colony was gripped by 'a land mania', which he regarded as evil despite its profitability.[9] The *Imperial Waste Lands Act 1846*, brought into operation in New South Wales by an Order-in-Council in 1847, created a means to dispose of land by lease in the pastoral districts. It has generally been seen as a victory of the squatters over Gipps, giving them far more security than the Governor had desired. Yet the Act did reiterate the 1842 power to create reserves for the benefit of Aborigines.

One possible reading of these Acts suggests that the term 'reserves' referred to discrete areas of land. Another meaning of the word, current in Earl Grey's Colonial Office at the time, and used also by the NSW Surveyor-General, was that a 'reservation' meant a restriction or limitation on a lease, a retention by the Crown of some power or rights which were not given over to the lessee when a lease was approved.[10] These two concepts of 'reserves' were at the heart of the humanitarians' 1840s attempt to recognise Aboriginal property rights in land.

The rapid expansion of pastoral runs and then their consolidation during the late 1840s placed severe pressures on Aboriginal landowners, as we have seen on the Gwydir. Chief Protector Robinson wrote to the British Secretary of State for Colonies, Earl Henry Grey, protesting at

> the probability that, unless suitable reserves are immediately formed for their benefit, every acre of their native soil will shortly be so leased out and occupied as to leave them, in a legal view, no place for the sole of their feet. If the occupation of Crown Lands is to be settled by the Crown granting Leases for years, the Natives will be deprived of all legal right to hunt over their own native lands, and according to the dicta of certain high legal Authorities, may be forcibly excluded by the Lessee from the tract of Country so leased.[11]

Grey's response was to attempt to formulate a co-ordinated policy to recognise the property rights of Aboriginal people in the colony of New South Wales. In his instructions to the newly arrived Governor Fitzroy on this matter, in February 1848, Grey expressed his deep concern that the property rights of Aborigines were being ignored. He went on to describe the options he saw operating in various parts of the Empire. One was to set up large-scale hunting reservations, in which Aboriginal people could continue to support themselves by traditional means. This had been the basis for the Protectorate a decade before, and it is a measure of the victories of the colonists over those years and the diminished scope of the humanitarian agenda that this was no longer regarded as realistic in Australia. Grey discarded this option, partly because he held a simplistic notion of the random nature of Aboriginal movement over the land and did not understand the regular and bounded nature of Aboriginal harvesting practices. He argued as well that pastoralism in Australia required huge tracts of land, and that the infertility of much of the Australian geography demanded that pastoralists have access to all available grazing land to maximise their flexibility in poor seasons.

Grey nevertheless insisted that Aboriginal people continued to possess property rights to the land occupied by pastoralists. He argued that the meaning of 'Crown Leases' under the 1842 and 1846 Acts gave

> the grantees only an exclusive right to pasturage for their cattle and of cultivating such land as they may require within the larger limits of this assigned to them, but that these leases are not intended to deprive the natives of their former right to hunt over these districts or to wander over them in search of subsistence in the manner to which they have been hithertofore accustomed, from the spontaneous produce of the soil, except over land actually cultivated or fenced in for that purpose.[12]

He went on to state explicitly that the British view was that Aborigines had 'mutual rights' with the pastoralists over Crown leases, and that much of the violence of the past decades could have been prevented by due recognition of this fact: 'A distinct understanding of the extent of their mutual rights is one step at least towards the maintenance of order and mutual forbearance between the parties'.[13]

Grey argued that the Crown lease to pastoralists allowed only limited rights, and that much of the rights of possession remained 'reserved' to the Crown. He was convinced that the recognition of Aboriginal property rights on pastoral land had been achieved under the 1842 and 1846 legislation, in their provision for the creation of reserves (presumably in both senses of the word) and in his reading of the nature of the Crown Lease itself. Grey wished no confusion to arise in the colony, however, and instructed Fitzroy:

> If therefore the limitation which I have mentioned above on the right of exclusive occupation granted by Crown Leases is not, in your opinion, fully recognised in the Colony, I think it is advisable that you should enforce it by some public declaration, or if necessary, by passing a declaratory Enactment.[14]

This constraint on the rights given to pastoral lessees was the element of Grey's proposal which would have affected the Australian colony most widely, but he insisted that there should also be a companion policy for 'setting apart small tracts of land . . . to be cultivated either by them, or for their advantage'.[15] This proposal shows the great distance between the British reformers' position and any recognition of the traditional meanings of land for Aboriginal people. In Grey's view, small-scale reserves were intended to constrain Aborigines and teach them 'industry', not because of any fences or barriers to them leaving the site, but because their small size would be deliberately too limited for hunting, and so the Aboriginal beneficiaries would be compelled either to cultivate or to seek outside paid labouring to survive. Either way, Grey saw these small reserves as being the tools for forcing major social and cultural change, to transform Aboriginal landowners into the mythologised agrarian ideal of yeoman farmers.

Few white groups in the colony were favourably inclined to anything Grey might propose. Despite a depression in the international price for wool, it was clear that the main hope for Australian economic growth in the 1840s was to be its pastoral industry. The squatters were heavily represented on the Legislative Council, and had made substantial gains in the Waste Lands Act in 1846, but they felt they had done this against pressure from Grey and others in England. They now saw themselves as aligned strongly with most of the major advocates for self-government in the colony. All these groups had been outraged by Grey's first attempt to devise a constitution for the approaching self-government of the colonies without consulting the colonists. By the time Grey sought to influence the colonies on native title to land there was firm resistance from the squatters against humanitarian meddling in colonial affairs.

Yet there was a real sympathy in government and among the growing number of urban and rural working class to the idea that squatters' rights to land were only temporary and partial. The Waste Lands Act had handed over 180 million acres in New South Wales to about 1800 squatters, an outcome which had gravely alarmed urban wealthy and working-class groups.[16] To further exacerbate tensions, the squatters' consolidation of their runs led them to advocate the reintroduction of convict transportation to allow them adequate labour for their remote leases. Grey supported renewed transportation, and a convict ship arrived in Sydney in June 1849, only to be met with a 'great meeting' of protest in which both Grey and the squatters were condemned. There was potential for interest in Grey's proposals only if they were seen as limiting the power or security of the squatters.

At the same time, Fitzroy was being made aware of the continuing demands of Aboriginal people to use their lands for hunting and harvesting, camping and ceremonies. A number of the commissioners for Crown Lands were informing him that squatters frequently, and often brutally, refused access to what Aboriginal people regarded as their own land. The Commissioner for Wellington, W. C. Mayne, put the case most strongly, in a recommendation written in June 1848, apparently without knowledge of Grey's proposals. Mayne argued that the Aborigines in his district, which included the recently penetrated Brewarrina area, were vulnerable to 'gross breaches of law or humanity' by remote squatters. He recommended a general clause in leases which would force lessees to allow Aborigines access to all pastoral lands for water, hunting, gathering and camping.[17]

Although often portrayed as sympathetic only to the pastoralists,[18] Fitzroy supported Mayne's arguments and instructed the Crown law officers in July 1848 to begin inserting clauses into all leases which would guarantee Aboriginal access to pastoral lands. The Governor's direction had significantly weakened Grey's concept of 'mutual rights' and talked only of ensuring 'the *privilege* of free access to land remaining in an unimproved state'.[19] Yet in the highly charged atmosphere, where any tinkering with the terms of pastoral leases was seen as a threat to squatting interests, even Fitzroy's mild proposal was rejected by Crown law officers as beyond the terms of the 1846 Act and requiring a new Order-in-Council. Fitzroy appealed to Grey, who had anticipated this in February 1848 when he gave Fitzroy an unequivocal direction to overcome any 'confusion' by a 'declaratory enactment'. Grey arranged for the Privy Council to issue the additional order on 18 July 1849. This gave Fitzroy the authority he had requested to change the terms of the leases as he saw fit.[20]

The commissioners for Crown Lands had been circularised in September 1848 with an abbreviated version of Grey's February letter. This version omitted any reference to restrictions on Crown pastoral leases, perhaps because Fitzroy believed the matter to be already under way in response to Commissioner Mayne's submission. The circular did, however, include Grey's strongly worded insistence that substantial numbers of small reserves were to be created. This was of course the element of the British proposal which was less likely to anger pastoralists.

The responses from all the commissioners and from the Surveyor-General are fascinating in that almost all of them proposed some form of constraint on Crown pastoral leases to guarantee Aboriginal access to pastoral lands. The commissioners were generally less enthusiastic about reserves in their regions, for three broad reasons. First, many of them pointed out that the lands they supervised were mostly unsuitable for small-scale cultivation, and indicated that larger, pastoral reserves were the only ones likely to be practical in providing real support for groups of Aboriginal people. Second, many pointed out that Aboriginal people were tenacious in maintaining their possession of their own particular land, disliking unauthorised entry by neighbouring Aboriginal groups but also, many noted, intensely resentful of the white presence. It was put to Grey that reserves would need to be created within each group's lands, to allow free residence and usage. Third, the more perceptive commissioners argued that it was impractical to expect Aboriginal landholders to confine themselves to small areas as long as they remained 'still in possession' of their lands, with either the reality or the hope of real access to all of their country for harvesting and ceremonies. As Surveyor-General Mitchell put it, 'the idea of a reserved portion for his use is less likely to please the wild Native than to make him sensible of exclusion from the whole range of [his] country'.[21]

Nevertheless, most commissioners did recommend sites for reserves. They were not sites on which the different groups were to be concentrated, but instead were chosen to allow some land within language (tribal) boundaries for each of the main surviving groups in the pastoral areas. Commissioners had been asked to consult or at least consider likely Aboriginal wishes, and to select sites which were favoured and frequently visited by local Aboriginal people. There was surprisingly strong pressure applied to the commissioners to inform themselves about Aboriginal wishes, and in some cases these administrators showed that they had established reasonable communication with the Aboriginal people in their area.

At least 40 reserves were recommended. Only one commissioner, Bingham from Murrumbidgee, insisted on recommending extensive hunting reserves. Some of the rest were merely paddocks for safe but supervised camping close to the commissioner's headquarters, but most were described as being blocks of one square mile (640 acres), with good water sources, and in areas significant to specific, named language or kin groups. Some were areas of intense significance to Aboriginal owners, like Nganhu, the Brewarrina fisheries: a complex set of carefully engineered fish traps, essential to the economies of the surrounding Ngiyampaa groups, believed to have been created by the deeply revered ancestral figure Baiame who left the mark of his footprint in the rocks at the edge of the fisheries.[22]

In Gwydir, Richard Bligh recommended reserves on known camping sites near good water for each of the four main dialect groups in his region, including one square mile for the Pikampul on a well-favoured campsite at Boobera Lagoon. His recommendation acknowledged the Pikampul interest in this site, and their determination to stay on their own land. This reserve, however, could only have offered ambiguous haven. It was on Carbucky station, the sheep property held by sympathetic leaseholders but where neighbouring cattlemen were continuing to intrude to murder Aboriginal workers during 1848.[23]

Only the Surveyor-General addressed himself to the situation within the 'settled districts', where he suggested that reserves allowing access to the harbour and coastline for fishing were urgently needed now that private ownership by whites had taken what had previously been public waterfront. Mitchell argued that earlier such grants and reservations for camping areas had not been attractive to Aboriginal people when there were many alternative access sites open to them. The situation, as he pointed out, was very different by 1848 and 'these Aboriginal natives could NOW appreciate the benefit and avail themselves of it'.[24]

So the commissioners for Crown Lands strongly supported the recommendations from Earl Grey to restrict pastoral leases, and, with less enthusiasm, to create small reservations of land in the squatting districts. By late 1849 Fitzroy had his land administrators' support, and the power by Grey's second Order-in-Council to impose limitations on Crown leases. The squatters, however, continued to be bitterly opposed to any form of recognition of Aboriginal rights to land use.

Fitzroy was not known for his deep interest in Aboriginal matters, and he came under intense pressure from squatting interests. In 1849 the Legislative Council established a Select Committee to inquire into the Protectorate and the state of Aborigines generally, a body strongly weighted in favour of pastoralists. Reporting in September 1849, it savagely attacked the Protectorate, recommending its cessation, then dismissed the concept of restrictions on leases and argued against even the small reserves. Such notifications of reserved land would compete directly with squatters' interests, and the committee argued that 'settlers would be ousted of portions of their runs'. Fitzroy was clearly in some sympathy with the pastoralists, and wrote with pessimism to Grey in November 1849 that he and the Executive Council agreed with the Select Committee's report that there was unlikely to be any productive outcome from the creation of further reserves.

Yet the Governor continued to pursue some elements of Grey's plan. In January 1850 Fitzroy decided with the Executive Council that the creation of around 35 new reserves in pastoral districts would be authorised, and, most disturbingly for squatters, that new lease conditions would be drawn up, 'to secure to the Aborigines and others the right to wander over the unimproved portions of the lands demised'.[25] Then the will to resist squatter pressure began to evaporate. An important but as yet unanswered question is just why the new conditions to Crown leases were never drafted. It appears that the Executive Council's decision met obstruction in the drafting process and was simply not followed up. This may reflect a fundamental lack of sympathy with the measure, on the part of either the Governor or the administrative officers involved, which can be put down to successful pastoralist pressure. It may also, however, reflect the rapid shifts which overtook the issue once gold had been discovered in the colonies in the following year. This generated many changes to Aboriginal–white relations, one of which was the sudden end to conflicts about whether Aborigines could freely come onto pastoral leases.

But the creation of Aboriginal reserves did go ahead (Map 4, p. 54). In February 1850 Fitzroy notified Crown Land commissioners that 'a suitable number of Reserves of moderate extent' were to be created for Aborigines in the pastoral districts, following closely the recommendations the commissioners had made in the previous year.[26]

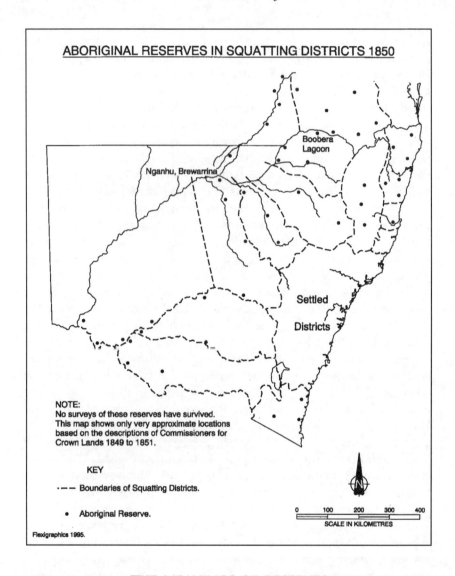

ABORIGINAL RESERVES IN SQUATTING DISTRICTS 1850

Boobera
Lagoon

Nganhu, Brewarrina

Settled

Districts

NOTE:
No surveys of these reserves have survived.
This map shows only very approximate locations
based on the descriptions of Commissioners for
Crown Lands 1849 to 1851.

KEY

·—— Boundaries of Squatting Districts.

● Aboriginal Reserve.

Flexigraphics 1995.

0   100   200   300   400
SCALE IN KILOMETRES

THE MEANINGS OF RESERVES

There can be no doubt that to Earl Henry Grey and the British Colonial
Office, as well as to the humanitarian reformers in England, the creation
of these reserves signified the recognition of Aboriginal property rights
in land. Henry Reynolds has reviewed exhaustively and compellingly
the vast documentary evidence which demonstrates this. Just one
indication is in the memo in Grey's office which recorded that his object
in the 1848 proposal was 'the conveyancing to the Natives the contin-
uance of their rights'.[27] As is clear even in this brief quotation, the rights

perceived by the British reformers were identical with those of bourgeois European property-holders. They were the rights of private, material property, which could be converted entirely into a monetary 'equivalent' to achieve complete compensation for dispossession and colonisation.

To the New South Wales colonial authorities and settlers, these reserves were, at the very least, ambiguous. The Executive Council did in January 1850 announce its intention to guarantee the *'rights'* of Aboriginal people to *use* pastoral land for subsistence and cultural purposes, and such usufructory rights were one type of property interest under common law. It fell short, however, of the commitment to recognise full property rights which was the humanitarian agenda in England. The 35 reserves created in 1850 were also ambivalently perceived by whites. The reserve over the Brewarrina fisheries, which forbade whites from taking fish, was treated as a serious matter by both Aboriginal owners and police, who were continuing to stop whites fishing there in 1906.[28] The belief that Aboriginal people were the 'the original and Native proprietors of the soil' was widespread among colonists in New South Wales, as was demonstrated by the reports of the commissioners for Crown Lands.[29] Yet the circular of the Chief Commissioner which announced the decision to create reserves spoke in terms of benevolence and charity, of 'the duty of the Government' to 'ameliorate the condition of the Aborigines', rather than of any recognition of past or continuing rights.

There were then significant differences between the British and colonial perceptions of the 1850 outcomes of Grey's proposals. The lease reservations appear to have been stillborn, but what did these 1850 reserves of land mean to Aboriginal people?

The commissioners were given emphatic instructions, repeated in later correspondence, that they must 'make known to the Aborigines by every available means that the tracts of land alluded to have been set apart for their special use'.[30] Bligh in Gwydir included in his annual report for 1850:

> I have in accordance with your letter of the 3rd September, 1850, #1697, endeavoured to apprise the Aborigines that these reserves have been set apart for their special use, but without much success, as it is difficult to make them understand the meaning of 'special reservation' of a square mile for their use . . . It will be easily seen that an effectively vagabond race of savages can have no very [great] sense of the advantage of a special reservation of a small tract for their use till the accompanience of the collateral receipts which the benevolence of the Government [offers] for them.[31]

A number of the commissioners reported, like Bligh, that they had followed instructions and tried hard to communicate to Aborigines the nature of these reserves. The way they explained them was to have a major significance in shaping Aboriginal interpretations of colonial land policy, and contributed to their later strategies for regaining their independence. To convey the meaning of 'Crown land', the monarch's ownership of all land in the colony had to be stated. Although there is little direct evidence, the later Aboriginal insistence that Queen Victoria promised them land suggests that the commissioners did stress the Queen's involvement; she was portrayed as the benefactress who now owned all 'Crown Land' and was offering these 'small tracts' to Aboriginal people. Certainly, too, the commissioners were emphatically directed to reassure Aboriginal people of the permanent security of these small areas of land. Given this strong interest on the part of the government to convince Aboriginal people of the security of the reserves, and to attract them to take up permanent occupation on them, there may well have been some echo of the promise implied by the squatters' lawyer, Richard Windeyer, to Mahroot only five years before: 'the land is yours and your children's forever and no-one can take it away from you'.[32]

It seems, however, that from Aboriginal perspectives, the reservations around areas of their land added no new meanings at this time. The significant sites such as the Brewarrina fisheries retained their complex economic, social and religious meanings, although the interdiction against whites using these harvesting places may have allowed Aboriginal owners to call on additional authority when asserting their prior ownership. The particular meaning of other small camping sites did not change simply because of being reserved, as long as the greater extent of their lands seemed still to be within the reach of their Aboriginal owners. Nor did the boundaries of the reserves offer real protection from marauding white hunters. In these stressful circumstances, there was little to interest Aborigines in the imaginary lines commissioners drew around small patches of their lands.

Yet it appears that Aborigines learnt that some areas of their traditional lands could be given back to them by Queen Victoria, and would be secure if they chose to live permanently or continuously on them. Despite the fact that these reserves were not particularly meaningful or useful in the circumstances of 1850, the process of their creation must have fostered an expectation among Aborigines that the colonial government's intentions in relation to Aboriginal owners were to see land as a central matter and that this government could and would act to ensure the continuing secure occupation by Aboriginal owners over at least some of their own country.

When the metropolitan, colonial and Aboriginal views are compared, it is clear that there were already very different perceptions of the meaning of the reserves created in 1850, long before they were marked on a surveyor's map.

5

Dual Occupation

At the time of the creation of these 35 reserves, Aboriginal people across the pastoral districts were 'still in possession' of their country, as the Surveyor-General was aware. But they were under intense pressure, as continuing violence and terrorism threatened to choke off altogether Aboriginal access to their lands. The reserves offered little to protect them, and were insignificant in comparison with the broader boundaries of their language areas and traditionally owned country. Like the Pikampul about whom Richard Bligh reported, Aborigines were desperately trying to maintain their contacts with their traditional country.

Then gold was discovered in February 1851 in New South Wales and later in the newly separated colony of Victoria. Among its many effects, this event dramatically and rapidly changed relations between landowners and invaders in pastoral New South Wales. White pastoral workers abandoned their jobs to try their luck at the gold diggings, drastically reducing the numbers of whites in most pastoral areas. The balance of power changed immediately on the frontier. In those districts where the invaders had only just begun to penetrate, such as the Paakantji lands of the middle Darling, and the areas to the north and west of Brewarrina, the Aboriginal landowners seized their chance and drove the remaining whites right out of their lands. The Paakantji were not to be invaded again for a decade.[1]

Just as suddenly, the Aboriginal landowners in the longer-established squatting districts found that the squatters who had attacked them only months before now began to court their favour, enticing them to come back to live again on their own lands as long as they agreed to care for the stock of the run. The pastoralists found that they desperately needed Aboriginal labour. They began to offer, for the first time, reasonable conditions and often cash wages.

But most importantly, they offered safe access again to traditional lands. The squatters had created barriers between Aboriginal owners and their country, and enforced the lines with cutlasses and guns. Suddenly these barriers disappeared, and Aboriginal owners could return to their lands. The cessation of hostilities allowed a restoration of Aboriginal occupation which could not have been anticipated during the debates about recognition of native title. The immediate outcome was that the newly created reserves faded in significance for all parties, as squatters stopped trying to exclude Aboriginal owners from their country, and Aboriginal communities reoccupied their lands as they took up work on their invaders' pastoral runs. This is the phenomenon referred to here as 'dual occupation'.

The extraordinary speed of these events was commented on repeatedly in the annual reports of the commissioners for Crown Lands. During the 1845 Select Committee inquiry into the conditions of Aborigines, squatter after squatter had complained that Aborigines refused to work in pastoral labour, that they could not be taught the necessary skills and that even if they did agree to work, their labour was erratic and unreliable. The reports from commissioners of Crown Lands in the squatting districts before 1851 either echoed these assessments of Aboriginal labour or at the least recorded the failure of employers to engage Aboriginal workers on a large scale.

In complete contrast, the same commissioners began sending reports from 1852 and on over the following decade, which were glowing in their praise of Aboriginal pastoral workers, and carried numerous testimonials from squatters grateful that their runs, whether sheep or cattle, had been saved by the generous attention and reliable care of Aboriginal employees. It became apparent that the change had not been in the skills of Aboriginal workers but in the attitude of squatters and in the conditions they were prepared to offer.[2] The commissioners' paternalism and their focus on pastoralists' needs is dominant in the following extracts, yet even so they offer glimpses of the varied but always dramatically new situation which unfolded with such speed in pastoral areas.

In Gwydir during 1849, Commissioner Bligh had reported widespread violence, which the whites had blamed on the 'savagery' of the Aboriginal owners but which Bligh had attributed after investigation to relentless white terrorism. In January 1853 Bligh wrote:

> No report of any outrage or aggression . . . in the limits of this district
> has reached me during the past twelve months . . . and I believe that
> the services rendered by the Natives to the Settlers during the difficulties
> consequent upon the present dearth of labour have been of the utmost
> importance amounting in some cases nearly to the absolute preservation
> of the flocks from the destruction which would have resulted from the
> impossibility of obtaining white men as shepherds.[3]

Commissioner Merewether of the the Macleay District was one of the majority of Crown Lands commissioners to describe in 1853 the rapid change over the past two years:

From what I could learn from the Blacks themselves, there has been a great demand for their services on the tableland, caused by the withdrawal of the whole of the labouring population to the different goldfields . . . The services of the natives have been indispensable. Indeed but for their presence most of the ordinary operations of the district would have been at a standstill and scarcely a single settler or squatter on the River is there, who has not had one or more in his employment under a written agreement at wages varying according to their degrees of usefulness and intelligence [from 30s to £15 per annum]. Many of these agreements have been entered into in my presence and to the credit of the Infidel be it said despite daily examples afforded them by the White man, I am not aware of a single instance in which they have been broken. The higher remuneration afforded to the Natives and the positive necessity to the Settler for their services have rendered them more mutually dependent, and the result has been in the one case greater pains bestowed in the training, and in the other, greater zeal in the performance of the task . . . The disposition of the Aborigines to be employed and of the Settlers to employ them have increased beyond expectations.[4]

From Commissioner Lockhart, in the Albert District on the lower Darling River:

The stock holders of the District having been obliged to fall back on the Aborigines for the labour necessary to tend their flocks it was discovered that the Aborigines were both able and willing to perform these duties . . . In the Albert District there are now 50,000 sheep and they are wholly shepherded by them. They are careful of the sheep committed to their charge. The sheep are in better condition and there occur fewer losses than formerly when Europeans were employed . . .

The experiment of employing the Aborigines of the Lower Darling as shepherds has been successful and . . . the flockmasters are now quite independent of European labour in this respect. The settlers located in this and in the neighbouring districts do not intend ever again to employ Europeans as shepherds and should European labour become available at some future period it will be reserved for those more laborious operations which require energy and a courage which the Aborigines do not possess . . .

The Aborigines now identify themselves with the interests of the Station . . . They do *most positively* feel a livelier interest in the welfare of their employers than European servants do . . . This year's clip of wool has at many of the Stations been principally shorn by them . . . Many of the natives have shorn from 800 to 1500 sheep and they clip much more closely and cleanly than it is possible to induce hired Europeans to do.

The widespread employment of Aboriginal people allowed them to travel over their lands, a practice remarked on by a number of the commissioners, including Lockhart:

> Feeding the flocks each day in a different direction they avoid the sameness which is so repugnant to their feelings and revisit scenes which recall occurrences of their past life. They have sufficient leisure on their extensive plains to amuse themselves in obtaining game and the very shifting necessary to the health of the sheep is highly agreeable to them. This shifting which is the cause of so much dissatisfaction and labour on a station where Europeans are employed affords the Aboriginal shepherds the greatest pleasure.[5]

Aboriginal women had already been widely employed for their skills as domestic and childcare servants, and were particularly valued in the general absence of white women. From 1851 this employment increased as Aboriginal workers were welcomed back onto the runs. But Aboriginal women were also drawn into the outdoor stockwork which was regarded as unsuitable for European women. This allowed Aboriginal women as well as men to have unfettered access to the whole expanse of their lands. In the north-western Bligh District on the Macquarie River, Commissioner John Robertson reported that the Aborigines were

> a very fertile source of labour to the squatters . . . In my official tours throughout the district, I have often met 'Gins' or female Aborigines herding or, as it is technically termed, tailing cattle in the bush and these females shepherd flocks of sheep with greater care and diligence than many European shepherds, so much so that some of the best flocks during last year have been under the guidance of the Aborigines. I have myself seen at farms or squattages other 'gins' or females performing all the operations required at a dairy while their husbands or brothers I found acting as stockmen . . . Indeed during the present great scarcity of Labour from the discovery of Gold I do not think the pastoral interests of the District could have been carried on without the Aborigines . . . Wherever I went, I found the Aboriginal labourer happy, well clothed, well fed and receiving fair wages from their employers.[6]

This renewed access to land allowed Aboriginal owners to continue ceremonial activity openly. They were now free to assemble in large numbers at ceremonial grounds, with less fear of ambush and pursuit. Everything from small local ceremonies to great gatherings with hundreds of participants continued in areas where dual occupation occurred for many decades, although they were sometimes shortened to accommodate the restrictions imposed by the pastoral timetable. Aborigines devised a way of taking part in ceremonies at the same time as being employed in stockwork: several commissioners recorded that Aboriginal workers would organise substitutes from within their community to do their work for them while they were away.[7] This was a pattern which was to be witnessed repeatedly in later decades in New South Wales and in later pastoral situations in, for example, the Northern Territory during the 1950s.[8]

The changes in relations brought about by gold were not shared equally across the colony. Aboriginal people whose lands included the goldfields immediately faced intolerable stresses as diggers began to flood in not only from pastoral areas but from overseas. Those whose country was near the diggings then began to suffer as previously pastoral land was turned over to cultivation to feed the diggers. At first, however, the most noticeable effects were the dramatic reduction in violence and the equally dramatic reopening of their lands to the Aboriginal owners in most squatting areas. Their incorporation into the workforce of these pastoral runs was so successful that a number of Crown Lands commissioners shared the conclusions of Richard Bligh, who saw some justice in the change of events: 'It is pleasing to observe that some share in the benefits which have accrued from the opening up of the auriferous wealth of Australia has not been denied to the original and Native proprietors of the soil from which it springs'.[9]

DUAL OCCUPATION IN PRACTICE

The particular qualities which pastoralists came to value in Aboriginal workers included, for the first time, a genuine recognition of the importance of Aboriginal knowledge of the land to locate feed, water and stock across vast distances. A number of other perceived benefits were derived from Aboriginal commitment to the land rather than from any decisions to become loyal servants to whites. These included their well-recorded 'faithfulness' to the employers on many runs, which reflected not only the importance Aboriginal people have consistently attached to personal relationships and obligations, but more significantly their faithfulness to the land and their assumption of responsibility for the people and stock who now lived on it. Another was their pleasure in the work of shepherding, which gave them the opportunity to travel over their well-known land and carry on their own lifestyle, whereas for white workers it was lonely, monotonous work in alien land.

A major difference in the way Aboriginal people were employed was that whites were taken on as individuals, whereas Aboriginal people were recruited from the extended family groups already resident on their land or seeking to return to it. They were embedded in a social network, which itself was directly attached to the land. This offered a strong continuity in labour for the pastoralist, rather than the often rapid turnover of isolated and lonely white workers. As accounts of Aboriginal stockworkers like Wilpi demonstrate, Aboriginal people also trained their young men and women in stockwork, as well as in the knowledge of the country which made their work so valuable. This allowed established skills to be maintained at the pastoralists' disposal in the permanent camp.

The Aboriginal workers were not only supported socially by their relations, they were supported materially. As long as the whole social group of Aboriginal landowners was living on the property, their hunting and harvesting continued, and much of the ongoing subsistence costs of the group as well as the employed workers could actually be met by the Aboriginal community. The pastoralists often counted their costs in employing Aboriginal workers as including the regular provision of meat to the whole group.[10] This encouraged the continued presence of all age groups, including the old and the very young even though these were seldom employed. This was done not as a charity but because it made good economic sense. The pastoralists' 'ration' was by no means enough to feed the group, but it was enough to ensure their continued presence. Then the rest of the daily food of the camp, including that of the workers, would be supplied by the hunting and gathering of those people not employed on stockwork. This was particularly the role of the older women, the grandmothers who cared for their grandchildren whose mothers were working in the squatter's house, doing his laundry or tending his flocks.

Aboriginal labour was not only being praised for the continuous work of shepherding during the early 1850s, but also for the work on cattle runs. Here there was less constant work needed: particularly once perimeter fencing became more common from the 1860s, cattle were mustered at regular intervals rather than tended all the time. In this discontinuous pattern of work, the employers needed only a few core permanent staff, but had to be able to count on a larger number of casual workers in busy seasons. The presence of an Aboriginal camp on the property continued to be very important in this irregular seasonal pattern. During the off-season, the Aboriginal community could largely support itself on bush tucker, but during the busy periods they could be recruited rapidly.

The viability of this dual occupation depended not only on an end to violence between invaders and Aboriginal owners but also on a substantial compatibility between the white and Aboriginal uses of the land. The most intense hostilities had flamed up in the agricultural areas around Sydney when the Aboriginal yam beds had been wholly taken over for the white farmers' crops. Around Bathurst and the early pastoral districts it was the intensive use by whites of Aboriginal economic resources and cultural sites which had forced Aboriginal owners into armed retaliation. Pastoral occupation of Australian grasslands eventually caused irreversible changes arising from the impact of hard-hooved animals on the continent's loose, shallow soils, the clearing of land, the introduction of rabbits and of course the interruption of Aboriginal firing. For a while, however, there was great compatibility between pastoral land use and Aboriginal traditional use.

The change in squatters' attitudes to Aboriginal workers involved a major conceptual shift: no longer were pastoralists seeking to change Aboriginal workers into whites in their habits and work patterns. It became much more economically attractive to try to keep Aboriginal workers living a traditional lifestyle, to conserve the economic, social and therefore cultural dimensions of Aboriginal society. As long as Aboriginal workers were still living on their own land and within their whole social group, they were much more likely to be available for both seasonal and permanent labour; they were more likely to be able to organise replacements during the times they had to be absent, to bring to the work the substantial skills arising from their intimate knowledge of the land, and to contribute to their own upkeep in food and accommodation.

Over time, pastoralists tended to portray the existence of Aboriginal camps on their properties as if they were the result of squatters' charity, the benevolence of the white victors in the grasslands wars. This construction of the past is belied when we see not only the glowing testimonials to Aboriginal workers which flow through the commissioners' reports in the 1850s and 1860s but also the steps pastoralists took to ensure their sources of Aboriginal labour even when white workers returned to the labour market. Rations 'to the tribe' continued on most properties, and as well as this pastoralists took on the distribution of blankets and medical aid with which the commissioners had been charged in 1850.[11] Squatters also took up the practice, started by Macquarie but then discarded as ineffective, of presenting 'king' or 'queen' plates to senior men and women, inscribed with the name of the pastoral run ('King of Kunopia' or 'Mogil Mogil') or the European names of rivers or regions ('King of the Barwon Blacks').[12]

Such 'king plates' may have been only symbols of the white belief that they could co-opt senior Aboriginal people into acting in white rather than Aboriginal interests. The pride with which such plates are remembered among Aboriginal families, however, and the authority with which elderly Aboriginal people can be seen to display the plates in late nineteenth-century photographs, suggests a real acknowledgment by the squatters of the authority structure of Aboriginal communities, where the elderly individuals who held greatest authority were those who spoke for the land. Endorsing the authority of these 'bosses' for the land with 'king' and 'queen' plates may have been most useful in securing continuing residence of the Aboriginal group.

The pastoralists also began to tolerate the cultural structure from which the elders' authority was derived, and after 1851 there are few reports of squatters refusing Aboriginal access to land for ceremonies. At times this meant camps of hundreds of Aboriginal people for weeks or even months, and while pastoralists may not all have been happy to host such gatherings, they seldom tried to intervene. Some went further, and provided rations for the camps, like the manager on Gundabloui in 1894, who gave beef to the *bora* (initiation) camp to supplement the Murris' own fishing and hunting.[13] Similarly, pastoralists are remembered as taking no part in affairs of the camp, never interfering in people's desire to speak their own languages, or in social matters such as discipline. When Ivy Green was asked if the Dungalear property management ever interfered with Murris, she replied in horror: 'They couldn't. It was their [Murris'] Law!'

Pastoralists also began to lobby government to regulate the contacts Aboriginal people had with whites, apparently with the goals of protecting their workforce. Particularly in the 1860s, it was pastoralist influence which succeeded in limiting the supply of alcohol to Aboriginal people in New South Wales. This was motivated less by a concern for Aboriginal health than by the fear expressed by a member of Parliament for the Lower Darling in 1868 that alcohol would make 'previously valuable' Aboriginal workers 'useless in pastoral and grazing occupations'.[14]

The continuity of these pastoral camps is a further indication that they played a structural role in the rural economy rather than existing as an expression of station owners' benevolence. The camps established during the 1850s on the big runs continued for as long as the properties remained large enough to require large numbers of seasonal workers, and to have a low enough stock density to allow the modified continuation of the traditional Aboriginal subsistence economy.

In the Walgett North Pastoral District closer settlement began to eat away at the edges of the big old runs through the 1890s, but pastoral maps from 1905 show that although nibbled and reduced around the edges, these properties retained a huge central core, where stock continued to be managed on the old patterns. The Aboriginal camps in this district were not scattered randomly, wherever charitable white owners happened to be in charge. Instead the nine Murri camps in the area were on nine of the thirteen largest properties out of a total of 49. In the Brewarrina District in the same year, the six Murri camps were on six of the eight largest properties out of a district total of 60. In the far west of the colony, the association of the presence of an Aboriginal camp and the size of the property is just as clear. Nor had these camps continued to exist on these big properties because of the links between the Aboriginal residents and a single benevolent owner. Instead, each of the properties on which a camp remained in 1905 had gone through a sequence of changes of ownership during the previous decades, and in the Depression of the 1890s, many had changed from individual ownership to company or bank ownership.[15] The owners had come and gone, but the camps had stayed.

These relations between pastoralist employers and Aboriginal workers have been described as 'internal colonialism', where instead of trying to change colonised workers into replicas of members of the colonising working class, employers try to conserve the traditional lifestyle and habits of the colonised group for as long as possible to exploit its particular qualities to generate more profits for the colonising economy.[16] The situation which developed in New South Wales after 1851 was certainly one where pastoralists no longer tried to destroy traditional life, but their presence and power could undermine custom. And the pastoral economy too was undoubtedly exploitative in the economic sense. Although Aboriginal workers were in some districts being paid high cash wages during the 1850s, in other areas they were paid only in kind. While most Aboriginal groups appear to have been eager to resume occupation in security on their own lands, this was not so where the white pastoralists in the area were cruel employers. The commissioners' reports suggest that this occurred only rarely when pastoralists were as dependent on Aboriginal labour as they were in the 1850s, but even then they record some occasions when coercion and violence was used to force local Aboriginal people to return to a property and work on it.[17] Accounts of this way of organising pastoral labour are available from the 1950s in the Northern Territory, and they make clear that there continued to be dangers and severe pressures on Aboriginal people living in and working from these camps, which ranged from the impact of diseases to the violence of coercive employers and rapists.[18] Aboriginal people in some areas in New South Wales have recorded stories about cruelty and coercion on properties, and they are often acutely aware of the exploitative nature of the pastoralists' interest in encouraging Aboriginal camps.[19]

In later years, as more white workers became available, pastoralists could play on the Aboriginal commitment to remaining on their land to reduce the cash component of wages to virtually none, or entrap it in the account books of the property store. By the turn of the century, Aboriginal workers from the resident camps were still making up around 30 per cent of pastoral labour in north-west New South Wales, but they were increasingly relegated to casual or seasonal jobs, and the better paid and permanent jobs were reserved for white employees.[20] And for all the profits made from these pastoral concerns, there was little more than a token paid to those who were 'the original and Native proprietors of the Soil'.

Nevertheless, living on these pastoral camps is remembered widely by Aboriginal people as being most often an experience of peaceful community life, in which they could travel frequently over their country, maintain traditional ceremonial and social traditions, eat healthy native foods as well as European rations, speak their own languages and teach their children about land, traditions and recent history. These are remembered as times when Aboriginal traditional knowledge was acknowledged by whites for its value to pastoral work, and when Aboriginal expertise at stockwork, horse riding and property management were widely respected.[21]

The strongest impression which arises from Aboriginal people's memories of pastoral life in New South Wales is of an immersion in the processes of Aboriginal life and philosophy which they missed when forced to move under more direct white supervision on missions or reserves.[22] The pastoralists could coerce and constrain, but they did not challenge or try to obstruct the dominance of Aboriginal paradigms, the power of an Aboriginal worldview.

THE LAND RELATIONS OF DUAL OCCUPATION

Aboriginal land use necessarily changed and developed under the impact of the new pastoral economy. There were limitations on traditional practices. The pastoral runs, though extensive, did not cover the whole areas of language groups, so the range of land which Aboriginal owners could visit frequently was restricted. Important tools of land management, such as mosaic firing of grassland, had to cease, as pastoralists feared the small fires and did not understand either their creative or their protective roles.

Pastoral managers wanted to have stockworkers and domestics close at hand. The convenience of both employers and the workers who had to assemble each morning for work, as well as easy distribution of rations, contributed to the increasing use of one site as the main camp, usually somewhere near the main group of homestead buildings. Other campsites continued to be used as outstations by smaller groups working with stock or hunting and harvesting, but the main camp took on a more permanent nature. This changed movement patterns over the land as well as changing the nature of social relations from a day-to-day focus on very small immediate family groups to wider extended family groups who now saw more of each other most of the time. This main camp had characteristics which, although derived from pre-invasion life, had developed to meet the new circumstances.

One was the burial ground, usually located at a short distance from the camp, which came to hold more burials in one place than had been usual during the previous more mobile lifestyle. The numbers of burials which took place there reflected the continuing toll taken on Aboriginal lives by the diseases of invasion, but the mode of burial and the attention paid to the graves was directly related to custom and tradition. On Yuwalaraay and Kamilaraay lands, for example, these pastoral burial grounds were decorated with clay, specially collected and shaped while wet to record and honour the dead.[23] As European materials became a constant part of Murri life, the potential of bottles and glass as grave decoration was recognised. Murris developed a technique of burning coloured glass bottles and plunging them into cold water until they crazed. When broken into small 3 or 4 centimetre pieces and embedded in the surface of graves, these glass sections shimmered like water in the sunlight. The graves close to centres of population today continue to be devotedly tended in memorialisation of the dead. The graves which mark the pastoral camps are now less accessible to be cared for, but they still shimmer, marking out the sites where Murri landowners occupied their land at the same time as they built up the pastoral runs of their invaders.

Births as well as deaths were recorded on the land. Aboriginal people brought up in the pastoral camps remember their birthplaces being affectionately pointed out to them. They recall them as a link between themselves, their mothers and the land. Again, these places tended to become more concentrated around the permanent camps as pastoral life began to shape the way people moved around their country. Birthplaces and occurrences at the time of birth were important in naming Aboriginal babies, and they were an important element in the process by which people identified themselves and established their relationships to other people and to the land.[24] Clusterings of birthplaces and the presence of burial grounds around main campsites thus intensified the associations and meanings of that place in a way which was a traditional process but which had been activated only in the particular circumstances of the new pastoral economy.

The timing and rhythm of land use changed too, as Aboriginal landowners became more engaged with the cycles of pastoral life. As the commissioners recorded, Aboriginal people continued to conduct ceremonies on their lands, initiating their young people into manhood and womanhood, and celebrating the great mythic dramas. Many large gatherings were reported in the later nineteenth century, bringing together people from different language groups to camp on pastoral land, sometimes for months, to prepare and carry out the important rituals.[25] The Aboriginal practice of finding substitute workers to replace them if they were needed to participate in ceremonies continued to be widely reported.

The smaller and more regular ceremonies, however, came to be rescheduled to occur in the quiet off-seasons away from shearing or mustering, or in a parallel rhythm to the Christian holidays, such as Easter and Christmas, which brought the European economy to a standstill. Many Aboriginal people in south-eastern areas remember 'Christmas camps', when they took the opportunity to escape the tedium of the main camp and regular work to travel out onto their lands and visit the places they had missed during the year. Sometimes these 'holidays' took people to the riverbanks or lagoons in the inland, to the remote rocks and their waterholes in the far west, or to the beaches on the coast, to fish, swim and relax as well as to cram in as much ritual, teaching and learning as they could.

The patterns of daily life changed, with pastoral work added to the experiences which caused challenges, successes and failures, generating jokes and long, funny stories as well as the tragedies of accidents and the dramas of personal conflicts. And these were patterns which took place in some forms of interaction with whites, either as bosses, respected or disparaged, or as workmates, trusted, hated or just eccentric. The close interactions with whites included sexual relationships, usually between white men and Aboriginal women, and ranging from brutal rapes to long and affectionate partnerships, although even these were seldom acknowledged by other whites. All these complex but changing aspects of pastoral experiences were linked by memory, retold and interpreted around fires in the camps, and became part of the new knowledge which was being woven into traditional knowledge about the land. There might be new experiences to recount, and new characters in the dramas, but the stories were told to illustrate traditional interests and were shaped into the familiar forms for oral transmission, and were invariably linked to the site on which they were said to have occurred. The stories told to Katherine Langloh Parker by Yuwalaraay people during the 1870s and onwards suggest some of these processes, and they are still clear in the stories collected by Roland Robinson on the coast in the 1950s.[26]

FREE SELECTION

The fragile accommodations between Aboriginal people and their invaders in the pastoral industry were almost immediately threatened in many areas. The pressures brought by the gold rushes began to expand like ripples. As the diggings became less profitable, the diggers flooded into the major cities or to rural areas, still seeking the golden future they had hoped to find on the goldfields. Their voices were heard loudly in the political debates of the time. Already, on the diggings, miners had formulated a vision of the future in which land was the shining goal. The Eureka Stockade in 1854 echoed to the cry of 'unlock the lands' almost as often as any demand for an end to miners' licences.

The desire for land was frequently expressed through the 1850s by the rapidly expanding Australian working class. With little appreciation of the environmental limits on the country, urban workers and artisans were intensely resentful of the hold pastoralism had on what seemed a vast and now empty land. The sense that so much land was simply waiting for proper use contributed to the ideal that a portion of land was the 'rightful inheritance' not only of the squatters who had previously claimed the land as their 'birthright' but also of the working men of the cities.[27] The cry became one for 'free selection': the right of whites to make their choice of any block of land, which they would then be entitled to own freehold if they could just meet low repayments and the residence qualifications.

This intensified the pressures on government to overturn the 1840s land laws, to release land from pastoralism and hand it over to the thousands of diggers and urban workers who were clamouring to reshape themselves as sturdy yeomen. By 1856, self-government allowed the new political alliances to challenge the squatters' hold on power and open the way for the first attempts to implement the agrarian myth by breaking up the squatting runs. New land laws heralded a series of changes which were to affect directly the relationship between Aboriginal landowners and the British in the south-eastern areas.

Although bitterly contested, these land laws came into force in New South Wales in 1861 and in Victoria in 1865, and both claimed to fulfil the cry for free selection. The shifts which occurred in the period from 1860 to 1890 can be seen as *intensification* of British land use. This was not just an economic process, but a major change in the social use of space in the colonies.

Invasions began again after the first distracting years of the gold rushes.[28] There was further white pastoral expansion into the area west of the Darling River in New South Wales, in which Paakantji people and then the Wangkumara in the corner country faced a renewed assault. These newly invaded lands then faced a different type of invasion, as minerals were discovered at Silverton and Broken Hill in 1882. In the central and eastern areas of Victoria and New South Wales, the 1860s saw the intensified use of land already taken over by whites. Some pastoral land was converted to agriculture, destroying the possibility of continuing native flora and game, while fencing obstructed Aboriginal access. The fences needed workers to build them, but once done there was little further need for shepherds or cattle tailers. Cultivation often required many hands at harvest time, but there was no space for an Aboriginal camp, and no longer the opportunity for indigenous hunting and harvesting. Other pastoral runs were cut up for smaller grazing selections. Here the work of shepherding was again made obsolete by fences, and the greater stock density damaged the ecology even more quickly, and so reduced the possibility of compatible Aboriginal and British economies. There was an obviously reduced need for stockmen and shearers.

In Victoria, despite heated conflict, a large amount of pastoral land had come under cultivation by the later 1870s, while in New South Wales the squatters retained a stronger hold; the Land Acts of 1861 were only effective in altering landholding in a few areas of the colony in the 1860s. The areas already affected by goldfields pressures continued to intensify, and the coastal areas, the Monaro and New England saw substantial sales of land. Some of these were to squatters exploiting loopholes in the law, but many were to selectors. The expansions of transport, with river steamers and railways developing through the 1860s and 1870s, along with the increasing recognition of the profitability of wheat in the western slopes and plains, contributed to a greatly extended cultivated area in New South Wales by 1880.

The 1861 Land Acts had forced squatters to buy as freehold much of the land they had previously held by lease. So although the Robertson Free Selection Acts were seen to have allowed the squatters to retain much of their land, the pastoralists had had to go deeply into debt in order to protect themselves from selectors. To cover their greatly increased mortgages, squatters across the remaining pastoral districts began to increase their rates of stocking. On the largely untouched old runs, these higher rates could continue for a while to be compatible with Aboriginal land use, although within two decades they were seen to have caused irreparable damage to the natural fodder of the western areas. The spread of rabbits exacerbated the land degradation on all runs, and on those which were being reduced in size by selection, the increasing stock density during the 1860s and 1870s intensified the pressure not only on the land but on the Aboriginal owners.[29]

Those Aboriginal people whose land remained as pastoral runs, in the west, north-west and the hinterland of the far north coast, were in a relatively stable situation even though the pressure on the environment was increasing. Here dual occupation continued, fragile but surviving, on into the new century. In the areas of intensifying land use, however, Aboriginal owners were once again faced with intolerable pressures.

Kooris near the goldfields and the adjacent lands which had been turned over to farming, those of the south coast and the areas around Sydney, faced sudden and simultaneous losses of native foods, jobs in the white pastoral industries, and access to their lands.

During the later 1860s and 1870s, it was the Aboriginal groups of the New England area and the Monaro who were more heavily affected, losing jobs and access to land as pastoral runs were cut up for small grazing selections and then increasingly for intensive wheat farming.[30] Those in the Riverina came under pressure as the wheat boom gathered momentum and the developing steamer transport along the Murray and lower Darling disturbed the fishing on which Aboriginal people increasingly depended as they lost pastoral work and access to game. The north coast was less directly affected by the 1861 Land Acts, but it was also undergoing intensification of land use, first with sugar in the 1870s and then in the 1880s with new grasses and the expansion of dairying through new technology. The upper reaches of most rivers were little changed in the 1870s, and pastoralism with dual occupation continued in the Macleay and other areas. The coastal plain was more rapidly affected, but even here the rate of white population growth was uneven. Settlement from Moreton Bay rapidly populated the far northern rivers area but left the middle coast, from the Hunter to the Nambucca rivers, to experience a much slower rate of development.[31]

There were further changes caused by the free selection fever over these years. The development of roads and railways to transport the new crops, and to construct the infrastructure expected for the dense settlement of the land, added to the process of penetration and dissection of Aboriginal lands into unfamiliar fragments. And the railways also brought a major new group of whites into Aboriginal lands, the large gangs of railway builders and then the fettlers who maintained the lines. These railway workers were the only working-class group other than station hands and shearers who were in touch with many Aboriginal people. Although rarely traced, the relations between Aboriginal people and railway workers were extensive in western New South Wales, and their fates were linked in that at times the NSW government saw Aborigines and fettlers as posing similar threats to morality.

The most powerful impact arose from the development of rural towns, growing out of the need to service the new selectors, and sustained by the links which the railways allowed. The towns represented a new social dynamic in rural areas, producing a different class and gender mix of whites, with middle-class merchants and professionals and many more white women and children than had ever lived on the squatters' runs. This new population made new demands on the state and the churches, such as schooling and the patterns of regulation which churches and law courts allowed. The towns created a focus of white occupation, a social invasion which was far more concentrated in its possession of the land than the invasion of the squatters or even the cultivators had been. The towns were residential and domestic space, the most protected symbols of security for individuals and communities in white society. Only some small segments of the squatters' homesteads were so sacrosanct, and in any event, with many Aboriginal domestic servants, even these domestic spaces were shared. The towns too came to rely eventually on Aboriginal women's domestic labour, but it was often confined to heavy cleaning and laundering, rather than the more intimate childcare which was so frequent an occupation on pastoral runs. Springing up through the 1860s, the towns depended for their fortune on the stability and success of waves of selectors, and these were precarious. While often flourishing during the 1870s and 1880s, many country towns began to decline with the Depression of the 1890s, and so their hold over the concentrated areas of land within their municipal boundaries was often tinged with insecurity even in the early days. The towns were to impose a very different set of relations on the Aboriginal owners of the land than the pastoral runs had done.

Part II

Regaining Land, 1860s to 1900s

6
Aboriginal Land Demands

As Aboriginal people faced these new pressures in the 1860s and 1870s, they needed strategies which would allow them to survive in some meaningful way. They were to have no support in this from the state, which after 1850 had no policy addressing issues that concerned them. As the realities of dual occupation in the pastoral areas overtook the hostile confrontations of earlier decades, the 1850 reserves slid into oblivion. There had been little survey work completed when they were declared, and the main demands on the Surveyor-General's Department during the mid-1850s were to chart the boundaries of pastoral runs and the new reserves for water, agriculture and town development beyond the settled districts. There appear to be no surviving maps which record the locations of these 35 Aboriginal reserves, with the notable exception of Nganhu, the Brewarrina Fisheries.[1]

The local Aboriginal landowners continued to use those reserved campsites or harvesting grounds which had previously been of significance to them, such as the lands around Boobera Lagoon near the MacIntyre River.[2] But the boundaries of these square mile reserves simply disappeared from white records as the struggle over pastoral land escalated after 1861. Only the pastoralists knew where they had lain, and they had no interest in identifying yet another piece of their land which was vulnerable to withdrawal. The power to reserve land 'for the benefit of Aborigines' was included in the 1861 and all later land laws, but otherwise, by default, the NSW government's policy continued to be the piecemeal ameliorative medical assistance and occasional rations which Earl Grey's instructions had laid down.

Yet Aboriginal people were under urgent pressure in many areas, and they began to take steps to protect themselves. Some people were pushed right off their country, notably those who migrated from the south coast in the 1860s and 1870s; impoverished and angry, they camped around the shores of Port Jackson, drinking, begging and demanding fishing boats and land, to the great irritation of the NSW government and the Sydney population.[3] Most, however, were still trying to stay on or near their own country. Aboriginal people may have remembered the promises of the early 1850s, but they had given them their own meaning. The commissioners for Crown Lands early in the 1850s had been instructed to explain the nature of reserves and try to entice Aboriginal landowners to occupy them. But Aboriginal spokespeople in the 1870s and 1880s showed little interest in the precise concept of reserves, which assumed retention of ownership by the Crown. What they had understood from the commissioners' explanations was that the government was prepared to secure some of their own traditional lands, free from white invasion and control.

The circumstances of 1851 had made the government's offer of reserves irrelevant, but ten years later, in areas where white land use was intensifying through free selection, the possibility of retaining some portions came to be increasingly attractive. Aborigines began to demand restoration of access in the areas where they were being hardest hit. They were at enormous disadvantages in power and resources and their spokespeople had to find ways of conveying their demands in a hostile climate. By the late 1850s the newer forms of the agrarian myth were drenching the free selection debates at the centre of contemporary white politics, and Aboriginal spokespeople appropriated language and concepts from this discourse to explain their desire for land to whites. Yet the Aboriginal-authored requests for land always included something more, a glimpse of a very different vision of the land's meaning.

There was no formal organisational link between Aboriginal communities themselves at this time. What appears in retrospect to have been a common strategy emerging among Aboriginal groups across the eastern half of New South Wales was in reality a series of separate community or individual decisions. But these decisions were taken with common needs and desires and in very similar conditions. Communication between Aboriginal groups continued, at ceremonies along the old cultural networks and as people travelled looking for work in the white economy. Aboriginal people eagerly followed the decisions and outcomes in other areas and referred to them in their own demands for land.[4] These years saw the first demonstration of a sense of common Aboriginal interest wider than the language group, on issues which were both traditionally based, in land, and were an engagement with the very new conditions of colonialism.

There were few actions to secure land in the remoter areas where dual occupation continued. Across the eastern half of the State, however, where land use was intensifying, Aboriginal landowners found they had three strategies open to them. The first was for Aborigines to make direct approaches to the government or the press, allowing us to read their own words about what they wanted and why. In the second, Aborigines recruited a local white figure, perhaps a policeman, priest or missionary, to convey their demands, which we therefore have only second-hand and perhaps distorted by the messenger. The third was where they took direct action, occasionally buying or leasing land, but more usually by reoccupying and squatting on some of their land and beginning to build huts and plant crops. We know of these actions only where tenure was retained or where the land was eventually reserved by the Crown 'for the use of Aborigines' in recognition of Aboriginal occupation, so it is still not possible to trace all the occasions on which Aboriginal communities took action to regain some of their land.

The earliest example of the first approach was in Victoria, where Aboriginal people faced the new pressures first and most intensively. In 1859, independent of the government protectors' activity in other areas, Goulburn Valley Aborigines began to petition collectively for some of their land to farm as compensation for loss of their traditional resources. These Taungerong and Woiwurrung members of the Kulin Confederacy met officials themselves and also recruited a series of whites to carry their demands to government. They chose 4500 acres of farming land close to a culturally significant site on the Archeron River. Driven off by local whites, the Kulin persisted, squatting on another site which was finally reserved for them as Coranderrk. There they began farming wheat and then hops, pioneering the crop in the area throughout the 1860s and 1870s.[5] At least some individual Aboriginal farmers in eastern Victoria also sought land, asking missionaries for help in petitioning the government.[6]

In New South Wales, the clearest example of Aborigines demanding land directly is that of Cumeragunja, on the Murray near Echuca. The Aboriginal community there was closely connected to the people of the Kulin Confederacy, some of whom had moved to the New South Wales border region when the Victorian government began interfering in Coranderrk affairs in the 1870s.[7] William Barak was a senior Coranderrk man who had been involved in leading a number of Kulin campaigns for independence, including the 1859 land demands and the earlier joint decision of clan heads to take part in the Victorian Native Police force, in an attempt to stem the loss of Koori life and gain negotiating power with La Trobe.[8] Barak was visiting Maloga (the mission forerunner to Cumeragunja) in 1881 when the Aborigines there formulated their demands, in wording very similar to that of the Kulin in 1859, for 'a sufficient area of land to cultivate and raise stock . . . that we may form homes for our families . . . and in a few years, support ourselves by our own industry'. Their requests were made, they argued, as compensation because 'all the land within our tribal boundaries has been taken possession of by the Government and white settlers'.[9]

The land at Cumeragunja was notified as Aboriginal reserve in 1883, but only a small amount was arable, and the community insisted that they wanted adequate good land for each family to be able to farm productively. The Cumeragunja people maintained their demands consistently, repeating them to a local journalist in 1886, after the newly formed Aborigines Protection Board had ignored calls to give land directly to family groups, then organising another petition which was presented to the Governor in 1887.[10] In the same year the local parliamentarian received letters from two Cumeragunja men, John Atkinson and his brother William Cooper, the latter to become a major political activist.[11] These letters amplify the demands made already, and their language is important in revealing the complexity of Aboriginal interests. Both Atkinson and Cooper were aware of the free selection debates and show their interest in operating in conventional working-class and selector roles within the colonial economy. At the same time, Cooper's letter in particular reveals the fundamentally different attitude to land which these Aboriginal men held.

Atkinson explained that he had tried to save money to buy a selection but had found it an 'utter impossibility' because Aborigines in the area could not gain constant work. As the area converted to intensive wheat agriculture, Aborigines were being squeezed out of the earlier permanent work they had gained in the pastoral industry.

> I want a grant of land that I can call my own and which I can leave at my death to my wife and children. I beg, however, to point out clearly that I do not want the power of being able to sell the land. Having for several years tried to save enough to pay for a selection I find it an utter impossibility . . . We know that grants of land have been made to the aborigines in other parts of New South Wales . . . Be good enough to give our tribe a trial.[12]

Cooper's letter, while repeating his brother's plea for secure, inalienable land as a source of economic independence, called on the government to secure 'this small portion of a vast territory which is ours by Divine Right'.

Cooper was using the language of the Christianity to which he had been recently converted, but the concept was not Christian: he was insisting on recognition of Aboriginal rights of prior ownership. This statement takes on even greater significance when we compare it with the discussion on reserve lands in the late 1840s, when Thomas Mitchell had suggested that the boundaries of the small reserves would remind Aboriginal landowners of what they had lost, rather than offering them a sense of possession. William Cooper had gone beyond this. He was suggesting that the 'small portion', while limited in area, nevertheless signified the whole of his people's 'vast territory'. The boundaries of his selection would certainly remind him of what he had been excluded

from, but the very existence of the 'small portion' would be an acknowledgment of the existence of that 'vast territory' and a testimony to the
continued responsibility its Aboriginal owners felt towards the largest
expanse of their lands.

While the Coranderrk and Cumeragunja people have left us the
greatest evidence of their own statements, there was not necessarily any
less Aboriginal agency in the second strategy, in which white officials
were recruited to articulate and convey Aboriginal demands. During the
early 1870s, this strategy was adopted repeatedly in the south-eastern
and mid-coastal areas. In 1872, on the Braidwood goldfields, Aborigines
from the south coast and the highlands areas met in a large ceremonial
gathering at which they also discussed ways of meeting the current crisis.
The local police officer, Martin Brennan, recorded the result:

> When the festival was over, sixty-two blacks called upon me. Jack Bawn
> and Alick were the leaders of the deputation. I asked Jack what they
> wanted. He replied, 'We have come to you to intercede for us in getting
> the Government to do something for us. Araluen Billy, our king, is old,
> and cannot live long; my wife Kitty and self are old, too. I have assisted
> the police for many years, and we want to get some land which we can
> call our own in reality, where we can settle down, and which the old
> people can call their home. Everyone objects to our hunting on his land,
> and we think the blacks are entitled to live in their own country.'
> . . . I replied that I would do what I could for them, and inform
> Jack Bawn of the result . . . On 29th March, 1873, I sent [the
> government] a comprehensive report covering eight sheets of foolscap,
> detailing their treatment, condition, customs and aspirations . . . Shortly
> afterwards I received instructions through the Police Department to
> survey forty acres of Crown Lands in whatever locality Jack Bawn
> desired as an Aboriginal Reserve. Jack desired the land fronting the
> Shoalhaven River at the base of the Jingeras, where fish, birds, and wild
> animals were plentiful.[13]

Jack Bawn and his people were unable to occupy this land because of
hostility from surrounding white farmers, but they continued to press
Brennan for land.

In 1872 also, three senior Aboriginal men from the Bodalla region,
Richard Bolway, Merriman and Yarboro, made formal submissions to
local officials for secure land around the entrances to Tuross and Birroul
lakes. Their demands were met with some confusion among Lands
Department officers, confirming that they were an Aboriginal initiative
rather than a response to the implementation of government policy. The
Lands Department eventually decided that these requests should be
dealt with as if they were requests for the creation of new Aboriginal
reserves. The lands were already within coastal reserves, however, so the
department argued that a further reserve was unnecessary and recorded

the Koori demands as 'permissive occupancies'. The three men, like Jack and Kitty Bawn, persisted in their demands for more security of tenure, and in 1878 they finally succeeded in having these three areas of land registered as Aboriginal reserves.[14] Just to the north of Sydney, similar processes were occurring, with Aboriginal people calling on local officials to record their desire to hold some of their own land in secure tenure. Willie Price asked for land in 1873 at Nelson's Bay near Karuah, and he too was told that as an existing coastal reserve was in force, his land would be secure enough if it was held only as 'permissive occupancy'. Although Price was unable to gain further security over the land, the Lands Department was still prepared to confirm his right of occupation in 1892 when it was queried.[15]

The Lands Department documents suggest that 'permissive occupancies' may have been a frequent outcome of Aboriginal demands for land during the early 1870s, wherever the land requested was already under one or other of the many types of reserves the Crown had established by that time over wide areas. This form of title is extremely tenuous, and tenants could be turned off their lands at the whim of the local Land Board officials. Such frail occupancies are unlikely to have survived the intense pressures on Aboriginal landholding which were to emerge after 1900, and so their only record may be in faint pencillings on old maps and in the memories of their Aboriginal owners. A few, however, were either converted to Aboriginal reserves or otherwise recorded within the Protection Board's Register of Reserves, and so we are able to trace their presence.

One of the most important of these was the land reoccupied by William Drew at Kinchela, near the mouth of the Macleay River, in 1880. Drew took up 26 acres of rich alluvial land close to the river, and began clearing and farming. His application for secure tenure was met by a decision of the Lands Department in 1884 to grant him 'permissory occupation' (*sic*), meaning that he was allowed to retain the land 'on sufferance until required by the Government'.[16] A later permissive occupancy over beachfront land was granted to William Ridgeway at Tea Gardens, on the northern side of the Karuah inlet, in 1905, adding to the possibility that there may have been other such Aboriginal requests to secure land between 1870 and 1905 which led to the same outcome.[17]

There had certainly been many other Aboriginal people appealing to local white officials through the 1870s to pass on their requests for secure tenure over some of their land. In 1882 the NSW government appointed George Thornton as protector to inquire into the conditions of Aborigines, and before he formulated or implemented any policy he surveyed local authorities to find out what the most appropriate aid for their area might be. His respondents returned many indications that Aboriginal people were asking for their land. He received a strongly worded response from Brennan, who was still trying to secure land for Jack Bawn and his people:

> I have known blacks in the Braidwood and Coast districts very intelligent, who have been and now are excellent farm labourers, and whose aspirations at all times were to be allowed some land which they might call their own in reality; which they might cultivate unmolested for the use of themselves and their families; and where the aborigines of the surrounding districts might meet periodically for the purpose of holding coroborees and other exhilarating games.[18]

And there were other responses which demonstrate similar Aboriginal decisions to recruit white men to convey their demands. At Lambton, a small Aboriginal family had lamented to the police 'that they had no homestead of their own'. From Marsden in the central west, police reported that Aboriginal requests were for 'some land for married people'. From Gundagai a reply to the question about what aid might be relevant came as 'some land to cultivate. They say they are driven away by owners of land . . . there are two tribes. A piece of land on the river for each'. The Nundle report was: 'Where there are tribes such as are at the Richmond River and other places, it would be a source of great pleasure for them to have hunting grounds reserved for their purposes'. From Moama, the area which would become Cumeragunja, the response was predictable: 'The Blacks at Maloga are desirous of getting land allotted to them to cultivate for their own support'.

At Armidale the conflict between Aboriginal aspirations and settler interests was evident: 'The half-castes who are rather intelligent are very anxious to get a grant of land from the Government, stating they are well able to manage it, but the general opinion is that they are better without it'. From Arakoon, the area at the mouth of the Macleay, where three Aborigines were reported to have begun cultivating vacant land well before 1883, the police commented: 'Aboriginals are very proud of calling a piece of ground their own'.[19]

These responses indicate a continuing desire for land in areas of New South Wales where white use was intensifying. They also indicate that although whites may have discarded the idea of land for Aboriginal hunting and harvesting, Aboriginal people themselves had not ceased to call for such expanses of land. The Armidale response suggests, however, that the hostility which the Coranderrk people and the Bawns' community had faced from white selectors were not isolated cases but examples of a perception of Aboriginal people as being in direct competition with whites for agricultural land in this period of free selection fever.

Recruiting officials to call on government for land was not the only option. Kooris in the Burragorang Valley won perhaps the most spectacular victory using this strategy in a different direction. They recruited the assistance of the local Catholic priest, Father Dillon, who raised enough cash in 1876 to buy a 70-acre farm called St Joseph's on the junction of the Cox's and Wollondilly Rivers. Partly freehold and partly conditional purchase, St Joseph's was handed over to the Aborigines, who from that time, entirely independently, made 'a very fair living rearing stock and growing maize' and supported an extended family group of around 50 people until the 1920s.[20] When the church tried to enhance its finances by reasserting its ownership over the freehold section in 1908, the Aborigines there said that they regarded the land as their own, refusing to recognise the church's authority over the farm.[21]

The danger of recruiting whites to convey Aboriginal demands was that the aims of government and church were not the same as those of Aborigines, so their demands were open to distortion. This happened in 1890 at Jervis Bay, where, like others on the coast, Kooris were seeking land but where missionaries were also looking for a foothold. Daniel Matthews was by then in conflict with Aborigines at Cumeragunja who rejected his authoritarian control, and he was considering a mission where he would 'gather together all the blacks on the coast between Port Stephens and Twofold Bay', that is, from two-thirds of the length of the New South Wales coast![22]

It was well known by the 1890s that such a relocation proposal would be resisted by Aborigines, but there were nevertheless south coast Kooris around Sydney and at Jervis Bay who felt the plan might at least give them access to some land for themselves. Sixteen Kooris were prepared to sign the petition asking the government for land, although they did not ask for missionary supervision. Matthews and the other churchmen involved had clearly had a hand in drafting the petition, but the result was an uncomfortable mixture, where the mission aims—'we want to learn to live like Christians'—were often swamped under the anger of phrases which appear to have arisen from more direct Aboriginal drafting:

> We, the native blacks about Sydney, ask you if you will be kind enough to give us a piece of land at Jervis Bay, where we can make a home for ourselves and our people. We have been hunted about a good deal from one place to another, and we find it hard to get a living for ourselves and our children, but if we get a chance and some help from the Government we might in time get a living. As it is we find it very hard. Drink and a hard life are killing us off. White people ought to be very good to us for they got our good country for nothing. We don't want them to pay us for it, but they ought to help us to live. We would like our boys and girls to learn to read and write like white children, and we

want boats and nets for fishing, so we can get money for our work and
learn to live like Christians.

We are left wondering if in any case the phrase 'to live like Christians'
had the same meaning to missionary and Aborigines, or if the latter
regarded it more as a level of material affluence or access to power.

Aborigines often chose the third strategy, direct action. Occasionally
they were able to buy land freehold, like the Bell family near Yass in
1881 or, in a few cases, secure a selection, like the Aboriginal family at
Coonabarabran who were running two or three hundred sheep on their
land in 1882.[23] Generally lack of funds or access to the bureaucracy
prevented such formalisation and Aborigines simply reoccupied their
own country, squatting, building, and planting crops. The decisions to
take such action were unrecorded, as were the events themselves, but
when the government began to make inquiries in 1882, the existence
of the reoccupations became clear. The Pelican, Shark and both Fattorini
Islands in the Macleay River near Kempsey, for example, were not
notified as reserve until 1885, but in 1883 police were reporting that
up to 40 Aborigines, of whom they named the heads of families, had
been in occupation for some years, clearing and cultivating the land.[24]
At Gloucester, 60 Aborigines were supporting themselves fishing and
growing vegetables on a portion of 50 acres of church and school lands
of which they had 'taken possession'.[25] Along with three farms at Port
Macquarie, where Aborigines had 'taken possession', another example is
Killawarra, near Wingham, where 100 acres had been occupied and
parts of it cultivated by Billy Johnston for a year before the land was
reserved in 1882.[26] On the south coast, the parallel situation was
commonly reported, as at Tathra near Bega, where the reserve was
notified in 1883 for 'George Cohen and family who have resided on it
for a number of years. Six acres cleared and enclosed, two acres under
cultivation'.[27]

These were not casual and transitory campsites but were the results
of active decisions to take back some of their land, like that of 'Frank'
at Nambucca Heads, who 'occupied Brushy Island nearly two years ago
[before 1883]' and that of the Kooris of Cabbage Tree Island, who were
farming the island in 1893 after 'they themselves took possession [of
it] a few years back'.[28] Some reoccupations may have been less recent,
with land occupied residentially from the early days of the invasion
becoming agricultural bases over time. This was the case with St Clair
outside Singleton, where Aborigines had been camping since at least the
1850s and where they had already harvested several crops of maize,
tobacco and potatoes, before the area was finally reserved in 1890.[29]
Rollands Plains near Port Macquarie was similar, where police reported

in 1887: 'Been occupied by the Aborigines for years and four acres roughly cleared in which they have planted maize and pumpkins'.[30]

There were three consistent elements in all these Aboriginal demands for land, shown in either the text of the formal applications or the actions taken. First, Aborigines were asking for land as an economic base from which to participate in the capitalist rural economy. They usually planned agriculture or small-scale grazing; the south coast Aborigines often planned the reserves as residential bases from which to fish for the market as well as for subsistence. This was not so different from contemporary white expectations of a selection, but the nature of the title Aborigines requested was different. They were certainly not asking for 'Crown land reserved for the use of Aborigines', but neither were they asking for simple freehold title. Rather, they called for full ownership but without the power to sell the land. This was explicit in the few Aboriginal-authored requests for land such as Atkinson's and Cooper's letters, and it was strongly implied in the desire for unmolested security expressed indirectly, like that of Jack and Kitty Bawn. They wanted what would now be called inalienable freehold, in order to ensure that they could pass the land on to their descendants.

The final element was unique and central to all the Aborigines' demands: they were not asking for just any parcel of productive land; they were asking for land within their traditional country. William Cooper's 'small portion of that vast territory which is ours by Divine Right' was the clearest statement, but the sentiment was strongly present in each of the requests, usually expressed as something like the right to land 'in our own country'.[31] Although the concept was not expounded in detail, it is clear that Aborigines were arguing that their ownership of land was sanctioned by tradition and religion.

THE NSW GOVERNMENT RESPONSE, 1860–83

The only colonial legal and policy precedent for responding to these Aboriginal requests was to fall back on the power to reserve Crown land for the use of Aborigines. So this is what officers of the Lands Department did, just as they had done eventually for Richard Bollway, Merriman and Yarboro on the south coast. The stimulus and the pressure to create these reserves came from Aboriginal decisions, but the tenure by which the lands were secured related only to white concepts of desirable uses and meanings for land. Certainly, however, these early reserves were not the result of any government policy to contain or segregate Aboriginal people. The government responded positively to Aboriginal demands because they were so in tune with the current political discourse of selection.

This had its dangers. Aboriginal fighting with squatters over land may have been over. But Aboriginal appropriation of the language of free selection emphasised that now they were in direct competition with white selectors. Despite the inclination of government to respond favourably, Aborigines did not get every piece of land they demanded, finding themselves always in conflict with local white land hunger and racism. The hostility towards Jack and Kitty Bawn on the Shoalhaven and towards Aborigines near Armidale was not unusual; a clear case was that of Bob Tobonts who requested land in 1886 on the Rous River on the far north coast. He was rejected after advice from the district surveyor that 'the land applied for is rich bush suitable for agriculture and if reserved would *lock up the land from settlement*, the habits and inclinations of the aborigines being not favorable to the settled and continuous labour required for clearing and cultivating the land'.[32]

This area was not only fertile but one where the local economy was booming with new technology and the expansion of dairying, and so the white population grew rapidly. With such competition, it seems that Aborigines on the far north coast could not formalise their tenure over any agricultural land on which they may have squatted, or even keep an informal hold, but instead were pushed onto less fertile, sandy campsites.

In general, however, officialdom responded positively to Aboriginal demands for land because Aborigines appeared to be doing just what Earl Grey had wanted them to do: recognise the reality of invasion, accept small agricultural patches of land as compensation, and settle down to be British farmers. The Aboriginal perceptions of their demands were very different, as we have seen. They consistently demanded land within their traditional areas, and it can be assumed that many, like William Cooper, were seeing any formalisation of their rights to even a small patch of their land as a recognition of their rights over the 'vast territory' of their own country.

Thirty-two reserves were created between 1861 and 1884, when the next major piece of land legislation was brought down (see Map 6.1). Most of these reserves were notified before the Aborigines Protection Board began functioning in 1883. The Lands Department passed over to the Board in that year the plans and details of at least 25 existing Aboriginal reserves, totalling 3500 acres,[33] and eventually all 32 were traced.[34] By laying these reserves out on the map it can be seen that their distribution does not correspond with the few areas of continuing armed hostilities, to the west of the Darling River or in isolated pockets of the far north coast hinterland. Nor did the reserves correspond with areas of highest surviving Aboriginal populations, which included the far north coast but also the north-west and far west. If the government

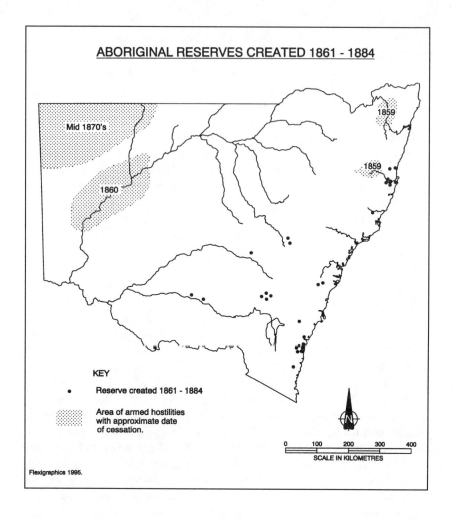

ABORIGINAL RESERVES CREATED 1861 - 1884

Mid 1870's

1859

1859

1860

KEY

•   Reserve created 1861 - 1884

     Area of armed hostilities
     with approximate date
     of cessation.

0   100   200   300   400
SCALE IN KILOMETRES

Flexigraphics 1995.

was responding to its own or to white missionary recognition of Aboriginal poverty and distress,[35] this again must have been localised. In the early 1880s Aboriginal people were not uniformly impoverished: in fact Aboriginal self-sufficiency was still high around 1880, with 81 per cent of the Aboriginal population economically independent from a mixture of wage or ration labour, farming, and more traditional subsistence foraging. The distribution of reserves actually corresponds closely to the districts most affected by the gold rushes and the 1861 Land Acts, where intensification had gone furthest in stripping Aboriginal landowners of land and resources.[36] But the outcome was not in most cases a proliferation of mendicants being offered indoor relief by charitable whites but a series of independent Aboriginal decisions about strategies to survive under these new pressures.

The greater proportion of these reserves, 27 of the 32, were created because Aborigines had demanded them or had already reoccupied the land and begun farming. If we include Cumeragunja, in spite of some involvement by the missionary Matthews, this makes 28 out of 32.[37] The creation of these reserves was not the implementation of a government policy to segregate but the achievement of a victory for Aboriginal communities in their attempts to regain some of their land, although the title fell far short of the inalienable freehold for which they were asking.

7

The Aborigines Protection Board

While the NSW government had shown no interest in Aboriginal people since the 1850s, the Victorians, stimulated by the more rapid and thoroughgoing intensification of land use, had been much more active. There the government had moved in the mid-1850s to establish a Board for the Protection of Aborigines which was empowered by a formidable array of legislation. This body began to intervene actively in Aboriginal community life, forcing people to move onto a small number of reserves under tight missionary control, then using its powers to expel some of them, on the basis of colour and descent as well as their degree of political resistance to missionary or government protector's control. Policies of removing children from their parents, 'to better their conditions', were also implemented early and actively, throwing Aboriginal families into turmoil. The independent Aboriginal farming at Coranderrk was viewed with deep suspicion by this Board, as it was seen as enhancing the Kulin community's solidarity and permanence. The Board's goal, on the other hand, had shifted from amelioration during the 1850s to become by the 1870s the removal of any long-term Aboriginal presence in the colony, by 'education' and 'employment', or any other means. In 1872 the Board tried to take over the independent Aboriginal farms on Coranderrk, and then when it faced strong and sustained opposition from the residents, it began from 1884 to dismantle the community by expulsions and removals of children.[1]

Pressure began to mount in New South Wales during the mid-1870s. The Parkes government was developing a body of legislative tools in welfare and social matters, but had got no further with Aboriginal affairs than Fitzroy's compromise steps in 1850. Aboriginal actions to demand land had begun to stir awareness within the bureaucracy, and missionaries were becoming more active in the south-west of the colony. Daniel Matthews had migrated from Victoria, and in 1874 selected land on the Murray at Maloga, where he began a small settlement in response to the distress of Aboriginal people caught in intensifying land changes and in loss of traditional game in the Riverina area. Close by, at Warangesda in an area of mixed pastoral and increasing agricultural land use west of Narrandera on the Murrumbidgee, the Revd J. B. Gribble began another small mission school and settlement in 1880. Both these missionaries petitioned the NSW government for urgent benevolent aid to Aborigines, whom they characterised as impoverished and without any alternatives.

Aboriginal people themselves, however, from the areas immediately around Sydney were the more effective stimulus to government action. Small groups of Kooris from the Illawarra region, the Burragorang Valley and the Hunter River began to come to Sydney. The Illawarra people often camped at La Perouse; the others camped in the boatsheds of Circular Quay. These were the Kooris drawn to the city because they were suffering increasing poverty and dislocation on their own lands. Their demands for land and boats attracted as much attention as their drinking.

Pushed by such diverse pressures, the Parkes government reluctantly appointed George Thornton in 1882 as protector to the Aborigines, instructing him to inquire into the actual state of Aboriginal people in New South Wales and make recommendations about further action. Thornton's surveys provide invaluable information about the effects of changing land use on Aboriginal people, and include fascinating glimpses into the demands Aborigines were placing on local whites, as well as into the attitudes of local officials towards them. Thornton recognised the need for ameliorative and benevolent action in some areas, although revealingly his main efforts were directed at repatriating the Aboriginal residents of the Quay boatsheds. His strongest positive recommendation was that the government should continue to respond to Aboriginal demands for land. He firmly believed in the redemptive powers of small-scale cultivation, and he seemed to expect that areas of 10–40 acres should be handed over to Aboriginal farmers without surveillance or control.

> I am strongly of the opinion that reserves should be made in such parts of the Colony, where it can be conveniently and usefully done, for the purposes of the aborigines, to enable them to form homesteads, to cultivate grain, vegetables, fruit, etc, etc, for their own support and comfort. I have every reason to hope and expect great success from granting reserves of from 10 to 40 acres of land for the uses of the aborigines in their own particular districts . . .
>
> This would provide a powerful means of domesticating, civilizing and making them comfortable.[2]

Thornton's support for the rapid expansion of the reserve network was quite separate from his acceptance of the need to have larger, supervised settlements with missionaries and teachers for a form of indoor relief. He also appeared to believe that lands handed over to

Aborigines were to be more or less permanent or at least secure. He acknowledged that the title to such lands would be 'Crown land reserved for the use of Aborigines', but most of the references in his report were to '*grants* of land for aborigines', implying a more permanent process of handing land over. His frequent use of the word 'grant' suggests that the police and land officials explaining these reserves to Aboriginal residents may also have used this ambiguous term.[3]

Alexander Stuart, as the new Premier and also Colonial Secretary, opposed Henry Parkes's inactivity on Aboriginal matters, and made more finance available, yet he still endorsed what was essentially a *laissez-faire* approach. Ameliorative work was to be accelerated in districts where it seemed necessary, but private charities and missions were to be encouraged to carry out such work even where subsidised by government. Stuart approved Thornton's recommendations for creating reserves for Aboriginal families and individuals. A Board for the Protection of Aborigines was to be appointed, replacing the lone Thornton with a group composed of interested private gentlemen and officials such as the Commissioner for Police who would oversee the work of all police who were to be appointed as protectors, but this board was not to introduce any major change of direction to the current state of affairs.[4]

The other approach which had been open to Stuart was laid out very clearly in the first report of this board. The new board echoed Thornton's pleasure at the existence of Aboriginal farming, and endorsed his suggestion that the numbers of reserves be increased. But in its view the most urgent need was for strong interventionist legislation on the Victorian model, which would vest all reserve lands in the Board, give it total power, *in loco parentis*, over Aboriginal children and allow it wide powers over the movement and residence of adults, who could only be freed from the net by 'exemption certificates'.[5]

Premier Stuart simply ignored the Board's pleas, finding such active intervention distasteful and unnecessary, and no doubt anticipating that it would be expensive. In a situation therefore very different from that in Victoria, the NSW Board began its existence without any legislative base, with virtually no power and with no clearly defined policy.

Ominously, while the Board endorsed the independently farmed Aboriginal reserves, it also resurrected another very different conception of reserves, which had been present in the earlier rationales for grants under Macquarie, as well as being part of the Victorian Board's perception of the use of reserves. This was the reserve as a segregation area, a buffer against contact between Aboriginal people and whites.[6]

The application the Board saw for such a reserve was significant. At Brewarrina, in the heart of a very stable pastoral area, a township was developing to service the pastoral industry. The site the whites had chosen for their town was the southern bank of the Barwon River, virtually opposite Nganhu, the rich fisheries constructed by the Ngiyampaa and their neighbours. The Ngiyampaa continued to camp at their fisheries on the land reserved for them there in 1842 and 1850, and confirmed under the 1861 and 1884 Land Acts. Whites were forbidden to take fish from the rock fish traps by the 1842 and 1850 reservations.

But the town had continued to grow, and like all towns catering to pastoral rather than selector populations, there were many more hotels and grog outlets than there were stores, churches or schools.[7] Aboriginal people camping at Nganhu, on the reserve which became known as Barwon 4, found alcohol readily available and used it freely. The abuse of alcohol allowed Brewarrina's white town residents to begin to demand that the whole camp be removed to a great distance away, arguing that it would be for the good of the Aboriginal residents to be removed from white influence, but also that it would remove an obstruction to town expansion and to white use of the fish traps.

The Aboriginal interest in the fisheries was, however, undeniable and the Protection Board had in any case no power to remove Aboriginal people to another location, so in 1885 it chose a compromise. It recommended the notification of a reserve over 2000 acres of land, later extended to 5200 acres, to be resumed from the pastoral property of Quantambone, 10 miles east of the town on the northern bank of the Barwon River. Here missionaries were invited to establish a ration station, in order to entice the camp residents out of town. At the same time the Barwon 4 reserve around the fisheries was reduced from 640 acres to 100 acres, on the northern bank of the Barwon only; the town was left free to expand along the southern bank.[8] The Murris of Barwon 4 did not, however, leave their favoured campsite. Some moved out to 'the Mission' as schooling was established there, but most stayed on the camp near Nganhu and eventually enrolled their children in the town school. The mission, however, became the home of the Murri pastoral workers who were working on Quantambone and who had formerly been living on a camp area closer to the homestead. This allowed some government subsidy for the wages bill at Quantambone, and most Murris went up each day to work at the station, which would always send down to the mission when extra hands were needed.[9]

The Brewarrina case demonstrates the forces operating from the beginning on the new Aborigines Protection Board (APB). It was a small administrative body, with little support or interest from the government, no legislative base and no policy. In reality it was a body which could only respond to the pressures put upon it. It could not ignore Aboriginal wishes or interests, as it showed when it declined to revoke the fisheries reserve, and it had no wish to obstruct such a worthy goal as independent cultivation. For these reasons the Board continued to respond to Aboriginal demands for land. Yet it also faced increasing pressure from white interest groups, who now had an administrative body to which they could channel their complaints or demands. One such group was the employers of Aboriginal labour, who began to advise the Board about where reserves might be located to conserve their labour sources most efficiently.

Another group was rural townspeople, whose perception of the nature of reserves was very different from those of either the Board or Aboriginal people themselves. The townspeople believed that reserves were places in which Aboriginal people should be confined, preferably under supervision, and although their labour should be available whenever required for domestic or other services, they should be kept firmly out of sight for the rest of the time, for ever. In the many statements made by many town authorities about Aboriginal reserves over the next century, there was occasionally the odd reference to reserves as places where Aboriginal people might receive medical aid, or rations, or education. But most were simply to reserves as places where Aborigines should be confined. Townspeople regarded reserves as always being 'somewhere else', where Aborigines rightly 'belonged' and to which they should be 'sent back'. Aboriginal people were seen to have no automatic right to a domestic dormitory area for themselves within the town boundaries nor any rights to access to the hotel, the stores, the school or the very streets.

The pressure of both these white interest groups influenced the Protection Board decisions on reserve notification over the next decades. A further important force was the Land Act of 1884, which addressed the limitations and weaknesses of the 1861 Act. The new legislation increased the pace of change in land use on the coast and began the penetration of selection and some agriculture onto the central and northern slopes, the northern half of what became the Central Division. The Western Division remained untouched, and so too did the form of labour organisation of the large pastoral properties there.

Between 1885 and 1894, when the next Land Act was passed, the APB recommended the creation of 85 reserves for the use of Aborigines; 47 of these were validations of Aboriginal occupation or responses to Aboriginal requests for land which was then occupied immediately. All of these reserves created on Aboriginal demand were on the coast or in the south-west, with the exception of two on the northern slopes. The south coast reservations were, like those of the previous two decades, usually on sandy coastal land, intended as a residential base from which to fish. All of the others were already under cultivation when notified or were intended for immediate preparation for cultivation.[10] The incoming Board was quick to take credit for having worked educative miracles in establishing Aboriginal farming; the fact that Aborigines had already been living on and farming many of these areas was conveniently overlooked in its later reports.[11]

Land use had begun to change in the north of the Central Division and there were some Aboriginal requests for land there. The most detailed records are about one which was unsuccessful, made in 1890 by a group of sixteen 'adult half-castes Aboriginal' (*sic*) with their nineteen children, for 100 acres on the Borah Creek near Narrabri, 'for school and agricultural purposes'. Their letter was written for them by F. L. Wortley, a man of Afro-American and European descent, who may have been married into the Murri group. As it was to do on later occasions, the Protection Board used Wortley's lack of Aboriginal descent to reject the claim of the 35 people there who were Aboriginal, although it did add that the land in question did not seem suitable for agriculture.[12]

Forty-five per cent of reserves created in this decade were not the result of Aboriginal request, for example those at Oban near Guyra and Burra Bee Dee near Coonabarabran. Although created because of advice by employers and local officials, these reserves are nevertheless extremely significant in that they record the continued presence of Aboriginal landowners on their own country during the pastoral period of land use in the area; they are the mapped traces of dual occupation.[13] Their notification as reserves, however, marked the local end of dual occupation, and the beginning of a severe constriction in the land readily accessible to Aboriginal owners. Aboriginal movement and residence were then focused more intensely on the campsite than at any time during the main phase of dual occupation.

Not only employers but also rural town authorities had recognised that reserves could serve their purposes, which were to have true segregation areas to contain Aboriginal town camps out of sight but not out of reach. Aboriginal women had become increasingly important for domestic labour and for heavy institutional labour like hospital laundries, while sexual relations between white and Aboriginal townspeople, exploitative or otherwise, were common although not often acknowledged.[14] Brewarrina was not the only town to begin to pressure the Board for reserves to contain the local population. At Walgett, just to the east, the long-favoured campsite for 100 local Murris, the Namoi Bend, was notified as a reserve after requests from whites to control and contain its population.[15] This first decade of Protection Board control of reserve creation showed the Board to be still highly responsive to Aboriginal demand but to act also on demand from white pressure groups.

The next attempt to implement closer settlement was the Land Act of 1894, implemented during the 1890s Depression, which threw many Aboriginal people out of work. This coincided with evidence of the destruction of the native pastures by pastoralism in the Western Division, and the economic and environmental stresses together forced a restructuring of the industry which shifted stock out of the ecologically fragile west to increase the stock densities of the smaller pastoral holdings on the northern slopes and plains. In the decade to 1905, the Protection Board proved less responsive not only to Aboriginal demand but also to white townspeople's calls for segregation reserves. Most of the 45 new reserves created in this decade were in the northern half of the Central Division, and these were reservations of land on which Aboriginal people were already living in pastoral camps. These reserves both recognised and trapped substantial Murri populations, and their names are central to twentieth-century Aboriginal history in the region. Kunopia pastoral camp on the MacIntyre became Euraba reserve until the Murris there were shifted east to Toomelah. Terry Hie Hie was home to the survivors of the Myall Creek slaughter, as well as to many other Kamilaraay Murris. Burra Bee Dee, Wingadee, Walhallow and the Mole at Quambone were just as significant for their Ngiyampaa and northern Wiradjuri landowners.[16]

Townspeople also called on the Protection Board to create segregation reserves in this period, although they found the Board reluctant to act. It did try to replicate the Brewarrina situation at Walgett in 1895. The town reserve at the Namoi Bend was revoked and a new reserve notified 6 miles out of town on the banks of the Barwon River on Gingie sheep station. Its intention to entice town Murris out to Gingie failed totally. They continued to camp at the Bend, and to enrol their children in the public school in town. The Murri residents of the pastoral camp on Gingie also declined to move to the new reserve, preferring to camp closer to the homestead. The Gingie reserve lay, unused and forgotten, for 30 years.[17]

The Board had no more success in Yass in 1901. There, in response to townpeople's demands that it remove the Aboriginal population from within the town boundaries, the Board tried to encroach on the independent farming of the Lewis family on land originally notified for them in 1875. It attempted to expand the family's reserved area, but only so that it could then transport the whole town Koori population out to their more remote land. The Lewises protested bitterly that the land had been set aside for their use only and the Board finally admitted defeat in 1903, in the face of Yass Kooris' refusal to move and the

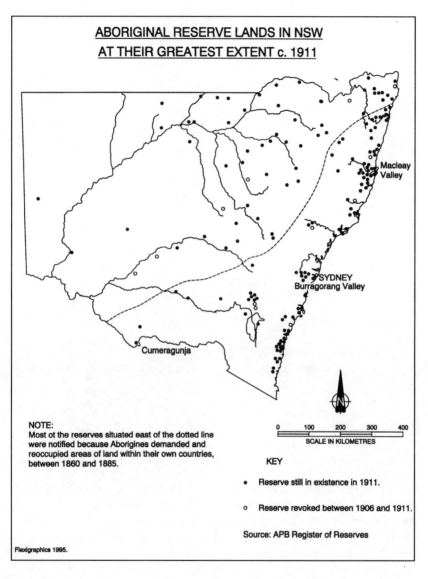

ABORIGINAL RESERVE LANDS IN NSW
AT THEIR GREATEST EXTENT c. 1911

Macleay
Valley

SYDNEY
Burragorang Valley

Cumeragunja

NOTE:
Most of the reserves situated east of the dotted line
were notified because Aborigines demanded and
reoccupied areas of land within their own countries,
between 1860 and 1885.

0   100   200   300   400
SCALE IN KILOMETRES

KEY

• Reserve still in existence in 1911.

o Reserve revoked between 1906 and 1911.

Source: APB Register of Reserves

Flexigraphics 1995.

Lewises' opposition to their loss of independent use of the reserve.[18] The Board severely criticised the Lewises for taking such an independent view of reserve lands, because it had become painfully aware that it needed to use existing reserves for its own strategies to manage Aboriginal populations.

By 1905 the lifting of the worst of the Depression and drought of the previous decade led to a revitalisation of the closer-settlement lobby, leading to new land laws. One early effect was to stabilise the creation of Aboriginal reserves. Aboriginal demand had slowed virtually to nil,

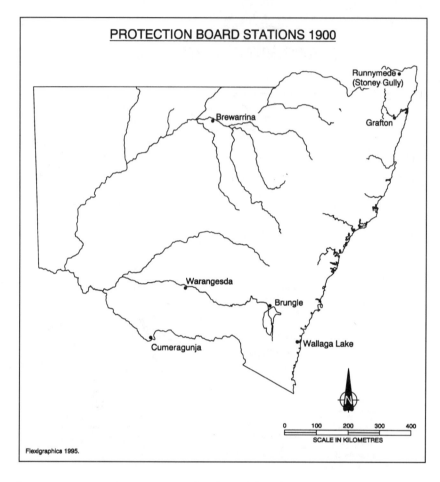

PROTECTION BOARD STATIONS 1900

Runnymede •
(Stoney Gully)

• Brewarrina

Grafton

Warangesda

• Brungle

Cumeragunja

• Wallaga Lake

0   100   200   300   400
SCALE IN KILOMETRES

Flexigraphics 1995.

but in any case there was no land available for reservation which was not sought also by white would-be selectors. Aborigines had to turn their attention from attempts to secure more land to defence of those pieces they had already won. At the height of Aboriginal holding of reserve lands in 1911, there were 115 reserves totalling 26 000 acres. Of these, 75 were created on Aboriginal initiative (Map 6, p. 95).[19]

Most of the reserves created on Aboriginal demand were farmed and managed by Aboriginal people themselves, and were never controlled by the APB. The three church-funded establishments in existence until 1892 had been on Cumeragunja, Warangesda and Brewarrina, only one of them the site of Aboriginal land demands. The Board took over these poorly funded 'Missions' in 1893, and proceeded to appoint four additional resident managers (Map 7, above). None of these appointments was over land reserved on Aboriginal initiative. While the Board had installed yet another four resident managers by 1910, only three

96

of their 'Stations' had been imposed on independently settled reserves. The Aboriginal-settled reserves were all in the areas where European land use had intensified but where there had been a rate of white settlement slow enough to allow at least some land for Aborigines to reoccupy.

The peak of Aboriginal demand for land in New South Wales and Victoria seems to have been from the 1860s to the 1890s. In South Australia Aboriginal moves to secure land by lease, purchase or reservation drew on methods very similar to those used in New South Wales.[20] Perhaps this can best be seen not as a phenomenon of one colony but as a movement around the temperate south-eastern agricultural belt. Despite differing policies in the various colonies, Aborigines in this region developed broadly similar strategies of using the free selection movement to regain some of their own land, for their own purposes.

8

The Aboriginal Experience of Regained Lands

Regaining some of their own traditional land and living on it securely had a powerful effect on Aboriginal landowners. The 75 independently claimed and farmed reserves were spread across the eastern and south-eastern part of the colony, setting up a physical chain of similar experiences of successful reassertion of rights to land (see Map 7.1). In 1910, between 1500 and 2000 Aborigines were recorded as living on or in direct association with these reserves.[1] This meant that around 25 per cent of the enumerated 7300 Aboriginal population had some knowledge of them. As Aboriginal people remember these lands, they usually recall them as being owned primarily by one man, or a married couple, but there were mutual expectations that kin members would come to live and work on the land and share its produce at different times of the year.[2] There were then even more people belonging to extended kin networks who had an experience of participation in using the reclaimed lands.

As a means to self-sufficiency, the reserve lands gave mixed results, but this reflected the variable quality of the land rather than limitations in the skills of Aboriginal managers. The south-western Kooris, particularly at Cumeragunja, were intensely eager to farm but were disadvantaged by their small plots of land and lack of capital. Although the reserve was notified in 1883, disputes between the missionaries and the government delayed any start to farming, prompting further Koori demands in 1887, which included Cooper and Atkinson's requests for a modest 100 acres each. What they in fact received was a 27.5-acre 'family farm block' on Cumeragunja in 1888. Neither Matthews' missionary body nor the Board which took over in 1893 could afford to put in adequate irrigation. Arable land on the original 1881 acres reserved was limited and the hostility of surrounding white landholders prevented expansion for some years. Modest extensions were made in 1893 and 1900, but all the land remained flood-prone. By 1898, however, twenty blocks of varying sizes existed on 300 acres of the reserve. The Kooris demonstrated their skills early, returning wheat harvests at or above the area's average in bushells per acre, but neither their skill nor their determination could provide returns adequate to support families.[3]

The Lewis and Wedge families at Yass were on land which was suited in many years to grazing rather than farming. These farms were nevertheless reported by local police to be producing a 'modest living' throughout the later years of the century. The Bells were on better land at Blakeney Creek and so were more successful, producing 15 tons of potatoes in 1894, with 10 acres under wheat and 200 fruit trees planted.[4]

In the Burragorang Valley, the fertile independent farm at St Joseph's continued to support a community of Kooris into the new century. A focal person in this community was one of the original Koori farmers, Mary Toliman (or Tolami). She was also the midwife for the whole valley, caring for both Aboriginal and white women in childbirth. Like Mary, many other St Joseph's farmers, including members of the Sherritt, Riley and Anderson families, worked outside the farm for wages in dairying or agricultural labouring but returned to work their own farm in the busy season.

The 1890s had been hard years for this area because as well as the difficulties of the Depression there were underlying economic shifts. Refrigeration and newly introduced grass varieties were allowing the north coast dairying industry to compete successfully with the Burragorang dairies. As the valley became more impoverished, local whites tried to improve the viability of their farms by increasing the size of their holdings, and the Aboriginal farm seemed an easy mark. This land came under threat in 1889, when the section which was conditional purchase was resumed for railway reserve and then applied for by a local white farmer. The Protection Board stepped in to defend Aboriginal tenure and secured a Reserve for the Use of Aborigines over that section, while the remainder continued to be owned nominally by the Catholic Church. The church too had become poorer, and it began insisting that Aboriginal farmers give up the portion of St Joseph's held in the church's name. Nevertheless, the Koori farmers continued to live and farm the land successfully until the early 1920s.[5]

The mid-north coast reserves were undoubtedly the most successful economically because the climate and the fertility of the soil allowed farming to go ahead with little capital outlay. Most were uncleared, and Aboriginal farmers undertook back-breaking labour to prepare the land for crops, making a mockery of the rejection of Bob Tobonts's 1886 claim on the Rous River because 'the habits and inclinations of the aborigines [are] not favourable to the settled and continuous labour required for clearing and cultivating the land'.[6] Herbert Davis, for example, recalled in 1937 how his family had cleared Rollands Plains, a reserve north-west of Port Macquarie:

> That was a standing dense scrub. That was cleared by me and my brothers . . . The land was given to us on condition that we cleared it. We fulfilled all conditions and cleared the land and fenced it off and resided on it for over 30 years. The land, when a standing scrub, was valued at £2 per acre . . . It is and was valued at £42 per acre after we had cleared it.[7]

Another family of Davises had similar memories about Euroka Creek, later called Burnt Bridge, which they and John Mosely had begun to farm in 1894. The APB originally assessed both Rollands Plains and Euroka Creek as 'suitable for grazing only', but after a few years of Koori labour reclassified the lands as 'suitable for cultivation'. In only two years, the Davis and Mosely families at Euroka had cleared and cropped 17 acres with maize, planted fruit trees and vegetables and begun raising chickens. By 1899 their maize crop yielded 800 bushells. The families had built barns for storing their produce and 'comfortable slab and bark dwellings' for themselves. As they later argued, the Moselys and Davises had transformed the lands to 'smiling properties' and 'very desirable farms without any assistance from the government'.[8]

A similar recognition of Koori labour and determination was made by local police in relation to the Forster reserve, in 1908:

> The Aborigines at Forster have been living on the reserve about 20 years and many of the tribe have lived about there for the last 50 years.
> Many years ago, several of the respectable residents applied to the Lands Department, when the present site was granted for their use. The Land was then a dense Scrub, and now the whole of the Reserve is cleared and securely fenced. The whole of the work of clearing and fencing has been done by the Aborigines themselves. The Aborigines have built several very good cottages on this reserve, and fenced off nice gardens where they are now growing Lovely Potatoes, Cabbages, Etc.[9]

Even the rich alluvial flats around the Macleay, Nambucca and Bellinger rivers required hard clearing before they could be made productive, as James Linwood and others recalled in the 1920s about their lands on Fattorini and Pelican Islands, where their labour in fencing and planting was often heart-breakingly washed away in floods.[10] These reserves were the ones which came nearest to fulfilling the Koori desire for self-sufficiency, where labour-intensive, under-capitalised farming could support an extended family. As the APB described the lower Macleay reserves in 1899:

> They are all cleared and cultivated, maize being chiefly grown. On the whole the Aborigines are in a fairly flourishing condition, having horses

and sulkies of their own. They have also provided themselves with boats, those supplied by the Government having worn out.[11]

* * *

If Aboriginal strategies to regain land had some economic success, how far was this at the cost of Aboriginal identity? These Koori small farmers of the north coast were using their profits to buy consumer goods similar to those bought by white small farmers; there were reports of Kooris furnishing their houses with curtains, pianos and other physical symbols of European culture. The Protection Board and local police assumed that this could not be consistent with an adherence to Aboriginal values. The Kooris of the Macleay, Nambucca and Bellinger rivers appeared to be living the perfect example of the 'civilised' lifestyle to which the Board hoped all Aborigines would aspire.

Yet the reality was far more complex. These farmers were involved in some of the most recent ceremonial activity in New South Wales, continuing modified initiation ceremonies in this area until at least the mid-1940s. During the earlier years of the twentieth century, some of the Kooris with the longest experience of secure tenure over reserves and independent cultivation were also those with the most detailed knowledge of traditional philosophy.[12] Some of the families who took part in the most recent ceremonies had been most tenacious in demanding and defending such rights; they, too, clearly regarded their reserve lands as a 'small portion of a vast territory which is ours by Divine Right'.[13] It might be argued that the success of their land strategy was one factor which had given these communities the security to create a lifestyle which 'made sense' in their own terms, developed from their own traditions as well as from what they found useful in European material and cultural life.

These reserves no doubt meant many things to Aboriginal farmers and residents. The Aboriginal petitions and letters suggest strongly that they wanted land which was part of their traditional country and that they saw the restored reserves as a recognition, however partial and inadequate, of their prior and continuing rights to land. It was from this period, the 1870s to around 1900, that the belief arose that portions of traditional land had been granted to particular Aboriginal people by Queen Victoria in a permanent restoration of title. These beliefs are geographically quite specific. They do not arise widely in western areas of New South Wales, for example, where Aboriginal people did not demand reserves in this period. Nor are they found to exist outside New South Wales. In Queensland the reserves were created in Victoria's reign but were always large institutions created without Aboriginal demand and run under dictatorial control. In Victoria a few reserves were created concurrently with those in New South Wales but they were under the direct control of the Victorian Protection Board, supervised by missionaries or Board managers, and seen from the beginning as places to concentrate the dispersed Victorian Koori population. With the notable exception of Coranderrk, most reserves in Victoria were not perceived at the time as being created for and then running under the control of the Aboriginal residents in the way that the smaller and more widespread reserves in New South Wales were understood by Aboriginal people.

The New South Wales beliefs about Queen Victoria having granted land have often been described rather patronisingly as reflections of Aboriginal people's gullibility in thinking that the monarch would either be interested in them or inclined to hand over land to them. A similar interpretation is that these beliefs are examples of Aboriginal naiveté in feeling gratitute and loyalty to the Queen for her benevolence and charity, while failing to recognise the British Crown as the cause of their dispossession. These readings severely underestimate the factual knowledge held by Aboriginal people in the period, and the symbolic power of their account.

Certainly the ameliorative measures such as the issue of blankets, which were the only real survivor of Earl Grey's 1849 initiative, were carried out with much use of exaggerated royal symbolism. Contemporary observers like Martin Brennan recorded that the annual presentation of blankets was made on the Queen's Birthday, and was described to Aboriginal recipients as 'the Queen's bounty', for which, in Brennan's view, 'the blacks felt grateful'.[14] The nature of reserves was no doubt explained by whites using the same loyalist language and symbolism. The Aboriginal remembrance of these lands as a recognition of their ownership rights is very close to the intentions of Earl Grey in his instructions to Governor Fitzroy from 1848 to 1850.[15]

By the early 1880s, when Protector Thornton was enthusiastically supporting the Aboriginal demand for farming reserves, he used the term 'grants' of land frequently enough to suggest that this impression of permanence in the title of the reserves may well have been conveyed to the Aboriginal residents and petitioners. It would then hardly be surprising if explanations by police and other white officials had not generated this belief in Queen Victoria's interest and in the permanence of the title which had been returned to Aboriginal hands. The widespread experience of independent control over most of these 75 reserves would again have confirmed that these lands had indeed been handed over directly to the Aboriginal owners.[16]

Yet there is a further reading possible, suggested by William Cooper's use of the boundaries of the 'small portion' to signify 'that vast territory which is ours by Divine Right', as well as by the way Aboriginal people have used the concept of royalty to assert the equivalent dignity of their own authorities and power structures.[17] The determination with which Aboriginal people have insisted that these grants were made by Queen Victoria reflects their conviction that Aboriginal rights to land had been recognised at the highest levels of the British state. So rather than a remnant of misplaced loyalty to a colonising Queen, these accounts demonstrate a further assertion of the dignity and solemnity of Aboriginal traditional rights to land, which Aboriginal people indicate were taken so seriously that they were acknowledged by the British Queen. It is not the British monarchy which is celebrated in these stories, but the permanence and dignity of Aboriginal land and its owners.

These beliefs about the reserves and their title represented a new layer of meaning about land, its ownership and its significance, which the experience of colonialism generated among Aboriginal landowners and which came to be inscribed onto the land itself. These concepts were not 'traditional', but they grew out of the strength of the emotional bonds between traditional owners and their lands, as well as continuing Aboriginal desires to organise their social future, their plans, residence and economy, around the land they regarded as their own. These areas of land, whether squatted on, 'permissively occupied' or actually reserved, symbolised the state of relations between invaders and landowners. Small though they were, they were lands won back, recognition achieved, and security ensured within 'their own country'.

The lands acquired a further layer of meaning which arose from the everyday experiences of their Aboriginal residents over decades. The people cleared land, built huts, fenced boundaries and in many cases planted and harvested gardens. They bore children on these lands, nursed their sick and buried their dead there. The reserve lands became focal points on the routes of those kin members who came to help with the harvest, or who camped on the land to get through the slow periods of the district's economy when little work was available. There were unquestionably many hard times on these small farms, which often had few implements and little capital, and where it was always necessary to go out to work or hunt to ride out drought and poor seasons. Nevertheless, these lands were places which for 20, 30 and sometimes 40 years were secure in spite of the mounting pressures all around. So the richness of daily life was experienced there repeatedly over those decades, and the memories of the everyday events, as well as the knowledge of the past meanings of the land, and the hopes for the future, were all embedded within the boundaries of those reserve lands. Thus an intense new web of significance and meaning was being laid down on these lands through this period of colonisation, adding to the traditional meanings for land.

9

Escalating Pressures

DENYING THE ABORIGINAL PRESENCE

It is ironic that in the very period when Aboriginal people in New South Wales were successfully regaining a hold over fragments of their country, the British and white Australians were symbolically removing Aboriginal people from Australian culture, law and the land itself. Representations and images of Aborigines proliferated in the period from 1860 to 1900. There was great diversity among them, but the dominant trend was to obscure and then erase altogether the detailed body of knowledge about Aboriginal people's culture and land relations which white settlers had accumulated by the 1840s. W. E. H. Stanner and Bernard Smith have both pointed to the 'cult of forgetfulness' which afflicted Australian history, literature, art and law. The groundwork for that cult was laid down in the 1870s and 1880s.

The gathering force in intellectual life in Britain during this time was what became known as Social Darwinism. This doctrine borrowed Charles Darwin's theories on the evolution of species among plants and animals, and applied them, inappropriately, to change in human societies. The possibility of regression by whites in remote areas was comfortingly removed by this doctrine, which explained that the behaviour, culture and relative power of different racial groups was biologically determined, and that 'inferior races', those who were lower on the old 'Great Chain of Being', were 'doomed' to 'fade away' in any encounter with the 'dynamic' 'higher races'. The diversity of early nineteenth-century settler experience with Aboriginal people seemed irrelevant in this framework, as the only significant fact was that the latter would inevitably disappear.

The mainland Australian colonies had now diversified. In the longer-settled colonies of New South Wales, Victoria and South Australia, conflict with Aboriginal landowners had ended, abruptly, in the 1850s, and had only been reactivated sporadically in the following decades. In these colonies pastoral employers continued to draw heavily on Aboriginal labour, but were aware that they were continuing to suffer great sickness and mortality because they were extremely vulnerable to European infectious diseases. Where selection was having a greater impact, the Aboriginal reassertion of land tenure was proceeding quietly, and often unnoticed, but in the most rapidly changing areas it was more often Aboriginal poverty which was seen by whites. This was in great contrast to the colonies of Queensland and Western Australia, where frontier brutality was flaring violently in the more remote pastoral areas, and Aboriginal people were being increasingly characterised as ruthless, treacherous and savage.

As the centenary of the British invasion approached, and the south-eastern colonies were booming economically during the 1880s, a number of histories were written, as white Australians sought to give themselves a new and suitably dignified historical basis for their prosperity. G. W. Rusden's *History of Australia*, written in 1883, was typical in its handling of the complex debates over Aboriginal property rights in the late 1840s and early 1850s. Looking back from the 1880s in the now subdued south-east, the issues were portrayed as terribly simple. Rusden ignored the widespread recognition in Australia and in England of the complex Aboriginal landholding systems which had been recorded by settler after settler in the early years of the colonies. He belittled the British humanitarian goals and power, and he dismissed Earl Grey's 1848 instructions as trivial. The colonial resistance was portrayed as rational and principled, while Grey was described as a dilettante whose alleged imprecision about the terms of his goal was ultimately the reason for its failure: 'as the Earl refused to declare that the native rights deserved respect, they would not be respected'.[1]

Few later historians bothered to explore this struggle between Britain and her colonies over native property rights even as far as Rusden had done. If the writer was following the views expressed in the colonies like Queensland which were still at war, then Aborigines were described as treacherous and savage foes who were resoundingly defeated. Writers from the southern colonies, on the other hand, tended to portray Aboriginal people as insignificant enemies, posing only a minor irritation to the onward progress of heroic squatters and selectors. This trend continued into the new century with James Collier's *Pastoral Age in Australasia* in 1911, in which he argued that it was 'natural' and 'irredeemable' for Aboriginal people to disappear because of their 'all-round inferiority and their inability to till the ground or even make use of its natural pastures'.[2] By 1924 S. H. Roberts could publish his *History of Australian Land Settlement* without any reference to Aboriginal people at all.[3]

This process of reinventing the past was to have major effects on the thought of generations of Australians in the twentieth century. Just as significant for the legal system was the effect of arguments put to Australian and British courts during the 1880s. There were many disputes between squatters and selectors over land ownership and use in this decade. In one of them, *Cooper v. Stuart*, in order to have the authority to sell or lease the land, the courts were asked to decide who owned it. An appeal to the Privy Council in Britain resulted in a decision in 1889 which for the first time laid out the legal fiction on which the whole edifice of real property law came to be based in Australia. Lord Watson declared that all property in Australia came to be owned by the British Crown in 1788 because the land at that time could be regarded to have been *terra nullius*. This he defined as meaning 'practically unoccupied, without settled inhabitants or settled law, at the time when it was peacefully annexed to the British dominions'.[4] This was not a decision which could have been reached in 1840, when there was such a wide acknowledgment of Aboriginal relations to land and when it appeared so necessary to recognise them; the adoption of *terra nullius* even as a legal fiction would have appeared inappropriate in the face of such detailed contradictory evidence. Yet by 1889 it could be readily accepted among whites as self-evident. This judgment went on to obstruct for decades Aboriginal legal actions to regain land in the middle and later twentieth century, until finally overturned in the Mabo decision in 1992.[5]

* * *

Cultural expression was flourishing in the colonies during the prosperous 1880s. The craft of photography was booming, with both studio and travelling photographers creating images of Aboriginal people along with those of whites in New South Wales. In the next two decades many of these photographs were made into postcards and widely circulated. Some were posed among inappropriate sets to present a fictional European view of tradition in Australia, but many of the rural photographs were in realist style and recorded Aboriginal people living on pastoral camps, and, occasionally, on their own cultivated farms (see photographs on p. iv). It has been suggested that these were interpreted by whites as reassuringly demonstrating the poverty of Aborigines,[6] but they must have had a very different meaning to the Aboriginal people who stood assertively in front of their lands to be photographed, often displaying with obvious pride the breast plates which identified the authority they carried for that country.

Another common genre of photography was portraiture, in which a convention known as vignetting was often applied to Aboriginal people. The person's head and shoulders were shown but the image faded out rapidly towards the edges of the frame. The effect was to show a head and shoulders decontextualised from any real landscape or background, and indeed detached from its own body.[7] This convention was taken up by painters of the period, and was also used frequently by them for Aboriginal subjects. Their portraits usually depicted a dignified and noble person, but also invariably a sad and melancholy one. The overall effect of both photography and painting in these styles was to sentimentalise and romanticise Aboriginal people, suggesting that they were passing away, regrettably but inevitably.[8] The white artists of this time chose to portray Aboriginal people as disembodied, isolated from their lost people and from their lands, and looking nostalgically back to the past, as if they had no hold on the present or the future.

This sentimental representation of Aboriginal people was common in literature too, with Kendall's maudlin poem 'The Last of His Tribe' an obvious example. Yet Kendall's later verse included many vicious caricatures of Aboriginal people, and the conflict within his work suggests the wider unease among writers when they addressed their relations with Aboriginal landowners. J. J. Healy has traced the way Rolf Boldrewood transformed his participation in frontier violence in Victoria in the 1840s when he wrote *Robbery Under Arms* in the 1880s. The Aboriginal servant Boldrewood created in his novel is irretrievably evil, but he depicted the process of 'settlement' as peaceful and essentially free of violence, as 'almost Arcadian in its simplicity'.[9] Charles Harpur had been more forthright in his haunting 'Creek of the Four Graves', in 1853, in which the deaths of whites in conflict with Aboriginal people 'become a geographic presence, endowing the landscape with melancholy'.[10] The continuation of this perception of the Australian bush as deeply melancholy is suggested by Marcus Clarke, who wrote in 1880, 'the Australian forests are funereal, secret, stern. They seem to stifle in their black gorges a story of sullen despair'.[11]

Bernard Smith has traced this persistent unease to a consciousness not only of the white dead in the wars over land, but to the awareness of the Aboriginal dead, with whites unable to resolve their deep although unacknowledged sense of guilt about the deaths on the frontier. It was this projection of guilt and pain onto the landscape which in Smith's view the Heidelberg school of painters and their successors tried to erase. Their landscapes and depictions of events are all washed by blindingly bright sunlight, reflected back from hard rock faces, open plains and shimmering beaches, or glimpsed in flashes through the gaps in shearing shed walls. There was no room for gloomy melancholy among these images, which sometimes depicted a hard land, but one in which everything was visible and open.[12] There were no ghosts of past Aboriginal or white dead, and there were also no living Aboriginal people. Landscapes painted during the late 1840s had still included Aboriginal people, often marginalised and as part of the natural world, but never-theless, alive and present.[13] Tom Roberts, during the early 1890s, painted a number of sketches of Aboriginal subjects, all decontextualised por-traits, but he never assembled them into the 'event' paintings he created, even though Aboriginal people were widely employed at the time in the occupations like shearing which he celebrated so well.[14] The Heidelberg school of painters chose not to include an Aboriginal presence in their self-consciously heroic depictions of Australian life and land.

While the 1870s and 1880s generated new ways to see, or to avoid seeing, Aboriginal people, they also witnessed white Australians explor-ing new ways to see the land itself. A growing appreciation of rugged and dramatic areas created an Australian form of the romantic vision of landscape and wilderness. The 'wild' country was no longer seen to be irrationally disordered but rather to reflect the divine order of God. By the 1870s the romantic vision of the beauty of God's work in nature had developed strongly, expressed most clearly in Baron von Mueller's words, but pervading an increasing number of white writings:

> The magnificence of a dense forest, before the destructive hand of man defaced it . . . the silent grandeur and solitude of a virgin forest inspires us almost to awe . . . It conveys also involuntarily to our mind a feeling as if we were brought before that Divine Power . . . before whom the proudest human work must sink into utter insignificance.[15]

The Romantic view of nature opposed it to 'the works of man', in yet another of Western philosophy's dichotomous views of the world. This wilderness which now inspired awe was a land perceived to have been without human 'defacement'. The emerging Romantic vision of wilderness had important practical effects because it became allied to the urban population's desire to escape temporarily their built environ-ment. This led to the creation of a series of national parks after 1879.[16] Both conceptions, of the 'national park' and of 'wilderness', relied on the opposition of nature and man, the assumption that the Australian bush was 'pristine' and 'unpeopled'. A third strand of thought was emerging too, influenced by developments in the United States and arguing that the environment was a resource which must be 'managed wisely', conserved to maximise future use and profit. This 'good man-agement' school argued that wholesale clearing of woodlands and forests was profligate, irresponsible waste and failed to conserve wisely for future generations.[17]

By the 1880s these three separate strands combined to influence the Lands Department to create reserves around potential future resources. Although the pressures to 'unlock the land' continued unabated, the Lands Department also persisted in its creation of reserves, some for 'villages' which might or might not come into existence, some for water catchments, but some also for forests and for 'national' parks.[18] These reserves were to become important to Aboriginal people in providing buffers for both significant sites and the people themselves against the rising pressure brought by intensification.

Yet the influence of these emerging streams of thought was just as negative towards Aboriginal people as the literary and artistic works of the time. All denied that the landscape was the creation of its Aboriginal owners. None sought to learn the meanings of the land and its patterns which Aboriginal knowledge held. And none recognised the continuing presence and interest of Aboriginal people in the land. The Romantic desire for 'pristine', 'virgin' and 'primaeval' wilderness, in particular, symbolically demanded an empty and unpeopled land just as relentlessly as the squatters and selectors had done in reality.

NEW PRESSURES ON ABORIGINAL GAINS

While Aboriginal attempts to regain land had achieved clear successes, there were pressures building to erode even the small independent economic and social base that had been achieved. These pressures led to increased populations on the reserves, reducing any chance of economic self-sufficiency. One cause was the worsening social confict between Aborigines and whites as Aborigines attempted to gain equal access to the services of country towns.

Schools were often the focal point of these tensions. The rhetoric of Henry Parkes's education system was that the schools were to be 'Free, Secular and Compulsory', in other words they were to be open to all. Aboriginal parents were aware of the potential advantages education might offer and they began to enrol their children in the new public schools as soon as they opened. In common with most white rural children, Aboriginal children were often unable to attend full-time, like those at the Drews' permissive occupancy at Kinchela who missed lessons for some months each year in the 1870s because they were helping their parents on the farm.[19] Nevertheless, Aboriginal parents clearly regarded the issue as important for their children, and sought enrolment with increasing frequency, so that by the end of the 1870s there were over a hundred Aboriginal children known to be enrolled in the public system.[20] This was seen by white townspeople, however, as a violation of their domestic 'town' space, and, even more emotively, as a threat to their children.

In later years, when white parents were forced to explain just exactly what sort of a threat they believed Aboriginal children posed, they would usually refer to the threat of infectious diseases. Whenever investigations were held, however, Aboriginal children were shown to suffer only from the same diseases of poverty as most of the white children at the school. The real anxieties of white parents were usually revealed to be fears that their children would grow up to form social or sexual relationships with Aboriginal people, which in the rigidly stratified world of country towns represented a major threat to social status. So although the schools were theoretically open to all, and were compulsory for all after 1880, they were a point of particular emotional sensitivity to both white and Aboriginal parents. In this situation, the tensions in towns about such diverse issues as Aboriginal access to the public streets, Aboriginal residence on an adjacent reserve, or Aboriginal competition with white workers for labouring jobs were all likely to flare up in a battle over whether Aboriginal children were entitled to attend the local public school.[21]

Although the Department of Public Instruction had no fixed policy on Aboriginal admission, the persistence of white parental complaints in areas of high Aboriginal enrolment forced the segregation of one 'public' school after another during the 1880s.[22] The first were at Yass and Brungle in 1883, but then the most persistent white complaints arose from the north coast, where independent Aboriginal farming was at its most successful during the 1880s, and Aboriginal parents had been confidently enrolling their children at the local schools. As the 'public' schools were closed one by one to Aboriginal students, the Department set up a series of segregated schools which it located for its convenience on the existing reserves, most of which were being independently farmed. The first was at Barrington near Gloucester in 1890, then at Forster, in 1891, Rolland's Plains, Pelican Island, Kinchela and Wauchope in 1892, and Cabbage Tree Island in 1893. By 1900 the five families at Burnt Bridge were seeking full-time enrolment for their twenty children in the Euroka Creek Public School, but whenever the children tried to enrol they were sent home because white parents objected. The Aboriginal families began petitioning for their own school in September 1900 and after persistent requests a 'special' school, for Aborigines only, was eventually opened in 1905 on the reserve.[23] There were 27 segregated 'special' schools established in New South Wales from 1883 to 1909, and fifteen of them were on the north coast.

The denial of access to an increasing number of north coast public schools and the location of usually the only alternative schools on reserves forced alterations in the residential pattern of Kooris, who were now faced with the decision either to move their whole family to a reserve or at least to leave their children there with relatives if they wanted access to schooling. On the far northern rivers, for example, it was segregation of the public school as well as the intensifying pressure of white settlement which forced Kooris, who had previously refused to have anything to do with the Protection Board, to move onto Dunoon reserve, 6 miles north of Lismore, where a 'special school' was established in 1909. These families, once forced onto the reserve, independently began cultivation there.[24]

For the families of the independently settled reserves in the Macleay, however, the imposition of the 'special' segregated schools created severe problems. Simply the presence of the school, with its white teacher there most days, increased the level of surveillance under which Kooris lived, changing the experience of independent control of their lives and farms. As well, the school was a magnet for Kooris who were suffering school segregations in other towns. The possibility that the farms could support the people living on them was diminished as numbers began to rise.[25]

These pressures of the 1880s worsened during the severe Depression of the early 1890s, and then the drought which affected most of New South Wales until the early 1900s. Aborigines found themselves facing high unemployment in most areas. In a period in which there was no general government unemployment relief, the only support was through subsidised charities. For Aboriginal unemployed the APB rations offered some assistance, although they comprised only a small dole of dry goods such as flour, but never meat, as Aboriginal people were expected to hunt and fish for themselves. It seems that many Aboriginal people who had previously been self-supporting were forced to apply to the Board's managers and the police for rations from 1891 onwards, and to move to a reserve for the duration of the slump.[26] This rise in population on independent reserves reduced their potential for self-sufficiency even further.

The encroachment of local whites was another and more ominous threat. The shock of the Depression dampened down most white demand for closer settlement. The bad seasons of the 1890s exposed the grave damage done to western pastures by overgrazing and the rabbit plague; many graziers went to the wall during this decade. Small selections too fared very badly, and there were many heartbroken families who simply walked off their blocks. The environmental crisis gave new impetus to the utilitarian 'wise use' approach to land management, and sowed seeds of doubt in at least some whites about the possibilities of endless 'development'. Yet locally the hard times generated desperate greed among whites for the land of those who were not regarded as legitimate agriculturalists. The confident presence of Aboriginal people on apparently secure land was envied by struggling neighbours, and the desire to grab land which had proven its capacity under Aboriginal farming began to emerge. There were only a few attempts to usurp Aboriginal holdings in the 1890s, and the Protection Board strongly supported Aboriginal farmers through this period, defending

Aboriginal residence against the slowly building pressure of local whites. But to have the Board defend your land often meant losing independent control over it. This bitter lesson was learnt at Kinchela, when whites challenged Aboriginal tenure of the richly fertile Drew permissive occupancy in 1899. The Board stepped in, securing the Drews' residency, but the cost was the transformation of the title into Aboriginal reserve.[27]

Part III

'For Land and Liberty': Defending the Land, 1910s to 1930

10
Land, Children and Power

When the drought finally broke in the early 1900s, the popular pressure for closer settlement pushed the government into new strategies to settle more farmers on the land. The 1905 Closer Settlement legislation was to make it even simpler to gain land in the eastern half of New South Wales, but four decades of intensifying land use had made agricultural land scarce indeed. Most large properties with suitable land had already faced partial resumption, and there were few left to carve up. The Lands Department was forced to turn back on its reserves, cannibalising the lands for which it had been trying to build up protection over the last twenty years. In 1906 it announced a policy of 'curtailment of reserves . . . to free as much land as possible for settlement', and it reported in 1907 and 1908 that it was pursuing this policy 'strenuously'. Forest reserves, water and travelling stock reserves were all to be reassessed and wherever possible 'freed' for sale, or, where they absolutely could not be revoked, they were nevertheless to be made 'revenue-producing' by leasing for grazing or cultivation.[1]

While Aboriginal reserves formed only a small portion of the Crown land reserved from sale, the proven quality of the more successful farms made them extremely attractive to selectors. The shift in Lands Department policy added to the vulnerability of all the Aboriginal-held lands when they fell under the covetous gaze of neighbours. White demands for these lands began to escalate from 1903, with Department endorsement of most white applications for revocation. The Protection Board, however, continued to defend Aboriginal tenure, contesting the Department's powers in 1906 when it unilaterally revoked a reserve at Booligal, on the Lachlan. The Lands Department retreated, reversing that revocation and agreeing not to revoke unilaterally in the future. But the pressure from whites only intensified, and some people believed they could just take over Aboriginal-held land. In the same year the Board had to 'threaten legal proceedings against a European who had illegally occupied a reserve'.

The motives of white usurpers were quite openly discussed. Calimo was a rapidly intensifying district near Deniliquin on the Edward River, where orchardists were moving into an area which had already begun to shift to smaller-scale pastoralism. In 1907 the Chief Secretary received a petition calling for the revocation of the Aboriginal reserve there and the removal of its residents to Cumeragunja, so that 'the land can be made available for settlement'. It was signed by neighbours of the reserve, many of them orchardists or town residents. The Aboriginal community opposed the move intensely, and argued that they were all employed by the large graziers remaining in the area, who had only the highest recommendations to make of their skills and character. The police agreed, recommending against the revocation of the reserve, because in their view the petitioners' accusations about Aboriginal intemperance and idleness were 'entirely without foundation, and are brought for no other purpose than the desire of one or two of the petitioners to acquire the land'.[2]

The strongest pressure was mounting on the north coast, where Aboriginal farming had been so clearly successful and where white population numbers were rapidly expanding. At Forster, in 1908, Kooris' land was desired by whites for residential expansion. A vicious campaign of slander was mounted by white neighbours, who lobbied politicians and wrote letters to the press, in the process exposing their underlying motives in demanding the revocation of the reserve and the removal of the Aboriginal residents. A white man signing himself 'Father of a Family' wrote:

> It is a disgrace to allow these few people to live in the centre of our tourist town and to insist that white folk must put up with them as nextdoor neighbours. They occupy a block embracing the choicest building lots in the town, and yet the Department sanctions this inconveniencing of the whole district. Further the reserve is the resort of the scrag of the district.[3]

The Koori residents protested strongly. The white strategy had been to demand revocation of only a section of the reserve, but as John Ridgeway explained in letter after letter to the Commissioner of Police, this was the only watered portion and its loss would force the Kooris to move elsewhere. Ridgeway argued that he and his kin had been living there constantly for at least 50 years, and had applied for the land to be returned to them in 1888. Since the reserve had been notified in 1891, they had cleared and fenced it, built houses and cultivated vegetables. None of them wanted to leave their homes.[4] They were strongly supported in this by the local police, who pleaded:

> Surely after doing all the improvement, for their own benefit, their land is not to be taken from them *because* it is cleared and fenced, to please the whim of any one man. The Reserve is a credit to the Aborigines, and in the Senior Sergeant's opinion it would be very unfair to remove

them and send them into the Bush to make a fresh start to clear homes for themselves.[5]

Aboriginal protests were rising from a number of different areas of the State where they were facing this pressure. Roseby Park Kooris, near Nowra, had also protested at the limited reserve lands they had been left with from the wider area which Alexander Berry had assured them they could occupy permanently at Orient Point. They demanded an enlarged area and a more permanent form of tenure, and their demands were among those which came to the notice of Joseph Carruthers, the Premier.[6] In July 1907 Carruthers pressed the APB to increase the number of independently held Aboriginal reserves and to develop a proposal for a form of tenure which would be more secure.[7]

To the Aboriginal protests about individual white encroachment were soon added the anger of Cumeragunja Kooris who were being confronted by Protection Board seizure of their family farm blocks. Diane Barwick has suggested that this fitted a pattern of attack on Aboriginal community independence, by removing first control over land and then over children, marking a shift in New South Wales from *laissez-faire* to the aggressive dispersal which had occurred in Victoria in the 1880s. Cumeragunja was first affected simply because greater existing control meant it was easier to implement the new policy before the board gained new legislation.[8]

The situation seems, however, to have been much more fluid than this. The APB had suffered a series of severe funding cuts from 1902, and it seems to have decided to expand its own resource base by developing farming for its own profit at Cumeragunja, initially on the land which was not yet under crop. It installed a farm overseer in 1906, invested heavily in rabbit-proof fencing, an improved water supply, a Massey-Harris cultivator, and other equipment for large-scale wheat farming. Cumeragunja presented the only large area of reserve land which would be suitable for profitable agriculture without huge capital expenditure. Before long, however, the Board decided that it needed more land and more labour, and this brought it into direct conflict with the Aboriginal farmers. Without warning, the Board moved in 1907 to resume the family farm blocks, on the spurious excuse that they had been 'neglected'. From then on, all land on Cumeragunja was to be farmed for Board profit, with wages being offered only to those former block-holders whom the manager chose to employ.[9] The outrage from Cumeragunja Kooris was intense and continuing.

The Board did not intend at this stage, however, to take over any other area of independent Aboriginal farming. Indeed, when the Premier began to pressure the Board in July 1907 to expand reserve numbers and security, it responded with enthusiasm:

> The Board concur with the Premier in thinking that the tenure over the land set apart for the Aborigines should be more secure, and an attempt will be made in the Draft Bill to deal with this phase of the question. It is considered too that more Reserves should be made available for their use, and of larger areas than hitherto, so that the Aborigines may not only be provided with a home but also with land of some use for farming and grazing purposes.[10]

The police had already been instructed to inquire into the whereabouts of suitable Crown land in all areas where there were any Aboriginal populations, and the Board assured the Premier that it would immediately apply to have such areas notified as reserves.

Yet as this quotation suggests, the Board was preparing a legislative base for itself. It had suffered a traumatic shock during the 1890s Depression and then the following drought. High Aboriginal unemployment had greatly increased the Board's ration lists. The Depression had generated intense debate among white Australians about the merits of unemployment relief, and there had been many who argued that any 'dole' would undermine a worker's motivation and capacity for further employment. The number of adult rations began to fall immediately after 1904, as the drought broke and there was once again a demand for labour, but the Board's concern was now that its policies of offering rations to Aboriginal workers had destroyed their economic independence, and it was resolved to take firm action to force Aborigines back into the workforce. It began to insist that there was a need to clear its reserves and especially its seven 'stations'—reserves where a resident manager had been installed—of 'undeserving' Aborigines.

But the Board was far more deeply disturbed by another issue. The need for unemployed Aboriginal people to come forward to claim rations had brought them much more systematically to its notice. The conclusion had become inescapable that Aboriginal people were not disappearing. The people called 'full bloods' by the Board were certainly reduced in numbers, but there had been a significant expansion in the numbers of those labelled 'half-castes', 'quadroons' and 'octoroons'. In 1882, only 26.7 per cent of the known Aboriginal population had been of apparently mixed Aboriginal and European descent. In 1900 this proportion had risen to 55 per cent.[11]

Contrary to the Board's expectations, these people of mixed descent were not separating themselves from the Aboriginal community, but were instead identifying as Aboriginal, living with their Aboriginal relatives, and being identified by whites as Aboriginal. At this time, with Social Darwinism at its height, biology was seen as a powerful determinant of behaviour and character, and the increase and cultural assertiveness of a racially distinct minority was viewed with fear and alarm. In the early days of Federation the chauvinistic ideal of a White Australia was widely embraced, and there were grave fears because the birthrate of whites was known to be falling. The rise of eugenics had contributed to concerns about the importance of 'racial hygiene' and 'purity'. This influential body of thought had fostered beliefs that disproportionately low birthrates among middle-class families should be addressed by limiting the birthrate of working-class people and undesirable social groups, often described as 'imbeciles' and 'defectives', who were said to be a 'menace' to white society because their biological make-up determined their 'antisocial' behaviour.[12]

In this climate the members of the NSW Protection Board feared that the ration issues and the security offered to Aboriginal communities on reserves had fostered an alien presence which was not only persisting but growing in numbers to endanger the new nation. R. Scobie, a Board member from 1901 to 1918, expressed their fears: the Aboriginal people 'are an increasing danger, because although there are only a few full-blooded Aborigines left, there are 6,000 of the mixed-blood growing up. It is a danger to us to have a people like that among us, looking upon our institutions with eyes different from ours'.[13]

These two fears, of having fostered an increasing financial burden of pauperised mendicants and an expanding alien cultural and racial threat, led the APB to revive its earlier campaign to gain a strong legislative base from which to disperse the Aboriginal population as had been done in Victoria. The Board had convinced the government in submissions from 1904 that it should have such power, and a draft bill had been prepared by mid-1907, ensuring that the Board would be able to decide who should and should not receive rations and live on reserves, as well as to exercise more control over Aboriginal access to alcohol and related matters. The Board did not see this as being any contradiction of its strong endorsement of the Premier's demand to increase the number and size of Aboriginal reserves, and the security of their tenure. In fact when the legislation was finally enacted it included a guarantee that Aboriginal farmers would retain the profits from any crop they grew on reserve lands. The policies of dispersal of adult Aboriginal workers and retention of independently farmed reserves were expected to proceed in tandem, as both were seen as achieving economic independence for Aborigines.

The Board's greatest worry in 1907 was that the Premier did not seem to understand the importance of one aspect of the Board's desired new legislative power, which was intended to remove all authority of Aboriginal parents over their children and give it to the Board. The Board had requested this power, to stand *in loco parentis* (in place of the parents), but the government had ignored this when it prepared the draft bill. The Board regarded it as the linchpin of its policy and would not abandon it. Only if it could gain control over children, it argued to the Premier, could it guarantee that they would be educated and indoctrinated into habits of industry.

The Board needed laws to do this. It had found already in 1906 that although Aboriginal parents were very interested in enrolling their children in public schools, they bitterly opposed the Board when it tried to remove their adolescent children from Warangesda and Cumeragunja and take them away to be 'trained' and indentured as 'apprenticed' domestic servants and labourers. Aboriginal parents may have been aware of the wider interests of the Board in pursuing this policy. The Board stated quite openly in its reports and minutes that it intended to reduce the birthrate of the Aboriginal population by taking adolescent girls away from their communities. Then it intended that the young people taken in this way would never be allowed to return to their homes or to any other Aboriginal community. The 'apprenticeship' policy was aimed quite explicitly at reducing the numbers of identifying Aboriginal people in the State.[14]

With Aboriginal parents in open defiance and the Premier unconvinced, the Board decided to gather more 'evidence' to persuade the government that it required total power over Aboriginal children. This task was enthusiastically undertaken by Board member Robert T. Donaldson, a member of State Parliament from Tumut and a man obsessively committed to 'saving the children'. In 1908 he produced a series of population surveys of Aboriginal reserves and stations showing the numbers of Aboriginal children and adolescents who, in his definition, were not 'under parental control'. His report shocked the Board, which was alarmed at the high numbers of 'half-caste' children, and at the numbers of 'girls at detached camps who are not under parental control'.[15] The government was still unconvinced. It agreed to allow the Board to increase its staff, with new managers and two full-time travelling inspectors, who would inform themselves of the conditions on reserves and stations, and oversee the implementation of the new law. It refused, however, to allow amendments which would give the total power the Board sought. When the new laws came into force in 1909, the Board still had only the power of the State Children's Relief Department to take control of children if they were judged by the courts to be neglected. The Board knew that these powers were not enough, for the simple reason that the children it wished to take were not neglected. It complained to the Chief Secretary in a further bid to gain the power it wanted:

> Under the law these children cannot legally be called neglected . . . If the Aboriginal child happens to be decently clad and apparently looked

. after it is very difficult indeed to show that the half-caste or Aboriginal child is actually in a neglected condition, and therefore it is impossible to succeed in court.[16]

The Board approached its new powers in 1909 with a clear commitment in all its documents to a continuation of the defence of Aboriginal tenure over reserves, to an expansion of reserve numbers and area, and to an increase in security of tenure for Aboriginal farmers. Yet the Board members were even more deeply committed to their goal of taking control of Aboriginal children. Donaldson's reports show a man repelled by Aboriginal social and cultural life, which he described as 'the evil influences of camp surroundings'. He took up the goal of gaining power over Aboriginal adolescent girls as a crusade, offering all his assistance in this 'urgent matter and one we should not shrink from'.[17] He made no mention of any positive aspect to life on Aboriginal reserves or farms. In fact it was Donaldson's understanding that 'the whole object of the Board is . . . the camps being depleted of their population and finally the closing of the camps and reserves altogether'.[18] So if other members of the Board had an interest in maintaining and expanding Aboriginal reserves and camps, it was certainly not shared by Donaldson. Yet it was Donaldson whose power was rising on the Board.

Meanwhile the pressure from whites to take over productive Aboriginal lands had intensified. The Lands Department began to insist more aggressively that the Board agree to revocation in favour of whites. The Board continued to reject this pressure, arguing again and again that Aboriginal people were entitled to secure tenure. There was no further action taken to notify new reserves, but for at least a couple of years there were no revocations.

An immediate consequence of the Board gaining its legislative base in 1909 was that its shortage of funds now appeared acute. A rapid increase in the number of resident managers imposed onto reserves around the State had drained the Board's resources as they funded the accommodation necessary to house the new staff and the fencing necessary to mark out the boundaries between manager and managed (see Map 8, p. 122). It had also acquired the old Cootamundra Hospital in 1910 which it intended to renovate as a Training Home for Aboriginal girls once it was empowered to remove them. The structure needed far more renovation than expected, however, and the Board was faced with the urgent need to increase its funds or abandon its goals.[19]

The Board decided to sacrifice Aboriginal land to fund its programs to take Aboriginal children away from their families. It was a momentous decision, but one it chose not to publicise. The annual report for 1910 had included the Board's often-repeated and impassioned plea for the security of Aboriginal land: 'the land already available to this unfortun-

121

PROTECTION BOARD STATIONS 1917

Angledool 1912

Brewarrina

Euraba 1912
(Old Kunopia)

Runnymede

Sevington 1910

Terry-Hie-Hie 1912

Grafton

Dunoon
1912 - 1917
Cabbage Tree
Island 1911
Ulgundahi Island
1911

Nymboida 1911 - 1917

Burra Bee Dee 1910

Walhallow 1906

Warangesda

Edgerton 1910 -1916
Cootamundra 1911
Brungle

Roseby Park 1906

Cumeragunia

Wallaga Lake

NOTE:
Dates of opening (and if appropriate closure)
shown for new stations.

N

0   100   200   300   400
SCALE IN KILOMETRES

Flexigraphics 1995.

ate race is so limited that every attempt on the part of Europeans to acquire these reserves for settlement purposes should be strongly resisted'.[20]

In 1911, however, there was silence. The APB had not only abandoned its earlier defence of Aboriginal land but it had begun to lease the reserve lands for its own revenue.[21]

The APB campaign for power *in loco parentis* mounted to a frenzy. The annual reports for 1910 and 1911 each began with horrifying accounts of the 'depravity' and 'vice' of Aboriginal camps and stations, although on later pages of these reports the very same stations were described as 'happy', 'contented' and 'moral' communities.[22] Donaldson led a deputation to the Chief Secretary in May 1912 in which he pleaded that Aboriginal parenting and community life was so corrupting that the only hope for children and adolescents was to be taken away regardless of their own wishes or those of their relatives.[23] This deputation was widely reported in the press as suggesting that the Board intended to remove all Aboriginal children from their families.[24] The obsessive tenacity of Robert Donaldson finally persuaded the government, and at this meeting the delegation was assured that the Board would now be clothed with all the powers it wanted. Although it took until 1915 to pass the amending legislation, the Board began from 1912 to remove as many children as it could. In the same year as the amending bill was finally passed, Donaldson resigned from the Board to take up one of the positions as inspector, which he fulfilled until 1929 by conducting a relentless routine of travels around the State, selecting children for removal. Known as the 'Kid's Collector', he was feared and hated by Aboriginal people more than any other man in all the years of APB rule.[25]

In 1916 the Board was restructured. The private philanthropists were replaced with busy public servants from departments like Child Welfare, Public Health and Education. Board meetings were no longer to be held weekly but only monthly, and power was rapidly devolved to the Board's permanent staff, the secretary, A. C. Pettit, and the inspectors.[26] Donaldson and Pettit had been the most vocal members of a policy review committee in 1915 which confirmed the increasing emphasis on the removal of children and the dispersal of adults. The committee's recommendations were unanimously endorsed by the incoming Board soon after the restructure. With Donaldson now in an unchallengeable position of power in its administration, any remaining possibility that the Board would defend Aboriginal land crumbled into dust.

Then a further pressure was added to those already threatening Aboriginal land. The First World War was taking a terrible price in lives and injuries in these years. As the surviving soldiers began to return, it seemed only right that they should be rewarded with the prize which white Australians had been struggling to attain for decades: a block of farming land. For the government, the possibility of self-sufficient yeoman soldiers offered a cheap solution to the massive costs of demobilisation and rehabilitation. For the soldiers, the myth of independence on the land beckoned, promising a just reward for the terrors of war.

So the Closer Settlement scheme of 1905 in New South Wales was expanded to encompass the Returned Servicemen's Settlement scheme of 1917, by which returned soldiers could select a small block of agricultural land in specified areas. The scheme held a powerful attraction. There were 154 New South Wales Aboriginal men who had volunteered and fought overseas in the war. In Collarenebri alone, a tiny town on the Barwon River in the north-west, there were five Murris who had served in Gallipoli, France and other theatres of war. Like Aboriginal soldiers across the State, they expected to benefit from the scheme, not only to secure a farm but to regain some of their own country. But the rosy promises of the Soldier Settler scheme turned out to be offered only to white soldiers. There were no discriminatory regulations or laws, but in practice, as applications were handled and ranked in dozens of Local Land Board offices, there was no Soldier Settler land for Aboriginal landowners. Only one Aboriginal serviceman, George Kennedy, managed to secure a block at Yelta, within his own country to the south-east of Wilcannia. One other soldier, George Kapeen, convinced the Protection Board to take the extremely rare step of leasing to an Aborigine, when he gained a personal lease over a family farm block on Aboriginal reserve land at Cabbage Tree Island near Lismore. No other Aboriginal soldier was able to use either the formal Soldier Settler scheme or the effusive public sentiment to regain any of his land.

Instead of securing more land for Aboriginal people, the Returned Servicemen's Settlement scheme accelerated the demand to revoke existing Aboriginal reserve lands. The goal of 'closer settlement' had been forceful enough, but when this was entwined with the call to compensate returning soldiers, it was irresistable. The Protection Board, like other government departments, found it almost impossible to deny requests for reserve land when the applicants were heroic diggers.

11
Dispossessions

Then began a relentless second dispossession, brought about by the increasing pressure of white land hunger and the APB dispersal policies. These dispossessions were experienced differently across the State because the Aboriginal history of regaining the land was different in each region and because local economies and political tensions varied, offering very different options to Aboriginal communities as they tried to respond and resist.

Continuing stability in the pastoral industry meant that there was in fact very little pressure to change the conditions of dual occupation in the Western Division, and in the inland areas of the north coast. The most severe disruption in the north-west was in the one area of high APB control, the Board's managed station 10 miles east of Brewarrina. Even here, the continuing existence of camps on the surrounding pastoral properties allowed places for safe escapes from APB interference.

For the Central Division, it was very different. In places such as the south-western Cumeragunja and Warangesda stations, intensive agriculture in the surrounding regions meant Kooris had very few places to go when dispersal policies and resumption of family farm blocks threatened to push people off their reserve homes. Here dispossession led to fierce community resistance, including court actions and violent confrontations. In other areas, such as the northern slopes, land losses generated great population movement, but Murris chose to avoid confrontation at first, because they could still find other living areas within their traditional country. Such alternatives did not run out until the following decades. On the coast the outcomes were different again: the massive scale of the dispossessions here not only generated individual and community resistance but linked communities throughout the region to create the first formal Aboriginal political organisation.

THE SOUTH-WEST:
COMMUNITY RESISTANCE AT CUMERAGUNJA[1]

By the early 1900s Cumeragunja was surrounded by wheat and mixed farming concerns, and for Kooris to find even short-term contract or shearing work on pastoral properties meant travelling long distances, sometimes up to 300 miles. The main source of employment close by was seasonal work on agricultural properties, and with this sort of land use there was no profit to the European landowner in permanent Aboriginal camps. What suited employers best was an itinerant work-force which could be compelled to move on once the harvest season was over. Aboriginal workers were therefore far more dependent on the reserve at Cumeragunja as a permanent place for themselves and their families to stay than were Aborigines at Brewarrina or even those at Warangesda, where a few pastoral properties remained nearby.[1]

The Cumeragunja people believed they had won at least a partial victory in their demand for land with the allocation of the first farm blocks in 1888. With the extensions to the reserve and the multiplica-tion of the blocks available to individual families in the 1890s the community must have believed that, despite the inadequacy of the blocks and of funds to develop them, the future would bring improve-ment. Meanwhile they used the blocks in the most sensible and economic ways possible to bring in harvests which equalled or bettered the local average yields. Their apparent security of tenure, as well as the independent income generated by the cropping or leasing of the blocks, gave the Cumeragunja community a solidarity and confidence found on few other stations.

The Protection Board seized the farm blocks in 1907 as it tried to increase its own income. It informed the residents that the land was now to be worked for Board profit. If they co-operated they could earn wages, but they were told they had no further rights of usage over the land. This action generated intense bitterness. Immediately after the land was taken there was a series of confrontations with the Board's manager. One was described by the local member of Parliament as occurring because the Kooris 'became a mob of howling savages and surrounded the manager's residence and shots were fired [by the man-ager]', a description which reveals a great deal about white attitudes. The Board's reaction to what it called 'disappointment' over the loss of the farm blocks was to forcibly remove the 'culprits' and 'undesirable residents' from the station, a measure which it was apparently able to achieve even without the powers of the 1909 Act.[2] The issue of the farm blocks was not, however, to be forgotten.

The other great area of conflict at Cumeragunja was over the removal of children. Aboriginal parents at Cumeragunja had already refused to agree to voluntary removal and indenture of their children and so they were alarmed by press reports in May 1912 that the Board intended seeking powers of summary removal. Their anger and distress were apparent to a NSW Children's Relief Department inspector who visited Cumeragunja two weeks after the newspaper coverage of the Board's intended new powers.

> It was impossible to see all the children. A 'mulga wire' had preceded me and on my arrival the camp was in a state of consternation. An impression was abroad that children were to be taken from their parents—'babies from their mothers' breasts' so it was said; some of the old hands were in tears and the women were lowering and sullen. Most of the boys ran off into the bush and were not seen by me during the day.[3]

Yet when Board member Thomas Garvin visited the station in June, he recommended the removal of 52 children he classed as 'quadroon' and 'octoroon'. On Garvin's list were the children of some of the earliest block-holders: Coopers, Atkinsons, Morgans and others. He expected difficulties because most of these children were 'living with their parents, who are apparently looking after them', yet he felt it 'a pity to have children who are almost white brought up on a "Blacks" reserve. Far better that they should be taken away from it and gradually merged into the general population'. But he stressed that more legislative power was needed 'as there will be great heart-burning and opposition to the separation of children from their parents, who will not give them up unless compelled by law to do so'.[4]

The Board began removing children in 1912 and accelerated this process when it finally achieved full power in 1915. Cumeragunja Kooris remember the removals and the escapes, with children running into the bush and mothers swimming the Murray clutching their children, and they remember the physical confrontations with the Board's officers as they tried to leave with the children they had managed to 'collect'.[5]

The disputes over the Board's policy on children added to the unrest which had continued on the station since the seizure of the farm blocks. The Board's records show an increasing amount of open conflict, very different from other managed stations over the period. At Cumeragunja police were called in in 1909 to 'keep the unruly elements within bounds'; there were expulsions of 'a number of undesirables' in 1911 for 'misconduct'; and continuing prosecutions for breaches of the peace such as 'abusive language' and 'disorderly conduct'. Aboriginal resistance to Board control did not end there, and at least one Koori from the station took legal action in 1914 to appeal against an expulsion order and won the case.[6]

The list of convictions gives an important indication of the tactics being used by Kooris. Many of them were for trespass, an offence against the Protection Act which carried a heavy fine or a month in gaol. It arose from Kooris defying the Board's authority by refusing to obey expulsion orders. The fact that these charges were laid at all indicates the struggle the Board was having to enforce its control over the station, and association with that specific land was obviously an extremely important element; a number of the men convicted of trespass were original block-holders, like Bagot Morgan.[7]

The options open to Aboriginal people in the surrounding area were also important. The only other station to have such a high proportion of trespass charges was Brungle, which was also located in an intensively agricultural area which offered few alternative places for Kooris to live and few remaining subsistence resources. For Kooris at Warangesda, enough pastoral properties remained on the claypan areas to offer at least temporary residence away from the reach of the Board. Around Brewarrina and other north-western stations, the continuing presence of the pastoral camps offered permanent and secure residence on significant country. The increasingly apparent disadvantage of the camps was the absence of schooling, which made them less useful for parents of young children. Nevertheless they offered a way of resisting the Board without a confrontation. Aboriginal people were finding that to defy the Board openly increased the risks that children would be noticed and taken away.

Cumeragunja Kooris, lacking such options, were forced into the most confrontationist forms of resistance. The Board was forced in response to strengthen its powers to prosecute for trespass and in 1915 to create the new offence of 'harbouring any expelled aborigine'.[8] Violent disturbances continued on Cumeragunja, however, into 1917, with the manager, who was armed with a revolver, reporting that 'the unsettled state of some Aborigines, and breaches of discipline, requir[e] numerous expulsion orders'.[9]

This manager resigned after failing to restore order, although he had received police assistance from Moama. The new manager was confronted with the same situation and dealt with it in a similar way: by firing on residents, by disciplinary expulsions for 'assaulting the manager', 'general bad behaviour', 'insolence' and 'defiance of the Board's authority' and by Police Court prosecutions. The continuing unrest, as well as police concern about the manager's use of his gun, forced the Board to dismiss this manager in late 1918.[10]

By 1919 expulsions and removals of children by the Board and the response of Kooris in taking their children away from the station had greatly reduced the population of Cumeragunja. This process had been even harder for the Board than at Warangesda, because the Cumeragunja Kooris were more desperate in the defence of their right to live unmolested on the station. Even with the reduction in population, the residents remaining on Cumeragunja were by no means subdued.[11]

In May 1919, in response to further conflict and the flight of more families across the river to escape removals of their children, the Board decided that to quell the unrest it must make some concessions to Aboriginal people. Its minutes show a decision to try more actively to gain the consent of parents, and to allow them funds to visit their children once a year, although it is not clear that any Aboriginal parents were told of this policy. Further concessions were made in June 1919. The community was promised renovations to all the huts and allocations of larger plots around each hut so that vegetables could be grown, but the main concession was that for the first time the Board decided to allow girls taken away to service to return to their families 'for a time' after completion of their 'apprenticeship'.

Yet these concessions were only a change of tactics: the dispersal program was to be slowed down but not abandoned. The intention was that all except full-bloods and half-castes 'were to be removed from the station', but that this was now to be done 'quietly'. In addition, the Board decided that wages should be paid only to 'full-bloods and half-castes', which meant that those men who had worked farm blocks but whose skin colour led them to be classified as 'quadroon' or 'octoroon' were now no longer even to have the opportunity of earning wages for working what they believed to be their own land. At the same time, and on the old assumption that all this disruption must be the work of individual 'troublemakers' rather than arising from deep and widespread distress, the Board tried to transfer Thomas James, a Mauritian missionary and trained teacher, who had married a Cumeragunja woman and raised a family on the station. James saw himself as a part of the Koori community and the Board believed that his presence 'would continue the friction and strife which had been prevalent'.[12]

More disturbances led to the sacking of yet another manager in January 1921 and to another inspection by a member of the Board, this time B. J. Doe, MLA. Again, there were some concessions designed to reduce the tension. The Board suspended some of its expulsion orders and withdrew its objection to Thomas James as teacher. As at Brewarrina, however, the chaos generated by the dispersal activities had disrupted attempts to work the land for the Board's profit and so despite the heavy capital investment which the Board had made in machinery, Doe's report recommended the complete abandonment of farming on Cumeragunja. The Board agreed and proceeded to sell off the stock and machinery. It then leased most of the 2800-acre reserve to whites and allowed a local white sawmiller the rights to timber from the remaining wooded areas. The Cumeragunja Kooris were herded onto a 14-acre corner of the reserve, watching the land they had cleared and worked being used to the profit of whites.[13]

This decision predictably led to still further conflict and more disciplinary expulsions. In August 1921, acting on the troublemaker principle, the Board moved again to end the employment of Thomas James as teacher, on the grounds that it was 'not in the best interests of the Aborigines' for him to stay. This time the Board was successful and James's services were terminated in December, although the Board was apprehensive that Kooris would remove their children from the school in protest. In August, also, the Board tried to expel James's son Shadrack, but he continued the Cumeragunja tradition and refused to comply with the order, seeking legal advice. The Board was forced in turn to ask the Crown Solicitor's advice and had to rewrite the expulsion order in different terms to protect itself from court proceedings. The political nature of the expulsion is evident from the Board's insistence throughout that 'the presence of [Shadrack] James on the Station is a menace to the good government thereof'. James, however, still refused to leave the station and the Board prosecuted him for trespass.[14]

By December 1921, although the population had been reduced by 52 per cent of its 1908 total, the resistance had not ended. The Board decided to act in two ways. Those defined as 'undesirables' were to go on being 'weeded out', but as discontent was so great, the Board reconfirmed its 1919 decision to carry out this process only 'gradually'. In a final attempt to restore order on the station, however, the Board decided to act aggressively and remove the veil of civilian government. For three months, from December 1921 to March 1922, a police station was established at Cumeragunja and the Kooris there were ruled by a resident police officer. This show of force did have an effect: the remaining residents were subdued, temporarily. Over the next ten years, conflict was noticeably reduced and no shootings or violent disputes between the manager and the residents were reported.[15]

The resistance was not over, however, but rather took less confrontationist forms. More and more families escaped with their children, and in 1927 the Board was so concerned that it sought legal advice on how it could regain control over children taken across the Murray into Victoria by their parents.[16] These Aboriginal tactics appear to have been very successful: the Board's Records of Wards do not show any children to have been taken from Cumeragunja from 1922 to 1928 when the records cease.

Some of those who left Cumeragunja went as far as Melbourne, where a community of exiles developed which was to form the nucleus of later political activity. Others found seasonal work in the agricultural areas to the north and south of Cumeragunja, while others again moved only across the river to the camp at Barmah. Over the next decade many Cumeragunja people moved between all three situations, but it appears that few lost their sense of identification as Cumeragunja Kooris. The Board had succeeded in creating the illusion that the numbers of Aborigines had decreased, but temporary dispersal did not mean disappearance.[17]

For those remaining on Cumeragunja during the 1920s, life was far from happy. By 1924 the dispersal program, the disciplinary expulsions and the Koori escapes to protect their children, had reduced the population by 63 per cent of the 1908 figure. The proposed 'renovation' of the houses took place from 1921 to 1926, but amounted to little more than the patching up of houses that had been built 20 or 30 years before. To further discourage 'light-caste' or able-bodied Kooris from returning to Cumeragunja after they had been engaged on seasonal work, 21 houses were pulled down or burnt by the management. In 1927 the inadequate water supply failed altogether and was not repaired until 1934, so that for seven years even the growing of vegetables around the huts to supplement the meagre ration was impossible. General health was poor and trachoma was raging untreated.[18] At no stage did Cumeragunja people forget that their land had been taken from them, and in 1927 they made a formal request to the APB for the farm blocks to be reallocated. They were, however, curtly dismissed by the Board, which informed them 'that the experiment of farm block farming was tried at Cumeragunja and proved a failure, and the Board has no intention of altering the present system'.[19]

The Board had succeeded in maintaining its control, but the bitterness and hostility generated by its policies and methods were to bear fruit in the desperate conditions of the 1930s.

THE WEST: CONFRONTATIONS DEFERRED

The pastoral areas of the far west, north-west and northern rivers were not subject to the pressure for closer settlement that the agricultural areas faced in the first decades of the century. Murris and Wiimpatjas there faced increasing APB interference, but the continued presence of alternative living sites meant they could avoid the risks of open resistance.

Their lives were greatly disrupted: families were forced into a turmoil of movement by threats to take their children. Escaping from the managed stations, they tried to gain access to town public schools, only to be rejected as the schools were segregated one by one. They then had to decide whether to try another town or to seek asylum on a pastoral camp at the cost of no schooling at all and so an increased risk of accusations of neglect. Murris remember the anguish of these decisions and the constant tension caused by the need to be vigilant against Board enquiries. Success in avoiding confrontation with the Board, however, was often at the cost of increasing confrontations with town authorities, and the local archives record the rising protests of alarmed white townspeople who recognised the determination of Aboriginal pressure for access to town services. The returned servicemen of Collarenebri, like Mick Flick, found that not only were they to be refused a Soldier Settler block but that their children were then denied enrolment at the racially segregated 'public' school. Flick's family recall him telling them that he 'started to see after he came back that he wasn't such a respected soldier as a white man'.[20]

During the 1910s and early 1920s, the community political expression in the western Aboriginal communities was muted because of the amount of disruptive movement within the region. Nevertheless, most people were able to find alternatives in areas that satisfied their interest in living on or near lands of significance. With virtually no loss of accessible camping grounds and reserves, the issues of land and residence were not prominent.

An important exception was Walgett, where Murris had tried to address the problem of lack of schooling on pastoral camps. Parents working on the adjacent Gingie sheep station had enrolled five of their children in the town's public school and they walked the 6 miles to and from the town each day to attend. Hostile white townspeople demanded that the school be segregated and all the area's Aboriginal community removed. The Education Department agreed to segregate the school in 1917, whereupon white parents began to complain that the Aboriginal children were neglected because they had no schooling. The Protection Board was reluctant to try to force the movement of the whole community of Murris from the Namoi Bend camp as well as those from Gingie. It reported to the Education Department that all the Aboriginal people in the area were fully employed, 'industrious', 'of excellent character' and the children 'healthy'. In any event, the Board pleaded, 'it would be practically impossible to move them to any other camp as it would be contrary to Aboriginal habits'.[21]

But, under mounting pressure from the townspeople and the Department of Education, the Board retreated and ordered the removal of the five Gingie children to its 'Training Homes'.[22] Their parents were distraught. As the children were forced onto the train at Walgett by the police, one father, George Driver, jumped in front of the train, his hands against the engine and his feet braced against the. sleepers, in a last attempt to stop the train moving off. He was dragged away as the steam shot out from under the engine, and his daughter Ruby was taken away 'for her own good'. Ruby Driver died in Sydney in 1922, after five years of 'service', without ever having seen her family again.[23]

Although missionaries had opened a makeshift school in a bag hut at the Namoi Bend, Murris at Walgett continued to try to re-enter the public school. In 1923 one family succeeded in enrolling their children, with strong support from the local branches of the Labor Party and the Australian Workers' Union. But white parents opposed the re-entry and reignited the calls for the whole of the Aboriginal community at Walgett to be removed 'somewhere else'. The Protection Board instructed the police to canvass the Kamilaraay families of the town to see if they would move to Angledool or Pilliga Board Stations 'at Government expense'. They all adamantly refused, explaining that there was no work for newcomers around the APB stations, whereas they were in constant work on properties around Walgett. They might have added that as Kamilaraay people they were unlikely to feel at home on Yuwalaraay or Ngiyampaa lands.[24]

Unable to gain consent, the Board resorted to force. The police informed the Walgett Murris that all their children were to be summarily removed to Angledool station, 60 miles to the north, under Section 13 of the Protection Act. Parents were contemptuously told they could follow if they wished. As Arthur Dodd of Walgett recalled the situation, 'No kids went to school in Walgett, that's why they hunted us all out. They took their kids and they had to follow their kids then'.[25] The missionary described the action as a 'forced removal', reporting on 'how hard it was' to see the unwilling children and women bundled into the mail trucks used to transport them. The Murris who were there recall weeping people trying to gather a few belongings while the local police hurried them along. Twenty-one children were removed and about 60 Murris were forced to 'follow their children' to Angledool. Only the Nicholls family remained at the Namoi Bend.[26]

Yet dispossession by forced removal proved intolerable for most of these Kamilaraay Murris. After about twelve months, most of them returned to Walgett, 'walked back, carryin' their swag, womens and kids and everything', defying the Board and the town.[27] Their defiance had brought them back to their home, but not to security. White hostility persisted and the missionary reported by 1925 that there was 'another move on foot to remove them altogether from the district'.[28] This missionary suggested as a compromise that the Namoi Bend population might accept removal to the disused reserve on Gingie station. The Protection Board eagerly embraced the idea and so the town Murris, and the bag hut school, were packed off to what became known as

Gingie reserve, 6 miles out of town. Again it was an unwilling move. As Don Nicholls recalled: 'They hunted 'em out from here [Namoi Bend]. They wouldn't have been out there at Gingie at all only for them white fellas hunted 'em out'.[29] Eventually some Murris from the Gingie pastoral camp moved onto the reserve to gain access to the school, but for many Murris the reserve was unsatisfactory, and they moved back, yet again, to what they considered their home at the Namoi Bend. By 1927 two Murri families had once more gained entry to the public school, and white townspeople and the Protection Board were still wrangling over their rights to admission when the Depression hit and distracted them for a few short years.[30]

This Murri community was clearly motivated by a concern to live on the land of their choice, for economic and cultural reasons. For most others in the west, however, the need to take such direct action to stay close to land of significance was not to arise until the 1930s.

THE NORTHERN SLOPES

A large number of reserves had been created when this formerly pastoral area was penetrated by agriculture in the 1880s. This could have caused the immediate disappearance of the Aboriginal pastoral camps of the region, but the great need for labour led to the camp lands being retained even while the pastoral concerns were divided up around them. These camps became reserves, from which Aboriginal workers provided the fencers and harvesters for the area's smallholders. The new wave of closer settlement after 1905 was too strong, however, to allow these small islands of Aboriginal land to survive. One by one they fell to either leasing or revocation, and the Murris on them were forced to move (see Map 9, opposite). The Protection Board acted to increase its control over a few reserves, like Pilliga on which it installed a resident manager, but it abandoned all the others to white demand. Some Murris sought a secure living space on the remaining reserves in their immediate area and in this way many families from Cuttabri, Redbank and other old campsites found their way into the tightly controlled atmosphere of Pilliga station.[31]

Others, however, were anxious to avoid Board interference and so they moved to the unsupervised campsites and reserves around the towns. An important example was Terry Hie Hie station, which was desired by local whites. The Kamilaraay Murris who lived there were in strong opposition to the Board's manager and the great tension there had already driven away many residents, so the Board withdrew its manager in 1924 and leased the reserve land to white farmers. Many Terry Hie Hie Murris moved into Moree, a town 24 miles to the

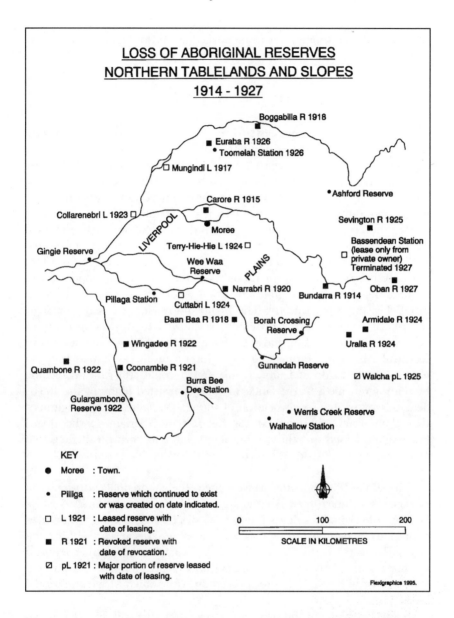

LOSS OF ABORIGINAL RESERVES
NORTHERN TABLELANDS AND SLOPES
1914 - 1927

Boggabilla R 1918

■ Euraba R 1926
• Toomelah Station 1926

□ Mungindi L 1917

•Ashford Reserve

Carore R 1915

Collarenebri L 1923 □

Sevington R 1925
■

Moree

Gingie Reserve

Terry-Hie-Hie L 1924 □

Bassendean Station
□ (lease only from
private owner)
Terminated 1927

Wee Waa
Reserve

PLAINS

LIVERPOOL

Pillaga Station

Cuttabri L 1924

■ Narrabri R 1920

Bundarra R 1914 ■

Oban R 1927

Baan Baa R 1918 ■

Borah Crossing
Reserve

Armidale R 1924

Wingadee R 1922

Uralla R 1924
■

Quambone R 1922

Coonamble R 1921

Gunnedah Reserve

☑ Walcha pL 1925

Burra Bee
• Dee Station

Gulargambone •
Reserve 1922

• Werris Creek Reserve
Walhallow Station

KEY

● Moree : Town.

• Pilliga : Reserve which continued to exist
or was created on date indicated.

□ L 1921 : Leased reserve with
date of leasing.

■ R 1921 : Revoked reserve with
date of revocation.

☑ pL 1921 : Major portion of reserve leased
with date of leasing.

0   100   200

SCALE IN KILOMETRES

Flexigraphics 1995.

north-west on Kamilaraay land, where their relatives already lived in a long-established camp from which they worked in the town and sent their children to the public school. Like the north-western Murris, these Kamilaraay were able to avoid direct confrontation because they had some alternatives. But they had lost their homes, and their bitterness and anger led them to entrench themselves tenaciously in their new locations. They did not fight their battles over land at this time, but they became determined not to be pushed away from a home site again. Their time, too, was to come later in the decade.

THE NORTH COAST

From the earliest white requests to the Board for revocation of reserves, the focus of white acquisition attempts was the reserved Aboriginal farming land of the north coast. As white settlement intensified all along the coast, high-quality alluvial land had become as scarce in the Macleay Valley as it had been for decades in the far northern rivers area. The fertile and proven lands of the Aboriginal farming reserves began to attract the attention of land-hungry whites, who appealed to the local Lands Boards to take up their case through the Department of Lands.

The Board continued to resist these demands for outright revocation, but only because its need for funds was so urgent. It saw opportunities to fund its dispersal program by using Aboriginal lands for its own profit. Leasing proved useful. The Board did not have to evict outright the Aboriginal residents, who could be allowed to stay camped on an acre or two, nor did it have to force newly dispossessed and very resentful Aboriginal farmers to work for its profit, as it had tried so unsuccessfully to do at Cumeragunja. Yet it could still gain an income by renting out most of the land. So while it resisted many of the 1910s demands by whites for revocation of the reserve lands on the argument that they were 'still required for the use of Aborigines', the Board increasingly leased out those same reserves for its own profit. Between 1913 and 1921 the Board's income from leasing increased by 500 per cent.[33]

The Board's opportunism weakened the Aboriginal position still further. As it interrupted Aboriginal farming to lease the land to white farmers, Aboriginal residents found it harder to defend their tenure over their lands by demonstrating their own farming skills and self-sufficiency. The 1916 restructuring of the Board (see Chapter 10) further reduced its interest in encouraging Aboriginal farmers or offering even nominal support to Aboriginal rights to association with some of their traditional lands.

Soldier settlement brought an accelerated demand for Aboriginal land which neither the Lands Department nor the APB could resist. On occasions the Board fought against the Department, but this was usually when the Board wanted to keep reserves to lease out for its own profit. The Board was of course no longer interested in defending Aboriginal landholding for farming or any other purpose. In any event, it was such a minor element of the bureaucracy that in any contest between it and the powerful Lands Department, such as occurred over the Ballengarra reserve, the victor would inevitably be the Lands Department and the whites it represented.

The result was a massive loss of Aboriginal-controlled land, either to APB or Lands Department leasing or to outright revocation. There had been over 27 000 acres of Aboriginal Reserve land in 1911; by 1927 more than 13 000 acres had been completely lost by revocation. Far more was then removed from Aboriginal control by leasing. In total, 75 per cent by acreage of all of the reserve lands revoked from 1913 to 1927 was from the fertile, Aboriginal-controlled farming lands of the New South Wales coast, from the Bellinger River in the north to western Sydney.[34] (See Map 10, p. 138)

BALLENGARRA AND ROLLANDS PLAINS

To gain an insight into the impact of this loss, we can trace the story of a cluster of families around the Macleay River whose experience of the second dispossession is typical. Percy Mosely was the son of John Mosely, who had occupied one of the Fattorini Islands and then moved to Euroka Creek, known as Burnt Bridge. Percy was related by marriage to the Fields family, and so by 1914 was farming the land at Ballengarra, originally reserved at the request of Robert Fields in 1894. Early in 1914, uneasily aware of intensifying local white interest in his family's land, Mosely applied to the Board for formal confirmation of his rights to occupy and cultivate the 20-acre reserve. In June he was assured by the Board that he could consider his occupancy secure, after which he began preparations for another maize crop. At about the same time, however, a white man applied to the Lands Department for a lease over this reserve and his application was approved.[35]

The Board protested on Mosely's behalf, but the Lands Department refused to change its decision, so the Board sent the police to ask Mosely if he 'might know of some vacant reserve to which the Board might remove him'. Mosely, however, refused to leave the land or the crop, so the Board decided, without consulting the Kooris of Rollands Plains reserve, that Mosely should be given a permissive occupancy of 6–10 acres there and 'transferred without delay'. Mosely still refused to move, and in February 1915 the Board offered him £10 'out of pocket expenses', to be paid only after he left the reserve. When Mosely refused to accept the money, insisting that the land and the crop now ready to harvest was his, the Board washed its hands of the matter and the police forcibly evicted him early in March. The white lessee then took possession of the land and the crop.[36]

Mosely moved his family north-west to Rollands Plains, so adding another to the four or more families living there. Mosely himself went

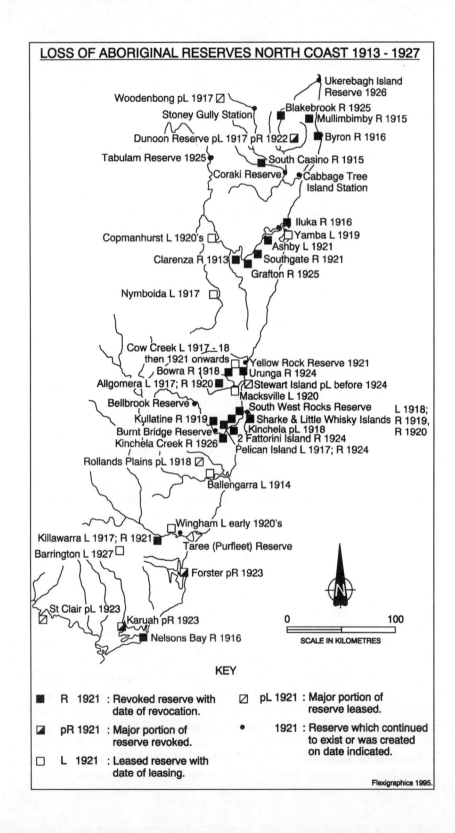

LOSS OF ABORIGINAL RESERVES NORTH COAST 1913 - 1927

Ukerebagh Island
Reserve 1926

Woodenbong pL 1917 ☑

Blakebrook R 1925

Stoney Gully Station

Mullimbimby R 1915

Dunoon Reserve pL 1917 pR 1922 ☑

Byron R 1916

Tabulam Reserve 1925

South Casino R 1915

Coraki Reserve

Cabbage Tree
Island Station

Iluka R 1916

Copmanhurst L 1920's ☐

Yamba L 1919

Ashby L 1921

Clarenza R 1913

Southgate R 1921

Grafton R 1925

Nymboida L 1917 ☐

Cow Creek L 1917 - 18
then 1921 onwards

Yellow Rock Reserve 1921

Bowra R 1918

Urunga R 1924

Allgomera L 1917; R 1920

☑ Stewart Island pL before 1924

Macksville L 1920

Bellbrook Reserve

South West Rocks Reserve

L 1918;

Sharke & Little Whisky Islands R 1919,

Kullatine R 1919

Kinchela pL 1918

R 1920

Burnt Bridge Reserve

2 Fattorini Island R 1924

Kinchela Creek R 1926

Pelican Island L 1917; R 1924

Rollands Plains pL 1918 ☑

Ballengarra L 1914

Wingham L early 1920's

Killawarra L 1917; R 1921

Taree (Purfleet) Reserve

Barrington L 1927 ☐

Forster pR 1923

St Clair pL 1923 ☑

Karuah pR 1923

Nelsons Bay R 1916

0   100

SCALE IN KILOMETRES

KEY

■ R 1921 : Revoked reserve with date of revocation.

◨ pR 1921 : Major portion of reserve revoked.

☐ L 1921 : Leased reserve with date of leasing.

☑ pL 1921 : Major portion of reserve leased.

• 1921 : Reserve which continued to exist or was created on date indicated.

Flexigraphics 1995.

on to Sydney, to explain to the Board in person 'his desire to again occupy the reserve' and his argument that the white lessee had received the proceeds of his labour. The Board was convinced to some extent, asking the white lessee to remit £7 2s 6d to Mosely, being one-third of the profits of the maize crop and suggesting to the Lands Department that the lease be terminated. Mosely remained immovable in his demand for 'repossession' of Ballengarra, despite the Board again offering him the choice of any vacant reserve land. The Board felt confident enough to assure him that at the termination of the Lands Department annual lease, he would be able to return to the reserve. But the Lands Department ignored the Board and renewed the white occupier's lease, over the protests of both Mosely and the Board, which as some consolation again offered £10 to Mosely, who again rejected the money.[37]

In the course of this dispute, the Board paid some attention to the situation at Rollands Plains, noticing that in the latter part of the year some of the Koori residents had leased a portion of the reserve for agistment. The Board itself had classed this land as best suited to grazing purposes; in any case cultivation in the severe north coast drought of late 1915 was extremely risky, all crops on the other Board reserves failing over this period. But the Board strongly disapproved of the Kooris of the reserve receiving a cash income from it in this way. By this time the Board itself needed extra cash to fund its child removal program. So after ordering the police to step in and end the existing Aboriginal-initiated lease at Rollands Plains, the Board immediately called for tenders for agistment on part of the reserve, with the fees now to be paid to itself.[38]

The Davis family, for whom the land had originally been reserved, began a twenty-year campaign for its return. They were still arguing their case in 1937, when Herbert Davis wrote the following letter to the Select Committee on the APB. His account is consistent with all the Protection Board's records.

> We consider that we ain't getting a fair deal by the Aborigines Protection Board regarding a piece of land situated at Rollands Plains. That was a standing dense scrub. That was cleared by me and my brothers. After we had cleared the land and put it into value, it was then leased to a white man, Mr Clarrie Avery by name.
>
> The land was given to us on condition that we cleared it. We fulfilled all conditions and cleared the land and fenced it off and resided on it for over 30 years.
>
> The land, when a standing scrub, was valued by the valuator, Mr H. Watters, at £2 an acre. It is and was valued at £42 per acre after we had cleared it.
>
> Several applications was made to the Board for to continue cultivation and were each time refused.

Some Aborigines tried to stem the loss of land by requesting leases themselves over the reserves. The Davises' applications for a lease of Rollands Plains were rejected in 1919 and again in 1920.[39] Percy Mosely, however, was one who refused to accept bureaucratic decisions as final. After the leasing of Rollands Plains, he returned to Ballengarra and organised an unofficial arrangement with the white lessee. This was still functioning in 1924: the white lessee used Mosely's pair of Clydesdales for ploughing and in return Mosely lived on the reserve, farming a share of the land.[40]

The Mosely and Davis story demonstrates the weakness of the Protection Board in relation to a powerful bureaurcracy like the Lands Department. It makes apparent the Board's desire to use Aboriginal land for its own financial interest rather than for Aboriginal interests. The story gives insights too into the tenacity of these Aboriginal farmers, their determination and courage in challenging government officials in order to try to restore their rights, and their independence in negotiating with local whites to regain at least their usage rights over some of the lands.

REVOCATION AND LEASING

All of the good-quality alluvial land reserved in the area north and south of the Macleay came under pressure. By 1918 Killawarra, Urunga, Cow Creek, both of the Shark Islands and Pelican Island were all partially or wholly leased. Even a portion of Kinchela reserve was under lease by this time. In the far northern rivers areas, land of similar quality came under the same pressure, and by 1918 most of Dunoon was under lease to returned soldiers and there had been repeated requests for either revocation or leasing of Grafton.[41]

On many of these reserves, Kooris had still been cultivating the land when they were revoked or leased. One example is the loss of the group of fertile islands near the mouth of the Macleay. As late as August 1919, Board Inspector H. L. Swindehurst had emphatically advised against revocation of the two Fattorini Islands and Pelican Island on the grounds that the Koori residents were farming the land efficiently. In June 1924, however, the decision fell to Inspector Donaldson, who was just as committed as ever to the closing of the reserves. He advised the Board that the Fattorini Islands' residents should be relocated to nearby Pelican Island and the Fattorini Islands revoked. Only months later, Donaldson recommended that Pelican Island too should be 'disposed of' and the residents of all three islands concentrated on Kinchela station.[42] Koori requests to lease their own farms were usually dismissed just as curtly as the Davises had been. Only at Cabbage Tree Island was the returned serviceman George Kapeen more successful, but even then he could secure no more than a small 'family block', and his success was perhaps simply because there had been no white demands yet.[43]

In the other area which suffered major reserve loss because of revocation or leasing, the northern slopes, Mungindi and Narrabri reserves, and part of Sevington, had all been leased by 1918. Only Kooris at Walcha reserve were successful in securing their occupation by lease in 1917, but even this was temporary and in 1925 the Board leased the reserve to a white man who made a more attractive tender. One of the original Koori lessees at Walcha described the conditions of the reserve after the transfer:

> Our complaint here is that the Aborigines Protection Board allows white men to run sheep, cattle and horses, on the Aboriginal Reserve, and they eat all the feed, so we can't keep horses for our children to ride to school. The fences around the reserve are cut and are falling down.
>
> Some of us tried to grow vegetables, corn, potatoes by the river-side, but the white people cut down the fences and let their stock in to trample down and eat what we planted with so much labour. All our work is gone for nothing.[44]

INCREASING APB CONTROL ON REMAINING LAND

With land lost by revocation and leasing, the area available to north coast Kooris was decreasing rapidly. At the same time the Protection Board greatly increased its interference and control. A greater number of children were taken from the north coast from late in the 1910s, but in this period as well the Board imposed resident managers on several Koori reserve communities of the mid- and lower coastal areas. Two examples were particularly significant.

St Clair

St Clair near Singleton was farming land worked independently by the Phillips, Murphy and other Wonnarua families, who had fenced and cleared 20 acres before 1890 and were growing maize, tobacco and potatoes.[45] From 1913 there were local white demands to revoke the reserve to 'open' the land for white farming, while at the same time white hostility to the Aboriginal presence in the town led to the public school being segregated. The Board resisted the pressure to revoke St Clair because it sought to use the reserve as a central point to exercise control over the area's Koori population, many of whom had been forced to move to the reserve to bring their children to the 'special' Board school there. A manager took up residence in 1916. Insistent white demands for revocation of St Clair now occurred at the same time as rising conflict between residents and manager, with expulsions and prosecutions which effectively disrupted the Aboriginal farming there. Finally the Board took the opportunity to gain from the lands and closed the station to lease the reserve to white farmers from 1923.[46]

Kinchela

At Kinchela, the hopes held by William Drew and others in the 1880s for economic independence had been almost completely destroyed. The Protection Board imposed a resident manager over the reserve lands in 1917, and by 1918 forced the lease of part of the 30 acres to a white farmer. By 1921 there were 114 Kooris on Kinchela, the two Fattorini Islands and Pelican Island under the Kinchela manager's control, with only fourteen of them being children of school age. These fertile but tiny reserves had been divided up into 'farm blocks' of unspecified size for individual families. Such blocks could only have been very small, with portions of Pelican Island and Kinchela already leased and the Board's manager having instituted maize farming for the Board's profit on another, again unspecified, area of the reserve lands. Nevertheless Kooris were successful in retaining most of the profits from the maize; in 1921 this amounted to £322 as against the Board's share of £177. The figure for private profit is impressive under the circumstances, but when divided among 114 people would not have gone very far towards self-sufficiency. In 1924 most of the residents of the Fattorini and Pelican Islands were forced to move to Kinchela, greatly increasing the population there. Later in the same year, the Protection Board imposed its new Boys' Home on Kinchela, with all its additional buildings. By 1926, in a final irony for this independently won and farmed Gumbaynggirr land, the Protection Board was referring to Kinchela as 'the reserve attached to the Home'.[47] Within fifteen years, this 'home' had become infamous after police investigation uncovered sustained cruelty and abuse against the young boys held there by a series of drunken and sadistic superintendents.[48]

So Kinchela farm, which had been for so long a flourishing symbol of Aboriginal independence and assertion, became Kinchela Boys' Home, a feared place where boys removed from their families were kept in loneliness and abuse, to teach them to forget their Aboriginality. This reversal was more extreme than most, but as the surveillance and control of APB staff over all the remaining reserves intensified, the new meanings being acquired by these pieces of land began to change. Aboriginal memories of these lands now became complex and strongly polarised. There were affectionate and affirming recollections which related to the independent period or to the social relationships and support between Aboriginal residents, but there were also bitter memories of humiliation and frustration under tightening APB control.

RESERVED AND NON-RESERVED LANDS:
THE FAR NORTHERN COASTAL RIVERS

The story of a number of Bandjalang families around Lismore suggests a common pattern in the coastal areas, which shows the relationship between the Aboriginal use of reserved and non-reserved land over this troubled period. Their story also shows the complex interaction of land issues with those arising from increasing Protection Board power and rising tension with white townspeople. The Lismore story is an example of the way the dispersal policy led to growing friction with townspeople, who tried to shut out the increasing numbers of Aboriginal people who came to the towns seeking asylum and access to services.

The situation of the far north coast was different from that on the mid-coastal lands. In the northerly areas from the 1860s to 1890s, Aboriginal people had not been able to secure much independent farming land; Cabbage Tree Island was an exception. Nevertheless the reserves which had been created without Aboriginal demand had come to have increasing significance as alternative living areas became less available.

Dunoon, near the town of Lismore, is a clear example of land which grew in significance over time. It was a reserve created on APB initiative in 1887, on land which was not of particularly good quality and which Kooris had not wished to use at first because they had other attractive campsites and many employment opportunities. By the 1910s, however, with fewer available campsites, they had begun to live on the land and to farm it. There was no direct Board supervision until a manager was imposed in 1914, turning the reserve into a station; this led to a series of conflicts between him and the Koori residents. Their alarm at managerial interference and threats to remove their children was so great that the Kooris, including those who had been farming the land, moved off the reserve to unreserved vacant land closer to Lismore, vowing that they would not remain under APB control. Alternative campsites and good opportunities for employment combined with the abundant resources of the subtropical coast allowed them to escape from the Board even in an intensively settled agricultural area.[49]

This Aboriginal strategy forced the manager to resign, the station to revert to unsupervised reserve, and the 'special' school to close in December 1916. Donaldson, by this time active in his travels as the Board's inspector, investigated the Lismore Kooris to try to force them back under direct Board control. He managed to remove some children classified 'orphans' but failed when he tried to take the children of families like the Robertses, who had left Dunoon. They had gained the support of the local police, who pointed out to Donaldson that these Aboriginal families had succeeded in enrolling their younger children in schools and their older children were already working or 'apparently looking after themselves'. After 1917, when it was clear that a manager would not be reappointed, Kooris began to return to Dunoon, although the Board by this time was preparing to lease the reserve.[50]

By then the Board's interventions into Aboriginal life on its managed stations on the north coast had intensified, with increasing expulsion orders and child removals. Because it was now free of managerial supervision, Dunoon reserve became a focus for migration as Aboriginal people tried to escape APB interference. Despite the fact that the Board leased much of the land in 1917, there was a substantial Koori population again resident in 1919, and by 1922 more people had arrived seeking refuge from managerial interference on Runnymede or Cabbage Tree Island stations. In an attempt to stop this movement, the Board decided to remove Dunoon as an alternative by revoking the reserve in May 1922. It met with sustained and effective Koori protest, expressed in letters to the Board from the Kooris themselves and from white supporters. The Board was forced to compromise. It revoked 30 acres of the reserve, but left a 10-acre strip around the existing huts. The Lismore police were issued with instructions to 'discourage' new arrivals. This still did not halt the growth in reserve population and in 1926 the Board reopened the 'special' school on the reserve in an acknowledgment that the Kooris there were not going to return to its managed stations. This, of course, increased the Board's power of surveillance once again, and a number of families moved to an unreserved campsite closer to Lismore called Tuncester. From here they sought access to the public school and for a while at least some families were successful, defending their rights of entry with letters of support and character references from lawyers, until eventually segregation of the school was reasserted in 1928.[51]

It was not only at Lismore that the dislocation caused by loss of reserves and intensified APB activity heightened Koori pressure for access to the precincts and services of the white towns. At Kyogle in 1919, Forster and Karuah in 1923, Wingham in 1924 and Taree and Kempsey in 1925, white townspeople were demanding removal of the increasing numbers of Kooris in the vicinity of their towns, while Kyogle in 1926 and Lismore in 1927 insisted that the government fund additional hospital wards to segregate Aboriginal patients. As in the western areas, such segregation demands reflected wider attempts to block Aboriginal access to the towns.[52]

In this context of heightened protest from white townspeople, the Protection Board became extremely anxious about the Aboriginal exodus from all its north coast stations throughout 1923 and 1924. It instructed its resident managers to 'dissuade' Koori families from leaving, but if that failed they were to institute prosecutions for 'abduction' of children and then summarily remove the children from fleeing families.[53] The maintenance of some alternative residence sites allowed Kooris the avenue of escape from the managed stations, where Board control was tightest, but this process in turn made alienation of the reserved station land more likely. At Grafton station, for example, it was 'loss of population' caused by the Board's own policies which placed the Board in the position in 1924 of being no longer able to resist the Lands Department, which had been demanding the revocation of the reserved land since 1918.[54]

Some Kooris were able to move to non-reserved camps like that at Tuncester or Greenhills near Kempsey. By the 1920s, however, people faced the contraction of vacant land as well as the closure of access to public schools which was by now general on the north coast. Many families decided in these conditions to move to the remaining, less closely supervised reserves where a 'special' school existed but where there was no resident manager. To the south, Purfleet at Taree was one such alternative, while in the Macleay Valley, Bellbrook and Burnt Bridge offered some refuge.

But even the presence of a Protection Board school with a non-residential teacher created a danger for Koori families, and children were taken from Burnt Bridge with increasing frequency after 1920. Jack Campbell has recalled being kept home from the reserve's school one day in 1925, when his parents had apparently received warning that Inspector Donaldson was arriving to 'kidnap kids'. As the inspector approached the Campbell's house, Jack's mother fired a shotgun over Donaldson's head, sending him back into Kempsey to fetch the police. It was clearly imperative for the family to escape the district altogether after this incident and so the Campbells went south down the coast in Jack's father's fishing boat. After a brief period at Putty Beach, the family settled in Sydney, but rather than live at the closely police-supervised La Perouse reserve, they lived at the non-reserved campsite at Salt Pan Creek, joining other refugees from APB control like Paddy Pitman, expelled from Wallaga Lake for defiance of the manager.[55]

BURRAGORANG

To the west of Sydney, the Burragorang lands were yet another example of the white pressure on Aboriginal farming land, but in this case it arose not only from white farmers and the Protection Board, but from the Catholic Church. This was the 70-acre farm called St Joseph's, which had been bought for local Kooris in 1876 from contributions made by parishioners. The farm was made up of the portion bought with these church funds, and another section which had been railway reserve, before being converted to Aboriginal reserve in 1898 when a local white farmer had tried to take it over.

The church-owned section was the piece of land which had become associated with Mary Toliman, now widowed and remarried to a Tharawal man from the south coast named Longbottom. This part of the farm was shared with Mary's daughter Selena, who had married an Aboriginal man named Archie Shepherd. They were adamant that the church had handed over the land as a gift and had no further claim to it. The churchmen were appalled by this but the tone of their correspondence suggests they were even more concerned because the men in the family, Longbottom and Shepherd, refused to give the church their allegiance. Speaking of Archie Shepherd, Father Considine wrote to Cardinal Moran in 1908:

> He is a very indifferent Catholic and does not attend to his religious duties. I informed him that unless his conduct changed, I should have to consider some fresh arrangements with regard to his tenure of St Joseph's farm . . . He said most emphatically that he refused to recognise the Church's authority over the farm . . . So defiant was he, that I consider some action must be taken to assert your Eminence's title to the property . . . And if the 10 acres could also be recovered from the Crown it would be very advantageous, as it would complete the farm.[56]

Mary Toliman and Selena Shepherd took on the role of negotiating with the Catholic Church from 1908 through to 1916. They were the ones who visited the priest and the bishop, they were the ones who conciliated. Mary and Selena argued that they had had a long association with the land, but they stressed also that they would go to church and continue to be loyal to Catholicism. While Longbottom and Shepherd held out a hard line throughout these eight years, Mary and Selena consistently agreed to negotiate. Both positions may have been elements of the one strategy to keep the land.[57]

But the pressure did not ease, and now pleas to assist returned servicemen were added to the demands on the Board to revoke the reserved area. All of St Joseph's was still being farmed in 1918 when local whites approached the police to request revocation or leasing. The Board resolved most emphatically that because they continued to farm the land, Kooris should be allowed to remain in possession of the reserve. By 1924, however, as it was doing elsewhere along the coast, the Board acceded to Lands Department pressure and revoked the farm reserve. The church moved in to regain its land soon after, and the farming community was dispersed. At least some of the Burragorang Kooris, the Anderson, Williams and Shepherd families, moved to Sydney.[58]

THE SOUTH COAST: BATEMAN'S BAY

On the south coast, lands had been reserved because they had been demanded and reoccupied by Aboriginal people, but their intentions had been mainly to use the land as residential bases, from which they had often been engaged in fishing. The pressure on these lands was also building throughout the 1910s, but it arose not from white farming interests but from demands for urban expansion. Bateman's Bay is a clear example of the complex tensions as well as collaboration between local white interests and APB policy in the pressure on Aboriginal lands in this area.

The main pressure on south coast reserves was from town expansion, which resulted in the revocation of Ulladulla reserve in 1922 and that at Tomakin near Moruya in 1925. As early as 1918, however, the Bateman's Bay Progress Association had informed the Protection Board that the reserve near that town was standing in the way of white residential development and requested its revocation and the removal of its inhabitants. The Board procrastinated until 1922, when it agreed to 'encourage' the reserve residents to move to a newly created reserve some miles out of town. The Kooris of the town refused to move from the site where they had built their own houses and from which their children could easily attend the public school.[59]

After further pressure from townspeople, the Board in 1924 agreed to revocation of the town reserve. This did not occur immediately because the Koori residents' total refusal to leave threw some doubt on the proposed development. The Lands Department now put pressure on the Board not simply to formalise the revocation but to remove the Koori community. The Board again capitulated, and issued removal orders in June 1925. The townspeople had by this time decided to take matters into their own hands: the local Parents' and Citizens' Association voted to segregate the school in order to force Kooris to leave the town.[60]

School segregations had become a well-tried tactic in the hands of white townspeople trying to force the removal of whole communities of Aboriginal people. In another south coast use of the tactic, the Huskisson school segregation had been initiated in 1921 to achieve the removal of the Kooris there to Wreck Bay. White fishermen at Huskisson were resentful of Aboriginal fishermen trawling in the local area, and had made a number of attempts to have the whole Koori population moved to reduce this competition. Kooris there had bitterly contested the segregation and the pressure to move, defying the police instructions to that effect. In 1925 too, as well as the segregation at Bateman's Bay, the school at Summer Cloud Bay, near Wreck Bay, was also segregated with the same goal of forcing removal.[61]

The Bateman's Bay school segregation left fifteen to twenty Koori children with no schooling at all. Rather than leave the town, however, their families mounted a sustained and well-coordinated campaign to have the segregation rescinded. Numbers of white supporters, who all stressed their ALP affiliation in writing to a Labor ministry, appealed to the government on the issues of the injustice of the segregation and the exploitation of Aboriginal school-age children's labour in sawmills owned by some of the P & C members who had voted for the segregation.[62] It was the Koori protesters, however, who put the school segregation in its context, linking it with the attempt to revoke the reserve as a means of forcing them out of town. Prominent in this protest was Jane Duren, whose grandchildren were among those excluded from the school. She appealed to the monarchy against the government, writing to George V in June 1926. Her letter referred to the hypocrisy of the Australian myth of 'fair play' and pointed out the contradictions of a system which declared itself committed to 'compulsory' and 'public' education and yet excluded Aboriginal members of the public from schooling. The land issue was, however, given priority in her final demand: 'Let them stay on the land that was granted to them also compel the children to be sent to the Public School at Bateman's Bay'.[63]

Early in 1927 Duren came to Sydney to see the Education Department officials. As it did often when a situation became too difficult, the Education Department called in the Child Welfare Department, but in this instance its inspector declined to remove any children from their families and in fact supported Koori demands for readmission to the school. An assurance was given by this inspector to white parents that 'an influx' of Aboriginal children from other areas would not occur and with State Departmental backing withdrawn, the two-year segregation collapsed. Kooris had won both the battle for access to the school and for security of residence in the town: in September 1927 the Lands Department revoked the out-of-town reserve which Kooris had 'absolutely refused' to occupy, and no further attempts were made to move this community.[64]

12

Fighting Back:
Aboriginal Political
Organisation

By 1915, Kooris on the north coast had demonstrated that they would take their disputes with the Protection Board to the public and the press. It was in that year, when the Board gained its new legislation concerning children, that Kooris at Grafton and Nymboida decided that the Board's stations were definitely unsafe and began to move away in substantial numbers, causing the Board to try to reassure them that it did not intend to take their children 'without careful enquiry'. Far from being reassured, Kooris took their case to the *Grafton Argus*, and gained sympathetic coverage.[1] Some families were forced into extreme defence of their children, either by fleeing from land they had considered their home, or by defying the Board as Jack Campbell's mother had done. One of these families, on the Hastings River, drew on traditional symbols of authority. They confronted Inspector Donaldson with spears and shields, signifying the depth of their anger and their right to resist. Such open use of traditional cultural symbols was to become a hallmark of the political movement which developed on the coast.[2] Then, in 1919, Koori returned servicemen from the north coast began to protest at the conditions they faced. Like other Aboriginal men who had served overseas, Koori soldiers returning to the north coast after World War I found that the facilities of the towns were still closed to them and their families. They organised a petition demanding 'Civic Rights' and they were supported by the Casino and Bangalow branches of the Returned Soldiers' and Seamen's League.[3]

The first Aboriginal political organisation to create formal links between communities over a wide area took shape in the early 1920s, in the midst of the second dispossession, the growing APB pressure on children and communities, and the spreading segregation of town services. The energy and membership for this organisation came initially from the north, but it expanded rapidly to include Kooris from right along the coast (Map 11, p. 150). It was known as the Australian Aboriginal Progressive Association (AAPA) and was first seen in the public media in 1924, but there are signs of its activity before then.

ACTIVE COMMUNITIES IN THE
AUSTRALIAN ABORIGINAL PROGRESSIVE ASSOCIATION
1922 TO 1929

• Lismore

Grafton

Coffs Harbour
Nambucca Heads
Bellbrook   Kinchela
Burnt Bridge   Kempsey
Port Macquarie

Taree

Singleton   Port Stephens
Newcastle

Salt Pan Creek   Sydney

Batemans Bay

0   100   200   300   400
SCALE IN KILOMETRES

Flexigraphics 1995.

Its chief spokesperson was Fred Maynard, a Hunter River Koori who was 45 in 1924. Maynard was the nephew of Tom Phillips, one of the original farmers of the St Clair land, lost by leasing to whites in 1923. His grandfather was a Mauritian, Jean Phillipe, who had married a Port Stephens Koori whose name was recorded as Mary. Their daughter Mary, Maynard's mother, had died giving birth to twins when Fred was five. Maynard's father had abandoned the six surviving children, and so Fred lived for some time in the home of a local Presbyterian minister. This informal arrangement was similar in many ways to the conditions of Aboriginal 'apprentices' during their indentures, with Fred and his young brother facing hard work and poor conditions on a small dairy farm attached to the presbytery. However, Fred had also spent some time with his uncle Tom and other Wonnarua relatives on the St Clair lands and remained in contact with them, although he eventually came to

150

live with his older sisters in inner Sydney. Fred Maynard was a self-taught man, receiving no formal schooling, and travelling Australia as a drover and stockman while a young man, before returning to Sydney to work on the wharves and take an active part in the Waterside Workers' Union during the First World War.

Among his Hunter Valley family connections was his cousin's husband, Sid Ridgeway, from the family associated with another of the farming lands, held by permissive occupancy at Tea Gardens.[4] Sid was to become an office-bearer of the AAPA, and so too were members of the Johnstone family, who had been involved with farming lands at Killawarra near Wingham, which were revoked in 1921.[5] Another friend from the area was Louis Lacy, who was also to become a prominent AAPA speaker. As early as 1922, these Hunter Valley Kooris were voicing their concerns about the pressure on their lands and the attempts by the Board to fragment their families. Their dissatisfaction was noticed in a small article in a Newcastle paper, *The Voice of the North*.[6]

The first activity of the AAPA was to try to help the children who had been taken from their families. In this they joined with a sympathetic white woman, Elizabeth McKenzie-Hatton, about whose earlier life we know only that she had come from Victoria, a single parent, possibly widowed, and looking after two daughters and a son. Hatton may have been aware of growing feminist interest in Aboriginal policy in the 1920s; this would be consistent with her later close contact with the Victorian Aboriginal Uplift Society, a missionary group unusually supportive of Aboriginal political activity. In her AAPA work, however, Hatton acted as an individual, determinedly creating platforms for its Aboriginal spokespeople. She made contact with these activist Kooris of the AAPA soon after arriving in Sydney and became a stalwart and vigorous member of the Association, and apparently the only one who was not Aboriginal.[7]

In December 1923 the group took imaginative but concrete action: they informed the Protection Board that Mrs Hatton was going to set up a 'home' for 'incorrigible Aboriginal girls' at her house at Homebush. They even asked the Board for a contribution towards the financial support of the girls. Girls were usually classified 'incorrigible' after repeatedly absconding or defying their employers. From an Aboriginal viewpoint, these were the girls most in need of support and an alternative to the Board's 'solution', which was to send them to Parramatta Girls' Home. Mrs Hatton's proposed 'home' had the potential to deflect the weight of Board punishment from those girls who resisted most strongly. Although there is no remaining evidence, there must have been an extensive sympathetic network within the Aboriginal community which directed girls in need to the home because it functioned throughout 1924 and into 1925, in spite of the fact that the Board refused to assist Mrs Hatton in any way.[8]

The Protection Board was particularly sensitive on this issue because the apprenticeship scheme had recently come under press and parliamentary attack. It was not the conditions of the girls' employment which raised white public interest, but the implications of separating the girls from their communities. Articles in two Sydney newspapers, in 1924 and 1925, accused the Board of hastening the disappearance of the Aboriginal people by isolating the girls in the city. The arguments were that these girls were unlikely to meet Aboriginal men and, it being unthinkable that they should marry white men, the result would necessarily be fewer Aborigines. This had been the stated intention of the Board, but it responded speedily to the criticism by ensuring publication of lengthy articles describing the benefits of 'apprenticeships' to the girls and the 'holiday' at the end of their indentures which allowed (enforced?) 'suitable' marriages with Aboriginal men. In this context of public criticism, the Board was most unhappy at signs of Aboriginal organising aimed at undermining the 'apprenticeship' scheme. It called repeatedly for police reports on and surveillance of the home as well as asking advice from the Crown Solicitor, who was unable to offer any practical legal remedy.[9]

After this year of indirect confrontation with the Protection Board, the AAPA was officially launched in February 1925. Its letterhead carried the motto 'One God, One Aim, One Destiny', suggesting a Christian influence and a unity of interest with whites which was not reflected in the Association's policy. The emblem was an image of an Aboriginal man circled by the words 'Australia for Australians'. The AAPA frequently used the word 'Australian' rather than 'Aborigine'. The emblem was a thinly veiled reference to an indigenous people's assertion of nationhood.

In the early months of the AAPA's public existence, Fred Maynard and Elizabeth Hatton made a number of trips along the north coast. The Protection Board refused them permission to visit reserves or stations, but its managers had little control over communications between residents and their kin and community living off the station lands. There was a ready audience and membership for the new organisation, particularly among the independent Koori farmers, carpenters and boat-builders of the Macleay, Nambucca and Bellinger rivers.

Mrs Olive Mundine, of Nambucca, remembered that her father John Donovan had already taken an activist role, sending so many letters to the Board and other authorities that he had built a desk especially for the purpose of writing them. She described the worried gatherings at her parents' home of the adults of the Whaddy, Buchanan, Doyle and

Kelly families, among others, all 'very serious in what they did, they liked to get their facts straight' and all outraged by the continuing dispossessions and the pressure on their children. 'They were so frustrated, so angry in themselves, that they all got together to decide what they was going to do.'[10]

Groups like this in every area on the mid-north coast gave Maynard and Hatton a warm welcome. Such community support ensured that news of the organisation spread far in advance of the organising visits. By August 1925, eleven AAPA branches had been set up on the north coast, meeting in homes like the Donovans', and together they had a membership of 500.[11]

Elizabeth Hatton wrote that her first impression had been that the burning issue for Aboriginal people was the threat to their children from the Protection Board. This issue continued to be of major significance to the organisation, but the experience of the north coast organising trips was that the issue of land was inevitably entwined with that of children. At Nambucca, for example, Hatton and Maynard were involved in helping an Aboriginal girl to escape from APB control on Stuart's Island, to the further alarm of the Board. This girl was a daughter of Fred Buchanan, one of those men who was taking part in meetings with the AAPA, and recently dispossessed of reserved land at Cow Creek, totally lost by leasing in 1917. For this family, as for many others, the land issue was just as pressing.[12]

When the AAPA gained its earliest substantial press coverage, in June and August 1925, it had refined its position. Its two central demands were clearly formulated: enough good-quality freehold land for each Aboriginal family to sustain themselves by farming and the immediate cessation of the removal of children from their families. The issue of 'apprenticed' children received some space in this press coverage, with Hatton writing:

> We are surprised to find everywhere such a resentful attitude to the administration now in force. Day after day, letters come from the people, pleading for their children, asking me to find their girls, long lost to them—in service somewhere in this State—taken away in some cases seven years ago and no word or line from them.[13]

After six months of intensive organising on the north coast, however, the AAPA clearly regarded the land issue as dominant and even more urgent than that of apprenticeship.

> Everywhere we find [Kooris] being thrown out, fenced out of the homes that have long been theirs—their lands, which have long been reserved for them, are being ruthlessly taken from them and sold to the highest bidder or leased to white people, already made wealthy by using the labour of these poor coloured people devoid of equitable recourse.[14]

Hatton explained to the *Macleay Chronicle*:

> The position in regard to selling their lands, which had always been
> considered as belonging to the Aboriginal people, was a cause of deep,
> strong and resentful feeling. People [were] huddled together in any old
> corner of the earth, housed in the most wretched fashion. They were
> asking for a small bit of land on which to build their homes.[15]

The position on land was becoming even more acute, Hatton
reported to the half-yearly meeting of the AAPA held at Surry Hills in
August 1925. Deputations of Kooris had approached her in many places
on the north coast and implored her to appeal to the government to
stop the sale of their land. She described one woman whose reserve
land had already been sold to a stranger, who had given the woman
notice to be prepared to move at any time, although she had lived on
that land all her life. In another example, Hatton spoke of

> several married men [who] came to me and told me that they had been
> ordered to move back into the bush by the police . . . They had been
> camped on this place all their lives and now a sale had been arranged
> and they were told to move away. They were given three weeks to move
> out back or they would be arrested.[16]

One of the urgent issues for the AAPA was the threat to the
long-standing camp on unreserved Crown land at Greenhills, 3 miles
outside Kempsey, on the bank of the Macleay River. Its population had
increased as Kooris were forced off the reserves of the district by
revocations or Board interference. As Kempsey township expanded, this
land had begun to look extremely attractive for white residential development. The Protection Board and the Kempsey Council tried on five
occasions from January to October 1925 to force the 120 Kooris at
Greenhills to move off the land, using removal and eviction orders
delivered by the police. This was yet another attempt to alienate
Macleay River Kooris from land they saw as their birthright. It was this
immediate issue on which the AAPA appealed, in June 1925, to the
press and to the Minister for Lands for each of the families under threat
to be given a 5 to 10-acre block of good farming land to allow them
to support themselves.[17]

The first country conference of the AAPA was held in Kempsey in
October 1925. This was a gesture of solidarity with the Greenhills
community as well as a reflection of the fact that the organisation's
most militant strength lay in the area where the greatest dispossession
had occurred. The three-day meeting was attended only by Kooris (with
the probable exception of Elizabeth Hatton) and dispossession was the
focus, as described by a sympathetic local newspaper:

> Many of these people, as well as their fathers and mothers before them,

have worked an area of ground close to Kempsey, yet a proposal has been made that this land should be cut up and sold to white people. The land is still the property of the Crown, and common justice demands that the Aboriginals who have worked it successfully should be allowed to acquire it as their property.[18]

The conference endorsed the AAPA demand for adequate freehold land as a basis for the economic independence of each Aboriginal family. Yet this call for land security was not a simple demand for an economic hold in the capitalist rural economy. The meeting was attended by a number of the Gumbaynggirr and Dhan-gadi Kooris who had retaken their lands in the 1870s and 1880s, such as James Linwood from the Fattorini Islands and John Mosely from Burnt Bridge. Each addressed the meeting in his own language, speaking with the authority of a landowner by traditional right as well as a farmer who had been working the land for decades. The *Macleay Argus* described one of these speeches:

Mr. James Linwood, from Fattorini Island, spoke in Aboriginal language to the people, urging them to join up and work together in the interests of their own race. He referred to the unjust procedure of late years, when many of them, after years of occupancy of certain portions of land, and after clearing it and cultivating it had been set adrift to begin again in some unwanted portion of the country.[19]

Making their demands for the restoration of their land in their own language was an assertion that their rights arose from their traditional ownership of that country as well as from their understanding of the commitments made to them by the NSW government.

The meeting moved then to issues which were subordinate but still urgent. Kooris there were gravely concerned about their communities' health and the segregation of hospitals and about education and the segregation of schools. Speakers returned again and again to the need to keep the care and control of Aboriginal children in the hands of their parents and they condemned the Board's apprenticeship system. The conference argued that Aborigines already discharged their duties as citizens but were being denied the protections and privileges of citizenship such as education and health care. The meeting moved unanimously that Aboriginal people must be accorded these full rights. Their motion was framed in the language and ideals of liberal democratic egalitarianism in Australia, but even on this occasion, the meeting asserted its separate authority as speaking on behalf of Australia's original people:

As it is the proud boast of Australia that every person born beneath the Southern Cross is born free, irrespective of origin, race, colour, creed, religion or any other impediment, we, the representatives of the original people, in conference assembled, demand that we shall be accorded the same full rights and privileges of citizenship as are enjoyed by all other sections of the community.[20]

WHITE NATIONALISTS AND LAND

In the campaign to gain public attention and support for the AAPA, Elizabeth Hatton apparently wrote hundreds of letters to the press, few of which were published. The main vehicle for the Association's publicity was *The Voice of the North*, whose editor, J. J. Moloney, was the AAPA's most active white supporter. Moloney was a nationalist, a member of the Australian Society of Patriots (ASP) and the Australian Natives Association (ANA). He was looking for symbols for his concept of the Australian nation and, unlike some others, he preferred his symbols alive rather than dead. His main hobbyhorse in *The Voice of the North* was the preservation and increase of both Aborigines and native fauna. The two were often discussed in the same article or editorial by Moloney and sometimes even in the same sentence, while a resolution from Moloney's branch of the ASP asked the Premier in 1926 for a new ministerial department 'for the better management of the Aboriginals and for the protection and preservation of Australian Birds and Animals'.[21]

Moloney's interests reflected the growth since the 1890s of an expression of national identity which drew on a sense of place to create its symbols and images. The Australian manifestations of the arts and crafts movements and associated movements in the visual arts were heavily committed to the use of native Australian plants, animals and landscapes to express a sense of 'nature' which had a specific link to place. The exploration of the Australian environment was just as strong in fantasy and decorative movements as in the imagery of the artists of the Heidelberg school. The Wattle Leagues were a prominent example of this broad movement.

This widespread interest in and celebration of native Australian flora and wildlife as national symbol paralleled the developing interest in lands perceived to be 'pristine wilderness', but it also encompassed the landscapes of pastoral Australia, the European-created scenes of fences and sheep flocks which were regarded as the monument to progress and development. The nationalist interest in land and place then had a deep ambivalence in its implications for Aboriginal people's interests in land. The work of some nationalists was very consciously focused on linking white Australian history to the land, and this often included the supplanting of Aboriginal history. In Victoria during the 1920s members of the Historical Memorials Committee traced out the steps of white explorers and built stone cairns in their memory wherever their paths crossed contemporary roadways. The commemorative ceremonies over these memorials were intended to foster a deeper sense of association with and belonging to the land among white Australians. At the same time a number of these gentlemen were collecting Aboriginal remains and stone artefacts, removing them to museums where they were classified and stored away. Such work was often claimed to be directed at the growth of learning about Aboriginal culture, but the immediate effect was to remove all evidence of the presence of Aboriginal people from the land.[22] There was an underlying desire among many environmental nationalists to erase an awareness of Aboriginal people's presence and interest in land.

The widespread belief in biological determinism and hierarchy was also deeply antipathetic towards the Aboriginal presence. Again, the Wattle Leagues and Clubs across the country were clear examples. The wattle of their emblems was chosen because it signified both the brilliant sunshine of Australia, but also its supposed 'purity' and innocence. The moral and social meanings of 'purity' were always, in these years, entwined with a biological meaning of 'racial purity', 'racial hygiene' and a commitment to the superiority of European, and particularly British, 'blood'. The ANA was quite explicitly committed to racial exclusivism in Australia. One of its three main objectives in the 1920s was a White Australia, along with increasing support for Australian manufactures and economic development.[23]

These important strands of the white nationalist movement in the 1920s were not often expressed as openly antagonistic to Aboriginal people. At its most superficial, nationalist interest in landscape and place, along with the desire to find symbols of Australia which represented its singularity and its distinctiveness from Britain, fostered an awareness of Aboriginal people as well as native flora and fauna. A recognition could then follow that pastoral development threatened the continuing existence of both native animals and Aboriginal people, and this led some nationalists to a new sense of urgency in conserving from extinction these now harmless 'symbols'.

In an associated trend, the rising ethnographic interest in peoples other than the conquering Europeans had led to a proliferation of amateur ethnologists in the 1890s and early 1900s. Some of the best material published in this period arose from long and sensitive observation, like that of Katherine Langloh Parker who had lived in Yuwalaraay country in north-west New South Wales for many years, and whose careful recording of mythologies and customs demonstrated in detail the links between the Yuwalaraay and their land. Other careful recorders included the surveyor R. H. Mathews, and in visual imagery, the photography of Thomas Dick on the Nambucca and Bellinger rivers. What distinguished all of these recorders, however, was their desire to describe what they believed was a rapidly disappearing way of life, and they wrote very little about the present lifestyle of Aboriginal people. Most of the ethnography produced in this time was far below the standard of these examples, at best nostalgic and romanticised, and at worst racist, patronising and sensationalised. Yet the early years of the century nevertheless saw a slow and painstaking rebuilding of white Australians' fragmentary knowledge about Aboriginal people, the rebirth of a dim perception of the richness and complexity of Aboriginal culture, social and religious practice. As this was occurring in the context of the strengthening sense of place in national identity, the recognition among whites of Aboriginal knowledge and meanings for the land were also slowly being re-established.

J. J. Moloney's views and the material he published in his *Voice of the North* reflected all these developing and sometimes conflicting trends in Australian nationalist thought. He wrote editorials about the need to save the 'childlike' Aborigines in 1922, at a time when few questioned the prevailing 'doomed race' predictions. Questions did begin to emerge in the mid-1920s, arising from three groups. Progressive missionaries claimed that their methods of mission settlement management were more effective than government control in stopping the decline in 'full-blood' Aboriginal numbers.[24] Anthropologists were rising in influence over the decade, offering scientific opinion that Aborigines were educable.[25] Feminists, although more prominent in Western and South Australia than in the eastern States, insisted on the responsibility of the new nation to educate its colonised minority.[26] There were differences in perspective: the anthropologists were generally more cautious in assessments of Aboriginal capacity to adapt to European culture than were the missionaries. The feminists insisted that Aboriginal women be assisted because they were being exploited by both white and Aboriginal men. In general, however, each group proposed the same model for reform, which amounted to segregation of Aborigines under benevolent white 'expert' control, whether missionary, university-trained anthropologist or professional 'woman protector'. There was little open conflict between the groups, with most missionaries and feminists who commented in public paying at least lip service to the value of the new 'scientific' expertise of the anthropologists.[27]

The convergence of missionary and anthropologist thinking, as well as the rising influence of the anthropologists, was symbolised in the person of A. P. Elkin. In the early 1920s Elkin, the Anglican minister at Morpeth near Newcastle, had completed a Masters degree at Sydney University which had included some psychology and anthropology. Even this early in his career, Elkin demonstrated a capacity to evangelise for anthropology as well as for Christianity and he regularly wrote articles for the popular press explaining anthropology for lay people. His 1920s articles popularised outdated theories but at least conveyed the impression that Aboriginal culture as well as skull shape was of scientific interest. Such information fostered the development of white public interest in a rather romantic, nostalgic view of Aborigines which became more pronounced over the decade in the south-eastern cities.[28]

Moloney printed Elkin's early material in *The Voice of the North*, and in later years he gave space to all the missionary-anthropologist arguments on the need for alternative policy. Yet unlike some white nationalists, Moloney was also very interested in Aboriginal opinion. He was impressed by Aboriginal speakers like Fred Maynard and Louis Lacy, as well as by Elizabeth Hatton, and he was prepared to print what they had to say, even taking up their grievances himself. As his contact with the AAPA developed, the references to 'childlike' Aborigines disappeared from the paper's editorial columns. Nevertheless, Moloney did not really appreciate the contradictions between the emerging Aboriginal position and that of the missionaries, anthropologists and feminists. He often printed, on the same page and apparently without any intention to expose the divergence, the Aboriginal demand for immediate control of and title to land and the reformers' proposal for segregation under benevolent expert control.[29]

Moloney's practical support for the AAPA involved some mobilisation of the nationalist groups. The ANA wrote to the Premier in July 1925, endorsing the AAPA request for 'repatriation of the Australian people upon their own land on a family basis'. In August Moloney's ASP branch protested against the attempted removal of the Greenhills community and proposed a farm block system for Aborigines. The Protection Board did consider this, but reconfirmed its decision to refuse Aborigines this security and independence in regard to land. It persisted in its attempts to remove the Greenhills community and decided also to exercise more direct control over the troublesome Kempsey area by installing a manager at Burnt Bridge, only to find that a shortage of funds made such a step impossible.[30]

The Board, however, was so alarmed by the directions in which the AAPA was moving that it tried to stop its registration as a company. The Board's stated objection was that the AAPA's aims usurped its own duties under the Protection Act. To discredit the Association, the Board resorted to its usual strategy of blaming individuals as 'troublemakers' and manipulating the stereotype of Aboriginal incompetence and poor character by referring to 'the unfitness of the promoters, who, with the exception of Mrs Hatton, are all Aborigines, certain available particulars concerning the character of whom' were 'to be furnished' to the Registrar-General.[31]

'CRYIN' OUT FOR LAND RIGHTS'

The AAPA had broadened its public platform by late 1925. On a speaking tour of the north coast, Maynard and Lacy addressed a meeting in Newcastle, where they included the call for freehold land and the cessation of removal of children in a comprehensive plan for reform. They wanted a royal commission to inquire widely into Aboriginal affairs and they demanded the abolition of the Protection Board. Maynard explained that the Board 'had outlived its usefulness' and that Aborigines required 'a new system of administration . . . without the foolish patronage which affects to regard them as children'.

During 1926 the organisational link was made between Kooris mobilising around these issues on the north coast and those involved in similar struggles on the south coast. Jane Duren, who had taken such a prominent part in defending Koori land at Bateman's Bay, as well as her grandchildren's access to public schooling, was speaking on the AAPA platform by November.[32]

The white press took little interest in 1926, but Koori political activity did not cease. At least some of this activity was generated from the Salt Pan Creek camp in south-western Sydney. Jack Campbell recalled that from the time of his arrival in 1926 until he left in 1932, the camp contained usually around thirteen family groups. There were not only the dispossessed Burragorang families, and the refugees from Protection Board control on the north and south coast, like Jack's family, but also some families originally from Cumeragunja including that of Jack Patten Snr with his sons George and Jack and their families, and Bill Onus, married to one of the Pattens' daughters. Jack Campbell remembers that the older men, particularly the Anderson brothers and old Jack Patten, would talk politics 'all the time': 'You'd see them old fellas sittin' around in a ring, when there was anything to be done. Specially when there was anything to be done with the Aboriginal Protection Board'.[33]

Around these general discussions were the younger men, Onus and the Pattens, who were to carry this political education with them into the next decades. A regular part of the talk was about a petition to the King, to expose their grievances. Joe Anderson told the young boys that he was going to speak to visiting royalty, such as the Duke of York, about Koori demands. The talk was not limited to the camp. The men used to go to Paddy's market on Friday nights and 'spruik' from a fruit box, like the Domain speakers on a Sunday. Jack Campbell would go down with another of the men from the camp who had a job as night watchman at the markets, and this was how he came to hear the speeches. He remembered that the prime issue was land: 'They'd only be spruikin' on land rights, that's all, on land rights . . . y'know, "Why hasn't the Aboriginal people got land rights?", they said. "The Aboriginal's cryin' out for land rights" '. When he was asked what sort of land they were asking for, Jack replied:

> Aboriginal land! They was askin' for the land they was on. That's when they were chuckin' 'em off. There was places around . . . 30 or 40 acres, 60 acres, what Aboriginal people was *on*, and they [whites] went into 'em, run a mob of cattle through their crops and that. They only had dog leg fences then. They were pushin' Lang, at that time, for land rights. That's what it was all about, and to break up the Aboriginal Protection Board.

If little white media interest was shown in these Koori demands in 1926, it was a year in which missionaries, some scientists (notably the South Australian physician Dr H. Basedow) and one Aborigine, David Ngunaitponi, gained substantial publicity for their proposal for a 'Native State'. This was to be located in Arnhem Land and Aborigines were to be allowed to live there as they wished, with minimal white interference, no separation of children from their parents and no compulsion either to enter or remain within the 'State'. The proposal did endorse cultural intervention: prohibiting 'cruel rites' to satisfy the missions and arranged marriages with older men which feminists believed exploited women. These intentions immediately imposed a framework of European value judgment, while incidentally necessitating a policing system. The work of Christian conversion and the teaching of agricultural skills, again without compulsion, were to be the priorities of the 'State's' administrators, who were initially to be Europeans. At some very distant time in the future, it was envisaged that Aborigines would take over the administration and that the 'State' would enter the Commonwealth on equal terms and with parliamentary representation equal to existing States. The models cited for the 'Native State' were Murray's administration in Papua New Guinea, considered by whites to be progressive, and the landholding and separate parliamentary representation of Maoris in New Zealand.

Although the Native State proposal clearly focused on 'tribal' and 'full-blood' people, and denied compulsion, the plan's organising committee had made an ominous suggestion in relation to people outside Arnhem Land, and it was one of which Kooris in New South Wales took note: 'Natives who have no regular approved employment or are hangers on to the fringe of civilization should be removed far away from possible contaminating contacts'.[34]

There were some superficial similarities in the 'Native State' proposal and the platform of the AAPA, such as guarantees of secure tenure of land, an end to the removal of children and at least the hope of ultimate autonomy. These similarities, however, sprang from totally different basic assumptions. The complete lack of common ground between white advocates of change and the AAPA became more obvious during the campaigns undertaken by both groups during 1927.

'FOR LIBERTY, FREEDOM, THE RIGHT TO FUNCTION IN OUR OWN INTEREST'

The AAPA program had been fully developed by the third annual general meeting in January 1927. This was to be a very active year for the Association, with more travelling by the organisers, meetings with the Koori communities in Kempsey, Grafton and Lismore, and a series of letters to the government protesting about Aboriginal housing conditions on the north coast, conveying general Aboriginal grievances, and calling for the 'emancipation' of Aborigines by the extension to them of 'full citizen rights'.[35]

The Association conducted an energetic campaign to gain concessions from the government, and as a result a number of its documents and letters have survived, giving insights into the intellectual and emotional basis of the movement as well as details of its program. The resolutions of the Association's third annual meeting were sent to the Premier in February, quoted almost verbatim in *The Voice of the North* in May and sent again to the Premier in the form of a petition in June. This carefully drafted platform had extended the earlier AAPA statements to make them more widely applicable.[36]

The first and chief demand was for land, as an economic base and as compensation for dispossession. The AAPA asked that the government 'restore to us that share of our country of which we should never have been deprived'. Specifically, each Aboriginal person capable of working the land should 'be given in fee simple sufficient good land to maintain a family'. By omitting any mention of an exact acreage, the AAPA had made its demand for land as an economic base appropriate to areas where land was less fertile than on the north coast. The petition insisted that those Aborigines who were incapable of working the land were only in that condition because of past government policies of oppression and neglect. These people must therefore be 'properly cared for in suitable homes on reserves' at the full expense of the government. These reserves, however, were no longer to be under the control of white men, but were to be supervised by Aboriginal people only, because there were already an adequate number who were 'educated' and possessed 'the requisite ability' to take over the reserves immediately.

The second element in the petition was the request that the removal of Aboriginal children from their families cease immediately. The Association sought the restoration of 'those family rights which are the basis of community life' in that 'the family life of the Aboriginal people shall be held sacred and free from invasion and that the children shall be left in the control of their parents'.

Finally, the petition demanded the dissolution of the Protection Board, and its replacement by 'a board of management comprised of capable, educated Aboriginals'. In its only concession, the Association stated that it was prepared to accept a chairman of this board who was appointed by the government and who would therefore presumably be white.

The petition mentioned the 'full privileges of citizenship' and stressed that Aborigines were a people perfectly able to manage their own affairs. Yet while the AAPA program clearly assumed that Aborigines were entitled to the full benefits of citizenship, it was not a simple civil rights campaign, because it did not assume an identity of interest or experience with white citizens. Its principal demands were based rather on the overriding rights of Aborigines as prior owners of the land and as a community whose integrity had been uniquely assaulted by the invasion of family life.

The Protection Board's response to the AAPA petition rested entirely on an assertion that Aborigines were not competent to handle their own affairs. The proposal to give freehold land was 'not considered at all advisable', it wrote, because 'the Board, knowing the nature of the Aboriginal, is of the opinion that in most cases the property would be quickly disposed of for more liquid assets'.[37]

The Premier was assured that Aboriginal family life was already 'held sacred', except of course where the Board deemed that children were exposed to 'immoral or contaminating influences'. The Board insisted that it offered benefits to Aborigines which were not only adequate but which were far greater than those provided for poor white men, and concluded with a further statement of Aboriginal incompetence, this time in relation to the proposal that Aborigines could supervise reserves or sit on a board of management. The whole idea, the Board insisted, was 'impracticable'.

Frederick Maynard's response revealed in more detail the basis of the Association's demands.[38] He first attacked the Protection Board's all-pervading assumption of Aboriginal incompetence:

> I wish to make it perfectly clear on behalf of our people, that we accept
> no condition of inferiority as compared with European people. Two
> distinct civilizations are represented by the respective races . . . That the
> European people by the arts of war destroyed our more ancient
> civilization is freely admitted, and that by their vices and diseases our
> people have been decimated is also patent, but neither of these facts are

evidence of superiority. Quite the contrary is the case. Furthermore, I may refer, in passing, to the fact that your present scheme of Old Age Pensions was obtained from our ancient code, as likewise your Child Endowment Scheme and Widow's Pensions. Our divorce laws may yet find a place on the Statute Book. The members of this Board [the AAPA] have also noticed the strenuous efforts of the Trade Union leaders to attain the conditions which existed in our country at the time of the invasion by Europeans—the men only worked when necessary—we called no man 'master' and we had no king.

After firmly asserting the value of Aboriginal civilisation, Maynard went on to say, just as firmly, that 'when the treatment accorded them was fully considered', Aborigines had already 'conformed reasonably well' to European systems. On this basis, he continued, 'we are, therefore, striving to obtain full recognition of our citizen rights on terms of absolute equality with all other people in our own land'.

Maynard was arguing, however, that Aborigines did not have merely equal rights with Europeans, but rather had overriding rights (which included the right of the indigenous people to the title 'Australians'): 'The request made by this Association for sufficient land for each eligible family is justly based. The Australian people are the original owners of this land and have a prior right over all other people in this respect'. He returned to the principle of equal rights in the argument for Aboriginal control of Aboriginal affairs. Here he used examples from contemporary Australian society, so that they would be recognisable to a white audience, and drew attention in the process to the existing diversity of ethnic, racial and religious structures within 'White Australia'.

> Our request to supervise our own affairs is no innovation. The Catholic people in our country possess the right to control their own schools and homes, and take a pride in the fact that they possess this privilege. The Chinese, Greeks, Jews and Lutherans are similarly favoured and our people are entitled to precisely the same conditions.

Maynard denied the Board's claims that it adequately provided for aged and indigent Aborigines, calling the Board's reference to the generosity of ration and blanket issues 'a sneer'. The falsity of the Board's position was proven by its refusal to agree to the royal commission which the AAPA had proposed in 1925. Maynard accused the Board of being afraid of the truths such an inquiry would uncover.

The Protection Board replied with an expanded version of its earlier letter, beginning, however, with a revealing statement of what it believed its role to be:

> The Board cannot concern itself with the controversy regarding the inferiority or otherwise of the Australian Aboriginal race as compared

with Europeans, its duty being to ensure that the remnants of that race now living within this State receive benevolent protection and every reasonable opportunity to improve its condition.[39]

The Board avoided the crucial issue with this statement, based again on the assumption that Aborigines *were* inferior. It then proceeded with a glowing account of its work, particularly in the area of 'rescuing' Aboriginal children from 'neglect'. The Board even argued that the 'larger proportion' of the children it removed had a white parent of 'essentially a low type', although this statement is demonstrably untrue in terms of the Board's own records, which show that most of the wards came from families where both parents were of Aboriginal descent.

The Board did, however, make the accurate statement that Aborigines in New South Wales already held full citizen's rights in theory, with the exception of access to alcohol. It was true that Aborigines in New South Wales were not technically denied the franchise, and some had indeed been voting since the 1860s. It was also true that Aborigines could legally purchase land and property. The Board did not mention the denial of Commonwealth welfare benefits to Aborigines whose homes happened to be on reserves, nor did it mention public education, from which Aborigines in so many places were excluded, nor its own methods of restricting the movement or domicile of Aborigines. Finally, it most carefully avoided discussing the real issue, which was the condition of actual access to the education, employment, health and housing facilities which white citizens regarded as their right. In the final analysis, this statement rested, as did the Board's earlier reply to the AAPA, on an assertion of Aboriginal incompetence. 'It would be impracticable', said the Board, 'for the Aborigines in this State to be allowed to supervise their own affairs'.

In a further effort to rebut the AAPA demands, the Board sought to discredit Frederick Maynard. First, it now claimed that he was not of Aboriginal descent at all, but rather a 'full-blood' American or South African 'black'. Second, it passed on to the Premier a letter intercepted by an APB station manager, written by Maynard to a 15-year-old Aboriginal girl who had been 'apprenticed'. This girl had been removed from the care of both her parents at the Dunumbral pastoral camp by the Angledool manager, on the grounds that she was 'of an age to be apprenticed out to service'. The girl was placed on a property remote from her family and within a year she had been sexually assaulted by a white man at her place of employment. She was sent to Sydney to have her child, who died shortly after birth and she was then returned, via Angledool station, to the same place of employment.[40]

Through the Aboriginal community network, the AAPA had heard of this girl's problems and Maynard wrote to her in October 1927, offering help in bringing the man responsible to justice. He asked her for the particulars of the assault, which would be necessary for a proof of paternity, and it was presumably this aspect of the letter, as much as its criticisms of the Aborigines Protection Act, which the Board felt would discredit Maynard. The Board's opinion of Maynard was that he was a man whose 'illogical views' were 'more likely to disturb the Aborigines' than improve their conditions.

Contrary to the Board's interpretation, the letter shows more clearly than anything else the degree of personal commitment Maynard felt to the girls whom the Board kept forcing into intolerable situations. It shows too the intensity of the hatred, bitterness and frustration generated by APB policy and white racism. Finally, it shows the tenacity of hope.

In the letter Maynard savagely attacked the Aborigines Protection Act, which contained no protection for Aboriginal girls against 'these white Robbers of our Women's virtues', who 'take our girls down and laugh to scorn' yet who 'escape their obligations every time'. He assured the girl that her case 'was one in dozens with our girls, more is the pity'. The Act and the Board it empowered insulted and degraded all Aboriginal people, and aimed 'to exterminate the *Noble* and *Ancient Race* of Australia'. These 'so-called Civilized Methods of Rule, under Christianized ideals so they claim, of Civilizing our people under the pretense of love' were 'nothing more than downright Hypocrisy' and 'Stink of the Belgian Congo'. Maynard continued:

> The tyrannous methods have got to be Blotted out. We are not going to be insulted any longer than it will take to wipe [the Act] off the Statute Book. That's what our Association stands for: liberty, freedom, the right to function in our own interest, as right-thinking, Civilized people and decent citizens, not as non-intelligents devoid of all reason. That is how we are placed under the Law of the Statute Book. Anything is good enough—A Blanket, a pinch of tea [and] sugar thrown at us.
>
> Are we going to stand for these things any longer? Certainly not! Away with the Damnable Insulting methods which are degrading.
>
> Give us a hand, Stand by your own Native Aboriginal officers and fight for liberty and freedom for yourself and your children.

MISSIONARIES AND THE NATIVE STATE

It was hardly surprising that the AAPA had been unable to penetrate the Protection Board's assumptions, but it fared only a little better with one of the groups of white reformers, the missionaries. In October 1927 a meeting took place between a number of churchmen, including the Bishop Coadjutor of Sydney, Revd D'Arcy Irvine, and the chairman of the Australian Board of Missions, Revd J. S. Needham, and seven Aboriginal representatives of the AAPA.[41] Maynard and Duren both stressed the urgency of the problems of the revocation of reserve lands and of school segregations. As the main spokesperson, Maynard addressed the meeting in the terms used in his letter to the girl at Angledool, accusing the Protection Act of degrading and insulting Aborigines. He demanded new legislation which would give Aborigines 'equal status in every respect with white people'. He explained the desperate position of some groups of Kooris in the Macleay River area, who would not approach the police for food rations 'as it was feared that the children would be taken away from the parents. That was considered crueller than starvation'. He argued the AAPA case that Aborigines must have land in their own areas, 'with their own communities, with schools . . . and should be supervised generally by educated and capable Aborigines'.

It is clear that Aboriginal people believed that the Native State idea, strongly supported by Needham among others, was indeed a proposal to move all Aborigines by force to the Northern Territory. This opinion was held on the north coast, and the strong opposition of Kooris there to the Native State was reconfirmed at an AAPA meeting at Lismore later in November, where the people stated that 'they preferred to live where their homes were'. This was, after all, the essence of the struggle which they had been waging for almost two decades against the revocation of their reserve land, and it had been the main motivating force in the development of the AAPA. So at the meeting with the missionaries, Maynard made very clear the Aboriginal rejection of the Native State proposal on the basis of adherence 'to their age-old tribal customs and the place of their birth'.[42]

At this meeting, missionaries who had been largely focusing their attention on 'full-blood' and 'tribal' Aborigines in remote areas were confronted by a group of people from the most densely settled areas of New South Wales, who were asserting their Aboriginality in spite of being of mixed descent, and who were refusing to acknowledge an inferiority to whites in any sense. They were stating that they were already civilised by virtue of *both* their Aboriginal culture *and* their ability to cope with European culture. They were demanding land in New South Wales on the basis of their Aboriginality and, therefore, of their prior ownership and because they had already successfully worked the land in a European sense. Above all, they were specifically rejecting the need for white control or supervision of any kind.

While this meeting was probably a factor in turning missionary attention to the need for reforms in the more settled States, the experience does not appear to have shaken the fundamental assumptions the missionaries held about Aborigines. Needham's response was the most publicised and he clearly remained unconvinced by the AAPA, concluding that 'some of their complaints are legitimate, but I am quite certain that a number of their requests cannot be granted'.[43]

The *Evening News* summarised the missionaries' position, saying, 'Church organizations are not likely to join with the Aboriginal Progressive Association in an assault on the State Government', but that they would instead continue to press the federal government for a royal commission and an Arnhem Land reserve.[44]

THE STRUGGLE CONTINUES

The AAPA disappeared from white public view after 1927 and did not have the opportunity to confront the anthropologists as it had the missionaries. This confrontation was to come in the following decade. No explanation has yet been found for the apparent break-up of the AAPA's organisational structure after 1927. Fred Maynard continued to work and take an active role in union politics on the wharves in Sydney. He married in 1928. Soon after, he was badly injured in an industrial accident, and his political life was restricted by the increasing difficulties of making a living for his family. Elizabeth Hatton lost her son in a road accident, and moved with her daughters to Tweed Heads on the Queensland border, withdrawing from political work for a time. In 1939, however, she was again taking part in the conflict between Aboriginal and white people. She wrote to the Uplift Society journal to record the inequitable practices in the law courts of the area, and documented her role appearing in court as 'friend' to Aboriginal defendants who had no legal counsel.[45]

As the Depression began in the late 1920s, individual members of the Association did remain involved in political activity. This intensified in Sydney as white pressure on land reached the metropolitan reserve of La Perouse.

As early as 1926, Randwick Municipal Council had notified the Protection Board that it wanted the La Perouse reserve revoked and its residents moved, arguing that increased tourism in the area was interfering with the privacy of the reserve and that it would be 'in the interests of the Aboriginals themselves' to be relocated. The Council was, however, clearly more concerned with the development of its tourist industry, wanting the reserve removed so that 'the appearance of the place' would be 'improved'. The Board agreed, and went so far as to select another site at Congwong Bay.[46]

While one objection raised by Kooris to this new site was that it was 'sloppy, greasy and boggy in winter', their protest was not based on this issue, but rather that of rightful ownership of the land at La Perouse. At the height of the conflict in April 1928, 53 adult residents of the reserve petitioned the Government:

> We, the undersigned Aborigines of the La Perouse reserve, emphatically protest about our removal to any place. This is our heritage bestowed upon us: in these circumstances we feel justified in refusing to leave.[47]

The Protection Board itself raised the issue of the long association of the Aboriginal residents with the reserve: 'They had been asked if they wanted to go, but they strenuously objected. It was stated that many of them were born on the reserve and these naturally recognised it as their home'.[48]

The conflict was eventually stalemated, as in so many other situations, by Koori refusal to move. With the Protection Board ambivalent after its obvious failures over the decade to remove Aborigines against their will, Randwick Council was forced into a compromise solution, to which, however, the reserve's residents were not party and did not consent. In this agreement between the Council and the Board, a portion of the reserve along the waterfront was revoked to become a public recreation reserve under Council control. For its part, the Board was to remodel the reserve housing to bring it into accordance with the Council specifications.[49]

The Council kept the Board to this arrangement, with the result that the La Perouse houses not only absorbed a great proportion of the Board's Depression budget but created Aboriginal housing of a far higher standard than that on any other reserve or station. La Perouse gained 3- or 4-roomed houses, all with water and sewerage facilities. Housing on all other reserves at this time had at best consisted of 2-roomed, unserviced, earthen-floored huts, and these deteriorated quickly under the impact of the overcrowding caused by the Depression. The government was not slow to see the opportunity presented, and the Board asked the director of the Botanic Gardens to assist with a tree-planting program 'to make the reserve an attraction' as 'the Government Tourist Bureau contemplate including the reserve in its itinerary for overseas tourists'.[50]

La Perouse Kooris were not, however, bought off by their unexpectedly improved conditions. Politicised by their struggle against both the Council and the Board for the retention of the land, La Perouse residents were prominent over the next decade in publicising the discrepancy between their housing and that on all other reserves in the State.

Kooris from Salt Pan Creek camp also sustained their political activity into the grim years of the Depression, when two of the Anderson brothers were convicted of fare evasion after scaling a train to see a sick relative in Wollongong. Their defence in court was 'This country belongs to us'. The public speaking activity around the city continued and eventually drew some white attention. Joe Anderson became a known 'character' and the white press occasionally used him to reflect the stereotype European images of Aborigines, on one occasion dressing him up in skins and photographing him holding a boomerang and a wallaby, and on others treating him generally as a comic character. Only once was Joe Anderson given the opportunity to speak for himself, in a Cinesound news film made in 1933, showing him standing in his own old overcoat among the tea trees at Salt Pan. The film has been heavily and clumsily cut, but something of what Joe Anderson was saying has been preserved.[51]

Anderson asserted the integrity of the Aboriginal community and its laws: 'The Black man sticks to his brothers and always keeps their rules, which were laid down before the white man set foot upon these shores'. He commented on the hypocrisy of white people in failing to live by their own maxim of 'Love thy neighbour', and continued: 'It quite amuses me to hear people say they don't like the Black man . . . but he's damn glad to live in a Black man's country all the same!'

In his most powerful statement, Anderson said:

I am calling a corroborree of all the Natives in New South Wales to send a petition to the King, in an endeavour to improve our conditions. All the Black man wants is representation in Federal Parliament. There is also plenty fish in the river for us all, and land to grow all we want. One hundred and fifty years ago, the Aboriginal owned Australia, and today, he demands more than the white man's charity. He wants the right to live!

Part IV

Under the 'Dog Act', 1930s

We were under the Dog Act altogether. Just like a dog, they'd get hold of the chain and lead him over there, tie him up over there. What they said, that was the end of it. They could send you anywhere, do what they liked with you.

Henry Hardy, Interview T50

13

Land as Prison:
Moree, 1927–33

The decade of the 1930s was one of momentous changes for Aboriginal as well as non-Aboriginal Australians, with economic and environmental crises which often accelerated earlier trends towards structural economic change or irreversible ecological damage. For Aborigines this was a decade of intense pressures, among which was the fact that land began to be used as a weapon against them, to control, to confine and to exclude them. Aboriginal people found that they had to modify the terms by which they publicly claimed rights to land, to protect themselves from their enemies as well as to shore up new alliances with white supporters. The outcome was that while land continued to maintain an important position in Aboriginal demands, it could not be the primary, urgent goal it had been in previous decades.

The dispersals of the 1910s and 1920s saw patterns of movement very similar to those of previous decades. Some Aboriginal people moved long distances searching for work and safety, but most tried to remain within reach of their own traditional country and their supportive kin. The Protection Board had aimed to make Aboriginal people disappear culturally and socially to become atomised, nuclear families of working-class Australians. Instead it succeeded only in a conjurer's sleight of hand, in which they disappeared from one locality only to resettle close by, no longer on the APB ration lists but still identifying with their own lands and communities. These new living areas were often the camps outside towns in the district, where Aborigines could hope to gain support from their kin while they tried to re-establish their work contacts and enrol their children in the local public school.

The steadily increasing Aboriginal populations of these town camps led to a rising tide of protest during the 1920s as white townspeople articulated their deep belief that their towns were residential and service centres for white Australians, not for Aboriginal landowners. The Protection Board seemed quite unprepared for the vehemence with which whites demanded that Aborigines be excluded from schools, shops, the streets and indeed the very boundaries of their towns. Aborigines, on the other hand, were to prove equally tenacious in their determination to remain on these relatively independent campsites in the area of their choice. They were increasingly desperate. Finding work was extremely difficult where they were not known to employers, and they could not expect to ride out the periods of unemployment without the support of their families, or the resources of the land they knew for hunting and gathering. Where they had settled in these camps recently, after escaping from repressive Board control, Aborigines often brought with them deep resentments over the fact that they had just lost what they had thought was a secure home on their own lands. These refugees were profoundly angered when they met with further attempts to deny them the right to live safely in the area of their choice within their own lands.

The increasingly frequent battles between Aboriginal people and rural town whites which mushroomed in the late 1920s were often expressed in public debate as being conflicts over equality of treatment for Aborigines and whites in the town, but they were at heart struggles over what land was freely accessible to Aboriginal people and from what other areas they were to be excluded. This was a new spatial politics of exclusion and entry, defined and controlled by the incoming town whites but fought out on the very earth of Aboriginal people's own country. It carried with it grave implications of access to the means to survive economically and emotionally, the power over work, food and children. White goals were not only to exclude Aboriginal people from certain bounded areas, the schools and stores, the work exchanges, the dormitory residential areas of their towns and indeed often the public streets and gathering places. They sought to confine Aboriginal people within the boundaries of the reserves sited on the outer perimeter of the municipal boundaries, beyond the residential area which would entitle the inhabitants to vote, but still close enough to allow white men access for sexual adventures, and not too far for Aboriginal women to make the long walk up each day to do the laundry for the hospital, the hotel and the other institutions from which they and their families were banned.

The saga of Moree was an example of many of these aspects of the escalating conflict over boundaries between white towns and Aboriginal landowners. The town was economically comfortable in the period, surrounded by stable sheep pastoralism and drawing considerable tourist custom to its artesian baths, which were thought to benefit sufferers of arthritis and other complaints. These baths were an important hygiene resource to the white working class whose housing was close by, but Aborigines were excluded. Murris continued to challenge this ban, but the Municipal Council reaffirmed it on numerous occasions. While the aldermen occasionally discussed 'contagious diseases', their segregation motions were framed simply in terms of exclusion by race. The 'White

Only' baths persisted as a symbol of the wider segregation which the town Council sought for those people it called 'niggers' in its minutes.[1]

Most Murris lived during the 1920s in what later became known as the 'Top Camp', a substantial community in established dwellings of tin and corrugated iron. Their numbers had been increased after 1924 by people forced off the APB station at Terry Hie Hie by expulsion orders or threats to their children.[2] The Council had never provided any services to the camp, in spite of its long standing. The camp was close to the garbage tip, like many in New South Wales, and the residents drew their water from the river and made their own sanitation arrangements. Many Murri women were employed as domestics in the town, and the aldermen wanted this service to continue. They did not, however, want Aborigines within the municipal boundaries. From 1921 to 1934 the Council conducted a campaign to remove the whole Aboriginal community from their camp area on the edge of town, to some place at least 5 miles away. The Council tried first to have the Protection Board make Aborigines move back to Terry Hie Hie, but as the Board was trying to close this station down, the most it would do was issue an ineffectual order to 'move away' from Moree. The Board suggested notifying a reserve around the campsite, but the municipality rejected the proposal as an unacceptable validation of Aboriginal presence.[3]

Murris had demonstrated their desire to stay on the camp, and the Protection Board was proving unhelpful, so the Council launched a major campaign in 1928, using its own powers in relation to public health and control over dwellings. Its health inspector condemned 30 Aboriginal camp homes as unfit for human habitation and called in the police to evict the families who lived in them. These families refused to move, so the police issued the eviction orders and then arrested and prosecuted them. Many were convicted in 1928 and early 1929, and although a missionary and two town merchants paid fines for some elderly Aboriginal protesters, most others served time in the lock-up for refusing to pay. While this was happening the Council workers moved in with police protection to demolish the huts. Still Murris defied the orders, building new camps as the old ones were pulled down beside them.[4]

Aboriginal people had a short respite in 1929 as a new Council began negotiations with the Protection Board. This time the Council accepted the Board proposal that a new reserve be created within municipal boundaries, and only 2 miles further out of town than the existing camp, although this agreement was reached without consulting or informing Moree Aborigines, whose numbers now approached 200. They refused to move. The Depression interrupted the campaign to shift the camp, but the Council acted to limit the Aboriginal voice in local affairs. The local government franchise had been extended by a residential qualification which should have entitled the Murris to a vote, but Council redrew the ward boundaries in 1931 so that 'the Blacks' camp' became an island in the middle of the municipality and its residents were left disenfranchised.[5]

In 1933 Council again demanded that the APB force Aborigines to move to the new reserve site. When the Board appeared reluctant to act, the Council moved aggressively. Using the opportunity of its health inspector's report on conditions at the camp, which was still of course unserviced, in May 1933 the Council called for the segregation of the hospital and demanded that the Department of Education exclude Aboriginal children from the school. The Department was more co-operative than the Board, and agreed immediately to segregate. Council then wrote to the Board, lamenting the Aboriginal children's lack of schooling and insisting that they be provided with their own school *on the reserve*. Finally the Board responded, building a shed for a schoolroom, with few windows, no water and no furniture.[6]

Aboriginal parents were, hardly surprisingly, appalled and angered. They refused to allow their children to travel to an unserviced shack 2 miles away in acquiescence to the Council's campaign. Murris demanded readmission to the public school and said they would otherwise not send their children to school at all. When white parents made similar threats, as they had done at Walgett, Yass and elsewhere, the Department invariably conceded. Aboriginal parents faced a very different response: a Child Welfare officer arrived and threatened to take their children away if they did not begin attending the APB segregated school. Knowing, like all Aboriginal parents, that their children were vulnerable, they had no choice but to concede.[7]

This inspector's report revealed an attempt to convince Murris that they had not accurately understood what was happening but were instead suffering some form of paranoid delusion:

> When I visited the school in March last and also called on several Aboriginal families, I found that the local Aborigines had the idea that an invidious distinction was being made against them, on account of racial prejudice, by the provision of a separate school.
>
> I endeavoured to remove this idea, and inculcate the feeling that a benefit had been conferred by the institution of a special school intended to meet the requirements of their own race and to help their children in their own particular problems.[8]

In spite of such pressure, only some Aboriginal families moved onto the new reserve. The hardships of the struggle in fact increased the determination of Aborigines in Moree to resist further attempts to move them out of town, as anthropologist Marie Reay observed in the mid-1940s. At what had by then become known as the Top Camp, she wrote:

> Many of the inhabitants are descendants of mixed-bloods who were gaoled some years ago for refusing to comply with an order to move from this site, and consequently the site has an emotional value for the present occupants. This gives the local group a common tradition and solidarity which finds expression whenever efforts are made by white townspeople to have this camp removed.[9]

While Moree demonstrated many aspects of the escalating tensions between Aboriginal people and white towns, it was also being made clear that boundaries around residential areas were not the only way to confine and exclude. As the 1920s proceeded, Aboriginal people were more assertive of their rights of access to towns as their needs became more urgent. In response, whites grew more anxious to protect their racially defined hold on local power and services. This led to a greater formalisation, or at least an increasing *de facto* rigidity, in the exclusion of Aboriginal people from public spaces in the towns. Police maintained a curfew against Aborigines in many towns, which effectively kept them off the streets after dark. There was never any law which even suggested that such powers existed, but local authorities such as municipal councils and justices of the peace instructed police to implement such curfews, and the police apparently maintained them by harassment and creative use of the laws which did exist. Aboriginal people recall that if they were found by the police in town after dark they could be physically assaulted and forced out of town, or would find themselves charged with drunkenness or a similar offence, for which there was no effective defence. As in Brewarrina in the 1930s, the case would often be heard by the very justices who in their roles as aldermen had called for more aggressive policing to maintain the curfew. The interlocking nature of local authority structures and personnel meant that these illegal and unofficial barriers were powerful indeed.[10]

There were further deterrents in the frequent presence of gangs of white youths, who made a practice of intimidating and assaulting Aboriginal people as they came into towns, often in broad daylight, and with the tacit support of the police. Aboriginal people from Brewarrina, Walgett, Kempsey and Taree remember such vigilante gangs operating in the 1920s and 1930s. Jimmie Barker, Ray McHughes and Val Mingo have all described these gangs in Brewarrina, explaining that the threat of violence made many Murris reluctant to enter town at all.[11] Don Nicholls has recalled a similar situation in Walgett, when white gangs regularly attacked Murris with hobble chains when they tried to go to the pictures in town, and the police would intervene only to arrest any

Aboriginal people who tried to fight back. Marie Reay observed these gang activities still going on in Walgett in the early 1940s, describing 'a group of headstrong white youths who continually provoke the aborigines to fight'.[12] Until the 1960s, Murris from Gingie reserve knew that they could freely walk no further towards the centre of town than a shop on a certain corner. They christened it 'Crows' Corner', laughing with bitter self-reflexive irony at the way they would congregate after they had bought their stores, like a row of black crows perched on a fence, watching the main street they could not enter.[13]

So even open space was coded in these rural towns. 'Public places' offered free access and safety to white citizens alone. For Aboriginal people, these same spaces offered only limited and conditional access and no safety at all. This coding of public space intensified through the 1920s as whites in many rural towns met Aboriginal pressure for access with a determination to erect racial barriers around the sites and spaces of the towns.

14

The Depression Crises and Cumeragunja

The economic Depression descended on rural Australia in 1927, but it was not the only crisis. In a number of new settler economies it was becoming clear that Western capitalist land management was damaging soil and ecological systems. Australia and America were both engulfed in dustbowls at this time, as drought and overcropping left topsoils exposed to the winds. But America was a far younger and more fertile continent, with deeper soils, better water supplies and so a wider margin of safety in environmental matters. In Australia these years marked the bitter acceptance that the simple agrarian myth had failed. The droughts of the 1920s showed how fragile the land of Australia was; overstocked and overploughed, the soil just blew away into the eastern skies and was not readily replaced. The failure of the closer-settlement schemes of the later nineteenth century to establish a dense population of small agriculturalists had always been excused as the result of poor administration or inadequate supplies of men or good land. By the mid-1920s the terrible collapse of many soldier settler farms was common knowledge. The returned servicemen themselves were cruelly blamed at first, but eventually it became difficult to avoid the conclusion that no small-scale farm could ever succeed in Australia simply by the honest labour of the farmer and his family.

These Depression years should have caused a retreat from intensive farming and pastoral industries in Australia, in the face of the evidence of severe stress which the land was plainly showing. Instead there was emerging in the 1920s a growing faith in the ability of 'modern' Western skills and technology to solve economic, environmental and social problems. In land management, this confidence manifested itself in the popular interest in irrigated agriculture. Now the goal was no longer a simple farm, but an enterprise which demanded higher capital input and greater infrastructure provided by government, but which was then expected to lead to the same unquestioned guarantee of prosperity.[1]

But first the severity of the Depression had to be faced. Irrigation and such intensification proposals could be held out as a panacea, but the early years of the Depression gave no indication that any easy solutions could be found for the deep pain of the world economic crisis. Unemployment was enormous in Australia, and took its toll on Aboriginal as well as all other workers.

The only Aborigines protected to some extent from unemployment in New South Wales were those living on the pastoral properties of the far west and north-west and on the inland areas of the far north coast. Where labourers were working from a camp, the cost of their keep and often of their wages was substantially less than for outside labourers.[2] They had as well a deep commitment to remaining on their land and close to their families, so they were less likely to protest and move away if their wages were cut. Yet at the same time the Depresssion was finally undermining this niche of colonial labour relations. The large pastoral properties were often heavily burdened by debt, and they had already been feeling the effects of subdivision from the decades of closer and soldier-settlement demands to slice away at their best-watered portions. The environmental crisis had driven home the lesson that earlier closer-settlement blocks had often been too small to be viable as family farms, and so the pressure was increasing for further subdivision to enlarge the blocks previously withdrawn from the large pastoral holdings. The days of the large properties and the camps on them were drawing to a close.

For all other Aboriginal workers, unemployment hit savagely. They often found they were last hired and first fired when there was any competition with whites. Jack Lang's Labor government in New South Wales introduced universal unemployment relief in 1930, and Aboriginal workers, many of whom were members of unions and the ALP itself, applied for the dole like their white fellows. But they found to their dismay that while the politicians did not discriminate between white and black unemployed, the bureaucrats of the Department of Labour and the dole-issuing officers, the police, most certainly did. Unemployed Aboriginal workers in Victoria, who were far fewer in numbers than in New South Wales, found they had ready access to the State government's unemployment relief food orders and work relief programs. Aboriginal workers in New South Wales bombarded the government and the Protection Board with complaints that they were being denied unemployment relief and being told that instead they had to apply for APB rations, which were valued at only half the dole allowed to white unemployed.[3]

The Protection Board had just suffered severe funding cuts itself, and a large part of its budget was still committed to remodelling the La Perouse reserve. Family endowment payments had been the only State or federal government benefit to which Aboriginal people had been entitled without discrimination. But the Board needed these cash payments to meet its ration and maintenance bills, so it took them over on the concocted excuse that Aboriginal people had not been expending their full allocations. It was in no position to support the many Aboriginal people who had previously been living from their waged labour in the mainstream economy, so in 1932 it strongly urged the incoming conservative government to remove the widespread discrimination being practised in New South Wales.[4]

The new government, however, was eager to seize any opportunity to cut costs, and so it endorsed its Labour Department's ruling that Aboriginal unemployed were only entitled to the dole if they could prove that 'they had done a white man's work' in the years of their previous employment. Such proof was often difficult to provide, and its acceptance was entirely at the discretion of the local issuing officers, the police. The most frequent result was that unemployed Aborigines were told they could only have Aboriginal rations, and that they had to move to the nearest APB station to get them. The denial of unemployment relief put a new and powerful weapon in the hands of local town authorities, who usually exercised enough influence over the local police to ensure that newly unemployed Aborigines were 'moved on' to a suitably distant APB station. This exercise of power was intensified in decisions about work relief, which although funded by the State government was administered by local councils. Aboriginal people across the State found they would only be allowed to sign on for work relief if there was some particularly arduous or unpleasant physical labour to be done.[5]

So within three years Aboriginal people had experienced a massive loss of civil rights, and a demonstration of the degree to which the NSW government was prepared to treat them with discriminatory contempt. They had lost their first social benefit, the family endowment, then they were denied the dole, and then work relief, but all they were offered in place of the meagre food orders of the white man's dole were the even more grossly inadequate Protection Board rations.[6]

Aboriginal people from all over the State protested about the injustice of exclusion from unemployment relief, which both whites and Aborigines saw as a denial of the Aboriginal role in the economy and as a disparagement of the value of Aboriginal labour. The issue was raised in Parliament after Aboriginal protests to politicians in December 1930 and again in February 1931.[7] The denial of recognition was often linked in Aboriginal protests to their dispossession and loss of income from the traditional economy. Kooris at Wreck Bay had supported themselves by fishing before the Depression had destroyed their market. They told anthropologist Caroline Kelly (see Chapter 16) in 1936:

The Government gets revenue out of us. We pay on the railway for our fish to go to market and we pay out fishing licences just like the white men. When the Depression came we had a terrible time. We couldn't get the dole although white people got it and this isn't their country. It's our country and yet we couldn't get the dole.[8]

The experience of Arthur Dodd was typical of Murris in north-western pastoral areas. After his stepdaughter was taken by Inspector Donaldson in 1919, Arthur had tried to keep out of the reach of the Board. School segregations had forced him to leave his wife and children on APB stations but he had spent the 1920s shearing, as an AWU member and on award wages. When he applied for food relief at Walgett the police refused him, giving him only APB rations. Asked if he thought he was entitled to food relief, Arthur replied bitterly:

> Oh yes, I did. But we had to take what's coming. No good arguing the point with 'em because they'd wipe you straight off, give you nothing. It happened to a couple of 'em, they was giving cheek back to the boss bloke [police]. They were strict that day.[9]

The work relief system itself, as well as the exclusion of New South Wales Aborigines from it, stimulated further protest. The Protection Board insisted that once Aboriginal people were on their ration lists, they must do a number of days' work to 'earn' their rations. Aboriginal unemployed insisted that, just like white unemployed, they were prepared to work for wages but not for food. Individual and small-scale protests in the early years of the Depression culminated in a wave of Aboriginal action, with stop-works, protests and strikes at Wallaga Lake, Menindee, Burnt Bridge, Brewarrina and Purfleet from 1936 to 1938.[10] There were some Aboriginal activists as well in the general unemployed workers' movement, involved in eviction struggles in the city and in organising unemployed workers in rural areas.[11] Bill Ferguson was an Aboriginal shearer from the south-west of the State, who had managed to be taken on for relief work at Cabramatta in Sydney. His participation in unemployed workers' politics led to his dismissal from that job after he had addressed a stop-work meeting.[12]

Yet despite some involvement in the white political activity of the times, in only one area were Aboriginal people able to direct the attention of white unemployed activists towards the situation of Aboriginal unemployed workers before 1935. This was in Dubbo in the central west, where Murris Tom Peckham from the town and Ted Taylor from Talbragar reserve 3 miles away were prominent in local unemployed workers' organisations. In July 1932 the Dubbo unemployed workers were the only white Left group to protest when Aborigines in the region, who had formerly received food relief, were refused it and issued only with APB rations.[13] Jack Booth, one of the white activists in the town, was an English immigrant who had worked as a railway labourer and stockworker around Bourke. He recalled how the Aboriginal men in the unemployed workers' camps would sit around the campfires at night, joining in the general discussions but then explaining to the whites there how the Protection Board had escalated its hold on the area in the late 1920s, imposing managers over Aboriginal residents at Carowra Tank in the west, on Cowra reserve to the south and Pilliga to the north, then in 1931 had placed a manager on Bulgandramine just 40 miles out of Dubbo (see Map 12, p. 184).

Peckham and Taylor convinced the white unemployed that what was needed was the abolition of the APB, and 'the sooner you do it the better!' Jack Booth remembered that while their main concern was for an end to the Board, the Aboriginal activists were not demanding a revocation of reserve land. He explained:

> When they attacked the mission, they wanted to get rid of them alright, but they wanted to be their own masters. They didn't want this idea of white supremacy, the white man master, so to speak. They wanted to be regulated by themselves, with their own elected leaders or whatever. They wanted their home or their tribal land that it was on, they were quite satisfied to remain there, [but] they didn't feel as *part* of it, because they were under the orders of the white overlord, that was the trouble.[14]

Booth's recollections suggest the struggle going on within Aboriginal people whose land was becoming increasingly the site for the exercise of Protection Board power. Not only were people finding that, as in Moree, reserves were being used to confine them, but that the experience of living on land they continued to regard as their own was more and more like living in a prison, under intense scrutiny and rigid controls. This must have contributed to a growing ambivalence towards these small patches of land, in which the meanings acquired by daily living and shared experience, which so often fostered community identity, were now being overlaid by experiences of repression and humiliation.

Then in March 1933, the Murri children of Talbragar were abruptly refused entry to the nearby public school at Brocklehurst. Even with Dubbo Murris' white Left connections, it took eighteen months to set up a campaign of support, with the Dubbo ALP eventually joining the protest against the segregation, along with the local clergyman and the Chamber of Commerce, in June 1935. These latter white supporters were asking for readmission to the school or for a separate school on the reserve, an option which was not likely to have represented Murri opinion. This was, however, the one taken up in April 1936.[15]

It was in Dubbo, with an established link between Murris and the white Left, but also a high degree of tension, suggested by the school segregation and its aftermath, that Bill Ferguson and his family had settled in 1933. Ferguson rapidly developed close relations with the

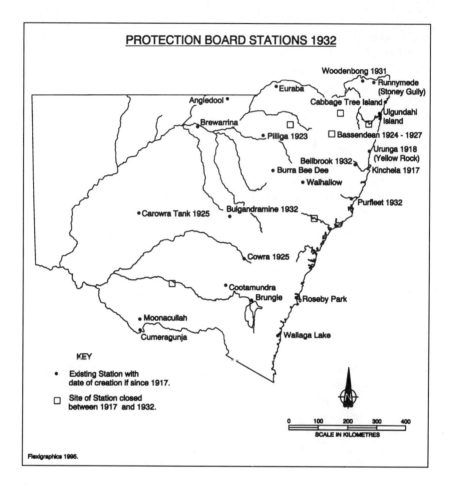

PROTECTION BOARD STATIONS 1932

KEY

• Existing Station with date of creation if since 1917.

□ Site of Station closed between 1917 and 1932.

town's white and Aboriginal unemployed workers' organisers, strengthened by earlier activity in politics and his association with the left wing of his union, the AWU. This union affiliation was very common among Aboriginal workers in the north-west, and although Ferguson's membership of the Labor Party was less common, there was much Aboriginal sympathy for the ALP. Ferguson's commitment to fundamentalist Christianity was not widespread either among Aboriginal communities of the western regions at this time, when compared to its high penetration in the coastal communities. He did not, however, support the work of white missionaries, regarding them as ineffective evangelists because they were alienated from and patronising to Aborigines. Ferguson favoured Aboriginal lay preaching, such as that being done by his brother Duncan along the Darling River at the time, because he believed that Aboriginal lay preachers' political partisanship allowed them to communicate the gospel effectively at the same time as actively supporting the Aboriginal community in its material and political interests.[16] In the west, however, the Aboriginal political movement remained informal over the first five years of the 1930s, as people struggled simply to survive the worst years of the Depression.

Kooris who lived on the border with Victoria were particularly aware of the discrimination of the New South Wales unemployment relief practices. By 1933 there was a large camp of around 200 Aboriginal people just outside Cumeragunja, refused the dole in Victoria because they were New South Wales residents, but refused the dole in New South Wales because they were said to be 'too black', and told they must go to the APB station for relief. But at Cumeragunja they were met by a manager clinging to the old APB rules, who told them that they were 'too white' to receive Aboriginal rations because they were not 'predominantly of Aboriginal blood'. The injustice of this proved to be a goad which pushed into life a political movement to address these urgent issues of the terrible Depression poverty and discrimination. The movement's underlying force, however, was the incessant hunger of Cumeragunja Kooris to get their land back.

THE AUSTRALIAN ABORIGINAL LEAGUE

The Australian Aboriginal League (AAL), which launched its challenge to the NSW Protection Board in 1934, was not formed inside the State borders at all, but rather in Melbourne. Unlike the extensive regional network of the Australian Aborigines Progressive Association in the 1920s, the AAL had a very tight community base, being made up largely of exiles from Cumeragunja. Some members of the AAL had close associations with other south-western New South Wales communities and there were long-standing relationships with Aborigines in Victoria, but Cumeragunja remained a focal point. Nevertheless the organisation made more claim to being a nationally representative body than the AAPA had done, and it addressed itself repeatedly to national issues. It is not known if the exile community in Melbourne had had contact with the AAPA, but their concerns were certainly running parallel and it was in 1927, the most active year for the AAPA, that the Morgan family had made its unsuccessful demand that the Protection Board restore the family farm blocks on Cumeragunja.[17]

The motivating force behind the AAL was William Cooper, who had applied to the government for land near Cumeragunja in 1887.[18] Through the disastrous years for the Cumeragunja community from 1908 to 1933, Cooper had remained there, witnessing the sustained refusal of both APB rations and food relief to many Cumeragunja families. He had left in 1933 only because his residence on the reserve made him ineligible for the old-age pension. At the age of 72 he moved to Melbourne and joined forces with the Cumeragunja exile community there. Cooper became secretary of the newly formed AAL in 1934 and was surrounded in the organisation by younger Cumeragunja people like Doug Nicholls, the treasurer, and Shadrack James, who had conducted such sustained battles with the Protection Board to stay on Cumeragunja. The AAL activists included Margaret Tucker, whose father had come from Cumeragunja although she had spent much of her childhood on the Brungle and Moonahcullah reserves on Wiradjuri land in southern New South Wales. Her grim experiences, and those of her sisters, during their 'apprenticeships' had given her good reason to fight the Board. There were, as well, families like the Morgans who had farmed the family blocks and whose bitterness and resentment of the Board for its resumption of those blocks was unabated after twenty years. There appears to have been regular contact between the Melbourne community and those of their families still at Cumeragunja; Doug Nicholls, for example, who had not been formally expelled, could move freely between the two places.[19]

The only white person in the organisation was its president, A. P. Burdeu, who was a unionist but whose associations and motivation appear to have been Christian. Burdeu acted as a close personal support for Cooper and worked to generate public interest by forming a white support group, the Aborigines' Uplift Society. He was in close contact with the Sydney-based all-white Association for the Protection of Native Races (APNR), an umbrella organisation in which many Christian and some specifically missionary groups participated. Canon J. S. Needham had been a vice-president of the Sydney organisation for some time before 1934, but in that year the missionary and anthropological reformist groups were formally united when A. P. Elkin became president of the APNR.[20]

There were also, however, some close personal connections between members of the AAL and individual members of the Melbourne branch of the Communist Party (CPA), although this caused conflicts with white Christian supporters and, indeed, with the Christianity of some of the Aborigines.[21] Burdeu was opposed to and worked against the involvement with the CPA.[22] In 1936, however, the AAL affiliated with the Peace Council, a 'united front' organisation with considerable communist membership, indicating that at this time associations with the white political Left were strong. Cooper commented in 1936 on the general nature of white support: 'Our friends among the white race are growing in numbers and interest, although we are often sorry to note that some of them regard us as inferior clay'.[23]

Some indication of the early activities of the AAL can be seen in the work of Mrs A. Morgan during 1934. She had been taken up by the white media in an example of its romantic interest in Aboriginal exotica from the safely distant past. Mrs Morgan, who was over 60, had given a number of broadcasts on Melbourne radio station 3LO, retelling the folklore taught to her by her grandmother. Eventually, however, like Joe Anderson, she was able to speak for herself about the conditions faced by Aborigines in the present. Mrs Morgan wrote a letter which was published in *Labor Call* in September 1934, in which she attacked the APB theft of Aboriginal land at Cumeragunja and the ensuing disciplinary expulsions of people like herself and her husband, who had 'protested against this injustice' and so were 'classed as agitators'. Using Cumeragunja as an example, she detailed the Board's dispersal tactics, and condemned the 'apprenticeship' system:

> At the age of fourteen our girls were sent to work—poor illiterate trustful little girls to be gulled by the promises of unscrupulous white men. We all know the consequences. But, of course, one of the functions of the Aborigines' Protection Board is to build a white Australia.

Like Jane Duren before her, Mrs Morgan used the contradiction between the Australian myth of 'fair play' and the conditions faced by Aborigines to expose the hypocrisy of white Australians. She denied that Aborigines lived under the British flag, declaring: 'We say that we live under the Black Flag of the Aborigines' "Protection" Board—we have not the same liberty as the white man, nor do we expect the same justice'. What Aborigines wanted, Mrs Morgan said, was better conditions and the 'abolition of the rule of the Black Flag', but above all, 'We want a home. You have taken our beautiful country from us—a "free gift" '.[24] Mrs Morgan called for support for the new Aboriginal organisation and early in 1935 she made at least one public speech, in which she attacked the 'poverty, prejudice and injustice' against which her people were struggling and stated that 'the Blacks of Australia are trying to emancipate themselves'.[25]

This national perspective was reflected in the first campaign of the AAL, which was aimed at the federal government and was an attempt to deal with the disenfranchisement of Aborigines at a federal level. Cooper drafted and circulated a petition to the King, which asked for 'royal intervention to prevent the extinction of the race', for better conditions and for federal parliamentary representation by an Aborigine (or, if that were not granted, by a white person of Aboriginal choice), to be elected from a separate Aboriginal electorate on the New Zealand model. This petition gained between 1800 and 2000 Aboriginal signatures before it was presented to federal Parliament in 1937. Cooper's petition had probably been circulating in Melbourne before he applied successfully to the APB for permission to collect signatures from New South Wales Aborigines in April 1934. Among those who spread the petition around New South Wales Aboriginal communities was Helen Bailie, a consistent white supporter of the AAL who was closely associated with the feminist groups active at State and British Commonwealth level in campaigns to change Aboriginal policy. Another petition worker was Bill Ferguson. By March 1935 the Protection Board had become alarmed at the political organising associated with the collection of signatures for the petition, and circularised all managers warning them not to let either Bailie or Ferguson onto any station without special permission from the chairman.[26]

In February 1935 the AAL agitation gained an audience with the federal Minister of the Interior for Cooper and four other Cumeragunja men, in which they presented their case for federal Aboriginal representation, a national department to manage Aboriginal affairs and administrations in each State composed, at least in part, of Aborigines.[27] There was little response, but the AAL clarified its position on national Aboriginal matters in the following year, when it requested of the Minister for the Interior that any 'concessions' made to Aborigines of mixed descent be made to 'full-blood' people as well. The minister apparently replied that it was not intended to make any concessions to 'full-bloods'.

The AAL responded by making the most unequivocal assertion of Aboriginal unity to be expressed at any time throughout the 1930s, totally repudiating the European thinking which classified and tried to divide people on the basis of skin colour. Its 1936 annual report stated:

> We should nail our colours to the mast in respect of this matter, making our slogan, 'Full equality for the dark race with the white race, and no differentiation between the full-blood and those of mixed-blood'.[28]

From February 1936 Cooper's extensive correspondence with the NSW Premier has been preserved, giving an insight into AAL policy and into conditions at Cumeragunja. Both of these elements are present and interrelated in each of Cooper's letters, but for clarity they will be dealt with separately here. AAL policy was made up of two parts: a demand for action to be taken immediately and then a proposal for the future development of the Aboriginal community. The immediate action the AAL wanted was the ending of all discriminatory practices against Aborigines, in 'civic, political and economic' spheres. The demand was for

> Full Citizens Rights to all Aboriginals, whether living on settlements or not. This to include the payment of sustenance, as to whites, for all

unemployed natives. We claim the right to work for full wages or the payment of full sustenance (dole) if unable to work.[29]

The recognition of Aboriginal participation in the economy by a guarantee of equal wages and equal unemployment relief was central to the AAL definition of full citizen's rights. Cooper related economic injustice to a sense of dispossession, as Cumeragunja people had done in 1889, when he pointed out that 'we are entitled to reasonable comfort, merely from the fact that this land was ours, with assured living, before the whites came'.[30] He was insistent, however, that the main basis on which the AAL called for equal unemployment relief was the fact that Aboriginal workers, when employed, provided labour of equal value to that of white workers and that this equality of labour must be recognised by equality of relief when unemployed.[31] The other elements of the citizen's rights concept which Cooper regarded as urgent were the ending of segregation in the New South Wales public school system, the cessation of child removal, and an end to the APB's power to sever Aboriginal people's contact with kin and land by the expulsion of reserve residents without any avenue of appeal.[32]

The long-term elements of AAL policy included a proposal for Aboriginal representation in federal Parliament, made with specific reference to the situation in New Zealand where Maoris had not one but four national representatives.[33] But the demand which Cooper and the AAL made most frequently was for self-sufficiency through land and for financial and technical assistance to develop that land to its full potential. This issue is referred to in every one of Cooper's letters in 1936 and 1937 and in the 1936 AAL annual report. It must be seen as the basis of the AAL program. The demand for land in the AAL view arose from Aboriginal prior ownership: 'There is room for us, and, in any case, who should have this right to land before the dark race itself'.[34]

Cooper referred the NSW government to the 1934 Indian Lands Development Act in the United States, which, although it fell short of Native American demands and was in fact used against them, seemed to Cooper to be an attempt to promote economic self-sufficiency. He condemned the waste of human resources which was occurring because Aborigines were refused sufficient land: 'Our men have been able to succeed in the past and given a chance we are sure that many of them will succeed in the future'.[35]

The details of the AAL proposal were that all existing Aboriginal reserve land should be fully developed, to be worked collectively or co-operatively by Aboriginal residents with the profits returning to them. More land would need to be acquired immediately for this purpose, but the AAL was also proposing that Aboriginal families be assisted to settle permanently on individual family blocks when confident of their skills.

It is not clear from Cooper's letters whether the final result was to be scattered family blocks or whether these blocks were to be adjacent and therefore comprise a larger block of Aboriginal-controlled land, in an expanded version of the old Cumeragunja situation, for each Aboriginal community.[36]

Cooper suggested that Cumeragunja be used as the experimental model for the AAL proposal, and to do this he used the language of the contemporary white popular view that irrigated small farms, relying on new technology and management techniques, could at last realise the agrarian dream. Well informed on this topic as on all others, Cooper urged on the NSW Premier a detailed and realistic plan of intensive agricultural development, which included tomato, vine and tobacco culture, citrus-growing, some cows and some experimental lucerne and pigs. He argued that with improvements to the water supply and with adequate government funds for seeds, stock and machinery, the station would easily become self-supporting. Cumeragunja was for Cooper a symbol of the waste and injustice of the existing system: 'Cumeragunja is potentially wealthy. The people are very poor. We feel that such poverty in such potential wealth is wrong'.[37]

The AAL policy can be seen to embody the same elements as that of the earlier AAPA, namely a call for the granting of immediate and full civil rights, although this time consciously addressed to the national as well as the State sphere, and a demand for land as the essential basis for future Aboriginal development.

Cooper received 'scant courtesy' during 1936, the APB having informed the NSW Premier that his criticisms of its methods were 'without foundation' and did 'not call for further notice'.[38] In frustration, Cooper limited the scope of his 1937 letters to an effort to achieve the implementation of at least the concrete first stage of the AAL land proposal: the establishing of Cumeragunja as a model agricultural experiment. This seemed to Cooper to be a very realistic proposition. Cumeragunja people already possessed agricultural skills and hungered for a chance to work their land for themselves again; the land itself was of good quality and there was a generous water supply close at hand from the Murray. The water supply became the focus of Cooper's demands, as he explained carefully to the Premier that the earlier tomato culture by Aborigines at Cumeragunja had ceased only because the water pump had failed in the late 1920s. This failure had not been rectified and now the water supply was inadequate not only for farming even the small amount of land left after the Board's leasing of the reserve but also for its Depression-increased population.[39]

There was at last some response: the Board was by 1937 in a better financial position and conveyed through the Premier its intention to build new houses and improve the domestic water supply at Cumeragunja. Cooper was far from satisfied, and insisted that there must be adequate water also for agricultural development. The next government response, in May 1937, seemed more promising. The Board was under growing pressure as white and Aboriginal groups began to gain publicity for their concern about Aboriginal conditions. It wished to demonstrate its willingness to undertake progressive reform and so instead of dismissing the idea of agriculture at Cumeragunja as it had done with the farm block request of 1927, it now indicated that it would 'investigate' the AAL farming proposal, although it had a far more limited scheme in mind, involving only part-time work for the unemployed men.[40]

Guardedly optimistic, Cooper turned his attention to the other urgent problems at Cumeragunja. Apart from the severe overcrowding, which he thought would be solved by the promised new houses, Cooper saw the first priority as increasing the ration issue to the full dole scale, and the second as rectifying the inadequate sanitation. On this issue, the current manager, Danvers, was in complete agreement. Danvers had been appointed manager at Cumeragunja in 1934, and had immediately acted to issue rations to the unemployed Aboriginal workers camped on the station boundary. He told the Board repeatedly of his concerns about the poor conditions on the overcrowded station, and had stressed the urgency of the sanitation problem to Board members. Nothing, however, was done.[41]

Cooper was not only concerned with the physical conditions on Cumeragunja, but also with the restrictions imposed on Aborigines' lives by Board control and the autocratic powers of the manager. Although Danvers was 'held in high regard' by Cumeragunja people, an opinion shared by Aborigines on other stations on which he worked, his total control was deeply resented by the Cumeragunja community. The entrenched bitterness in the station's population was revealed in an exasperated report by Danvers during 1936, when he wrote: 'The greatest trouble that [we] have to contend with on this Station is the fact that certain families set themselves against any authority by the Board's officers'.[42]

He then recounted as an example an incident in which a woman had shown 'the gross impertinence of her attitude towards the Board' and had acted, so Danvers believed, 'for no reason except that she wished to show that she was not under the control of the Board'. When he was later asked why Aboriginal people had held such deep resentment, Danvers acknowledged that the fundamental grievance among people at Cumeragunja continued to be 'that the land was taken from them'.[43]

This, then, was the degree of hostility under the management of Danvers, a man widely acknowledged by Aborigines as the most reasonable of the Board's officers. By July 1937, Cooper, the AAL and the Cumeragunja community had good cause to be hopeful, having been given assurances that the housing and water supply at the station were to be improved and that the agricultural proposals would be paid some attention. What they did not know, however, was that the manager who was about to replace Danvers was A. J. McQuiggan. He had been the superintendent of Kinchela Boys' Home for six years, but had finally faced an investigation after repeated complaints to the police by the boys held there for 'training'. The report of two senior police officers showed that McQuiggan was an indebted drunkard who had regularly punished boys at the home for minor infractions by tying them to the fence and beating them with hosepipes and stockwhips. The Commissioner of Police was the *ex officio* chairman of the Board, and he argued strongly for McQuiggan's sacking in disgrace. The Kinchela superintendent was saved from dismissal, however, because he was supported by B. C. Harkness, the Education Department representative on the Board, who argued that McQuiggan's offences had all taken place outside school hours. Harkness, with the support of his brother, E. B. Harkness in the Chief Secretary's Department, arranged for McQuiggan to be transferred rather than sacked, and so he became the replacement for the sympathetic Danvers.[44] The result of this change in managers could only be heightened tension. Conflict did not explode until 1939, however, and by that time much activity had occurred in the rest of the State.

15

The 'Dog Act' in the West: Menindee and Brewarrina

The Depression had hit the Protection Board just as it was despairing because of the rising pressure of townspeople's complaints about 'dispersed' Aboriginal people camped on their boundaries. Then the denial of the dole to Aboriginal workers began to reverse the processes which had allowed even a temporary dispersal, and the unemployed were forced back onto Board reserves and stations. Under these pressures, the Board demanded major amendments to the Aborigines Protection Act, which were passed in 1936. Although the name of the Act did not change, these amendments gave the Board substantial new powers, and allowed it, for the first time, to confine Aboriginal people against their will. This new form of the Protection Act was widely known among Aborigines as 'the Dog Act' because, as Henry Hardy explained, they felt that now they could be penned up and shifted around just like animals.

The Board had had to admit by 1931 that its 'dispersal' had been an illusion. Aboriginal people, far from disappearing, had reappeared in greater numbers than ever before. The police were not only the officers issuing food relief but also the recorders of the annual Aboriginal census. They had had to develop a sharper awareness of Aboriginality in order to make decisions about who should be allowed the dole and who must be forced to accept only APB rations. This heightened consciousness was translated into a dramatic increase in the recorded numbers of Aboriginal people, from 6788 in 1927 to 10 467 in 1937, an increase of 54 per cent.[1] The discriminatory unemployment policies were now forcing many of these Aboriginal unemployed into the remaining reserves and the 22 managed stations which the Board by this time administered across the State. The proportion of the known Aboriginal population which was living under managerial control had risen from 15 per cent in 1927 to 33 per cent in 1936, and this, because of the rise in population, represented a great increase in absolute numbers, which had caused a housing crisis by 1931.[2]

Aboriginal people faced intolerably crowded and insanitary conditions on the reserves and stations, because between 1930 and 1936 the Board simply had no funds to build emergency accommodation or to improve the water supplies and other infrastructure; this had fallen into neglect over the previous decades when it had expected that all the Aboriginal residents would be finally 'dispersed'. Such population pressures led to rapid deterioration in living conditions and public health. In the early 1930s the largest Board stations were swept with major epidemics of respiratory and eye infections, which attacked the residents all the more aggressively because their nutrition was so poor in Depression conditions. Those Aboriginal unemployed who had been able to avoid being pushed onto stations and reserves were living in impoverished conditions in town camps. Their conditions and health were actually better than those on the Board stations, but there were indications by 1933 that the clamour from towns to have Aboriginal people in camps removed and confined was about to be renewed.[3]

FORGING THE 'DOG ACT' AMENDMENTS

The Protection Board began to formulate a new policy direction which could be achieved within the limits of its very small budget. Board members consistently blamed the failure of the 'dispersal' policies on Aboriginal people, arguing that they had behaved in ways which antagonised white townspeople. So the solution which the Board proposed was to take more control over adult Aborigines to force them to conform to white expectations. In some ways this was a liberalisation of the Board's approach, because it had previously argued that only children and its young 'apprentices' were capable of being educated. But the nature of the Board's proposed education for adult Aboriginal people was entirely punitive, as its title of 'disciplinary supervision' suggested.

The crucial change was that the Board decided it would gain this extra control by enforcing the transportation of residents from all the town camps, smaller reserves and stations in the State, to concentrate them on a few centrally located and tightly controlled stations. It argued that its limited funds could be used more efficiently to provide healthy accommodation on a smaller number of more accessible facilities. Forced removal was a policy option which the Board had attempted unsuccessfully on a small scale in the past, when for example it had tried to move Walgett Murris to Angledool in 1923, only to have them all walk back home within a year. It was well known and widely commented on by prominent political figures like the former Premier Jack Lang that Aboriginal people bitterly opposed removal from their own lands.[4] In fact the Board had often explained to white townspeople that it was virtually impossible to force Aboriginal people to move, and so it had in the past always tried to avoid using this tactic. If this new policy was going to succeed, the Board knew it needed greatly increased powers, because it not only wanted to force people to move away from their homes but intended that they should remain confined on the 'concen-tration' site to which they would be taken. As it announced in its 1931–32 report:

> The Board, realising the inadequacy of its powers under existing legislation, contemplates seeking certain amendments to its Act, which will enable it, among other things, to concentrate on its Reserves, *persons of Aboriginal blood*, who are now living on stock routes and alongside of towns, and maintain a definite control over them, so that *they will not be at liberty to leave without permission*.[5]

Not only were new laws needed, but the Board believed it required control over a far wider population than ever before. After years of insisting that only people who were 'predominantly of Aboriginal blood' were to be recognised as Aboriginal, it now demanded that anyone who was even 'deemed to have Aboriginal blood' by a justice of the peace or a local magistrate could be brought under its control. The Board intended confining Aboriginal people until they 'had graduated to the standards of the white man'. Indeed, its reports repeat the work 'gradually' so often when discussing this topic that the reader can be left in no doubt that the Board intended to incarcerate Aboriginal people for a very long time indeed.[6]

This plan to imprison the majority of Aboriginal people in the State was little more than a surrender to the demands of white townspeople, who had for some years been calling for the permanent removal and confinement of local Aborigines. Yet there were differences. The Board, although grimly determined to round up and confine Aboriginal people, still insisted that it was intent on changing them, so that in the end they would no longer identify or be identified as Aboriginal, and could then be finally 'dispersed' and removed from reliance on the government ration books. Townspeople had never displayed any interest in an eventual release, and they saw only that the Board had finally become responsive to their calls for removal and confinement.

Then a third group entered the discussion. Just as those interested in land management had embraced the new technological advances of Western capitalism, governments were increasingly embracing the newly emerging disciplines of sociology, psychology and anthropology. All these strands of 'modernist' thought argued that European rationalist approaches could successfully overcome the problems faced by govern-ment administrators. The social science disciplines offered bureaucrats an optimistic confidence that the application of 'scientific' management could solve entrenched social problems and conflicts. The APB developed a mutually beneficial relationship with Professor A. P. Elkin, who headed the Anthropology Department at Sydney University and who was eager to influence Aboriginal policy in northern Australia. While he was not particularly interested in Aboriginal people in New South Wales, whom he dismissed as mostly 'clamant paupers', Elkin recognised that a place in the NSW administration offered him a springboard from which he could lobby the federal government on Northern Territory matters. For the NSW Protection Board, Elkin offered a more 'modern' and appealing rationalisation for a policy which it had really been forced to adopt by Depression conditions and the racism of white country towns. Under Elkin's influence, the terms 'disciplinary supervision' and 'concentration' disappeared from the Board's policy, to be replaced by 'training', 'education' and 'the development of social cohesion'.[7] But the Board's plans for enforced removal and compulsory imprisonment continued uninterrupted.

When the Board approached the NSW government in 1934 with its preferred amending legislation, it found to its surprise that politicians were not sympathetic. While the government agreed to most of the draft act, even conservative politicians found the confinement powers the Board wanted far too harsh and feared that these powers would 'interfere with the people'. The Labor opposition was concerned about the confinement section too, and made repeated attempts to obstruct the passage of the Bill during its early stages in Parliament.[8] The Protection Board began to fear it would not achieve its new powers, and it chose to inject an emotive element into the debate, as it had done in 1912 when it wanted to ensure government agreement to its powers over Aboriginal children.

The APB strategy, as the Bill went to Parliament in 1936, was to publicise the widespread epidemics of infectious disease raging on the Board's own stations. It then implied that such levels of illness were present among other Aboriginal populations too, and suggested that the eye disease from which many Aboriginal adults and children were suffering was 'gonoccocal ophthalmia'. This disease can occur in new-born infants who may come into contact with gonoccocal infections at the time of birth. The diagnosis would have been very difficult to confirm during the 1930s, and has been disputed by ophthalmologists commenting on the available evidence in the 1980s, who believe that it was most likely that the severe eye infections then present were trachoma.

Even if the Protection Board in 1936 believed that the infections were gonoccocal in origin, its members had no medical support or evidence for the charge which they then laid before Parliament. This was that whites were affected much more severely by the disease than were Aborigines. It quite deliberately raised the groundless fear that all uncontrolled Aboriginal populations could spread a virulent, blinding infection to surrounding white communities, while escaping permanent damage themselves. The fact that the disease was venereal in origin resonated powerfully with the deep fears and guilt held by whites about interracial sexual contact among adults, and their desire to prevent their children becoming sexually involved with Aboriginal people in the future, an anxiety which had permeated the debates about school segregations. So the Board found many new supporters when its parliamentary representatives argued that powers of compulsory and indefinite confinement were needed to protect the medical safety of the State's rural white populations. An edge of hysteria had entered the parliamentary debate, and although there continued to be strong opposition, the Board won all the removal and confinement powers it had wanted.[9]

These amendments to the Protection Act were passed in 1936. Yet the Board actually began to force Aboriginal people to move into confinement in 1933, very soon after it made its decisions about the directions it wanted its new policy to take. It did not have to wait for confirmation of its desired new laws because it already held considerable power over Aboriginal communities, which had only intensified in the sudden crisis of the Depression. The Board's power to remove children, used so effectively against the Murris of Walgett in 1923 and those of Moree in 1933, could be mobilised to force bitterly protesting families into reluctant consent to enforced temporary moves. When there was no longer work available for most Aboriginal people, and little likelihood of being allowed the dole, Aboriginal people were much more heavily dependent on Board rations and other support than they had been in the 1920s. These very real powers were to remain a central weapon in the Board's armoury against Aboriginal communities through the decade.

Yet even with such powerful weapons, strengthened by the new laws of 1936, the 'concentration' policy was only implemented very unevenly. The areas most severely hit were the far west, the north-west and the inland areas of the north coast (see Map 13, p. 198). The Board was still extremely short of funds, and it could not undertake such a major relocation and imprisonment program without a great deal of new building and infrastructure, so it was to be expected that its first interventions would be limited. It continued to be a body which responded to demands placed on it, and there were close correlations between the location of school segregation disputes in the 1930s and the Aboriginal communities which were targeted for compulsory removal and imprisonment (see Map 14, p. 199).[10]

Yet the underlying reasons for these high levels of local conflict may

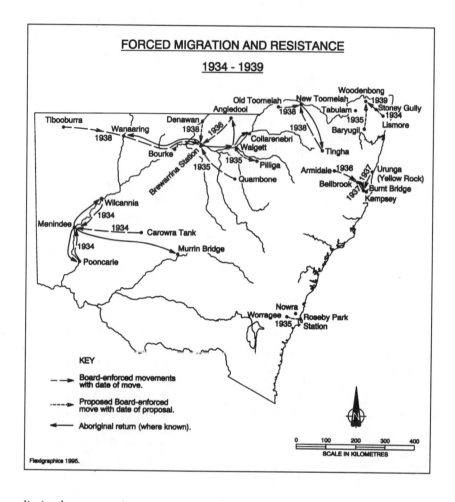

FORCED MIGRATION AND RESISTANCE
1934 - 1939

lie in the economic restructuring which had quickened its pace with the Depression. Each area affected by the concentration powers was one in which the remaining system of large-scale pastoralism was being challenged by economic and environmental decline and by closer settlement, with more intensive agriculture entering the region. The legislation which finally acted to break up the large properties of the Walgett North and Brewarrina Pastoral Districts, for example, was enacted in 1934. Within these districts, the properties marked for land withdrawals were, of course, the largest, and these were the holdings on which Murri camps were located. Gundabluie, Dunumbral, Angledool, Bangate and Gingie were all to lose between 30 and 38 per cent of their acreage, while Dungalear and Boorooma were both to lose 27 per cent. In the Brewarrina District, Weilmoringle was to suffer the greatest loss. Withdrawals were to begin in 1935.[11]

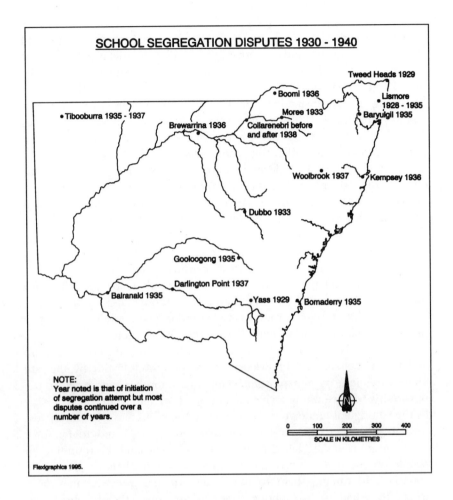

SCHOOL SEGREGATION DISPUTES 1930 - 1940

Tweed Heads 1929

• Boomi 1936

Lismore 1928 - 1935

• Tibooburra 1935 - 1937

Moree 1933

Baryulgil 1935

Brewarrina 1936

Collarenebri before and after 1938

Woolbrook 1937

Kempsey 1936

Dubbo 1933

Gooloogong 1935

Darlington Point 1937

Balranald 1935

Yass 1929

Bomaderry 1935

NOTE:
Year noted is that of initiation of segregation attempt but most disputes continued over a number of years.

0   100   200   300   400
SCALE IN KILOMETRES

Flexigraphics 1995.

This quickening economic change had exacerbated movements of Aboriginal people within each region, as their jobs were lost and they were encouraged or forced to leave pastoral camps. This economic pressure had combined with the continuing desperate flights of many Aboriginal families away from Board control in the 1920s, and the search for schooling, to accelerate the growth of Aboriginal population in the camps of the surrounding towns, and it was often a sudden growth in the numbers of Aborigines in the town camp which triggered a demand by white townspeople to tighten the colour bar at the school.[12]

These structural economic changes undermined the large-scale dual occupation of land by Aboriginal and white capitalist economies and cultures. Even when pastoral camps had been operating securely, there were pressures acting to change traditional life. The decline in numbers of people who were fully trained and confident in traditional Law, continuing constriction of opportunities to teach such knowledge and the encroaching demands of government, such as involvement in the education system, had already begun to erode the practice of ceremonial life. Large ceremonies were still being held in the northern areas bordering on Queensland in the 1910s and in the far western corner country during the 1920s, while on the north coast of New South Wales ceremonial activity continued even longer.[13] Even under the dual occupation of large areas which the pastoral economy had allowed, however, ceremonial activity had declined in many places by the 1920s. But changes did not mean that traditional knowledge had disappeared.

The sustained presence of Aboriginal people in pastoral camps on the lands they knew to be their own in the north-west had allowed the teaching of a wide range of traditional knowledge about land, environmental and social relations, along with a confident sense of belonging which was revealed in the tenacity with which people resisted removals and is clearly still present in the memories of those people who grew up in these situations. Moreover, the skills of Aboriginal pastoral workers were something of which they were also proud and confident. The long period of dual occupation had allowed the development of a new form of Aboriginal belonging to the land, one which drew on both tradition and the new skills and knowledge of pastoral work.[14] But by the late 1920s, the loss of one pastoral camp after another cut away at the possibilities of sustaining active dual occupation, and dealt a severe blow to the Aboriginal landowners as they were forced to move to the nearest town camp. Then the APB's 'concentration' policy acted to reinforce the separation of Aboriginal landowners and their land, by rounding up people on the town camps and reserves nearest to their original home country and forcing them to move even further away, to alien land where they had to live among strangers and obey the dictates of an increasingly authoritarian regime.

The Protection Board did not act innocently in this process. The government was well aware of how deeply Aboriginal people would resist the breaking of their connections to their own country, their homes. Throughout the 1920s, the APB officers, even the relentless Inspector Donaldson, had been prepared to bow to this tenacious Aboriginal determination to remain on their land. In the 1930s, however, the Board decided that it would no longer allow Aboriginal affiliations to land to determine the geographic framework and structure of its operations. Aboriginal people's identification with their land and kin was a characteristic which the Protection Board saw as fundamental in defining 'Aboriginality', and it believed it was this set of behaviours which had destroyed the 'dispersal' policy. Its new 'disciplinary supervision' was designed to eradicate offending Aboriginal behaviour, and so there was

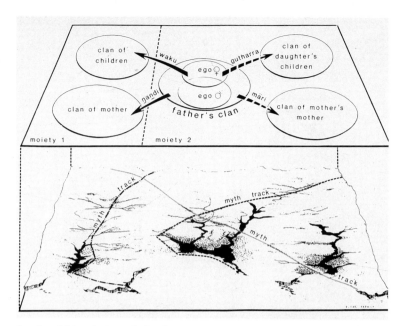

Land and kin relations: In fertile coastal Arnhem Land, a congruence between clan relations and land ownership may occur. Nancy Williams has explained this overlaying of Yolngu kinship and land relations in her diagram: 'The top portion of the diagram shows kin terms used to express the relations of individuals to groups and also of relations among groups. The landscape below shows how these kin labelled groups are related to each other in terms of the estates they own.' (DRAWING BY RICHARD BARWICK. SOURCE: WILLIAMS, 1986:77. REPRODUCED WITH KIND PERMISSION FROM NANCY WILLIAMS AND AIATSIS)

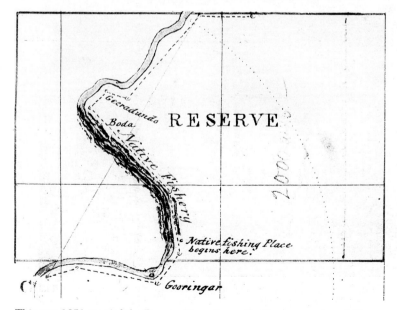

This rare 1851 map of the Barwon River shows the first reservation of Crown Land at Brewarrina 'for the use of Aborigines', dedicated to protect Nganhu, the extensive Ngiyampaa stone fish traps. (SA MAP 6009)

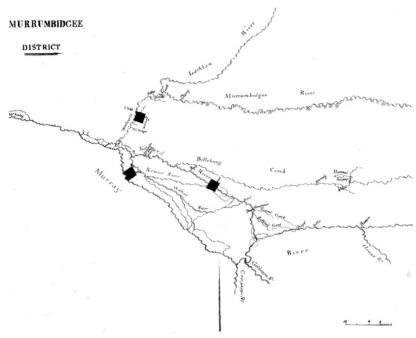

MURRUMBIDGEE

DISTRICT

These three Aboriginal reserves in the Murrumbidgee Pastoral District were among the 35 dedicated in 1850 on the advice of Crown Lands Commissioners. (SA 48/14196, IN CSIL SPECIAL BUNDLE 4/1141.2)

Dual occupation: Gingie Homestead. Some of the exploitative disadvantages of dual occupation are demonstrated in this photo of Gingie property homestead, near Walgett, during the 1880s. The image suggests the constraints and cultural isolation in which Murri domestic servants could be forced to work. (COURTESY MITCHELL LIBRARY SMALL PICTURES FILES)

Dual occupation: Dyrraba camp. The strengths of dual occupation are suggested in this 1890s photo from Dyrraba, in the north coast cattle country. There is assertiveness in the central position of the elderly man wearing the 'king plate', which indicated to Aborigines that the wearer carried authority on that land. The stance of the young stockmen on the right suggests the pride of skilled workers and those in rightful possession not only of the camp but of the surrounding land. (COURTESY AIATSIS N3156.7)

Starting for the Archeron: This is a reenactment of the 1859 decision by Goulburn Valley Kooris to regain control over traditional lands. The trek to Archeron and then, after hostility from surrounding whites, on to Corranderrk (near Healesville) was of intense significance to the Aboriginal farmers of the region. They participated in this reenactment during the defence of their tenure at Corranderrk in the 1870s and 1880s. (COURTESY AIATSIS N2438.2)

Land owning farmers—Hawkesbury. Most Aboriginal farmers were in independent control of their farming lands. Here, an Aboriginal farmer was photographed in his corn garden on the Hawkesbury River at some time before 1930. (PHOTOGRAPH DEPOSITED IN THE MITCHELL LIBRARY IN 1930. COURTESY MITCHELL LIBRARY SMALL PICTURES FILES)

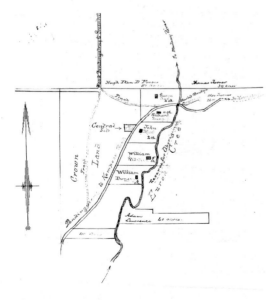

Land owning farmers—Burnt Bridge. The only surving diagram to indicate how independent Aboriginal farmers allocated the lands which were set aside as reserve. There was no APB or other white supervision at Burnt Bridge before 1937. This map was drawn up from Aboriginal · information by an Education Department inspector in 1900, reporting on Koori requests for a school to be established 'for their children. (COURTESY NSW STATE ARCHIVES OFFICE)

Ruby Driver, photographed while working as an 'apprenticed' servant. She was one of the young girls removed from Walgett against her family's wishes by Inspector Donaldson in 1917, after the school segregation, in an attempt to force the relocation of the town Murri population. Ruby Driver died while 'in service' and never saw her family again. (WITH PERMISSION WALGETT COMMUNITY. COURTESY NSW STATE ARCHIVES OFFICE)

A Christmas greeting from Protection Board Inspector Robert Donaldson. The most active and widely feared of all the Board's 'Kids' Collectors', Donaldson was also heavily involved in the massive revocation of reserve lands between 1917 and 1927. (COURTESY NSW STATE ARCHIVES OFFICE)

Fred Maynard, President of the AAPA, with his sister Emily in the Rocks in Sydney, during the 1920s. (PERMISSION OF MAYNARD FAMILY)

Elizabeth MacKenzie-Hatton. This earnest, formal photograph appeared in the *Voice of the North* in 1925. (HELD MITCHELL LIBRARY)

Granny Ellen, the elder from Angledool who danced in the firelight at Brewarrina to protect her displaced people in 1936. This photograph shows Granny Ellen at Angledool in 1921 singing and using wooden implements as clap sticks. (COURTESY AIATSIS N3925.28)

Denied schooling at Collarenebri, these children and their families were threatened under the 'Dog Act' concentration provisions with removal to Brewarrina or Pilliga stations in 1938. Isabel Flick is in the front row. The photgrapher was probably P. R. Stephenson. (*ABO CALL*, AUGUST 1938. COURTESY MITCHELL LIBRARY)

One of the truckloads of Tibooburra people, photographed at Wanaaring, during their forced removal to Brewarrina Station in 1938. Jimmie Barker was driving. (*NEW DAWN*, JANUARY 1974, HELD AIATSIS)

This page of Pearl Gibbs' scrap book recorded the Cumeragunja Strike in 1939. The article with photographs is dated but unsourced. The lower photograph shows one of the strikers' huts. Above, the strikers' children are shown with Hilus Briggs, a young woman striker who ran a school for them throughout the strike.
(PHOTOGRAPH HEATHER GOODALL)

This photograph, taken at the Day of Mourning, 26 January 1938, demonstrates the regional partners in the south eastern Aboriginal political coalition of the time. Bill Ferguson (with sign), Pearl Gibbs on the left and her mother Mrs Murray on the right, were there from the western-based APA; Jack Patten (with hat) from coastal APA and Margaret Tucker (second from left) from the AAL. (*MAN MAGAZINE*, APRIL 1938, HELD MITCHELL LIBRARY)

This photograph of a tough and determined Pearl Gibbs was taken in 1954 when she was taking up her position as elected representative of Aboriginal people on the Welfare Board. In 1981, she chose to have it rephotographed in front of her press clipping scrap book, which recorded the activism in which she was so deeply involved during the 1930s. (PHOTOGRAPH HEATHER GOODALL)

Lola Dodds, a Coonamble camp resident studying for her Leaving Certificate, photographed with activist Ray Peckham during the 1960 campaign for town housing land. Lola died a few years later, without ever living in a 'town house'. (CECIL HOLMES: 'A TOWN FINDS ITS CONSCIENCE', *PEOPLE*, 26/10/1960. COURTESY *PEOPLE* MAGAZINE)

Helen Hambly talks with a Coonamble Aboriginal woman outside her camp home, during the dispute in which the town's Council refused to sell land for the purpose of housing Aboriginal families from these camps. (CECIL HOLMES: 'A TOWN FINDS ITS CONSCIENCE', *PEOPLE*, 26/10/1960. COURTESY *PEOPLE* MAGAZINE)

Lyn Thompson played a key role in the intense political activity around land in the early 1970s. She is shown, third from left, in Moree during 1971 with her father Eric Craigie on her right and her young daughter Yeena being held on her left. (PHOTOGRAPH PETER THOMPSON)

The Journey for Justice. Lyn Thompson, Frank Roberts Jnr, Lester Bostock, Bronwyn Penrith, Chicka Dixon, and other activists at the beginning of the Journey for Justice, in May 1971. The young men in the foreground left the Sydney Town Hall steps to walk to Lismore to draw attention to Aboriginal demands for land and civil justice. Their itinerary highlighted the intense activity around land which had been occuring on the north coast in the preceding decade. Lyn Thompson's placard reads: 'What have you done to our land'. (PHOTOGRAPH PETER THOMPSON)

Mrs Milli Boyd, in front of Bull's Head Mountain, for which she was the custodian. This mountain is one of the sites of intense significance to the Gidhabal (Bandjalang) people of Woodenbong. (PHOTOGRAPH HOWARD CREAMER)

Jack Campbell's life spanned his involvement in the independent farming days at Burnt Bridge in the 1920s to his leadership of the Land Rights movement in NSW in the 1970s and 1980s. He is shown here on the right, with Peter Thompson of Wilcannia, at a 1981 demonstration calling for Land Rights legislation in NSW. (PHOTOGRAPH HEATHER GOODALL)

now a very pressing reason to disrupt the links Aboriginal people had with their lands, because these were seen to sustain an active, identifying Aboriginal community network.

THE 'DOG ACT' IN PRACTICE IN THE WEST

There were two western sites where major 'concentration' actions succeeded, at least for a short time, in forcing Aboriginal people into imprisonment under intensified APB control. Menindee in the west on the Darling River and Brewarrina in the north-west each suffered in this way and each had an impact on Aboriginal political development in the late 1930s, although we will examine only Brewarrina in detail. There, the story of the 'concentration' of north-western Murris exposes the complex interactions between State and local white power as well as offering insights into the diversity of Aboriginal experiences under the 'Dog Act'.

Menindee

The Paakantji Wiimpatjas and their neighbours of the far west had faced relatively little Protection Board intervention in their lives until the later 1920s. The sheep properties on the Darling and the more remote cattle properties to its west had continued to require much Aboriginal labour, and so dual occupation had been more widely sustained than in the north-west. There had been some reduction in size of the large properties with soldier settlement, but the huge Kidman runs such as Yancannia and those even further west still operated with most of their labour drawn from a camp of Aboriginal landowners. The Wangaaypuwan areas to the east of the Darling were less favoured, however, and the arid zones around Ivanhoe had suffered more severely under economic recession and drought in the 1920s. The Protection Board had established a ration station with a teacher-manager near Trida at Carowra Tank in 1927, and a camp had developed there composed of around 100 Wangaaypuwan and some Wiradjuri people who belonged to the surrounding country and had lost work with the onset of the Depression.[15]

As the drought persisted, the remote nature of this station invited the Board's attention, and in 1933, even before it acquired any new powers, it decided to implement its desired new policy by removing the Wangaaypuwan and shifting them to a better-watered site at Menindee, where it proceeded to 'concentrate' also the Aboriginal residents of reserves at Poonindee to the south and Wilcannia to the north. 'Concentration' under a Board manager was disliked by each group, but at least Paakantji Wiimpatjas from the Darling River towns were able to remain in Paakantji country. The Wangaaypuwan and Wiradjuri Murris from Carowra Tank were forced entirely away from their own land. The movement to Menindee brought them into a situation where they were on alien country and, because traditional hostilities had limited contact with the Paakantji, into a place where they felt themselves to be among strangers.

Problems resulted immediately. With APB funding so limited, the station buildings had been hastily and inadequately constructed, with no water supply other than the river itself, and no other facilities. The 40 tiny iron huts were never enough to house the 250 people who were dumped there, and these conditions alone could have been expected to generate social tensions. The situation was made immeasurably worse, however, because the station was located in a sandhill area which had been a Wiimpatja burial ground. Human bones were visible and bone dust was believed by all the Aboriginal people there to be a powerful poison. It was assumed to be mixed in the gritty sand which frequently blew across the station, piling into drifts against the huts and penetrating clothes and food. Tuberculosis was prevalent on this station and the highest death rate was among the Carowra Tank Wangaaypuwan, the very people who felt least secure because they were away from their own country. Paakantji river people eventually had a means of escape as employment opportunities improved in areas along the Darling, and some of these people moved away from Menindee as such alternatives allowed. For the Wangaaypuwan there were fewer employment opportunities in their drier country to the east and so to a greater degree than the Paakantji they were trapped at Menindee.

When the NSW government began to plan its 1938 celebrations to commemorate the 150th anniversary of the arrival of the First Fleet, it chose Menindee people to take part in the re-enactment of Phillip's landing at Sydney Cove in 1788. This re-enactment was widely criticised by Aboriginal political activists at the time, as was the whole celebration, and William Cooper conceived of holding a Day of Mourning to refocus attention on the great costs of the invasion. The government may have chosen Menindee people to take part because they were known to have a high degree of traditional knowledge and could therefore add 'authenticity' to the re-enactment, but it may also have been because they were so vulnerable to pressure because of their remoteness, and their distressed and disorganised state.

This difficult situation was an important factor in generating political activity to the east as well as on the station itself. Duncan Ferguson, the lay preacher, had moved with his Poonindee parishioners into the Menindee station, but he had been placed under police surveillance early in 1936 because of his active support for the dissatisfied station residents. His brother, Bill Ferguson, was the shearer and unemployed workers' activist who had become involved with William Cooper's campaign to send a petition to the King (see Chapter 14). Duncan's reports to his brother in Dubbo on the poor facilities and deteriorating health conditions on Menindee station formed a significant portion of the information revealed by the Aboriginal political movement in 1937 which so effectively embarrassed the Board. When the appalling conditions were finally publicised, however, the white press treated the matter as an example of the 'primitive superstitions' of 'simple people', who believed the land was 'under a hoodoo'. While this publicity assisted the Aboriginal movement to press for improved management by the Protection Board, it also left the activists angered and deeply suspicious of the disrespect with which the white media would respond to evidence of Aboriginal traditional beliefs.[16]

Brewarrina, 1935–38

In the mid-1930s the Murri population of both Brewarrina town and station was composed principally of Ngiyampaa-speaking river people, who belonged to that country, and Murawari-speaking people, from the land to the north-west, who had been forced into Brewarrina in 1911.[17] The town Murri population had risen over the Depression, from around 70 in 1927 to 150 in 1934, while that on the mission had risen even more sharply from 70 in 1927 to over 200 between 1931 and 1934. White townspeople's anxiety at this increased population in both locations was reflected in the Municipal Council demand in 1934 'that the Black population be removed from the town of Brewarrina to the Mission'.[18]

To the south-east, the Wailwan-speaking Murris of Quambone were suffering the same problems faced by other Aborigines over the Depression in towns with no reserve and no work. They had been refused State food relief and the local police were issuing them only APB rations as well as controlling their family endowment. The police took care to carry out the Board's instruction for all able-bodied Aborigines to support themselves where possible. If Quambone Murris refused work offered by surrounding pastoralists at under-award wages, their rations were cut off and they were forced to go to the resident missionaries for aid. When they did receive rations, however, the police followed Board instructions that Aborigines should perform two days' work in return.

Aboriginal involvement with left-wing organisers in the north-west pastoral industry had finally generated white interest outside Dubbo. Murris in Coonamble established contact with Norman Jeffries, a member of the CPA organising for the Pastoral Workers' Industrial

Union, who investigated the Quambone situation and wrote about it for the *Workers' Weekly*.[19] This was the first evidence that CPA members (other than the Dubbo unemployed organisers who had joined the party only in 1935) had developed personal contact with New South Wales Aborigines. Jeffries' attempt to open a campaign for Aboriginal rights in New South Wales had rapid but unforeseen consequences. The press report apparently drew the Protection Board's attention to Quambone, from which it had had no town protest nor any other local stimulus for intervention, and the group of around twenty Wailwan Murris there became the first people to be 'concentrated' on Brewarrina station.[20]

There are few records of this move, which took place before June in 1935. Jimmie Barker, then handyman at Brewarrina, was ordered to drive the manager to Quambone in the station's lorry. There the manager and the local police coerced the Wailwan to move. Roy Barker has remembered their arrival at the Mission. Crouched on the back of the truck, the women and children had pulled blankets over their heads and were moaning and wailing in distress. The Brewarrina people came to meet them hushed and sombre, believing that there must have been a death.[21] The Quambone Murris did not stay longer than a couple of years at Brewarrina. With the exception of Emily Lee, who married into the Sullivan family, the others returned to Quambone, Warren or Dubbo, where one family, the Carrs, had relatives. The Dubbo Carr family were prominent in the developing political activity there from the mid-1930s, and the events affecting their relations in Quambone in 1935 fuelled their opposition to the Protection Board.[22]

The Municipal Council at Brewarrina was, meanwhile, becoming more anxious about the increasing numbers of Aborigines in the town. During 1935 it instructed the police to use their powers to remove 'the disgraceful humpies' Murris had built near the Bourke road and to maintain the curfew more strictly.[23] There were no laws permitting a curfew over anyone, but the Council members clearly believed they were entitled to impose one, and expected the police to work out the details of how to implement their instructions. Brewarrina Murris remember frequent conflict with the police over this period, as they were either harassed in the street with bag searches or with threats of arrest or violence if they did not make themselves scarce. They remember too a rising tide of informal threats, as gangs of white thugs became more active in intimidating people coming in from the mission.[24]

The next group of people to be moved to Brewarrina were the Angledool Murris, most of whom were Yuwalaraay-speaking people living on their own country, although some Kamilaraay-speaking people from the land to the east of the Barwon also lived at the station. Angledool was an obvious target for 'centralisation'. It was the Board's only managed reserve in the Walgett North area, and by 1936 it appeared that subdivision was going to reduce the need for pastoral labour in this district, so there was no pressure on the Board to continue to supply services such as segregated schooling and rations during seasonal unemployment, to ensure an accessible Aboriginal workforce in the area. With subdivision in the offing, the Board also had no interest in encouraging the continued residence of the Yuwalaraay on their own country by improving the poor housing conditions of Angledool station. Trachoma was epidemic among its substantial population of 180, and the township of Angledool had no doctor and was inaccessible in wet weather. The Board's argument for the move was that it could treat eye disease and improve housing conditions more efficiently if the station was closed altogether and the population moved to Brewarrina.[25]

Closing the station at Angledool and moving over 100 people was a major exercise, and preparations at Brewarrina took a couple of months. Over that time the Angledool manager and APB Inspector Smithers held a number of meetings with station residents, in an attempt to convince them of the benefits of the move, with promises of improved conditions and 'fine houses' at Brewarrina. The angry Murris held their own meetings, and a letter of protest signed by all the station residents was sent to the Board. Angledool Murris, too, wanted better housing, but they wanted it at Angledool, on their own country. Although a few of the men had travelled through Brewarrina for work, most of the women and children had never been out of their Yuwalaraay country. They did not want to be forced to move to a community of strangers where it would be extremely difficult to get work.[26]

Ike Handy was an African-American married to a Murri, and he and his family used to camp outside the mission fence so their children could attend the school. Ike was literate, and so he had been asked by the Angledool Murris to scribe for them. He read out some of the letter to his family, and his daughter Donnas has remembered the issues:

> The bit of it Dad was reading out [said] that the people didn't want to move from the mission and that's where they were getting work and everything like that. The men were known on the stations, every man sort of had a station.
>
> Old Henry Hardy and all of them were regulars out there, see, so if they went to Brewarrina where would they go? See, they'd have to get used to being on Yarrawin and Gilgoan, they already had Brewarrina men, so . . . that's the reason why they didn't want to go . . . They put that down there—an excuse that they didn't want to go.
>
> They had their people buried in the cemetery there. And dark people are like that, you know, they don't like leaving their dead people . . . they like to get buried there with them, see . . . I reckon that'd be a strong reason because they've got their own little cemetery up there.[27]

There were also protests from the town whites of Angledool, who feared the effects on their businesses if well over a hundred residents were removed overnight. The Board pressed ahead with its plans, however, and Angledool Murris began talking of going to Collarenebri or Walgett, towns on the edges of Yuwalaraay country where they had relatives and which were accessible to the Walgett North pastoral stations. These two towns were also causing the Board problems.[28] At Collarenebri Murris were bitter at their exclusion from the public school, and their demands for access were becoming more insistent and aggressive.[29] At Walgett white calls had been renewed for the removal of the town Murri population and the Board was making plans to move them to Pilliga station.[30]

Henry Hardy's family was one which was split over the painful decision. Two of Henry's daughters had been left with permanent eye damage by the epidemic at Angledool, and he and Evelyn were now anxious about being so isolated from medical attention. This made them more vulnerable to the demands that they go with the mission to Brewarrina, but Henry's sister Eadie Weatherall and his mother Nancy Hardy were far less swayed. Rose, Eadie's daughter, remembers worried late-night conversations between uncle, mother and grandmother, with voices rising as the anxiety generated conflict about whether the whole extended family group should try to escape to the east. The Weatheralls chose escape: Rose remembers that one morning the children were hurriedly gathered together and with the help of another uncle, the Weatheralls and their children piled their belongings onto a dray and headed off to Collarenebri.[31]

Pressure on the Angledool Murris intensified as their mood became obvious to the Board's staff. Henry Hardy has described Smithers' methods of persuasion:

> A lot of 'em didn't like comin' down but they had to come down. A lot of 'em started bailin' up, talkin' they weren't goin' to go, they'd go to Collarindabri, Walgett.
>
> But this Smithers come there then. He walked round and put a revolver on and hung it around his hip, walkin' through the crowd . . .
> They're lookin' then and they started gettin' the wind up.
> And he stopped it that time.[32]

As Henry described it,

> We were under the Dog Act altogether. Just like a dog, they'd get hold of the chain and lead him over there, tie him up over there. What they said, that was the end of it. They could send you anywhere, do what they liked with you.[33]

It was, however, the groups most vulnerable to Protection Board threats who were really 'under the Dog Act'. First there were the people with children whom the Board could remove. Then there were the very old like frail Granny Ellen, who had spent all her life on the camps at Yeranbah sheep station, but who was no longer able to work among the sheep or to survive independently on traditional subsistence resources and so was dependent on rations. But for the rest, as Henry Hardy pointed out, Smithers had 'only bluffed 'em' with his gun: 'A lot of 'em just stopped there and he didn't do no more about it. He was just frightening 'em to come this way [to Brewarrina]'.[34]

Apart from those who escaped like the Weatheralls, the Murris who successfully defied Smithers by staying at Angledool were all middle-aged people, able to get pastoral work, but safe from the threat of removal of their children. Henry's own parents stayed; his parents-in-law, his older sister and others of that older age group made up the half-dozen families who were able to resist the move.[35]

For 110 Angledool Murris, however, there appeared to be no choice on 26 May when Smithers, the Brewarrina manager and three Brewarrina Murris, Jimmie Barker, Dudley Dennis and Billy Moore, arrived to load them onto two semi-trailers and a Bedford truck. The iron from all of the huts was stripped and loaded onto one semi-trailer, and the frames were burnt. The other two trucks were so crowded with people that there was little room for belongings other than a few clothes and blankets. After the trucks had gone, those Murris who had refused to leave simply moved closer to the town and began building their houses again. For those travelling to Brewarrina, the miserable trip took hours, with only one stop along the road to make tea and stretch cramped limbs.[36]

The trucks arrived at Brewarrina late on that cold night. Jack Barker, Jimmy Barker's son, has recalled the scene as the truck his father was driving pulled up.[37] He had pestered his mother to allow him to go and watch, wrapped in a warm dressing gown. In contrast, the distressed Angledool people were stumbling down from the trucks, wrapped in thin Board-issue 'Gubby' blankets, searching for wood to light fire buckets against the cold. Jack remembered vividly the glare of the flames as people hurriedly poured petrol on the firebuckets to get them started quickly. Then, in the fires' glow, he saw Granny Ellen rise and begin to dance, singing in Yuwalaraay. For the Brewarrina children this dance was a great excitement. But Granny Ellen must have had a different purpose. She may have danced to reassure and protect her Angledool kinsfolk, or to ask permission to camp on this strange land, or to announce their arrival in the proper way by dancing one of the stories for the Yuwalaraay land to which they belonged. Her reasons were only dimly understood, but the younger Murris watching have carried that image of her solitary firelit corroboree as a symbol of their painful journey.

For many the priority was not to get warm but to find a house. Henry Hardy and a mate jumped off the truck as soon as it stopped, leaving their families to help themselves down, while they rushed over to the row of tiny half-completed houses to select ones next to each other and at the end of the row for quietness. Jack Barker has described the houses in similar terms to Henry: 'They had two-roomed tin shacks half built for 'em. They was about 10 feet by 20. No doors and no windows and it was a cold night'.

Frieda Hardy, one of Henry's six children, has remembered the family's first night in their new house:

> It was cold. Open fires was all we had, there was no stoves. There was only two little rooms with cement floors, no windows, just the squares [holes]. We slept inside on the floor, we'd made sure of our blankets.
> There was no mattresses, just laying on cement floors. I don't remember if we had a fire bucket inside—there wasn't any room for us, let alone a fire bucket.[38]

These were the 'fine houses' promised the Angledool Murris. The next day the families set about digging their own pit toilets and were issued with hinged, woven-iron beds and palliasses which they had to stuff with straw for mattresses. Eventually tin flaps were placed over the holes in the wall for 'windows' and doors were added, but not for a long time. Through the winter months little was done; visiting Board members reported in August, 'much work remaining to be done on huts for Angledool people'.[39]

Those who had protested against the move but who had been forced to come anyway were not forgotten. The Murris who had drafted the letter of protest were called up to the manager's office, where the manager and Smithers abused them and threatened them with expulsion from the station (without their families) should they continue such activities.[40]

Angledool Murris' fears about employment proved justified. Little was offered around Brewarrina, and Henry Hardy, with other Angledool men, was forced to travel back to the properties around Angledool for work, necessitating longer absences from his family. At Brewarrina they found the same unstable and violent manager, R. R. Brain, who had served at Angledool until 1935 and who was widely believed to be manipulating for his own benefit endowment and other monies sent to the station. The Board, too, believed this charge, giving it as one of the reasons for Brain's dismissal in October 1936. For those Angledool Murris who could not find work, there was only work-for-rations on the station.[41]

In terms of relationships with Murris at Brewarrina, however, Angledool fears had not been fulfilled. Although there was some friction, there were enough traditional cultural similarities and enough shared experiences from the recent past to form the basis of relationships between Brewarrina and Angledool Murris. After a fairly short time, political alliances developed and people from both communities were involved in confrontations with the manager over issues like the poor water supply and the work-for-rations system.[42]

Yet things had changed for Angledool Murris. There had always been more singing (in the language) and 'corroboreeing' on the pastoral camps than on Angledool, but even the Yuwalaraay cultural expression which had taken place on that station ended when the people were moved to Brewarrina. The old people did not do so much singing and the dead were no longer buried with the smoke and the ritual which had been carried out at Angledool.[43]

Some of the older people died at Brewarrina. As time passed the Angledool Murris moved off the station, family by family, as their children grew a little older and so less vulnerable, as employment conditions improved. When they left, most of them headed home. As Billy Moore observed, 'They were contented for a while, but not living on your own place makes you different, see'.[44]

Some were back in Angledool before June 1938. Others went to Collarenebri, Walgett and Lightning Ridge where they are today. Some Angledool families stayed on Brewarrina station while their children were young, but as soon as possible moved to camps near the town, away from the direct control of the Protection Board and precisely as town whites had feared. For these families, links had been formed with Brewarrina Murris in struggles against the Board and later through marriages, and so for them Brewarrina as well as Angledool came to be seen as home.[45]

Although few Angledool people appear to have left Brewarrina station before the end of 1937, whites in Brewarrina had intensified their campaign for removal of the town Murris with the first rumours of the alleged gonococcal ophthalmia outbreak at Angledool and then with news that that station was to be moved. As in other towns where an appeal to the Protection Board had proved futile, the Brewarrina Council sought to draw in other State authorities and, using the gonococcal ophthalmia scare, called for the exclusion of the 32 Aboriginal children attending the public school.[46]

The Council found an enthusiastic ally in the regional inspector of schools, J. N. Harrison, who explained the elements of the town plan in a series of reports. Once the Aboriginal children were excluded they would, it was hoped, be either removed to the station dormitory or bussed daily to the station school. It was then assumed that 'it would not be long before the parents permanently settled themselves at the station' and this would 'clear the Blacks from Brewarrina'. That the aim of the exercise was removal of the town Murris rather than segregation of the school was made even more obvious when a separate 'special' school near the town was proposed. The town reaction, as conveyed by Harrison, was total opposition: a special school would 'aggravate the problem' by attracting more people from the station into town.[47]

The Protection Board was already finding itself in difficulties providing adequate facilities for the Angledool population and could not have hoped to provide accommodation at the station for the town population, which was approaching 200. It prevaricated by explaining to the Council that it did not yet have the legal power to confine Aborigines (although this was not stopping the plans to move the Angledool population) and repeated that its aim remained the eventual 'mergence' of Aborigines into the general community.[48] The Board had few arguments to offer when the town raised the Board's own exaggerated information about ophthalmia, but neither could it provide facilities on the station to satisfy town demands, so nothing at all was done. In August 1936 the Council broadened its line of attack, calling officially for support from the P & C Association and the Hospital Board for total segregation of both school and hospital. The intention remained the removal of town Murris, as was stated bluntly in the Council-initiated petition: 'That a separate hospital and school should be in operation for Aborigines. These should be established at the Mission'.[49]

Tension between whites and Murris was running extremely high over this period as the town's authorities attempted the closure of essential facilities to Murris. The conflict broke out on many occasions in street violence. Val Mingo, a Queensland Murri who lived most of his life in Brewarrina, remembered that Aboriginal people had to be very cautious about entering town:

> they were nervous to tackle with the mobs here, they were sort of a clique. They had a set on Aboriginals, they was up against 'em, didn't want to see 'em here . . . they'd tear into 'em, specially if they had the numbers, like, sure of defeating 'em.

Immediately after the arrival of the Angledool mob, a serious fight broke out near the fisheries between whites and Murris from the town. Val and others remember it as a Murri victory:

> A couple started a fight here one day, and there was a white bloke and a dark bloke and of course a lot of us started looking on, and then they [the whites] started into *him* [the Murri fighter] and we other dark fellas were about so we into *them*. Anyhow, we belted the tripe out of them!

Things were better from then on, 'cause they could see that we could hold 'em at any time.

Even if this did allow some respite from street harassment and violence, the fact that the hostility between the town's racial groups was so openly displayed suggests that all other aspects of life in the town must have been tense and difficult too.[50] Despite this intimidating atmosphere, Aboriginal parents tried to protect their children's access to the school, going in a deputation to the headmaster, where they insisted that their children's right to education be maintained.[51] Their views were not passed on to the Education Department, but this deputation must have added to the general uncertainty on what would happen about segregation.

The Education Department was in considerable confusion over the state of its own policy at this stage and by early 1937 was leaning towards the idea of a separate school in the town, but delayed any actual segregation.[52] The Board was more sympathetic to town calls to remove all the town camp Murris, but it was still in extreme difficulties because of the shortage of housing and the problems caused by poor staff on the station. Yet because it wanted to be seen to respond to town concerns, it placed even harsher restrictions on the mission residents. The town calls for hospital segregation were met by refusing hospital treatment to most people on the mission, who were now to be treated by the manager's wife. Only in the most urgent cases were Aboriginal people from the station to be allowed to gain a doctor's services in the town hospital. It also agreed to admit any of the town Murri children to the station school if their parents agreed.[53]

The town camp population continued to increase and with it Aboriginal enrolments at the public school. In mid-1937, 45 of the school's 90 enrolled students were Aboriginal. The white townspeople pressed their argument for segregation and removal through Inspector Harrison but without apparent success. As an internal measure, however, the Council, at the instigation of the aldermen who were also the town's JPs, again instructed the police to enforce the curfew strictly and ensure 'that aboriginals not be allowed to congregate in the streets'.[54]

There were, therefore, many angry Murris in and around Brewarrina when activist Bill Ferguson came there in the early part of 1937. Some Quambone and most Angledool people were still on the station, so there were two groups of people who didn't want to be there at all. For the disadvantages of loss of employment or greater travel for work, Angledool Murris had found conditions only marginally better at Brewarrina than at Angledool: they were still living in two-roomed tin huts, the only difference being that the new ones had concrete rather than earthen floors, while the 'running water' at Brewarrina in 1937 consisted of four taps for the use of 310 people. No one at the station was much happier with the new manager, E. Dalley, than with Brain. Dalley was in the habit of firing his gun at any movement after dark and there were persistent rumours about sexual abuse of the girls in the dormitory. Murris in town were under intensifying pressure as the Council attempted to close the school, the hospital and the streets to them to force them out to the station. Murris from both the town and the station talked with Ferguson. The issues they stressed were those of Board interference in their choice of where they lived, the intolerable managerial control, the poor food and conditions and the dormitory system at the station and the denial of access to the services of the town.[55]

In September 1937 the Council renewed its call for segregation of the school. When it gained little response from either the Protection Board or the Education Department it appealed to yet another government department, this time that of Health, insisting that an inspector be sent to investigate the housing of Aborigines 'on the outskirts of the town'. The Council apparently received little response to this appeal either, but by the end of the year the Minister for Education, D. H. Drummond, had become alarmed at recent medical reports which indicated a high incidence of trachoma among children in special Aboriginal schools. With dubious logic, the minister insisted that this report supported the arguments for exclusion of Aborigines from public schools—the purpose, presumably, being to send Aborigines to the overcrowded special schools where they would suffer greater risk of trachoma. An Education Department doctor was sent to Brewarrina to ascertain the 'caste' of the Aboriginal children, as a preliminary to the exclusion of all children of 'predominantly Aboriginal blood'. In his report, Dr Donnellan concluded that the Aboriginal children in town suffered a relatively low rate of trachoma and that there was 'very little risk' to white children from infection. He did, however, note the continued hostility of the town whites to Aborigines and the violence endemic in the white children's actions towards Aboriginal children. The Department then decided that physical segregation within the classroom was the most sensible solution and so refused to exclude the Brewarrina Aboriginal children.[56]

Murris on the station had been protesting at their conditions over this period as well. Jimmie Barker, among others, had maintained contact with Bill Ferguson and had sent him information which Ferguson was using in the current hearings of the Select Committee into the administration of the Board. Over Christmas 1937, Pearl Gibbs returned to Brewarrina, where she had grown up, to stay on the station with her relatives. She brought with her the clippings from the Aboriginal movement's successful press campaign in October and the newspapers were secretly passed so eagerly from person to person on the station that they disintegrated from handling while Pearl was there. Intending to gain further evidence for the Select Committee, Pearl spoke mainly with the women, who talked of the poor food, the sexual abuse of the dormitory girls and the insanitary conditions of the treatment room. It was while Pearl was there that the men working for rations refused to continue, telling the manager that they would work for wages but not for rations. The strike was short-lived: the manager simply denied food not only to the men but also to their families and they were forced to return to work. Pearl took all of this information back to Sydney, where Bill Ferguson was able to use some of it at the Select Committee hearings and Pearl exposed it in the press.[57]

Despite such great dissatisfaction among Murris on the station and among whites of the town, the Protection Board early in 1938 was organising the 'concentration' of yet another group of people. The Wangkumara at Tibooburra were about to be moved to Brewarrina.

The Wangkumara had been camping near Tibooburra in increasing numbers since the onset of the Depression, with the camp population rising from around 30 in 1928 to 148 in 1937. The only relationship the Wangkumara had with the Protection Board was that when they applied for unemployment relief they were given Board rations. Even when unemployed, however, the Wangkumara were able to add to their income by 'specking' for gold in the hills around the town. Employment had improved by 1937 apparently, and a number of the Wangkumara were working on surrounding pastoral properties again, leaving their families in Tibooburra so that the children could go to school.[58]

Conflict with town whites over access to the school had reached the point of actual segregation in 1935, only to fail in an embarrassing confusion over who was white and who black. A newly arrived teacher had excluded as 'black' the children of some of the 'white' parents petitioning for segregation. All the children were allowed back into the school, and the Wangkumara had assumed this to be the end of the affair, but some white townspeople pursued the matter. By late 1937 the demand for segregation had been renewed on the altered grounds that the Aboriginal children were carriers of trachoma, a call which must have been generated at least in part by the Board's own widely publicised scare about 'gonoccocal ophthalmia' in 1936.[59]

The teacher at the school agreed that 'some' Aboriginal children suffered from trachoma, but pointed out that all of them had the disease in its chronic stage, in which there was no discharge from the eyes, and which Education Department medical guidelines specified as non-excludable, as it was not usually infectious. Moreover, the teacher stated

213

that he also had many white pupils who suffered from this stage of trachoma. He had had difficulty in gaining permission for medical treatment from both white and Aboriginal parents and in his view the solution to the 'problem' lay in compulsory medical examination and treatment for all his pupils.[60]

This would appear to have been a clear-cut case for the Board to use its new powers of compulsory medical examination acquired under the 1936 amendments to enforce just such treatment. This was not done. The townspeople had enlisted the support of the regional Child Welfare Department inspector to achieve their stated aims of a separate, segregated school or removal of the whole Aboriginal population to Menindee station. This inspector proved co-operative, as he had been in 1935, and in his report to the Child Welfare Department in January 1938 he transformed the Wangkumara children into ones 'living under conditions of intolerable neglect' and 'practically all infected with, and spreaders of, trachoma'.[61]

This convinced the secretary of the Department, who transformed the children still further into 'diseased, dirty and verminous children undoubtedly carrying infection'. In turn, this argument convinced APB member B. C. Harkness and in March 1938 the Board decided to remove the whole Wangkumara population in Tibooburra to Menindee. This brought an urgent protest from white residents of Menindee, who probably knew of the prevalence of tuberculosis on the station there, but who had also heard rumours, spread by the police, that the Wangkumara were all suffering from (of course) gonococcal ophthalmia. The destination of the Wangkumara thus became Brewarrina, 350 miles to the south-east.[62]

By 1938 the Board was well aware of the difficulties it faced when trying to force Aborigines to move, and the Tibooburra removal was the largest the Board had yet attempted with an independent community. With pastoral camps still in existence in the area, there were places to which the Wangkumara could go, and so the police were careful not to alert them to the planned move. There were no 'consultations' as there had been with Angledool Murris.

It was therefore a total surprise when, in late April 1938, Inspector Smithers arrived in Tibooburra, with three Brewarrina Murris driving the trucks which the Wangkumara were told were going to take them to Brewarrina.[63] Jimmie Barker and Dudley Dennis were still employees of the Board and could not avoid assisting with the move, but Billy Moore had refused to be used again:

I'd seen enough at Angledool. I didn't like the way people were being shifted about from their homes. It wasn't a fair deal for any of the

214

people . . . young or old, they all wanted to go back to their own original homes.[64]

This was no longer a consideration for the Protection Board, however, and Smithers, again wearing his gun prominently, and with the police beside him, strode from camp to camp at Tibooburra, giving the bewildered Wangkumara three or four hours to gather their belongings. The situation was chaotic and if there was individual resistance it was futile. A few people had time to contact relatives working on properties nearby, but many did not. Families were not able to take many possessions and all were forced to leave the camels, horses and plant which were the hard-earned means of their livelihood. Both Lorna Dixon and Eadie Edwards, who were 16 and 14 at the time, have recalled the intense distress of the move, with many people crying as they packed under police surveillance and then were forced onto the trucks, some of the old people clutching dogs which they refused to leave behind. 'It was compulsory', Eadie said. 'We just had to go. But we didn't like leavin' our home, see.'[65]

The group of 130 Wangkumara who made the two-day journey were given nothing to look forward to at Brewarrina. Smithers is remembered to have warned them not to 'play up' at the mission or they could be 'shot like a dog'.[66] When they did finally arrive, they were greeted with an elaborate welcome, perhaps reflecting an attempt by Angledool Murris to make the Wangkumara feel a little more secure than they themselves had done. Eadie was one who was touched by the effort involved, but it did not comfort her against her overwhelming first impression: 'It was just like a gaol!'[67]

Lorna Dixon also remembered Brewarrina as a prison. The houses for the Wangkumara were better than those for the Yuwalaraay but were still tiny and too few in number to accommodate all of the families, many of whom spent some weeks sleeping in the schoolhouse. The Wangkumara had had enough to eat at Tibooburra and, despite some trachoma, they had felt they were healthy. This opinion was confirmed by the Brewarrina doctor, who found the new arrivals 'well-nourished' and in 'good general condition'. At Brewarrina, their health deteriorated: not only did their eye disease become worse but the children developed sores on their arms and legs which had not occurred at Tibooburra. The Wangkumara attributed this in part to the scarcity of food on the station. There was never enough meat and at times they boiled flour and water with sugar in it for their main meal to stretch their food until the next ration issue. In part also they felt their deteriorating health resulted from the lack of the right traditional remedies: the herbs they needed did not grow in the country round Brewarrina and, as Eadie recalled, the medicine there 'was all that whitefellas' turnout'.[68]

Time and again in their accounts of life on the station Eadie and Lorna returned to their sense of the oppressive confinement they felt there. They were not permitted to go into the town unless under the manager's supervision and, unfamiliar with the country, they found 'no trespassing' signs confronting them whenever they tried to find game. Their only source of food supplementation was fishing, but they were told that this was permitted in only one area of the river, in a spot visible to the manager so that he could 'keep an eye on them'.

George Dutton arrived after his family. He had been working on a property outside Tibooburra when word reached him that his family had been forced onto the trucks to go to Brewarrina. He was furious that he had been forced to leave in such a hurry he didn't have time to collect the £75 owing to him and had still received no reply to his letters asking about sending the money on. He explained his views about the move later in the year at Brewarrina to the visiting anthropologist Norman Tindale, who noted Dutton's words down verbatim. This account is direct confirmation of the memories of both Angledool and Tibooburra people that the most powerful weapon which the Protection Board held over people was its threat to their children:

> Object to idea of being brought from Tibooburra. Want to go back and will soon go back. Nothing here for a man to do.
>
> The treatment we get here is no good. We can do better in Tibooburra. Much more meat there, better conditions. We should be treated for bad eyes in our own country; not taken away to a strange country.
>
> No work here for us. On the Paroo, I can get work.
>
> We [were] told that if we did not move to Brewarrina they would take our children away from us. That's the only reason why we came.[69]

The Wangkumara, experiencing managerial control for the first time, would probably have felt confined at any period of the station's history. Their arrival, however, had increased the restrictions placed on all the station residents. Brewarrina townspeople had panicked at yet another increase in the station population. Within days of the Wangkumara arrival, another petition was circulating among whites demanding that the Board remove all the town Aborigines to the station and that station residents not be allowed free entry into the town.[70]

The Board made no reference this time to its aim of 'mergence' and appeared just as anxious as white townspeople at the increase in the town camp population, which was approaching 300. By May 1938 the Board had stretched the resources of the station beyond its limits: there were over 400 people there, still with only four taps; housing and schooling accommodation were acutely overcrowded, and all of this was compounded by what the Board now recognised as gross managerial unsuitability. While it could not comply with the demand to remove the town camp, the Board could restrict the movements of station residents and it directed that no Aborigine was to be permitted to go from the station into town 'except for very special reasons'.[71]

The Wangkumara felt isolated at Brewarrina. Not only was the country different but they had only the fact of dislocation in common with the Quambone and Angledool people. The Wangkumara shared little in traditional terms with the people to the east of the Paroo River: their ritual and ceremonial links were, like those of their language, with the people to the north and west of Tibooburra. Their colonial experiences had more in common with people in the desert cattle country of Queensland and South Australia than with those of the north-western New South Wales sheep country. On an intolerably crowded station, Eadie Edwards remembered, 'we kept away to ourselves as much as we could 'cause we weren't used to too many people'.[72]

There was little work for the Wangkumara men. No major droving routes passed through Brewarrina to allow them to pick up work in their usual occupations, and the surrounding pastoralists preferred men they knew to the strangers. The Board had no plans in this regard and made enquiries as to 'the prospective employment and future disposal' of the Tibooburra people only after it had dumped them at Brewarrina.[73] Murris there remember the Wangkumara as 'dejected', 'unhappy', 'homesick' and increasingly anxious as the death toll mounted among members of their community despite (or because of) 'all that whitefellas' turnout' at the clinic and hospital.

The man who made most impression on Murris at Brewarrina was Fred Johnson, who had followed his people across from Tibooburra bringing his donkey team with him. He thus had a means of support independent of the Board and made his living at Brewarrina carting wood. Those who were children at the station while he was there remember riding the donkeys when the team wasn't working, but Fred Johnson made a greater impact.

As a senior man, addressed by most people as 'Grandfather', Johnson expressed his people's anger by being active in the western political movement which was developing in late 1938. With both Brewarrina and Angledool Murris he organised meetings between Bill Ferguson and the station residents, although these meetings had to be held outside the station fence as Ferguson had been denied entry to any reserve. Early in 1939, Johnson officially took on the job of organiser for the movement. In February and March he travelled with Ferguson and Jack Kinchela, who had been organising at Burra Bee Dee and Pilliga stations, to Goodooga and the large pastoral camp at Weilmoringle. They went on to Collarenebri and Walgett, both towns where Murris were under threat of Board-enforced movement, and then to Moree, where Murris were still facing intense town pressure and where Johnson took the dominant speaking role at a large meeting attended only by Murris.[74]

*　*　*

The practice of the 'Dog Act' had had devastating effects for Aborigines in the whole of the western and north-western regions. In relation to Brewarrina alone, three communities had been uprooted and 'centralised' on the station where all the residents then had to share the continued poor conditions and increased restrictions on their movements. Managers who were unsuitable provided no 'training' but plenty of 'disciplinary supervision'. At the same time pressure on town Murris had intensified. The moves not only exacerbated the insecurity of the town's whites but had given them examples of the way the Board was prepared to deal with Aborigines from other areas. In doing so, the Board had in fact generated calls for the removal and confinement of even more people. In their response to white pressure and to the Board's moves and threats, however, Aboriginal people in the west had formed inter-community political links which spanned half the State.

16

The 'Dog Act' on the Coast: Burnt Bridge, 1934–38

The adoption of the concentration policy meant that the Protection Board began to change the general way it responded to problems and calls for action from 1933 onwards. As well as the factors which limited its activity to certain areas of the State, there were other matters which obstructed its intentions even in those areas where it did decide to act. One obvious matter was Aboriginal opposition, which it had certainly anticipated. Even with its new laws and new determination, however, the Board found it had particular difficulty in managing Aboriginal communities which were not already under Board control. Another obstacle arose because there were a significant number of local disputes among white interest groups about whether the Aboriginal population should be removed. Local employers of Aboriginal workers, for example, would disagree with the parents of white children who were demanding a school segregation in order to force a removal.

On the north coast, the Board's activity confirmed the long evident end of its interest in independent Aboriginal farming of reserves. The imposition of managers at Woodenbong, Purfleet and Bellbrook reserves had indicated the Board's intention to assert more control over a region with a large, and for the Board a troublesome, Aboriginal population in an area where mechanisation was reducing labour requirements. Bellbrook had been one of the few remaining independent agricultural reserves, although cultivation had been difficult with the crowding of the Depression. Burnt Bridge alone remained independent of managerial control by the middle of the decade and then in late 1936 even this reserve was chosen as a site for concentration.[1]

For the north coast the remaining small reserves appeared to the Board as simply a waste of its resources. A manager on one large station could 'discipline', 'supervise' or 'train' the residents of a number of small reserves more easily and cheaply once they had been concentrated. As well as the moves or threats indicated on the 'Dog Act' map (p. 198), the Board considered the 'amalgamation' of Kooris from Purfleet and Forster at Tuncurry in 1937 and those from Nambucca Heads, Stuart's

Island, Bowraville and Ulgundahi Island on an unspecified site in 1939.[2] The far northern rivers area, however, provided a clear example of the difficulty the Board experienced in moving Aborigines who were not already under managerial control.

In 1934 John Howard, the new manager at Stoney Gully (Runnymede) station, was instructed to use 'any reasonable means' to end the dispute at Lismore between Aboriginal people and the town whites and to centralise the large number of separate Koori communities of the area on Woodenbong and Stoney Gully stations.[3] At Lismore the Board had gone ahead with the creation of a reserve around the Tuncester campsite, and the Dunoon school had been transferred there during 1932. The Kooris who had earlier tried to have their children admitted to the Lismore public school included a number of the Roberts families who had left Cabbage Tree Island station after conflicts with the manager there.[4] Frank Roberts Snr was, like Duncan Ferguson, a Christian lay preacher. He wrote an accurate description of the events at Tuncester once Lismore town protests were revived in 1934. The dates on which the Board's minutes show its authorisation of Howard's actions have been inserted into Roberts's account:

> Howard, on his first visit to Tuncester, stopped the rations completely, starved the inhabitants, acting on instructions by his Board [12.9.1934; 16.11.1934] . . . He then attempted to bluff the people, saying that the Aborigines' Protection Board is forcing them to another reserve and if they don't comply with his instructions he, or his Board, would take the children away from their parents [16.11.1934]. Next step was to demolish the school at Tuncester [5.2.1936] and remove it to another settlement 52 miles away [Woodenbong, 6.5.1936]. The result is now the thirty-five children are without a school.
>
> Words cannot express what is scandalous treatment by the Destruction Board.[5]

After the segregation of the Baryulgil public school in 1935, Kooris there were similarly refused rations and instructed to move to Woodenbong.[6] Like the Tuncester Kooris, those at Baryulgil refused to move, although 29 of their children were being denied access to schooling. The numbers of children involved in both cases would have been adequate to justify establishment of an Education Department 'provisional' school, but the Department was at this stage still denying responsibility for the education of Aborigines. In view of the virtually universal segregation of public schools on the north coast, the Board's removal of the Tuncester school and its refusal to establish a school at Baryulgil must be seen as intended to enforce its confinement aims.

In 1938 both communities were still holding out against Howard's pressure and finally the Board decided that the best it was likely to

achieve was the amalgamation of Woodenbong and Stoney Gully stations themselves, a move undertaken in 1940.[7] The painful loss felt by
the Koori owners of Stoney Gully was to bear bitter fruit in the 1960s.
The Baryulgil and Tuncester communities had, for the moment, won
their battles to stay in the area of their choice, suggesting the possibility
of successful resistance in their circumstances of a prolonged conflict
and the absence of residential supervision. The victories had not been
easy, however, and at one stage in 1938 Frank Roberts appealed to
Aboriginal activists in Sydney for urgent support and the dispatch of
an organiser. The Board pressure had intensified, with further threats
to children and, Roberts wrote, 'the people are shaky'.[8] As well as
indicating the conditions for successful resistance, the northern rivers
area also demonstrated which communities were likely to become targets
for the centralisation policy. Through all these years of pressure on
Tuncester and Baryulgil, the Kooris of Tabulam appear to have remained
undisturbed, although this small residential reserve was no further from
Woodenbong than was Tuncester and was far closer than Baryulgil. At
Tabulam, however, there had been no white protests against the presence
of the Koori community.

The south-west and the south coast also escaped the centralising
activity almost completely. Shifts towards more intensive European land
use and a reduced need for labour had occurred earlier in these regions
and so the Board's operations were already geographically limited. The
south coast had in fact seen an increase in demand for casual and
seasonal labour as pea and bean-growing became more widespread. This
created an interesting situation in the one instance on the south coast
where the Protection Board did attempt to concentrate Kooris.

Worragee, a non-reserved campsite west of Nowra, provided the only
documented four-cornered conflict. Not only were there the usual
combatants, Aborigines, town institutions, and the Board, but in this
instance out-of-town employers also became involved. Nowra Council
strenuously argued in 1935 for the enforced transfer of Kooris at the
camp to Roseby Park station, 10 miles to the east. This, however,
brought the town into conflict with the interests of the local small-scale
pea farmers who depended on Koori labour. The emergence of a second
white interest group placed the Board in a dilemma as to which group
of whites it should support. An awkward compromise was eventually
proposed in which the Board agreed to pay for the cost of transport for
the concentrated Kooris from Roseby Park each week to the farms round
Worragee. In the event, the Board was spared this subsidy to the pea
farmers by the flat refusal of Kooris to move and, as they had the tacit
support of their employers, the Board took no further action.[9]

BURNT BRIDGE

The struggle for Burnt Bridge played a significant role in the developments of 1937, when the Aboriginal political movement emerged dramatically into (white) public view. The nature of this particular dispute also suggests the source of some of the dissimilarities in political aims between western and coastal Aborigines, and indicates the differences in the white groups to whom each regional movement looked for support.

Most of the high-quality alluvial land reserved for Aborigines on the north coast had been lost by 1927, so with the mid-1930s revival in the capitalist economy there was not such intense white interest in reserve land for economic use. The pressure caused by town expansion was, however, renewed. As one example, townspeople at Karuah had attempted to have what remained of the reserve there revoked in 1929, in favour of subdivision for white residential use.[10] Such plans had been laid aside during the Depression, but by 1936 the campaign for revocation had begun again. White intentions were made very clear to the Karuah Kooris, who included the Ridgeway family, prominent in the AAPA in the 1920s. The political link between north coast Kooris and white nationalists was reactivated with this renewal of pressure on reserve land, and the resulting submissions to the Premier from old supporters like J. J. Moloney, alongside some local publicity, were able to stave off revocation. They failed, however, to prevent the leasing of most of the reserve.[11]

To the general pressure from local whites on reserve land was now added the new pressure of the Protection Board's concentration and confinement policy. In August 1936 the Board decided to establish a station at Burnt Bridge, adding a new area of reserve land adjacent to the two original reserves there. This station was intended to 'absorb' the population of Urunga (who had been relocated already from the island to the mainland at Yellow Rock in 1921), the Kooris of the Greenhills camp who had given the Board so much trouble in the 1920s, the residents of the old Burnt Bridge reserves, and eventually all those on the station at Bellbrook further upstream on the Macleay. The first step for the Board was the leasing of a portion of one of the old reserves which it did not feel was necessary for the new station, thus taking financial advantage of revived white interest in land.[12]

The land to be leased was that portion on which the Davises had settled in 1893 and which was notified as reserve in 1894. It was Chris Davis, therefore, who made the first protest, writing directly to Prime Minister Lyons in January 1937 and asking for intervention to stop the leasing. Davis explained that his family had been told in 1893 that if they cleared, cultivated and continued to live on the land it would remain in their possession. The family had fulfilled these conditions, he argued, and so their rights to the land must be acknowledged. This letter set off a flurry of correspondence between the Prime Minister, the NSW Premier and the Protection Board, resulting in the proposed leasing being delayed.[13]

The Board went ahead meanwhile with its plans for the station. John Mosely was still living on the second of the old reserves, notified for him in 1898. He was by this time an elderly man, and during the Depression his son Percy had come back up to Burnt Bridge to manage his father's affairs. In 1937 the extended family group was farming corn on the reserve. As the preparations for the station were made, Percy Mosely was faced, for the third time in 23 years, with impending dispossession of land which he or his people had cleared, worked and been assured was theirs in perpetuity. Using the networks of the 1920s movement, Percy Mosely had already contacted Moloney for support before the station was officially established.[14]

Early in June 1937, the Urunga community, some Kooris from Greenhills and Bellbrook and some who had already been moved from Armidale and Walcha to Bellbrook were forced onto the new Burnt Bridge station site. There they found a few rough huts, a water supply that was totally inadequate and no sanitation at all. These people faced similar problems to those of the dislocated communities at Brewarrina, the main one being that there was no work to be had in the area. Kooris at Urunga had been among the few in the State to be admitted to work relief, but they found themselves excluded from the Kempsey system. Their only alternative was work-for-rations on the new station, which they bitterly resented.[15]

The Moselys, however, refused to move down to the central station complex, insisting that the land was theirs and denying that the manager, J. Jacobs, had authority over them. On 30 June, without prior notice, Jacobs arrived at the group of cottages and other buildings that the Mosely family had built over the years. Acting undoubtedly to intimidate the residents into moving to the main station and on the grounds that all structures erected on reserve land were legally the property of the Board, Jacobs began to demolish and remove the buildings. The following day, Percy Mosely wrote to Moloney:

> We have again been interfered with. The Manager of the A. P. Board came out on 30th June and took possession of the place and took away the W.C. from the school. Father protested and asked him who had given him permission to remove the buildings and he said we had no right to question him. When he had gone with one load, we nailed up the fence and stopped him from coming in the second time, so he went

in and brought the whole of the police force out to help him break the fence.

> After they had broken down the fence and taken away the second load, the police headed by the Inspector came down to the house and gave the manager permission to take the tank off the place. Then I asked the Inspector what his duty was here, to which he replied, 'Give less cheek or I'll lock you up'.[16]

Moloney sent an urgent telegram to the Premier, followed by a series of letters, and the issue received some sympathetic coverage in the local white press, leading to a hasty denial by the Board that it intended to evict the Moselys and other families.[17] Percy Mosely read this denial, but when Jacobs came back later in that same week to take away the church building, Mosely wrote again to Moloney, saying: 'I have read in the paper that no evictions will take place . . . but I want to know if it is not evicting to take away our tank and houses and church. I call it plain robbery!'[18]

The demolitions continued, however, with Jacobs taking whatever he wanted from the old settlement to try to make the new one habitable. The labour needed was reluctantly supplied by Kooris from the central station, forced to carry out the work for rations for themselves and their families. Among them was Jack Campbell, who had returned to the Macleay communities from which his family had fled in 1927 to escape their children's removal. Jack described himself as being young and fairly thoughtless at the time, and he did not expect that his kinsman would seriously object to the work the manager had ordered them to do. But when they began to build a fence across Mosely land, Percy Mosely had had enough. He followed the workers with a razor-sharp axe and as they erected each fence post he chopped it to pieces behind them. Losing patience even with this tactic, he went back to his house and returned riding his blue pony and firing his shotgun over the heads of the Koori workers. The men scattered and the work was stopped, although only for as long as it took Jacobs to fetch the police to arrest Mosely. Then the shaken workers were ordered back to begin the dispossession once more. Yet Mosely's grim battle for his family's land was not wasted. It left a lifelong impression on many of the younger men at the station. Campbell explained that it was this incident which revealed to him the fundamental importance of land to the older people of his community, and set him off on his life's long journey through ceremony, law and politics to learn about his country and to win it back.[19]

The repercussions of the Board's actions continued into August, as more white support was mobilised. The issues were broadened from the specific one of the seizure of the Burnt Bridge reserve to a platform of demands based on the 1920s AAPA program for land and full citizen's rights, with the Depression-stimulated addition of a call for a guaranteed basic wage or full food relief for all Aborigines.[20] After consultations with Mosely and other Kooris, Moloney put these demands to the Premier early in August on behalf of the ASP. Other letters from white north coast supporters of the same platform followed, referring to the publicity being given by the local press to Aboriginal issues.[21]

It was not only on the north coast, however, that Burnt Bridge became a focal point for organisation. North coast Kooris were in touch with those in Sydney, and Moloney maintained his contact with Sydney nationalist groups and associated individuals like Michael Sawtell, who had once been a member of the International Workers of the World but had left this anarchist ideology behind him by the 1930s. Sawtell by then regarded himself as a nationalist as much as a socialist. His interests were eclectic and ensured that his connections ranged from the far Left to the far Right of Sydney politics. Having had contact with Aborigines in the Western Australian pastoral industry, he developed this interest also in Sydney, joining the APNR, but as this organisation had little direct contact with Aborigines, Sawtell established his own links with the growing Sydney-based Aboriginal movement. Sawtell was alerted to the Burnt Bridge issue by Moloney, the nationalist connection, and probably by Sydney Kooris.[22]

From the considerable number of Kooris involved in community politics in Sydney by the mid-1930s, the individual who emerged as the most impressive public speaker and the most effective organiser was Jack Patten Jnr. He had been a child at Cumeragunja and then grown up on the highly politicised camp at Salt Pan Creek near Peakhurst in south-western Sydney, surrounded by the angry and dispossessed Andersons from Burragorang and the political refugees fleeing from the Board on the north and south coast such as the Campbells and the Pitmans. He had learnt more about the north coast experiences when he travelled in search of work into the Bandjalang country of his wife's family around Baryulgil. In the mid-1930s the Pattens were living in the inner city and Jack Patten was developing his links with Kooris at La Perouse as well as those at Salt Pan. Earlier in the year, Patten had made another trip to the north coast, travelling as far as Tabulam, and so he was well acquainted with the current concerns of north coast Kooris.[23]

Michael Sawtell had been accompanying Patten to the Domain on Sundays for some time before this, speaking with him in support of Aboriginal demands, and had introduced him to the various nationalist groups in Sydney. A link had been established between Patten and a friend of Sawtell, P. R. Stephensen, a central figure in the Australia First group.[24]

Sawtell, however, played the pivotal role in mobilising white support in Sydney because of the diversity of his connections. Early in August he wrote the first of a series of letters to the Premier on the Burnt Bridge issue, protesting at the prohibition on Aboriginal ownership of reserves (and, so Sawtell believed, on any other land) and calling for full citizen's rights for all Aborigines. He effectively communicated the north coast information to his broad range of contacts, eliciting support for Burnt Bridge Kooris not only from Australia First and the Theosophical Society (of which Sawtell was an active member) but also from J. B. Steele, a left-wing activist associated with the International Labour Defence organisation.[25]

When, late in August 1937, Percy Mosely yet again made the journey to Sydney to argue for independent Koori control over reserve land, it was Sawtell whom Moloney had organised to help Mosely gain interviews with the Board and the Premier. Mosely met only the Board's secretary and the Premier's secretary and received no more from the interviews than yet another denial that an 'eviction' was being carried out. The Board, of course, did not wish the Moselys to leave Burnt Bridge, but it wanted them to relinquish their claims to the land and remain there as subjects of managerial control. The Board pushed ahead with its station, formally absorbing the old reserve lands into the station boundaries and forcing the previously independent Koori families into subservience to its manager.[26]

It was on Burnt Bridge that the Protection Board asked Caroline Kelly, a graduate anthropology student working for Elkin, to undertake investigations in August and September 1937 to lay the groundwork for the practical incorporation of anthropological expertise into administration. Kelly became aware immediately of the extent of dissatisfaction and anger on the station, but she also recognised the extensive and pervasive influences of Dhan-gadi culture among the Kooris there. She was perceptive enough to realise that a major concern to Kooris was Protection Board power, and one of her key proposals was aimed at combating 'dissatisfaction' and 'apathy' towards the station management. This proposal was to form a 'club' or 'lodge', which would follow what anthropologists then believed to be the traditional hierarchies of kinship, with older men holding the senior positions and young men being 'initiated' into membership. There was to be a parallel, but subordinate, 'lodge' for women, run along the lines of a women's auxiliary. Kelly argued that the lodge would have a role in running the station, but final decision-making in her scheme rested firmly with the manager on all matters, including membership of the lodge itself. Advancement within the lodge hierarchy was to be a reward for 'success' in such Protection Board goals as 'the tidiness of and improvements to [a member's] house'. In what could only be called a parody of the traditional advancement by degrees of initiation, advancement in the lodge was to be by 'degrees' also, to be recorded on a paper certificate to which 'gold, silver and coloured stars' would be affixed as the member progressed. We can only be reminded of the demand Frederick Maynard had made in 1925 for an end 'to the foolish patronage which affects to regard us as children'.

The lodge was not only to be divided into hierarchical degrees, but also to be vertically segmented into 'totemic groups' which, as Kelly noted, had been 'in olden times . . . charged with the increase of the species', that is, with a central role in economic and social life. In Kelly's scheme, these 'totemic groups' would each be responsible for a particular settlement job, such as 'road maintenance, sanitary collection, amusements and the care and surveillance of young people'. Kelly suggested that anthropologists could be invaluable in supplying the 'correct terminology' for the club's organisation. She had apparently not considered that Aboriginal people could supply this, as she was proposing a role in which anthropologists were to be inserted as the indispensable mediators and interpreters between Aborigines and whites in power.

The lodge proposal was little more than a means of co-opting Aboriginal social structures to reinforce managerial control. Membership was to be only for the 'law-abiding' and could be withdrawn as a punishment for any 'offence' defined by the manager. Kelly claimed to be proposing 'an initial attempt to solve the native problem in a scientifically planned manner'. What she was in fact offering to the Protection Board was a respectably academic and attractively 'modern' justification for the old system of total managerial control.

Kelly had also recognised that land was an area of tension, although she minimised its importance. She must have witnessed much of the battle over the old reserve lands, but in her reports she merely observed that the Aborigines there suffered 'a sense of insecurity' about land tenure. In a later interview with the Premier's secretary she made no mention of the land issue at Burnt Bridge at all, concentrating instead on the problems more obvious to her: Aboriginal 'social pathology', poor housing, poor water supply and lack of employment. Kelly had failed to communicate her concern over even these issues to Burnt Bridge Kooris, however, who regarded her work with 'much amusement', Jack Patten reported, because 'our people live in the Tin Hut Age, not the Stone Age'.[27]

She did make recommendations to the Board on the land issue, however, which were endorsed by Elkin, and reflected the same fundamental weaknesses as had the lodge plan. Kelly proposed a 'training' scheme, to overcome the land 'insecurity', by which Aborigines would be allowed 'leases' over small areas of land on stations. These leases were to be conditional on the approval of the manager and would be surrendered for any misdemeanour, as defined by the manager.[28] Percy Mosely and Caroline Kelly were not talking about the same things.

Unaided, then, by the anthropologists or their associates in the APNR, but helped by an expansion of the old nationalist networks of support, the Kooris of the original Burnt Bridge reserves continued their campaign for restoration of independent control over their land. In one reflection of this continuing struggle, a member of the Davis family wrote to the newly convened Select Committee in November 1937, protesting at the seizure and now-completed leasing of the family's reserve by the Board.[29]

A partial victory was eventually won in mid-1939, when Percy Mosely and two members of the Richie family were each allowed permissive occupancies over small portions of the original reserves. Even this victory was flawed. The Board had eagerly adopted the advice offered by Kelly and Elkin and had set up only the illusion of land ownership as proposed in Kelly's scheme for 'leases'. The families' occupancies of the reserve land were strictly conditional on the continued approval of the station's manager. In 1940 Percy Mosely's persistent refusal to submit to managerial authority led to his expulsion from Burnt Bridge altogether, 'in the interests', so the Board claimed, 'of the peace and good order of the station'.[30]

The battle for Burnt Bridge went on, then, long after 1937, and continues today, but by September 1937 Burnt Bridge with its context of similar if less dramatic threats to the remaining north coast reserve land had led to a repetition of the 1920s situation. The attempt to defend independent Koori control of reserve land had again provided a focus for an emerging political organisation and had contributed to a developing alliance between Kooris and white groups, more diverse than in the 1920s but among which white nationalists were still prominent.

Unlike the AAPA, however, the as yet unnamed Sydney coastal Koori movement in the 1930s was developing in a situation where Aboriginal political support existed in other areas. It is probable that Patten was aware of the Melbourne organisation of William Cooper and the other Cumeragunja people, and there was definitely contact between the Sydney group and Murris in the west, where the Dubbo group had formalised their organisation under the name of the Aborigines Progressive Association in June 1937.

THE 'DOG ACT' POWERS IN REVIEW

The outcome of the 'Dog Act' concentrations demonstrated over and over again through the 1930s that Aboriginal people in New South

Wales strongly desired to live on or near the land which they held to be significant and which they called home. There were clear reasons for this in terms of the conditions of colonised Australia. Aboriginal people were more likely to find work and to be able to enrol their children in schools if they were known in the area than if they were new to town. Yet when Aboriginal people tried to explain then why they did not want to be shifted, and when they recall those times now, they always add another dimension to these practical reasons for not wanting to move. They talk about 'home', about their own place, their country. They include in this the desire to remain in touch with relatives and community. Even when whole social groups were forced to move together, even this was not enough to stop people 'worrying for their own place' or 'worrying for the old people' who had been buried in the lands back home.

If these days of enforced movements showed Aboriginal desires to sustain their relations with their own country, they also saw a rapidly changing Aboriginal relationship to those patches of land which were under APB managerial control. These 'missions' or 'stations' had always been home to some people, but even for those long-time residents, life on these areas could now only be seen as imprisonment. The incidents of repression, of humiliation and violence under poor managers, and the stress of rapidly deteriorating health and housing conditions from which people could not escape, all laid down experiences of pain and distress onto earlier memories of a more relaxed life on those same reserves, and onto the traditional knowledge about the land itself. Such growing ambivalence towards the mission sites meant that for some people these places have been too painful to revisit, stirring memories which cause too much corrosive anger. For others, the memories are bitter-sweet, as recollections of sadness and repression are balanced by stories of small and funny victories won behind managers' backs, or of family life sustained despite the pressures to undermine it. And for many of the people forced together on these 'concentration' sites, the experience of resisting Protection Board control was in itself an affirming process, building links between people otherwise separated by language, kin and previous land affiliation. In spite of the ambivalence, then, life on these missions in this intensely repressive time welded loyalties not only to fellow residents but to the places themselves, which grew always richer in meanings.

17

'The Big Fight': Land in Aboriginal Politics, 1937–38

This was the big fight, not with your fists but with your brains.
　　　—Pearl Gibbs, recalling the 1937–38 period in 1980

As well as the courageous attempts of individuals and communities to stay on their land, the times also catalysed another type of resistance, a resurgence of the formal politics of the 1920s. This political activity is now well known, with William Cooper's brilliantly symbolic plan for the Day of Mourning in 1938 being recognised as a turning point in capturing white public attention. The names of the activists are also now deservedly familiar, with Cooper joined by the younger Marg Tucker, Doug Nicholls, Bill Ferguson, Jack Patten and Pearl Gibbs. But the movement they led was much more than a handful of activists. Rather than a single organisation, there were three bodies, each representing a regional network of local communities linked by kinship and land affiliation as well as similar experiences of colonialism. The Australian Aboriginal League under Cooper was the best established of the three. The western communities incorporated into the Aboriginal Progressive Association looked to Bill Ferguson and Pearl Gibbs as spokespeople, while the coastal communities, although initially linked in the same organisation, were re-establishing the old 1920s Australian Aborigines Progressive Association network, and looked more consistently to Jack Patten as spokesperson. The platforms of the three organisations of the late 1930s differed from each other in ways which reflected the differences in regional experience, needs and goals.

These organisations nevertheless shared many fundamental demands and goals, and so a coalition was welcomed by them all. The Aboriginal movement burst into the white press in October 1937 with a dramatic campaign of public speeches, support meetings and press interviews. The activists were united in their attacks on the discriminatory unemployment relief system, the increases in APB powers and the appalling conditions on APB stations and reserves. So effective was this Aboriginal press campaign that for the first time the NSW Premier's attention was caught and he set up a Select Committee to inquire into the policies and administration of the APB. This public inquiry had Aboriginal representation, with Ferguson empowered to question witnesses, and it heard many Aboriginal witnesses as well as disgruntled APB staff. Yet although the stimulus for this inquiry had been the Aboriginal campaign, the activists found during 1938 that the real decisions about changes to bureaucratic practice and legal powers were to take place in Parliament and the bureaucracy. The 1937 Select Committee lapsed without reporting as white politicians withdrew their interest. A Public Service Board inquiry during 1938 was to have far more effect on changing administrative structures than the public Select Committee hearings, but this inquiry was conducted effectively behind closed doors, consulting 'experts' like APB staff and anthropologists but failing to call on any Aboriginal spokespeople or indeed any Aboriginal residents of the APB stations it visited. Not only did the Aboriginal movement find how hard it was to penetrate State government decision-making, but it was also disrupted by the trauma of conflict between coalition partners.

The members of these organisations were scattered across two States, and the distances between them were made all the more formidable because of the poverty they shared, which made travel and telephone or telegraphic communication often impossible. So the association between the three bodies depended heavily on relations between the small number of activists, and in the pressurised circumstances of the times such relations were often strained. The days of formal coalition were therefore short-lived, stretching from 1937 only until the middle of 1938, when relations between Ferguson and Patten broke down and the APA split into two bodies with the same name. Yet the division was along regional lines, not those of personal loyalty, and Ferguson continued to speak for the western communities while the coastal movement endorsed Patten as spokesperson. Informal collaboration continued long afterwards, with strong links maintained between Patten and Cooper, both from Cumeragunja, and between Cooper and Ferguson on the basis of their shared involvement with moderate left-wing Christian allies. Such affiliations and a regular flow of information ensured that in most cases the common interest of the Aboriginal membership of these movements continued to be well represented.

In each of the three organisations land had a developing role. Certainly their membership pressured them to address the issue of land. Pearl Gibbs was from Brewarrina originally, and did not have a personal experience of farming independent Aboriginal land. She recalled, however, that as soon as she joined Bill Ferguson and Jack Patten in the first week of heavy campaigning in October 1937, she met people from the coastal areas who asked her to help them search for the deeds to the lands they knew Queen Victoria had handed over to their grandparents.[1] Following the land issue through the stormy politics of the later 1930s offers a sense of its continuing underlying presence on the political agendas of activists and ordinary people, but it also shows the interaction of land issues with other matters of great urgency and significance.

The AAL was a direct outpouring of the community dissatisfaction at Cumeragunja and the desires of its network of exiles to re-establish their community's independence (see Chapter 14). It was made up largely of these exiles, though it spoke also for the needs of other Kooris in the south-west. It was unique in being led by a man who was elderly and so had personally experienced the whole process of demanding land and winning it, farming it in relative independence, and then facing the bitter years of dispossession and violent repression on the station. The AAL concentrated on the immediate distress of the Depression. Its short-term platform was for restitution of the economic rights which had seemed secure in the 1920s, then for their guarantee in a formalised way, by a government recognition of Aboriginal people's rights to civil equality, and by the achievement of sectional representation in federal Parliament. Even its plans for a short-term solution to the economic crisis involved land, however, in its appeal for the application of the new technology to Cumeragunja's farming land, to place economic independence again in the hands of the station's Aboriginal residents. The calls for equal civil and economic rights were therefore strongly entwined.

THE APA: ALLIANCES WITH THE LEFT AND THE RIGHT

The other two bodies, the two wings of the Aborigines Progressive Association, were in quite different situations. The western communities were becoming rapidly politicised as they faced the trauma of enforced moves and intensified APB repression, but their intercommunity links were only just beginning to be forged. There was general endorsement of Ferguson's leadership, but the channels for conducting community views and demands to the spokespeople had not yet become strongly developed.[2]

Bill Ferguson was a man who had always been proud of his Aboriginal ancestry, but his fair skin had meant that he had never been formally under APB control. This changed dramatically in 1936, when the amendments to the Protection Act suddenly brought Ferguson, Gibbs and many other previously independent people under the potential control of the Board. Just as significantly, Ferguson's south-western origins had given him little experience of life within Aboriginal communities living on their own land. Although his shearing had put him in touch with Aboriginal communities all over the pastoral areas of New South Wales and Victoria, his early life had not included long periods in large Aboriginal communities on pastoral camps, which had all been long dismantled in that area, nor on APB stations after Warangesda was closed down. He had had no experience of the independent farming reserves on the coast. His brother Duncan had gained a far more concentrated view of Aboriginal experience under institutional control when he took up lay preaching at Menindee. Ferguson relied initially on his brother and deputies like Gibbs, who returned to work in her home community of Brewarrina, to inform him about conditions among Aboriginal communities under APB managerial control.

Ferguson's great strength lay in his courage in leadership, his long involvement in union activity, and his developing contacts and common language with white unionists and Left political activists. He was able to force awareness of Aboriginal issues among these groups, who could then mobilise funds and support for the APA platform and for the substantial cost of organising trips over long distances. Ferguson lived in Dubbo at first, but during 1937 and 1938 he made frequent trips to Sydney, extending and consolidating his white alliances and speaking on radio and to the press about the new organisation's concerns and goals. He was therefore most conscious of the need to establish effective communication with whites in the general public and among political groups. Although he initially shared Jack Patten's contacts among white nationalists, the allies with whom Ferguson had longest association were Left-leaning Christians, the more progressive feminist groups, Left unionists and, among them, some members of the NSW branch of the CPA.

All these allies shared a deep commitment to the liberal-democratic ideal of equality of opportunity and potential between all humans. Only the communists had a party policy which recognised ethnic and cultural difference, but it was not regarded as directly relevant. The CPA had been very slow to address the issues of Aboriginal rights and of racism in Australian politics. The Soviet Comintern reprimanded the Australians over this tardiness in 1929, and by 1931 the CPA had adopted a Draft Program on Aborigines which called for equal rights for all Aboriginal people, as well as land for economic independence in remote areas and, if appropriate, for political autonomy. But this policy did not stimulate party members to make new contacts with Aboriginal people, with the notable exceptions of the journalist Norman Jeffries and the Dubbo Unemployed Workers group, whose Aboriginal alliances arose from prior personal contacts. Instead the CPA in New South Wales tended to wait until Aboriginal people contacted them, as did Ferguson and his other union allies.[3]

The CPA ideas were, however, very important in formulating white motions and demands which endorsed the Aboriginal activists' campaign in 1937 and 1938. An important example was the meeting of the NSW Labour Council addressed by Ferguson in October 1937. After Ferguson's impassioned speech, a motion of support was moved by Tom Wright, a member of the CPA and secretary of the Sheet Metal Workers' Union. This motion reiterated almost verbatim the 1931 CPA Draft Platform on Aborigines, but significantly the only sections left out were those in the original which called for independent Aboriginal control of land and which stressed rights for Aborigines which were separate and distinct from those of whites. The sections retained were those which stressed equal and identical rights for all Australians regardless of race.[4] It was clear that white left-wing supporters regarded the issue of special rights to land as relevant only to the more remote areas of the Northern Territory and Western Australia, not to New South Wales and Victoria.

Bill Ferguson was suspicious of any whites who thought they could dictate to Aboriginal people on what they should be demanding. He distrusted Jack Patten's nationalist allies and he was angered when the CPA complained that the Aboriginal movement was making the error of 'separatism' when it insisted that its organisations were for Aboriginal members only and that the Day of Mourning meeting was open only to Aboriginal people.[5] Nevertheless, the general Left interest in equality of treatment, rights and opportunity for all Australians, regardless of biology or skin colour, found deep agreement with Ferguson's public stance and with his past experience. Ferguson made important statements on land during 1938, but it was only when he began to take a more active role in organising trips to the north-west early in 1939 that his political demands broadened to include acknowledgment of cultural differences and to increase his emphasis on the need for a special policy on land.

Ferguson may have felt pressure from white allies to tailor the public expression of APA demands to fit the ideology they recognised and endorsed. But there was a far more powerful force acting on Aboriginal activists in the 1930s to push them into altering their public statements. This force was the new element in the political opposition which Aboriginal people faced which had not been effectively present in the 1920s. The entry of anthropologists into the public debate over Aboriginal policy, with their expressed goal of becoming accepted into administrative roles, altered the language and the issues in that debate. The arguments of Professor Elkin and his protégé Caroline Kelly were that anthropological studies ensured practitioners had special skills in interpreting the current conditions and future needs of Aboriginal people. The attempts Kelly made to demonstrate such interpretive skills had led only to a childish parody of traditional knowledge at Burnt

Bridge in 1937, but the Protection Board had been delighted to have someone come up with a rationalisation for 'concentration' and a blueprint for future 'training'. The adoption of Kelly's proposals convinced Aboriginal activists that the anthropologists wielded real power.

Kelly's work attracted many feminists, who rallied strongly to demand change in the APB during 1937, but remained committed to professional expert administration over Aboriginal people. Mary Bennett was almost alone among feminists in crossing political lines to support the Aboriginal activists on the Day of Mourning in their call for Aboriginal control of their own affairs.[6]

Elkin was on many occasions dismissive of the existence of Aboriginal traditional culture in New South Wales, suggesting it had 'shattered' under the impact of so many years of intense colonial experience, but this did not stop him arguing that anthropologists were better able to interpret and administer Aboriginal people than they were themselves, in New South Wales just as much as in the more remote areas. Elkin's position was simply that New South Wales Aborigines were still in some sense 'traditional' and therefore must be controlled by those people who understood them best, the anthropological 'experts'. As he commented in relation to Papua New Guinea as well as Australia, 'the more we know of these peoples, the better can we govern them'.[7]

With such formidable opposition, the Aboriginal activists were extremely reluctant to make public assertions of the strength and continuity of any aspect of traditional life. They were demanding the abolition of all special administrative controls and they feared that if they admitted the continuity of tradition in New South Wales this would lay them open to the argument that they needed anthropological expertise to manage them until they had been educated to make the transition to a 'modern' lifestyle. Their relations with the anthropologists were hostile and tense. Kelly's questions at the 1937 Select Committee inquiry into the APB had virtually all been aimed at establishing that strong traditional lifestyles continued to be present among New South Wales Aboriginal communities, and in particular that at Menindee. Ferguson was intensely aware of the way traditional affiliations to land and kin had increased Koori and Wiimpatja distress in the enforced concentrations at Menindee. Yet he was so suspicious of the use to which the anthropologists would put information on traditional beliefs that he refused to answer any of Kelly's questions, and rejected contemptuously her plaintive cry, 'Mr Ferguson does not understand that I am trying to help him'.[8] Ferguson and Patten attacked the anthropologists' interventions in their pamphlets and newspapers, arguing that these white experts used any evidence of 'tradition' among contemporary Aboriginal people as an excuse for continued white control and interference. At first they treated the anthropologists with derision. Then, as it became clear that Elkin and Kelly were negotiating with the NSW government to become a part of the restructured APB, Patten's tone reflected his bitterness: 'We are not savages, sinners or criminals. There is no need for anthropologists, clergymen or police to look after us specially'.[9]

The confident and proud public assertions of the value of traditional civilisation which Fred Maynard had been able to make in the 1920s were therefore not to be heard in the 1930s political statements. This made it difficult to argue for any rights to land which arose from prior possession based on traditional law and from continuing traditional affiliation. Ferguson tended to campaign for Aboriginal people to be able to enter closer- and soldier-settlement schemes on terms of equal opportunity with whites, rather than on the basis of prior rights or affiliation to particular areas of land. His awareness of the older argument was made clear in his important statement at the Day of Mourning meeting, in which he referred to the existence already of practical skills in farming held by 'most of our people' in New South Wales and demanded they be given secure ownership of adequate land for agricultural development in 'the land that our fathers and mothers owned from time immemorial'.[10] On all other occasions during 1937 and 1938, however, he was very cautious about any acknowledgment of tradition or rights of prior ownership.

* * *

The eastern coastal wing of the Aboriginal Progressive Association had a different history from the western wing, and its spokesperson too was a man with a different background and alliances. Jack Patten was younger than both Cooper and Ferguson, but his experiences in the Salt Pan Creek camp of political activists and refugees meant that he was already aware of the independent farming reserves and the brutal dispossessions of the 1920s when he married Selena Avery, a Baryulgil woman from near Grafton. This strengthened even further his links with the traditions of north coast land demands and assertive political organisation. On the basis of these regional affiliations, Patten gained consistent support from the nationalist allies of the old AAPA and the more radical nationalists of the emerging Australia First movement.

Australia First offered new forms of support for the Aboriginal activists. The most important link was P. R. Stephensen, a publisher whose strongly radical right-wing nationalism had led him into political and economic partnership with W. B. Miles, an affluent man who sympathised strongly with the social and racial policies of the German Nazi Party.[11] Both Stephensen and Miles were openly racist, advertising their anti-Semitic and anti-Asian views in the *Publicist*, a magazine which Stephensen edited for Australia First. Indeed Stephensen used biology as a strong theme in much of his social analysis, arguing for example that there had been 'a decline in physiological standards in the Australian community' which had led to 'mental decadence'.[12] Yet the Australia First movement was fiercely anti-imperialist too. Stephensen's university experience in England had led him not only to shift his politics from Left to Right but had left him with a virulent Anglophobia, which was shared by Miles. Stephensen had returned to Australia intent on exploring the particular identity of his nation, and his *Foundations of Australian Culture* celebrated the development of a unique Australian literature. His Anglophobia and anti-imperialism, however, forced him away from a biological explanation of national charactistics towards the strand within nationalist thought which held to environmental determinism. He began to argue that it was the impact on its inhabitants of the climate and natural surroundings which created the unique characteristics of the nation, and his slogan became 'Place Not Race'.[13]

Stephensen, like the 1920s nationalists, wanted icons to represent the unique qualities of Australia. The emblem he chose for *Foundations* was the silhouette of an Aboriginal man with winged heels, spear and headband, an indigenous Mercury. His interest in Aboriginal people was strongly shared by another sympathiser with the Australia First movement, Xavier Herbert, whose *Capricornia* Stephensen published and publicised. These two nationalists went beyond the search for mute symbols of an Australian nation. They were interested in both contemporary social relations and a traditional Aboriginal culture which had a primary interest in place and land. The cultural meanings Aboriginal people had developed about this 'place' they saw as shaping the new Australian nation. They were far more receptive to Aboriginal demands for special rights to land based on assertions of prior rights and spiritual or cultural associations, and in fact Stephensen is an example of the shift in white public interest from the outer forms of Aboriginal life to its inner meanings. He reflected an assertive and chauvinistic nationalism which nevertheless desired not to erase the Aboriginal presence as the Victorian Historical Memorials Committee had done, but to embrace and draw on the presence and knowledge of Aboriginal landowners. The rising interest in Aboriginal philosophy can be seen in the anthropology of the period as well, but although the nationalists had a strong inclination to sympathise with traditional lifestyles, they were not trying to salvage or restore a pristine traditionalist past. In the same way that J. J. Moloney had come to recognise and defend contemporary Aboriginal demands in the 1920s, Stephensen moved to acknowledge and try to improve Aboriginal contemporary life.

Stephensen's involvement with Aboriginal people went beyond opportunism. He was heavily influenced by the Australian literature of the bush, and he made frequent trips into inland and north-western New South Wales, celebrating these trips in the *Publicist* and in his regular broadcasts on 2SM as romances with the Australian bushman and the Australian land. What he did not publicise was that he made increasingly frequent contacts with Aboriginal people on these trips; the anonymous 'Traveller' who exposed the scandal of the Collarenebri school exclusion in the August and September 1938 editions of the Aboriginal-controlled *Australian Abo Call* was Stephensen himself.[14]

His closest Aboriginal friendship was with Monty Tickle, a Wiradjuri man from Cowra who testified at the Select Commission hearings in November 1937 about conditions there, including the refusal of work relief and the APB prosecution of Aboriginal families for 'abducting' their own children as a way of forcing them back to the managed station.[15] Stephensen's personal papers are dotted with photos of Tickle and his wife Mary, together with Stephensen and his wife Winifred, depicting the two couples enjoying apparently numerous picnics in bushland settings, perhaps at the Stephensen's 'country place'.

One wing of the APA was therefore supported by white left-wing groups which included both moderate ALP members and members of the CPA. The other wing was supported not only by moderate nationalists, who were aligned with the centre and right of the ALP, but by extreme right-wing nationalists, who had expressed sympathies with the Nazi Party in Germany. Hardly surprisingly, the Aboriginal activists had to face not only internal tensions, but conflicts between their white allies. In general the tension between Right and Left supporters was restrained, only bursting destructively into public view over the Cumeragunja strike in 1939. This tension may, however, have had effects long after the collapse of the Right extremists during the Second World War. Until late in the 1950s there continued to be a mutual suspicion between New South Wales communists and Aboriginal activists, which was significantly at odds with the warm relationships in Victoria. At the same time this may have strengthened the emphasis on equity and civil rights issues among all Left allies because traditional cultural assertion and land matters had become tainted by the Australia First involvement.

A NATIONAL POLICY

Despite the pressures of its diverse allies and opponents, the Aboriginal political coalition of 1937 was still faced with the monumental burden of economic discrimination and the savage reduction in civil rights which Aboriginal citizens had suffered since the 1920s. The statements and

policies announced during that year and early in 1938 reflected the
urgency of a situation in which Aboriginal people were facing enforced
moves, indefinite imprisonment, starvation and appalling health, without adequate food or clinical or public health facilities. The documents
most often publicised then and later were these initial urgent demands
of the joint movement, and in particular the pamphlet *Aborigines Claim
Citizens Rights!* written by Bill Ferguson and Jack Patten to publicise the
coming Day of Mourning in January 1938.

The urgent pressures of the 1920s had been the loss of people's
homes and land, as well as the removal of children. In the 1930s few
revocations were occurring and almost all of the independent lands had
already been lost, so the short-term focus of these political movements
was not on the land issue but on the denial of unemployment benefits,
the rapid widening of the net of APB control around ever more
Aboriginal people, and the increasing severity of its powers, coupled
with the deteriorating health conditions of those many people so
recently imprisoned under the new APB powers. The activists demanded
the abolition of the Board and an end to all forms of discrimination.

Yet each of the three coalition partners in the Aboriginal movement
distinguished between their urgent short-term goals and their longer
aims. When their consciously long-term policy statements are examined,
it becomes clear that what had occurred during the 1930s was a
relocation of the land issue, from short-term demand to long-term goal.
The AAL had of course retained land matters very close to the centre
of attention on both its short- and long-term platforms. Both the
western and coastal APA groups took part in formulating a policy
statement to be presented at meetings organised with the NSW Premier
and the Prime Minister during January and February 1938. This joint
statement was intended to be relevant to all States, and was significantly
different from the many statements of protest which each of the activists
had made in the preceding months. It demanded the abolition of all
State Protection Boards and the recision of all existing legislation, and
insisted on a unified national policy under the control of the federal
government. It proposed the establishing of a federal Ministry of
Aboriginal Affairs, in which the minister would be advised by six people,
at least three of whom were to be Aboriginal people nominated by the
AAL and APA.[16]

The national policy was to be directed toward two aims. The first
was the achievement of full citizen status by all Aboriginal people in
the Commonwealth in all spheres, namely in education, labour awards
and conditions, health, housing, rights to ownership of property, control
of personal savings and receipt of Commonwealth and State welfare
benefits. All the elements of this first policy aim were therefore directed

towards the attainment of equal and identical rights with white Australians. The second aim was land. The joint statement called for a 'Special Policy' of land settlement, based on the unique right of Aboriginal people as prior owners of the land but to be implemented on lines recognisable to Europeans, such as the Soldier and Immigrant Settlement schemes. There was a continuing mobilisation of agrarian mythology as well as a reference to past Aboriginal experience of farming reserves in this policy, with agriculture being proposed as the main form of land 'development'. The statement called for financial support for 'expert tuition' and establishment expenses so that Aboriginal families could become self-supporting. This call for land settlement was, however, placed firmly alongside a call for the retention of existing reserves as 'sanctuaries' for those Aboriginal people who were unable (because of past government 'neglect') or unwilling to take part in the general Australian community and economy. This allowed at least the suggestion of an alternative to European agriculture as a way for Aboriginal owners to use the land.

After the split with Patten in April 1938, Bill Ferguson and Pearl Gibbs worked most closely through their white Left allies in Sydney and Dubbo as they tried to maintain pressure on the NSW government to achieve Aboriginal goals. In the attempt to maximise white support, they both became the captives of the interests of these white organisations. While both Ferguson and Gibbs strongly endorsed the causes championed by the white Left, which had been focusing for some years on racism in the United States and on discrimination and poor conditions for Aboriginal people in the Northern Territory, they spent far more time during 1938 speaking to white groups on these distant issues than they did in raising awareness further about the New South Wales crisis. More significantly, they had no time in 1938 for rural organising trips of the kind Gibbs had made to Brewarrina in December 1937, when she took back home the press clippings of the October campaign, and watched them passed around so eagerly among the Murris 'concentrated' on the mission. The western APA did not address itself to long-term policy again until it had been forced late in 1938 to recognise that the NSW government was not going to involve Aboriginal activists in the process of reforming the Protection Board. Only then did Ferguson and Gibbs begin again to travel among their western constituents, and their statements from that time began to show the impact of the concerns expressed to them.

In December 1938 the first rural meeting of the western APA for some time took place at Talbragar, the riverside Aboriginal reserve near Dubbo. The meeting moved for support for the agricultural development of the three suitable reserves near Dubbo: Talbragar itself, Nanima at

Wellington and Burra Bee Dee at Coonabarabran. Then, early in 1939, Ferguson made a series of trips among north-western communities from Weilmoringle in the west through Brewarrina to Moree and Boggabilla in the east. Brewarrina and Tibooburra people took part in organising and speaking during these trips, and so they became better acquainted with the similarities in experience between their own areas and others like Moree and Boggabilla where concentration had occurred. The expansion of structure and policy was obvious by April 1939, when the western APA held its second annual general meeting in Dubbo. Over 60 Murris attended, even though wet weather had made the blacksoil roads from Collarenebri and Moree impassable. The policy arising from this meeting reflected more accurately and specifically the current needs of western communities, criticising not only APB control, its inadequate rations and its power over Aboriginal children, but also white town actions in segregating schools and hospitals. Apart from their intrinsic injustice, these issues were the very real weapons the Protection Board and town authorities had held at the heads of Aboriginal families in the north-west to force them to submit to concentration.[17]

The most substantial development was that the issue of land as it affected Murris in pastoral areas was finally addressed. For the first time, the western APA addressed the devastation caused by the 'Dog Act' concentrations and demanded a guarantee from the government that Aboriginal people would have security of residence in the area of their choice. It insisted that there be an end to the leasing of reserves, that more land be added to enlarge existing reserve areas, which would then be the basis for a housing scheme similar to the government's Homes for Unemployed. The reserves were to be handed over to their Murri residents, free of all APB supervision, and then Murris were to be helped to build 'proper' serviced houses which were to be transferred on a low-rental/purchase scheme, while the land of the reserves was to become the property of the Murri home occupants.[18]

The coastal APA under Jack Patten had a more rapid expansionary progress during 1938. Funding from a skeptical W. B. Miles, for a strictly limited time only, had allowed Patten to continue the movement's broadsheet, *The Australian Abo Call*. Stephensen provided editorial assistance, but had surprisingly little influence on the *Abo Call* when this is compared to the strident racism and general style of the *Publicist*. Patten seems to have been able to retain a firm control over the paper.[19] It gave him not only a vehicle to publicise the movement's goals and strategies but also a forum for interaction with the APA's growing membership.

In June 1938 Patten set out on a major organising trip, travelling with two Kooris from La Perouse and a white friend, well known to

241

them through his marriage to an Aboriginal woman. Sharing the driving of the old car this white friend owned, they set out to Newcastle, where they spoke to a meeting of white railway workers. After this, as they headed north, they concentrated on organising meetings among Aboriginal people. The group stopped in at least ten towns along the coast, and the APA membership grew as most of the people who formed the politically active nucleus of each community joined up. Many of these new members were from families which had been active in the 1920s AAPA, while others were involved in current struggles with either local white towns or the Protection Board. Percy Mosely joined, as did Herbert Davis of Rolland's Plains and some of the Kooris from Urunga and Bellbrook who had been concentrated at Burnt Bridge. The response from the far northern rivers areas where towns and the Board were exerting pressure was just as strong. By the end of July, the *Abo Call* could name 118 active members in nineteen New South Wales communities, twelve of which were on the north coast, three on the south coast and the others, including Moonahcullah and Cumeragunja, in the south-west.[20]

The coastal APA expanded further when the organising party in June crossed the State border, putting its national perspective into practice and gaining members in five Queensland communities. Just as significantly, the organisers met not only with Kooris but with Islanders living at Tweed Heads, 'extending them a hand in friendship' and promising to alter the constitution of the APA to include them in its membership. This was the first time an Aboriginal organisation had formally recognised that South Sea Islanders faced similar pressures from white Australians.

The organising party brought with them a revised version of the long-term policy which had been formulated in January. This confirmed the fundamental dual strands of the first, but made important points. First, the Aboriginal demand for equal representation and voting parity on any new board was reasserted, a point on which some white allies were retreating at this time. Second, the roles of the three white members of the APA-proposed Board were to be strictly defined: one was to be an expert in education, one in health and the third was to be a specialist in land settlement. This gives some indication of the importance the coastal APA attached to the question of land restoration and management in what it hoped would be the immediate future. This policy was discussed and endorsed by each of the Koori communities visited and then adopted by a general meeting of the APA in Sydney on 16 June. With a strong mandate from at least one region, the coastal APA then approached Government and Opposition members for support. J. T. Lang, then Opposition leader, seems to have had good relations with Patten and the coastal group, and he asked a series of questions in Parliament on matters they raised with him. He did not, however, prove particularly helpful in the matter of pressing Aboriginal views about reform of the Protection Board, while the Government refused to meet the Aboriginal delegation at all.[21]

The *Abo Call* was an extremely important vehicle for the movement, distributed far more widely than its organisers could travel and enabling contact with Aboriginal people in the Northern Territory and in remote areas of Queensland. After the first edition, much of it was devoted to readers' letters and their reports of news items. These pages opened up the slogan 'full citizen's rights' to reveal the range of issues which it in fact represented. Direct conflict with whites over school segregations and over pressure on reserve lands, the refusal to allow Aboriginal people to control their own family endowment payments and the galling denial of access to alcohol were all raised alongside personal accounts of conflict with the police and the Protection Board. This flow of information in turn stimulated the coastal APA to lobby on a wider range of issues than that of the restructuring of the Board. The Education Department, for example, became a focus of protest over its continued support for the segregation of public schools. Significantly, as the circulation of the *Abo Call* extended beyond the coastal movement's original membership, the letters coming in from western regions began to expand the APA vision to incorporate concerns and goals which were appropriate to those places, as well as to draw out the areas of common struggle across geographic boundaries.

This dynamic can be traced in the reporting of the pressures on a series of communities over the time the paper was being published. In the June edition, the situation at Bellbrook on the upper Macleay River was described in letters sent from that community. The Board was exerting pressure on the families remaining at Bellbrook by limiting ration issues and insisting that conditions would only be improved if they moved downriver to the 'central' station at Burnt Bridge. The *Abo Call* protested at 'this moving of our people, like pieces on a draughts board', and pointed out that Bellbrook Kooris 'do not want to be moved from the district where they were born'. Bellbrook people already knew of the lack of employment and poor water supply at Burnt Bridge and they demanded that 'instead of being moved from our own place, we want conditions to be improved here, on the spot'.[22] This was very similar to the arguments raised by Angledool Murris against their enforced move in 1936, but the coastal movement was not so conscious yet of western conditions.

The more immediately obvious parallels with Bellbrook were the situations at Baryulgil and Tuncester, which were pointed out in the

July edition of the *Abo Call*. The additional element in both places was the segregation of the local public schools; the paper drew very clearly the connection between the segregations and the Board's ability to exert pressure by threatening to remove children. Its positive proposal, other than desegregation of the schools, was that 'the Government make good land available to Aboriginal settlers in the farming districts'. Using the example of the Kooris currently farming cane on Cabbage Tree Island to 'provide an answer to the lie that Aborigines do not become good farmers', the *Abo Call* asserted that ' "Farms for Aborigines" is our cry'.[23] In the August and September editions the *Abo Call* ran its leaders on the similar situation in Collarenebri. It reported that the Collarenebri Murris were well aware of the events at Angledool and Brewarrina, and so, like the Kooris at Baryulgil and Tuncester, they did not want to be forced under Board control 'to be bullied and half-starved'.[24]

In all four places Aborigines were demanding not only the right to be free of Board control but the right to have secure residence in localities significant to them. Just as Bellbrook was 'our own place', Collarenebri was the 'home town' of the Murris there; it was their 'birthplace' and the location of their elaborate burial ground. In addition to the call for farming land in agricultural areas, these final editions of the *Abo Call* stressed the rights of Aboriginal people to have secure residential land in the area of their choice. In this way the paper's position on land expanded to include the rights of association with traditional country alongside access to farming land, which gave this regional movement a platform which finally addressed the land concerns of Aboriginal people across the State.

In an attempt to support the communities under pressure, Patten wrote to the Minister of Education as well as to the Premier, pointing out that the threats to Aboriginal parents at Collarenebri and Tuncester over their children and their place of residence were a direct consequence of the school segregations.[25] In August the *Abo Call* offered encouragement to Aboriginal people facing such pressures: 'Pending new legislation, we advise all Aborigines to resist intimidation . . . and to refuse to be "bluffed" into moving away from their present homes to Government Reserves'.

The 'new legislation' was still pending when the paper went out of existence after its September edition. W. B. Miles had refused to give further funding, and Aboriginal community resources had not proved sufficient to support both the newspaper and the organising costs. All the Aboriginal organisations were constantly short of cash. The May organising trip of the coastal group had raised a fair sum of money from sales of the newspaper, for example, but when they returned to Sydney the car they had used was repossessed and the next organising trip had to be made by train. Functioning from April to September, the *Abo Call* had provided not only a record of attempts to influence government, but with each edition had reflected the increasingly bitter disillusion of the Aboriginal movement as it was realised how profoundly the government was intending to ignore Aboriginal proposals. By August Aborigines had become extremely anxious and the *Abo Call* condemned 'the "skilled lobbyists" like the anthropologists and missionaries' who were 'pestering Members of Parliament' and whom the government was indeed consulting at the same time as it was refusing to meet any Aboriginal delegations. By September, although there had been no government statement of its decision, there had been enough hints given by Chief Secretary Gollan to the press to indicate that there was to be no Aboriginal consultation about or representation on the new Board. It had also been made clear that the anthropologists had secured themselves a role in the NSW administration and were to be represented by Elkin.

Despite its pessimism concerning the new legislation, the *Abo Call* closed on a determined note, announcing that Patten and other members of the APA would continue organising and recruiting. Patten appears to have been strengthening his contacts with his father's people at Cumeragunja and he was able to gain press coverage in December 1938 to expose the extremely bad physical conditions there. He stressed the land issue, pointing out that a major portion of this potentially productive reserve was still under lease to a white man, despite the skills and the continuing desperate need for employment among the Aboriginal residents.[26] Patten's involvement with Cumeragunja deepened, and he went down there to take a more active role in events. This exposed a problem in the structure of the organisation, which had allowed a concentration of either the skills or the contacts for publicity in Patten's hands. No other coastal APA member emerged as spokesperson for the organisation to give a response when the final announcement was made early in 1939 about the government's plans to modify the Protection Board and rename it the Welfare Board, although the *Abo Call* had quite accurately predicted that the new Board would retain, and indeed strengthen, all the most repressive legal mechanisms of the 1936 'Dog Act' amendments. Even more serious, there was no alternative APA spokesperson left in Sydney to mobilise supportive press coverage for the escalating crisis at Cumeragunja, in which Patten himself was playing a significant role.

While the western and coastal APA groups had undergone a widening of membership and vision during the difficult years of 1937 and 1938, the Cumeragunja-based AAL, which had had the most clearly developed and the most wide-ranging policy from 1936, went through a rapid contraction of its focus of interest and its demands on the NSW government during 1938. In mid-1937 the AAL and the station residents at Cumeragunja had had good reason to believe that the manager replacing the moderately well respected Danvers would assist them with the building of new houses, with the installation of a pump to improve the water supply and with the fulfilment of their long-held hopes for renewed agricultural development.

Within months such beliefs had all been dispelled, the government promises all found to be empty. The saga of Cumeragunja was moving rapidly into its next, tragic, act.

18

The Cumeragunja Strike, 1939

The new manager, A. J. McQuiggan, had arrived at Cumeragunja in 1937, transferred to cover up his cruelty to the boys at Kinchela Home (see Chapters 11 and 14). McQuiggan brought to Cumeragunja only arrogance, threats and violence. The new 'houses', rather than an improvement on the old four-roomed cottages, were found to be two-roomed slums, built of mill-rubbish, with tin rather than brick chimneys and wooden shutters instead of windows. There had been no improvements to either the water supply or the sanitation and not the slightest indication of a renewal of farming. Despite the heavy AAL involvement in lobbying both federal and State governments and in planning the Day of Mourning, William Cooper felt it necessary early in January 1938 to pass on the Cumeragunja protests to the NSW Premier, pointing out that 'while all the papers are talking housing reform, the natives are getting hovels'.[1]

On 16 January a young Cumeragunja child was diagnosed as suffering from polio, then prevalent among the white population and receiving much publicity. This diagnosis seemed to confirm all the fears of the Cumeragunja residents about the dangers to health posed by the station conditions, and many began preparations to leave, both in protest and for safety. McQuiggan stopped this movement only with the aid of seven police officers and the declaration of a state of quarantine. The incident, significantly, was portrayed in the white press as a result of irrational 'panic', caused by interpretations of earlier press coverage of the disease. The implication was that Aboriginal people were prone to groundless fears because they were unable to understand western medical explanations and so acted out of 'primitive' simple-mindedness. McQuiggan took the opportunity to assure the public that the station residents 'live in their own homes contentedly' and 'have similar educational, religious and social facilities as residents of an ordinary country town'. No further cases of polio were diagnosed and by the time the quarantine was lifted the Cumeragunja people had decided against a walk-off but appealed to the AAL to intensify the protests on their behalf.[2]

Cooper had been informed by this time from the Premier's Department that the new 'houses' were the Board's 'standard design', which had been approved by the government architect, and that the station's sanitation was considered satisfactory. The next letter Cooper wrote to the Premier was at the end of March, after the disappointment of the federal government rejection of the AAL petition and after further appeals from Cumeragunja. Cooper's bitterness was reflected in his strongly worded letter, which scathingly pointed to the difference between the Board's 'standard design' house and those at the 'show window' at La Perouse. He went on to attack the whole attitude of the government, which he said was 'usually one of domination and oppression, of take it or leave it, and the last ones to be considered are the natives themselves and their feelings are not considered at all'.[3] Finally he invited the Premier to inspect Cumeragunja for himself but warned that he should not expect to be able to speak freely to the station residents as they had reason to fear retaliation from McQuiggan.

Cooper did not receive even an acknowledgment to this letter, and in May, in response to more pleas for help from Cumeragunja, he visited the station to find it in a disastrous condition, as he wrote to the Premier immediately on his return to Melbourne.[4] Cooper had heard innumerable complaints from the station's residents, but the one he was most angry about was that the pumping plant, promised ten months before, had still not been installed. The problem of water supply for even domestic use had been acute in 1937, but in the drought conditions of 1938 the Cumeragunja water shortage had created a very real emergency. Drinking water was contaminated and there was no feed or water for the stock, with the result that the few milking cows were no longer capable of supplying milk for the children. The residents were in extreme physical distress, all of which, Cooper pointed out furiously, could have been avoided if the government had kept its promise to install the pumping plant in mid-1937. He demanded the immediate installation of a pumping plant and urgent aid.

Cooper did not, this time, write merely one letter. As he had received no reply to his last letter in which he addressed a number of issues, he suggested that it might 'facilitate investigation' for the officials if he confined himself to one issue per letter. So on 23 May, he wrote four letters, each in uncharacteristic and sarcastically simple language. One addressed the problem of the water shortage, another the problems of sanitation, the third condemned the 'building of slums' on the station and the fourth demanded an end to all discriminatory legislation. These May letters were acknowledged, but not until mid-July. The Premier's Department asked the Chief Secretary for information a week after this again, but had received no reply at all by mid-November.[5]

By this time, however, conditions on Cumeragunja had become even worse. There had been no improvement in physical facilities, and relations between the station residents and McQuiggan had reached irretrievable breakdown. The lack of response to Cooper's letters on their behalf had convinced Cumeragunja Kooris that they must take matters into their own hands, although they maintained close contact with the AAL. They therefore formulated a petition stating their grievances and, knowing the risk they faced of retaliation, a 'very representative' number of Kooris signed it.

The main demands were for the immediate dismissal of the McQuiggans because of their arrogant, offensive and abusive behaviour and for an urgent inquiry into the conditions and management of the station. The rest of the petition was a ventilation of all the complaints which Cooper had already relayed to the Premier, including those of long standing like the continued paucity of rations and the denial of control over family endowment. Cooper sent a supporting letter to corroborate each of the charges made in the petition and added, on McQuiggan: 'The people are frightened of him at any time, for we have been cowed down so long, but the fact that he carries a rifle about with him makes matters worse. We have been decimated by the rifle among other things and fear the result of one being carried now'.[6]

The original copy of the petition is not available to give an exact number of signatories, because the Cumeragunja people still had some faith in the use of the proper administrative channels and so they sent their petition to the Protection Board in mid-November. They received no acknowledgment and no direct reply. The Board did what it always had done in such circumstances and sent the petition immediately to the manager of the station from which it had come. The Cumeragunja people first learned that the Board had received their petition when McQuiggan pasted it up on the door of the station office and then 'invited those who wished to remove their names to do so'.[7]

Cooper's response was intense anger. He wrote to the Premier, tersely describing the events and saying:

> I submit that this is not in accordance with British tradition and would not be done for a fully white community and in itself constitutes a further grievance . . . We are not an enemy people and we are not in Nazi concentration camps. Why should we then be treated as though we are?[8]

Cooper was a man who believed in working through the correct bureaucratic procedures and who had shown, by the very number of the letters he had written to governments, that he believed that reasoned argument and presentation of the facts would lead to equitable solutions. He probably believed personally in the ideals of 'British justice', in addition to his political judgment that exposure of the discrepancy between those

249

ideals and the actual practice of British settlers in Australia could awaken the conscience of whites. Cooper's situation late in 1938 was symptomatic of the effects of the pressures facing the whole Aboriginal movement.

In 1937 both Ferguson and Patten had been calling for the immediate and total abolition of white boards of control. During 1938 both had been forced, by government intransigence or by the pressure of white supporters, to limit their demands to lobbying over the composition of the inevitable 'new' Board. First the coastal movement and, somewhat later, the western movement were able to counter this pressure by the expansion of their community base. The AAL, however, had always been tied far more closely to a single community in New South Wales than had the other two movements. That one community suffered a classic example of the rejection of their 'rising expectations'. As Cooper himself had said, 'we were being encouraged to expect something decent, but it appears that we are to be dehumanized'.[9]

The conditions and, more importantly, the hopes at Cumeragunja deteriorated so rapidly that the AAL became entirely absorbed in the urgent and immediate needs of that community. Few of Cooper's letters during 1938 refer to any long-term policy or even to the agricultural development of Cumeragunja itself. Instead they refer increasingly to the day-to-day injustices occurring under McQuiggan's rule. Cooper, who in 1936 had been proposing imaginative, constructive plans for the positive and independent development of all Aboriginal communities, had been forced by late 1938 to limit his vision and focus all his energies on the attempt to have one manager on one station dismissed.

For many members of the Cumeragunja community, McQuiggan's use of the petition to intensify the victimisation of those who had signed it marked the end of their confidence in Cooper's methods, although certainly not in Cooper himself. They began to consider other methods of forcing the government to concede to their demands. Talk of a protest walk-off was revived and contact was made with Jack Patten, whose brother George and other family members were living on the station. Patten was asked to take the more radical step of generating publicity in the white press about Cumeragunja. The coverage he achieved early in December 1938 effectively exposed the alarmingly high death rate on the station, particularly among infants. Significantly, however, Patten's focus in his press statement on the issue of the leasing of the reserve showed that for his Cumeragunja correspondents, even 30 years and McQuiggan's intolerable behaviour had not driven the basic land dispute very far below the surface.

Talk of a walk-off had intensified after McQuiggan's victimisation of the petition signatories and as conditions worsened with an increased population over the holiday period. Jack Patten had arrived at the station late in January, and had stayed with relatives there. By all accounts, including that of McQuiggan, Patten had spent his time explaining the political campaign of the last year and its failure. He had also described the powers gained by the Board under the 1936 amendments, which included the power to confine Aborigines against their will on reserves. This was a power which had not yet been exercised in the south-west as had been done in the west and north of the State, and there can be no doubt that a simple description of events at Angledool or Burnt Bridge would have been alarming. Patten himself could only have been pessimistic by this stage about any chance of government response to formal Aboriginal proposals, and his analysis of the situation may well have proved the final argument for Cumeragunja people that they must take direct action to force even a hearing of their demands.[10]

The hard decision to make the walk-off was taken on the morning of Friday, 3 February. This was the form of protest attempted a year before, and its enormous symbolic significance cannot be overstated. In walking away from Cumeragunja, the people were walking away from land they had been fighting to regain for 30 years. At this early stage, however, few could have believed they would have to walk away forever.

As Cumeragunja people prepared to leave, Patten went to Barmah to telegraph an urgent message to the NSW Premier demanding an immediate inquiry into McQuiggan's 'intimidation, starvation [and] victimisation', which, he said, was the cause of the protest.[11] McQuiggan, as he had done a year before, called the Moama police and when Patten returned, he and his brother George were arrested for 'inciting' Aborigines to leave the station, an activity which had, of course, only been made an offence by the enactment of the 1936 amendments.

The walk-off continued. Two hundred of the 300 Cumeragunja residents crossed the river into Victoria, set up camp at Barmah and vowed they would not return until McQuiggan had been dismissed and the inquiry they had asked for was begun. Many of the Cumeragunja strikers believed that this action in itself would win them a hearing. The Protection Board, however, chose to treat the matter with total public dishonesty and in precisely the same way that the entirely different personnel on the Board in the 1910s had treated the major community disturbances at Cumeragunja in that decade. Rather than viewing the issue as one of widespread protest among the whole station population, requiring serious investigation, both sets of Board members looked for individuals to be made scapegoats with the usual label 'troublemaker'.

On Saturday, 4 February, the Board issued a statement to the effect that the 'incident' had been caused by 'an agitator' and that there had been no previous complaints from Cumeragunja residents. This statement was broadcast on radio. While the 200 strikers had few possessions with them and little food, they did have access to a wireless. The broadcast proved to them that their actions had not even gained an honest response from the Board, let alone acknowledgment of their demands. It was this broadcast which convinced the strike camp that a brief, token demonstration was not enough. They spent the following day making arrangements for a more permanent camp and a school for their children, while dispatching a delegation to Cooper in Melbourne to mobilise political support.

So began a strike which lasted nine months. The initial demands of the strikers were those of their petition of November 1938, but by August the focus on McQuiggan had broadened to a reassertion of the longest-standing Cumeragunja and AAL demands. The strike call became one for a royal commission, not just to have McQuiggan removed but to gain the return of the farm blocks to the Cumeragunja owners, for support in agricultural development plans for the whole reserve, for the abolition of all boards of control and for full citizen's rights.[12]

The strike had reversed the process of 1938 in which attention had been restricted to immediate concerns, and mobilisation around the long-term, double-stranded policy had begun again. The closest political working alliance during 1939 was between Jack Patten and William Cooper, although, perhaps for tactical reasons, Jack Patten played a minor role for the duration of the strike. His brother George became the strikers' chief spokesperson. As far as Jack Patten remained in contact with the coastal APA network (and the extent of such contact is not clear) the *de facto* coalition of regional movements had shifted.[13]

The white press, encouraged by McQuiggan, the Protection Board, and local white landholders, tended to portray the strike as it had done the polio incident a year before: as irrational panic, the product of an agitator's lies on superstitious, primitive and simple minds. The notable exceptions were the articles written by journalists who visited the strike camp and who could not fail to be impressed with the sincerity and determination of the strikers.

The most politically inflammatory coverage of the strike, however, was in the Sydney *Daily News*, of which Bill Ferguson's supporter Albert Thompson was a board member. On the obvious grounds of Jack Patten's association with Australia First, the *Daily News* article implied that Patten was working for the Nazi Party and had caused the strike to assist German claims for a return of the mandated territory of New Guinea. Thompson was interviewed in the same article, and repudiated Patten, accusing him of 'fomenting trouble on aboriginal reserves'.[14]

Either Ferguson's continuing antipathy towards Patten or his cultivation of ALP support led him to make a statement to the Dubbo press three days later which was similar to that of Thompson.[15] When Ferguson made this statement, there had been enough coverage of the strike in the New South Wales press for him to have been aware that there were 200 Cumeragunja residents involved and that the strike had the full support not only of Patten but of Ferguson's oldest allies, William Cooper and the AAL. Ferguson, however, refused to make any supportive public statement for the whole nine-month duration of the strike. The coastal APA group in Sydney was apparently unable to mobilise New South Wales press support and Ferguson and his white allies were not prepared to do so. The New South Wales press was dominated by the stream of false public statements issued by the Protection Board, describing Cumeragunja in idyllic terms and McQuiggan as an 'able and humane' manager.[16]

In contrast, the campaign mounted in Melbourne was by far the largest and most organised of any yet undertaken by an Aboriginal body. It began as a collection of food and blankets for the strikers, who were of course being refused endowment and APB rations. The campaign broadened to include, at its height, groups as diverse as the Women's Christian Temperance Union and the Young Communist League. The main white supporting bodies were, however, the Australian League for Democracy and Peace and (despite the refusal of the Melbourne Trades Hall to endorse the campaign) the left-wing unions, notably the national Australian Railways Union. Melbourne press coverage was consistently more sympathetic than that in Sydney and probably helped the AAL convince the Victorian government to provide unemployment food relief for the strikers through the harsh winter months.[17]

Yet, in spite of the magnitude of the campaign, it had absolutely no effect on the NSW government. The lack of press mobilisation in New South Wales undoubtedly made it easier for the government to avoid the issue, but in fact it had in hand a perfect set of answers to the strikers' demands. It deflected the pressure it received over the strike by pointing out that it had already held an inquiry and it was already committed to 'new' and reformed legislation and administration (although the details had not yet been made public). Moreover, its plans for reform had been approved by that most 'progressive' group of experts, the anthropologists.[18] As Premier Stevens noted in June on yet another petition supporting the strikers and containing hundreds of Victorian signatures, 'the real "cure" is to introduce the new legislation'.[19] The government found, however, that it had more pressing business and so the 'cure' was delayed still further.[20]

With the government feeling under little real pressure, the Protection

Board was left with a free hand to deal with the strike. This actually occurred in three phases over the nine months. When virtually all of the 200 original strikers had held firm for six weeks against McQuiggan's withholding of aid and his threats to move other families into their station houses, the strike camp was eventually visited by the newly appointed full-time superintendent of the Board, A. W. G. Lipscombe, and its vice-chairman, S. L. Anderson. These two highest-ranking APB officials promised an inquiry (although its exact nature was left unspecified) and assured the strikers that no retaliations would occur if they returned to Cumeragunja.[21]

Having received some Board attention and with food short and autumn weather setting in, the strikers returned to the station on the seventh weekly ration day since the walk-off. They were met with immediate reprisals from McQuiggan, who had indeed reallocated houses and who began to manipulate the ration issues of the strikers. After five weeks of such action and with no signs of the promised inquiry, 80 people walked off, absolutely determined that they would not return from the Barmah strike camp until their demands were met.[22]

For weeks, the Board made public statements to the effect that no second walk-off had occurred at all, quoting McQuiggan's report that 'the inhabitants are now happier than they have been for a long time'. When it did finally admit that the strike was continuing, the Board insisted that no more than a couple of families were involved and in all its public statements sought to minimise the effects and ridicule the demands of the strikers.[23]

The Board's public dismissal of the strike as a minor incident did not, however, reflect its actual opinion. The strike dominated the Board's meetings for months and shook the Board to such an extent that it seriously decided to take the impossibly expensive and impractical action of moving the station. The Cumeragunja population was to be 'concentrated' with that of Moonahcullah and both were to be resited at a new location, well away from the Murray River. In this way the Board hoped to solve the recurrent problems it had faced with Aborigines 'absconding' into Victoria and to end the land dispute at Cumeragunja forever by revocation of the reserve and the permanent alienation of the land. This action was never taken because the Board simply could not afford it, but the fact that such a move was considered at all indicates the anxiety which the strike had generated.

The strike was finally broken in October 1939, when the NSW Protection Board convinced the Victorian government to withhold food relief to strikers and to deny their children access to the Barmah public school.[24] Even this, however, did not force the strikers to return to the station, where McQuiggan still held control. Instead, they moved to surrounding areas in New South Wales or Victoria, very bitter and highly politicised people. They had indeed been 'dispersed' but they had by no means disappeared (or 'merged' or 'assimilated') as the Board wished they would do. They were a new generation of Cumeragunja exiles, who retained their sense of community association and who have continued to play prominent roles in Aboriginal political activity both in New South Wales and Victoria and nationally.

Although in October 1939 the strike appeared to have been a total failure, resulting only in the loss to the station community of its most politicised activists, one of the strike objectives was achieved. A. J. McQuiggan and his wife were sacked in February 1940, as a direct result of the strike but too late for the strikers to claim victory. The Board's grounds for dismissing the couple were not, however, their treatment of the station residents. The McQuiggans were sacked for their political ineptitude in failing to squash rapidly a dispute which had embarrassed the Board and two State governments.[25]

Superintendent Lipscombe, whose appointment had been announced in February 1939 as the first step in the 'new' 'assimilation' policy, had been at work for long enough by this time for the directions he was taking to be obvious. Aborigines did not have to wait until the amendments to the Protection Act came before Parliament in mid-1940 to learn that the old Board's 'concentration' policy was going to be pursued even more vigorously. Had Aborigines seen Lipscombe's first reports they would have been even more alarmed. In his statement to the Chief Secretary, in December 1939, Lipscombe stressed that 'assimilation' could not be attempted before 'families now living on camps on the outskirts of country towns' were 'urged, even forced, to reside on stations'.[26] In the event, every one of the 1936 'Dog Act' amendments was included in the 'new' legislation.[27] As the Board's intention to dismiss the McQuiggans was not public by the end of 1939, none of the organised political movements could have felt themselves to be in a position of strength. They had suffered defeat at the level of lobbying government and, in relation to Cumeragunja, defeat at the level of support for a single community.

YET THE RESISTANCE CONTINUED . . .

Jack Patten's attention had been focused on Cumeragunja during 1939 and he sustained these south-western links until his enlistment and overseas military service early in 1940. The coastal APA had been left with few resources after the collapse of support from Australia First. It was the western APA which had been finally undergoing major community expansion during 1939 and was the regional movement with

255

greatest impetus. In a situation of weakness, unity between regional movements was the preferred situation and was advocated by Cooper. The western APA appeared to be the most viable base for a single New South Wales organisation, and the formal coalition was re-established early in 1940, with Dubbo as the structural focus.[28] Activists on the coast like lay preachers Frank Roberts, Bert Marr and Harry Connelly, who had all previously used Patten as a spokesperson, found they had much in common with Ferguson on a personal level. More direct alliances between at least the activists of the coast and west were formed. The public political struggle, however, essentially had to begin all over again. Ferguson launched the January 1940 meeting of the APA with a call 'to oppose the policy of Mr Lipscombe regarding the segregation of all those of Aboriginal blood'.[29]

The war economy, however, rapidly changed the conditions which had made Aboriginal people so vulnerable to the 'Dog Act' powers. Improving employment opportunities offered real alternatives to those who had been compelled to remain under Board control because they were denied the dole. Many Aboriginal men enlisted themselves, but the enlistment of whites previously employed meant that there was an increasing reliance on the Aboriginal workers who remained in rural areas. The interests of employers then became the retention of workers, not their 'concentration' on distant Board stations. The Aborigines Welfare Board, as the re-formed APB was named, continued to try to concentrate Aboriginal communities. In 1941 the Murris on Weilmoringle pastoral property north-west of Brewarrina faced enforced transportation into the reserve at Goodooga. Jack Orcher, a stockman there, recalled that a conflict arose with the pastoral station management because Aboriginal workers wanted to build decent housing for their families on the property, to replace the camps and tin huts which were the only dwellings they had previously been allowed to erect. The new Welfare Board must have been asked to fund the building, and their response was to send the police out to Weilmoringle to force the Murris there to move onto Board-controlled land. As Jack Orcher described the confrontation:

> They [the Murris] didn't want to go, they were making them move with the police. The police told them that if they didn't move they will take them and lock 'em up . . . They told them they're going to give them a certain day to pack up and shift their camp to Goodooga . . . Well, some of them packed up and waited for the police. They asked me to pack up too, so I said, 'I won't be packed up when you come out'. I said, 'My camp'll still be there'. And so it was, but he never came near me.[30]

The intransigence of Orcher and others allowed time for the Sydney-based Weilmoringle owners to be contacted. They disagreed with the Welfare Board's decision, and instructed their managers on the property to go into Goodooga and bring the workers who had already been forced into town back out to the camp. The property management at Weilmoringle continued to rely heavily on Aboriginal labour throughout the war and into the 1950s.[31] The expansion of the economy meant that for at least some time to come, 'concentration' had ceased to be a rational strategy in these remote rural areas.

Just as an improved economy meant that resistance like that at Weilmoringle could be successful, it also offered a chance of escape for the people who had been trapped on Board stations in the worst years of the Depression. The Wangkumara suffered at Brewarrina for more than two years. They had been afraid of the guns and the threats to their children, but by November 1940 too many of their family members had died for them to feel they could stay any longer. They chose the risks of escape rather than face what they believed would be the inevitable further deaths if they stayed away from their country. Eadie Edwards has described her family's role in the escape:

> My old great grandmother died there [at Brewarrina] and my granny she worried for her mother and her stepfather . . . And then my aunty died, that was my Mum's next oldest sister. So Mum said to Dad, 'This is no good, all the old people worryin' for home and I lost my sister, so we might as well pack up and go back to Tibooburra'.
>
> The biggest half of 'em followed back, like Granny Ebsworth and her sons and daughters. They was all very close and they wouldn't leave one another. So when my grandmother lost her mother and her stepfather there and my aunty died there, well that just done everything then, so they just packed up and come back. They said the Mission manager wouldn't hold 'em there. They said the police wouldn't even hold 'em there.
>
> So what couldn't ride in the buggies, walked. A lot of us teenagers walked along the road. And we walked along the road till we hit here [Bourke], and different cars used to pass us. They'd say, 'Oh, there's a circus comin' in from Brewarrina to here'. Well, we was the circus!
>
> So we all headed back here. When we got to here, we headed out to Wanaaring. We was going on to Tibooburra but when they got to Wanaaring all the men folks and the younger boys all got jobs there so that's where they hung out there then.[32]

The Wangkumara were 80-strong when they walked off Brewarrina station. The Cumeragunja people had been forced to walk away from their land, but the Wangkumara walked home. They did not reach the Europeans' town of Tibooburra but stopped instead, after walking 190 miles, at Wanaaring on the Paroo River where they were able to find pastoral work. Employment was not their only reason for stopping at the Paroo. The Wangkumara were more closely associated with land to the north-west, but by traditional protocol could move freely on the Paruntji speakers' land on the west of the Paroo. Only if the Wangkumara wished to travel east of the river was formal permission required. The Wangkumara had defied the Board and the police to reach country of significance to them at Wanaaring.[33]

The long trek of the Wangkumara was a sign that Aboriginal resistance was to continue.

Part V

Border Wars, 1948 to 1965

19
Shifting Boundaries

In New South Wales Aboriginal politics during the 1930s, land continued to be held as an important long-term goal in most regions despite
the sense of crisis over the rapid erosion of civil rights. Yet assumptions
persist, in both scholarly and popular accounts, that in the following
decades of the 1950s and 1960s this politics was focused exclusively
on civil rights, in the form of equal and full access to the benefits and
protections of citizenship. The period is assumed to have had a high
degree of control over the Aboriginal movement by white left-wing
supporters. The prevailing wisdom continues to be that land rights was
only placed on the agenda of south-eastern Aboriginal organisations with
the emergence of land-focused politics in the 'traditional' Northern
Territory at Yirrkala in 1963 and then at Wattie Creek in 1966. The
challenge by some Aboriginal activists to the large white involvement
in FCAATSI in 1969 has strengthened the assumptions that the
organisation had been previously dominated by whites who were interested only in civic equality, and who were obstructing the emergence of
authentically 'Aboriginal' issues such as land rights and cultural resurgence.

Like all interpretations arising from intense contestation, these
assumptions need to be questioned. Part V explores the political issues
relating to Aboriginal people through the 1950s and 1960s. It opens up
the complex interaction between Aboriginal interests in achieving access
to the rights of citizenship and in being at the same time acknowledged
on the basis of their cultural difference, of which a fundamental source
was their original and continuing ownership of the land. Yet while this
pattern echoes those of the 1920s and the 1930s, there were changed
circumstances: rapidly shifting economic demands and bureaucratic
constraints, and a broadening range of alliances with white groups.
Aborigines often found themselves at odds with their allies as well as
their enemies; they were constantly challenged to educate their white
supporters as they carried them along in more confident assertions of
the urgency of their goals in relation to both land and civil rights. These
more expansive demands for land from the later 1950s allow us to

explore the range of meanings for which land was significant to Aboriginal people after nearly 200 years of intense colonisation.

ABORIGINAL ORGANISATIONS IN THE POSTWAR YEARS

The Aboriginal organisations that had struggled to end APB domination in the later 1930s had been undermined by their inability to influence the new Welfare Board and then by the Second World War. William Cooper had died in 1941, and while the Cumeragunja community continued their political activity, with Pastor Doug Nicholls as spokesperson, the links with New South Wales politics were less active until the 1960s. Jack Patten had returned from his overseas war service to take up a new life with his relations from Cumeragunja in their Melbourne exile.

The western Aboriginal Progressive Association, headed by Bill Ferguson and Pearl Gibbs, had addressed itself more directly to New South Wales matters in the war years, linking up with coastal allies of Jack Patten such as Frank Roberts Snr, a lay preacher in Lismore. Bert Groves had emerged as a key speaker in the organisation, and now shared many public speaking roles as Ferguson took up his hard-won position as the 'half-caste' Aboriginal member on the Welfare Board. The divisive rivalries of the prewar period had eased and the APA now had links with communities from each of the main areas in the State, although regional differences in conditions continued to influence priorities and goals. Yet formal unity made political organising no easier, because changed conditions disrupted the older political networks.

ECONOMIC CONDITIONS

The high demand for labour during the war and throughout the 1940s had freed Aborigines from the 'Dog Act' restraints, and like the Tibooburra people, many now felt confidently able to walk away from Welfare Board imprisonment to find a place to live in parts of their own country where work was available. Towns which saw rapid increases in Aboriginal population and the corresponding growth of 'uncontrolled' camps included Coffs Harbour, Kempsey, Nowra and Bega on the coast, and Yass, Griffith and Cowra, especially for the harvesting seasons, Wilcannia, Coonabarabran and Moree in the inland, again particularly in times when seasonal workers were greatly in demand.[1]

Political organisation was difficult in conditions where people had to move to find work and then re-establish themselves in new towns. Despite considerable recruitment of Aboriginal workers into public

262

utilities such as the post office and the construction of roads and railways, much of the work available in rural areas continued to be seasonal. From their new home sites, men in particular travelled on the seasonal agricultural harvesting and pastoral circuits which took them often far beyond their own kin and land. The rapid spread of irrigation along the Murrumbidgee and Murray, for example, offered much work for Aboriginal labourers, but it demanded constant travel for only short-term work. The mobility enforced by the increasing seasonality of labour presented a major difficulty for rural Aboriginal families and for their political organisations.

The 1950s were boom years for some non-Aboriginal Australians, but they did not continue to support much Aboriginal employment. The Welfare Board recorded an alarming drop in this from the 1946 level of 96 per cent to 76 per cent in 1952.[2] Postwar immigration programs brought many Europeans to the irrigated farm areas of the Riverina, and into some of the north coast agricultural industries. The new immigrants became involved in family farming as well as in providing a large number of labourers to work during busy seasonal picking, and this soon pushed Aboriginal workers out to the most marginal of roles in these industries.

Mechanisation continued to erode the need for agricultural labour. Silo construction made redundant the armies of bag sewers who had accompanied wheat harvests all along the inland slopes, while mechanised corn harvesting replaced the jobs of many Aboriginal workers on the north coast, where Aboriginal unemployment had become serious by 1958. The pastoral industry in the western division had not collapsed as predicted, and many Aboriginal stockworkers and shearers continued to find work throughout the 1950s, involving themselves more frequently with AWU union politics and campaigns to gain better conditions for Aboriginal rouseabouts. Yet here too, jobs were being eroded by increasing use of trucks for droving, and four-wheel drives then motor bikes for mustering. The slow reduction in pastoral work, and the eventual closure of most of the remaining Aboriginal pastoral camps in the Western Division, led to the growth in Aboriginal populations in towns like Wilcannia and Walgett. The widespread conversion from horses to internal combustion engines throughout rural industries further decreased the need for fodder corn crops on the north coast, and so undermined still further an important source of jobs for Aboriginal workers.[3]

While wool prices boomed in the 1950s, the increasing mechanisation was an indication of the industrialisation of agriculture. The companies prospering were the larger and the more highly capitalised, not the small family farms. So the meanings of land for white Australians were undergoing profound changes over these years. The vision of the Australian inland densely settled by a myriad yeoman farming families disappeared, along with the paintings of sunlit flocks among the gums. More compelling images of rural areas were the recent ones: the Depression memories of drought-stricken farming country tramped by destitute unemployed, of soldier-settlers walking away from their barren lands. The land of the cities increasingly attracted the attention of settlers, as the suburban sprawl accelerated. Working families and those with a small amount of capital looked to the quarter-acre suburban block to allow them to call a piece of Australia their own. There were rising incomes, the rapid expansion of the availability of consumer appliances on which to spend those incomes, and the naively enthusiastic belief that modern science would conquer any climatic and environmental problems. The forbidding desert itself now appeared vulnerable to conquest by modernity, as the air-conditioned townships, equipped with every convenience, were set up overnight in the early 1950s to house the uranium miners at Rum Jungle and the rocket technicians at Woomera.[4] At the symbolic level, as Australians searched for visual images which would signify the essence of the postwar nation, the iconic rural scenes of grasslands and eucalypts was being replaced by the more uncompromising harshness of the Central Australian desert landscape.

THE POLICIES OF THE ABORIGINES WELFARE BOARD

The Aborigines Welfare Board had seriously tried to continue its predecessor's concentration policy. The incoming Board went so far as to contact all local government authorities in 1941 asking them to assist it in an aggressive policy of removing all town camps on unreserved land in order to concentrate the residents under the necessary 'supervision' for 'training'. With Professor Elkin as a member, the Board had a strong commitment to adult education and resocialisation, and it was felt this could best be achieved under residential managerial supervision. Yet by 1947 the Board had to admit that the booming job market had defeated it: Aboriginal people had so many employment opportunities that they were able to walk away from any supervised Board station and their employers would support their doing so. The Board's only alternative was prosecution under its 1939 Act, and then formal imprisonment, but it knew that the courts would be reluctant to take such action, which would have been both politically and economically unacceptable. In 1948 the Board announced a shift in policy direction, but it never abandoned its desire to see as many Aboriginal people as possible incarcerated in managed stations where they could be 'trained' before eventual release.[5]

The new policy was to direct money away from enhancing the infrastructure of a small number of concentration stations to the establishment of a network of district welfare officers (DWOs). These officers would be posted in towns which had seen a rapid growth in the Aboriginal population, and there they would 'assist and guide' the Aboriginal people by keeping 'in constant contact with them'. These were people who had come to live in these towns to gain work but often also quite explicitly to escape Welfare Board control. Now the DWOs were ordered to keep under constant observation precisely those people living most independently of the Board: those 'living privately in houses in towns'. The DWOs were expected to exercise 'vigilant oversight over the substandard homes' of those living off reserves, just as vigilantly as over those on a reserve. They were to form a web of surveillance, to meet the Board's inability to confine Aborigines by extending the boundaries of constant surveillance to entrap people who had thought they could escape.[6] The Board truly sought to '[make] it prison, most everywhere we go'.[7]

By 1961 there were thirteen DWOs (eight men and five women) positioned in eight locations in addition to sixteen AWB station managers (see Map 15, p. 266). The DWOs were placed in those towns which the AWB felt were most 'troublesome' and they had as their specific goal to 'assist and guide' Aboriginal people towards 'successful assimilation'. This meant quite simply that Aboriginal people were expected to accept the values and behaviour of the dominant European society, and the Board insisted that Aboriginal people demonstrate this by not only earning an independent living, and showing they could save money in a bank account, but by avoiding contact with other Aboriginal people and refusing to participate in community-oriented activities such as sharing resources with kinsfolk and travelling to visit relatives and country.

The Board was particularly anxious to force Aboriginal people away from any demonstration of commitment to their cultural and social networks. Time and again the Board's reports criticised Aboriginal people for 'clinging together in groups' and 'segregating themselves among their own kind'.[8] This meant that the Board condemned Aboriginal interest in maintaining contact with their own country as well as their own community.[9] In a characteristic approach, the DWO in Moree complained that Murris there had caused the discrimination against them by refusing to move away from what he termed a 'saturated' town, that is, one with too many Aboriginal residents. He explained this refusal in terms of

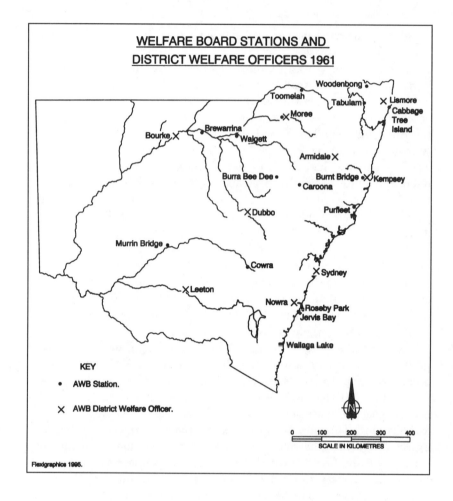

WELFARE BOARD STATIONS AND DISTRICT WELFARE OFFICERS 1961

KEY

• AWB Station.

✗ AWB District Welfare Officer.

0   100   200   300   400
SCALE IN KILOMETRES

Flexigraphics 1995.

the determination to live in the town of their birth, despite strong prejudice within that town . . . In fact, they cannot bear the thought of leaving relatives, completely severing themselves from old associations and serving as pioneers . . . It is this deference for the past and determination to stick together not unmixed perhaps with the white population's efforts to drive them together, that constitutes the greatest barrier to effective work on the part of the Welfare Officer.[10]

Economic self-sufficiency alone was not enough to avoid interference by the Board. It regarded the independent Aboriginal farming of reserve and other lands as an illusion of successful adaptation, because Aboriginal farmers had not abandoned traditional kinship and cultural commitments. The Board dismissed the widespread experience of Aboriginal farming by saying in 1951:

In a few instances very small gazetted reserves are occupied by single

266

families who live there over a long period and have come to regard themselves as quite independent. At the same time, these people cannot be said to be assimilated although they would probably be accepted by their neighbours.[11]

The Welfare Board, far more than the Protection Board, was determined to intervene in the lives of the broadest possible section of the Aboriginal population of the State. The Protection Board had been happy if adult Aboriginal people could demonstrate economic independence, and until 1936 refused to have anything to do with Aboriginal people who were not living on reserves. For the Welfare Board, this was not enough. It was resolved to intervene in the lives of all Aboriginal people, at the most fundamental levels, wherever they lived and however successful they might have been previously in escaping from Board influence. In its determination to erase all evidence of cultural identity, the Welfare Board was firmly of the view that Aboriginal commitment to their own country was an undesirable obstacle to 'progress' and 'successful assimilation'.

To achieve its aims, the Welfare Board developed a crude carrot-and-stick behaviour modification program, whereby if Aboriginal people could convince the DWOs that they had cut themselves off from family, culture and land they would be rewarded with an 'Exemption Certificate'. This, the Board said, would make it easier for them to achieve the very real benefits of easier access for their children to public schools and Commonwealth pensions and unemployment benefits. All these made it more likely that Aboriginal children would be safe from removal, and that economic security was a little closer. The other major prize was the promise that an Exemption Certificate, and careful attention to the DWO's 'guidance', would make Aboriginal families eligible for a house in town.

The Board believed that when it offered houses it was offering the status and improved health and material conditions of a 'proper', 'respectable' dwelling. Its aim was to use such houses as behaviour modification tools in themselves, to be inspected constantly to ensure the Aboriginal residents had paid adequate attention and expenditure, made a proper commitment to the material appearances of 'stability'.[12] The houses were to be 'pepperpotted' too, an arrangement by which the Aboriginal house would be surrounded on all sides by white residents, guaranteeing that there would be no Aboriginal neighbours. So 'assimilating' families faced constant scrutiny and judgment from their all-white neighbours as well as from the DWO.[13]

For Aborigines, the offer was intensely attractive but for different reasons. They were desperate for security of residence in the area of their choice. Every shift in the economy and every decision of the

Protection Board since the turn of the century had made it harder for them to stay in the town or on the land where they had previously reached some equilibrium, however tenuous, with the settler colony. The dispossessions and dispersals of the 1920s, the constant threats to children and the enforced concentrations of the 1930s had each caused a tumult of reluctant migrations.

Even when people moved only to the next town, seeking asylum within their own country, they usually found only temporary residence, in even less secure conditions than those they had been forced to leave. A few rural Aborigines had managed to buy a block of land in town, but many were lost to local government to pay for land rates in years when employment was bad. Most Aboriginal families who tried were looking to rent, but were confronted with an informal and unspoken alliance between landlords, real estate agents and local councils. There were sometimes slums on offer, but much of the time there was a strange absence of any rental accommodation whenever Aboriginal people enquired.[14] So the Welfare Board had a powerful attraction indeed when it announced that if Aboriginal families could demonstrate that they would live in 'conformity to the standards of white people' the Board would secure a house for them in town.[15]

The possibility of access to rental accommodation within towns was an important challenge to the way in which white rural townspeople had used space and land definitions to exclude Aboriginal people. The Welfare Board had failed to appreciate the depth of commitment which rural town whites held for the segregation of both public space and residential areas. Segregation was an edifice which had been built up from at least the 1880s, when Aboriginal people had begun in numbers to demand access to the services and institutions of the new liberal democracy being established. 'Public' schools had been only the most formal of the closures. Over the years, hospitals had been closed down to Aborigines, and in particular women had been made aware of this medical segregation. The Protection Board had attempted to intervene in Aboriginal health as well as culture by sending increasing numbers of Aboriginal women to hospital to have their babies. In response, white townspeople demanded that labour wards must be denied to them. Many Aboriginal women remember the discomfort and humiliation of giving birth on the hospital verandah or in a makeshift area at the rear of the main buildings.

Leisure was now strictly segregated, with picture shows, swimming pools and tennis courts usually closed to Aborigines, and Aboriginal football teams denied a place in the local competition, all on the grounds of fictitious 'health risks'. The limits of this 'petty apartheid' were bizarre. Lake Cargelligo spent a decade over the 1950s trying to preserve their 'Whites Only' public toilet. These white townspeople demanded that the manager of nearby Murrin Bridge station bring its Aboriginal residents into town for shopping for no more than two hours, so that they would not use the town's 'amenities'. Otherwise, the town demanded, the Welfare Board must build a separate, 'Blacks Only' toilet block, which was to be surrounded by seating, so that Aboriginal shoppers would only be allowed to rest in the same strictly limited area.[16]

The keystone of this whole system was the segregation of residential, dormitory areas. Exclusion of Aboriginal people from the 'real' town meant they could always be defined as 'outsiders', like the Murrin Bridge shoppers in Lake Cargelligo, and always denied the access accorded to 'real' citizens. It was this fundamental core of the rural structure of racial hierarchy and power relations which the Welfare Board expected to breach when it boasted to Aborigines that it could provide them with 'a house in town'.

For both Aboriginal people and for rural whites, there were therefore many tensions raised by the Welfare Board policy after 1948 around the issue of land and what might be called spatial politics, where conflict occurs over who controls and has access to the various places in which public and domestic life are conducted. It could be expected that there would be contradictions in the implementation of such a policy, and intense conflicts around its outcomes.

ALLIES: THE JINDYWOROBAKS

The alliances Aboriginal groups had with whites after the war were just as polarised between Right and Left as they had been in the 1930s. They were diversifying, however, and the whites involved were often changed dramatically by their contacts with Aboriginal activists and their engagement in the increasingly heated politics of desegregation.

Although the differences between Right and Left political philosophies were very sharply drawn during the Cold War, both groups shared an interest in Aboriginal politics until the later 1960s. Their interest arose from different sources, however, which meant that they had differing responses to the Aboriginal demands for rights which were based on cultural grounds. The left-wing organisations, including the Communist Party but also the many non-communist unions and some church organisations with socialist sympathies, were committed to the concept of human equality across racial lines. They all firmly believed that differences between human societies and individuals were the result of social and cultural conditions, of 'nurture' rather than 'nature', and their political aims were to achieve the recognition of this underlying commonality between all humanity. They believed that inequalities were the result of oppressive social, political and economic forces, and if these repressive conditions could be changed, then it was expected that all people could take equal and identical roles in society. The CPA had had to confront the issue of ethnic minorities in the Soviet Union, and had a policy which recognised their rights to land and political autonomy (within limits!). As mentioned earlier, in Australia communists regarded this policy as directly relevant only in the 'remote', 'traditionally oriented' areas of central and northern Australia. In the south-east during the 1950s and 1960s, the CPA still tended to treat Aboriginal people as a category of the working class, who only needed the removal of legal and economic discrimination to take up their place as full citizens indistinguishable from white Australians.

The right-wing groups, however, like P. R. Stephensen in the 1930s, continued to look for essential characteristics in both races and cultures. Their position was always on the 'nature' side of the debate. Their racism was based on assumptions that physical differences indicated underlying, biologically determined and 'essential' characteristics for different groups, and they were often engaged in the search for an 'essence' of the Australian 'culture' and 'nation'. Ironically, while the Liberal Party and other conservative political groups drew on the support of the major capitalist concerns in the country, which were pushing ahead with industrial modernisation and technological innovation, the Right nevertheless had an ideological commitment to seeking out the 'traditional' in its own and other cultures. This was so whether the group admired Britain, like Robert Menzies, or detested the British imperial influence, like Stephensen and the later Jindyworobaks. Each in their own way was constructing a romantic history for its conception of the 'essential' Australian character. This interest in 'traditionalism' in any culture, and the search for 'essential' cultural and social traits, made the Right, at least until the later 1960s, far more receptive than the Left to the assertions by Aboriginal people that they had entitlements based on their differences from white Australians, a major one being their traditional association with land.

The interests of P. R. Stephensen in symbols of unique national identity which differentiated Australia from Britain had made him attractive to the emerging literary nationalists of the 1930s. Rex Ingamells in Adelaide was one who found Stephensen intensely interesting, and formed a close friendship with him in the years after Stephensen's internment in 1941. Ingamells was searching for a body of literary symbolism which was 'free of alien influences', which to him meant British influence. He shared Stephensen's interest in Aboriginal imagery as the best way to represent the unique qualities of the coming

Australian culture. He took up the word 'Jindyworobak' from the glossary of James Devaney's *The Vanished Tribes*, where it was unsourced but said to mean 'to annex, to join'. This became the banner under which he gathered a group of writers and poets interested in a new, uniquely Australian art, in which their European style of individualist poetry was engaged with the symbols of indigenous Aboriginal cultures.

Yet Ingamells and most of the Jindyworobak writers were little interested in any real encounter with Aboriginal people of the past or the present. While Stephensen had at times been strident in his white nationalist stance, he had developed lasting personal relationships with Aborigines like Jack Patten and Monty and Mary Tickle, and he had used his travelling in the bush to report on some very current matters for the Aboriginal press. Rex Ingamells, however, paid no attention to what was known of Aboriginal literature, and was not interested in contemporary Aboriginal artists or activists.

Most of the Jindys were more closely aligned with artists like Margaret Preston. In the 1930s she was one of the first Australian artists to use stylised forms of Aboriginal imagery to produce what she argued was uniquely Australian art because it drew on the authority of the land's ancient culture. Preston's art played an important part in familiarising white Australians with the power of Aboriginal visual imagery, because her work appeared in accessible, everyday situations such as popular magazines and prints from her woodcuts. From the mid-1940s on, this growing artistic use of Aboriginal imagery contributed to the slowly growing popular Australian awareness of Aboriginal cultures.

Yet Preston and many later artists were, like the Jindys, interested primarily in the outward forms of Aboriginal culture. They felt little need to understand the philosophies behind the creativity of Aboriginal Australians and saw no contradiction in appropriating language and imagery without consultation or permission from the creating societies and artists who continued to exist. For Ingamells and Preston, Aboriginal cultural expressions were the heritage of the new nationalist Australian artists, to be used respectfully, but nevertheless to be used for nationalist purposes.[17]

There was one writer among the Jindyworobaks who wanted something more substantial than a simple appropriation of decorative 'primitive' symbols. Roland Robinson was born in Ireland in 1912 and emigrated to Sydney as a child. During the 1930s, Robinson travelled around coastal New South Wales, fishing and camping with many Aboriginal men who were to become respected leaders among their communities in the decades to come. After the war, Robinson frequently revisited men such as Percy Mumbulla and his kinsmen from Wallaga

Lake and the far south coast; the community at La Perouse, where many coastal and inland people would come to stay for extended visits; and the north coast communities from Purfleet to the Bandjalang communities from Yamba and Baryulgil to Woodenbong. There he stayed frequently with Alex Vesper, a Bandjalang man who had been driven off the Stoney Gully land at Kyogle when that station had been 'concentrated' with Woodenbong in 1940.

In 1958 he published *Black-Feller, White-Feller*, and in 1965, *The Man Who Sold His Dreaming*, which each record stories told to Robinson by these Aboriginal friends in New South Wales. Such stories offer a glimpse of the way Aboriginal people expressed their understanding of their cultural heritage in the mid-twentieth century. The stories all spoke of strong involvement with traditional concerns about law and social regulation, about land and ownership and responsibility, and about punishment and retribution for transgression of laws about social and land responsibilities, yet all are set within the context of contemporary living. Many of them told of Aboriginal people's encounters with legendary figures or with the still-present spirits of the land as they went to work on a neighbouring farm or came home after collecting rations from the local police. The themes and concerns of the storytellers were not located in a pre-invasion golden age, but were the narratives they saw as part of their experience under colonisation in the present.

All of the narratives are anchored to the country of the storyteller, with the events located at particular named sites, as the storyteller explained their formation or the nature of the spirits who continued to live within those sites. Although full of potentially everlasting resources, the land these stories describe was also full of danger and powerful forces, which needed to be acknowledged. These stories consistently affirm the power of the 'Clever' men and occasionally women, the *wirringun* or *wee-un*,[18] whose learning allowed them power to manage the dangers of the land as long as they respected its laws and punished transgressors. These Aboriginal storytellers of the mid-twentieth century constantly affirmed the central significance of land to the well-being of Aboriginal societies.

The question arises of the extent to which Robinson's selection and editing of these stories reflects his interests and desires rather than those of the storytellers. Other compilations of 'legends' at the time, like that of Devaney, decontextualised stories so that their storytellers and land of origin was obscured. Even K. Langloh Parker, while carefully recording the sites of origin, never attributed stories to individual speakers. Robinson, however, was scrupulous in naming the storytellers, in conveying their distinctive narrative styles and in laying out text to reflect their individual rhythms of speech. This suggests he was trying to convey their voices rather than his own.

Yet it is also true that Roland Robinson was part of a wider movement among white Australians of the time, whether they called themselves nationalists or whether they were just developing a stronger sense of difference from England and a desire to be a part of the new Australia. The extreme right-wing direction which Stephensen had taken had been discredited, but his deep interest in developing a sense of unique national identity, tied to the landscape, but without any reformist social agenda, had permeated widely into the general population. The centre and right of the ALP, for example, had a strong commitment to the construction of an anti-British and unique Australian identity which could be recognised in working people's experience of work and leisure in their country.

The 'popular nationalist' trend can be seen in the 'bush walking' clubs of the mid-century, which flourished as urban dwellers searched for a direct relationship with the 'unique' and the 'wild' in their landscape. My grandfather was a part of a less formal experience. Throughout his life, he spent his leisure time fishing on the south coast where he frequently met Aboriginal fishermen, learning from their expertise and sharing yarns. Despite his commitment to a White Australia, these Kooris peopled my grandfather's holiday stories, as comfortable companions and respected, knowledgeable fishermen. Their presence at this level of white family stories may have been uncommon, but it was not unique, and it allowed threads of contact to be sustained through these years when Aboriginal symbols were valued more highly than living Aboriginal people.

Roland Robinson took on more than a casual relationship with his Aboriginal friends. He became increasingly involved in their political struggles. Like Stephensen, he became an advocate, and spent more and more of his travels in New South Wales conveying political news from one community to another, or between Aboriginal activists in rural areas and their supporters in Sydney. He was a founding member of the Aboriginal Australian Fellowship in 1957, wrote frequently to the news-papers advocating changes to the administration of Aboriginal affairs, and he took to travelling around New South Wales in the old car of Helen Hambly, a CPA member, to gather information on Aboriginal conditions. So Robinson's personal relationships with Aboriginal people and their politics took him across the lines of political affiliation, teaching him, as others were to find also, that engagement with Aborig-inal matters did not sit comfortably within the categories of political alignment which white Australians fashioned for themselves.

ALLIES: THE LEFT

On the left of Australian politics, support for Aboriginal political organisations continued, but attention was more often focused on dramatic events in distant and remote areas of the country than on the mundane details of the petty but relentless hostilities in rural New South Wales. The Pilbara strike of 1946 had drawn wide interest, as Aboriginal groups undertook what left-wing activists could recognise as working-class industrial action in striking for better conditions in the Western Australian pastoral industry. The Pindan Mob's demands for land and independence were less often noticed. The British Atomic Testing Program, started in 1947 with a rocket-testing range, then graduating to nuclear explosions in 1952 and 1953, began to draw left-wing interest to the impact of this activity on Pitjantjatjara and other people in the Western Desert. These issues aroused a great deal of interest in Aboriginal conditions among white Australians concerned about atomic warfare or about their own safety from nuclear fallout from the tests. But the response of the Commonwealth and State governments was to brand any expression of concern about Aboriginal welfare on the test site as a communist-inspired attack on British and Australian defences. Such Cold War suspicions complicated the processes of planning and mobilisation of support for public campaigns.

The Communist Party in New South Wales remained interested in Aboriginal affairs, but as an organisation it still kept its distance from Aboriginal bodies, which reflected its suspicions over right-wing white support during the 1930s. Individual members of the party, however, became involved during the 1950s in what became deep personal commitments. Con O'Clerkin was one such member, an Irish immigrant who had spent the 1920s in Goondiwindi and the 1930s on the north Queensland canefields, until he returned after the war to live in Sydney where he continued the interest in Aboriginal affairs that he had formed in Queensland.

Other members of the party became involved through other organisations. Helen Hambly, for example, was a communist who was deeply involved with Jessie Street's Union of Australian Women, and had become aware of Aboriginal issues in that body. Hambly had been a domestic servant before her marriage, and after her two children were of school age she had bought a small car and begun to work as a real estate agent, taking an active role in local government at Lane Cove. She was asked by a neighbour to participate in the early meetings of the Aboriginal–Australian Fellowship, and her access to a vehicle allowed her to undertake country research and activism for the Fellowship, during which she developed close personal links with Aboriginal communities and individuals.

This common personal and political interest drew O'Clerkin and Hambly together on many occasions, although in conflicts within the party they took opposing sides, O'Clerkin supporting the Moscow line during the 1960s while Hambly leaned towards the Maoist faction. Yet their personal relationships with Aboriginal friends and associates continued to form a stronger link than the communist factional politics which divided them. In the 1950s these two white activists shared the general CPA commitment to economic and social equality for south-eastern Aboriginal people.

There were, however, new influences abroad. Postwar immigration had brought to Australia the cultural diversity of European refugees. Jews and others who had suffered under fascism brought with them an interest in social justice which nevertheless recognised cultural differences and could form a base from which to question assimilation. In the aftermath of the exposure of the Holocaust and other racially based crimes, left-wing and liberal Christian groups experienced a revulsion against the previously fashionable eugenic goals of 'racial hygiene'. There was a slowly growing awareness that racial inequality and persecution was widespread in Western societies and required action to redress.

This shift in public awareness was fostered by the emergence into public view of cultural anthropologists who popularised a more respectful view of Aboriginal culture and educability. The major figures of the 1950s took opposing political positions. Elkin, committed as ever to the anthropologist's role in government policy ('the more we know of these peoples the better can we govern them'), lobbied for and took up roles as an adviser on both Papua New Guineans and the Aborigines. Similarly, he took part in the federal government's cursory inquiries into the effects of British rocket and atomic testing in central Australia, in 1947 and in the early 1950s, and reassured the government on both counts that no damage would be done.

A quite different but similarly high-profile approach was taken by Donald Thomson, who had researched in northern Australia and was deeply opposed to British atomic testing and the dislocation caused to the Pitjantjatjara and Ngaanyatjara peoples of north-west South Australia to make way for the test range and then for the associated Giles meteorological station. Thomson was viciously attacked by the federal government, and along with Dr Charles Duguid, the Presbyterian founder of Ernabella mission, was pilloried as a 'communist'. Yet as rising concerns were expressed about atomic fallout contaminating Aboriginal and non-Aboriginal populations across the country, particularly from 1956, and as film of the conditions of displaced Ngaanyatjaras from around Giles were circulated in the same year, general awareness of Aboriginal issues was influenced as much by Thomson's work as it had ever been by Elkin's. Both, however, contributed to the wider sense of the need to take some action in relation to Aboriginal conditions generally.

In New South Wales in the early 1950s, these various influences were just beginning to identify the issues for sympathetic liberal or left-wing whites. These seemed to be that poor Aboriginal education and poverty, along with white ignorance, were obstructing Aboriginal equal participation in Australian society. In 1956 the Welfare Board sought to draw on what Elkin and others perceived to be a fund of goodwill in local rural areas to facilitate their assimilation policy. They called on sympathetic whites to form groups which would encourage social functions and try to break down the great social distance which then existed between local whites and Aborigines in country towns.[19] Self-styled 'Assimilation Committees' did form in many towns, and the whites in them usually endorsed the expectations of the AWB that the best interests of local Aborigines would be served by their rapid assimilation, which for most meant their access to education and separated, 'pepperpotted' housing. The membership of these groups was extremely varied, often including members of the CPA, as in Taree, along with some Christians and liberal-minded professionals and businessmen, such as the lawyers and chemists who made up the committee in Coonamble. These committees were to undergo often profound changes through the 1950s and early 1960s, as they found themselves confronting their white neighbours and clients in the struggles to gain decent Aboriginal housing within town limits.[20]

The same confidence in the government's assimilation policy was displayed in the first constitution of the Aboriginal–Australian Fellowship (AAF), which formed in 1956 after discussions between Pearl Gibbs and Faith Bandler.[21] Gibbs was trying to expand the white support base for the Aboriginal activist organisation she and Bert Groves had continued to lead after Ferguson's death in 1950. She was able to draw together in the early membership of the Fellowship a diverse group of middle-class Australians, some of whom were members of the Communist Party, while others were from left-wing artistic or Christian circles. Among the founding artists were Muir Holburn and Roland Robinson. There were a number of highly committed Jewish immigrants including Hans Bandler, whose wife Faith was from the Mussing family, of South Sea Islander descent, with an intense involvement already in fighting racism in northern New South Wales. Then there were Jack and Jean Horner, who were aligned with the Christian Socialist Movement, and counted Mary Bennett and Charles Duguid as their 'social history' tutors. The communist Helen Hambly also became involved through Jessie Street's organisation.

Closely involved too were a number of officials from major unions in the State, including the Waterside Workers and the Builders' Labourers, which had many Aboriginal members. The union role increased after 1957 when the Federal Council for the Advancement of Aborigines (FCAA, later FCAATSI) was formed. Unions could then formally affiliate with this body, on the lines of the structure of Trades and Labor Councils.

A number of Aboriginal people, including Pearl Gibbs and Bert Groves, were involved from the earliest days. They brought to the organisation another western Murri, Ray Peckham, whose father Tom Peckham had been a supporter of Bill Ferguson in Dubbo in the 1930s. Peckham was to become an active AAF member, travelling widely, on the AAF executive in 1960 and 1961, a member of the Builders' Labourers' Federation and the Communist Party. Charlie Leon from Purfleet and also, for a while, a member of the Communist Party, was another extemely active member, and their group drew in the highly respected Redfern activist Ken Brindle.

This assorted group at first endorsed a constitution in 1956 which pledged them to co-ordinate the efforts of individuals and groups in order to assist the NSW government and the AWB in the implementation of their stated aim of assimilation. After just two years of intense activity, including much rural travelling and engagement with the Aboriginal activists, the AAF had moved a long way from the confidence in government expressed in this first constitution. Bert Groves took part in 1959 in the formulation of the first constitution of the FCAA in Adelaide. In 1960 the AAF endorsed a new constitution which replaced completely the clause about supporting assimilation and incorporated the FCAA clauses calling for equality and full citizen's rights in education, wages, social services and the franchise, and finally, 'the retention of all remaining native reserves, with native communal title or individual ownership'. While this was still far from Aboriginal demands of the time, it was a great advance on the 1956 position.

20
Spatial Politics: Surveillance, Segregation and Land

The Welfare Board policies of the 1950s were implemented unevenly, so that people in different areas experienced very different effects. Yet each outcome limited the access Aboriginal people had to their country, as well as changing the way they could experience the remaining accessible land.

The experience of the Dhan-gadi in the Macleay Valley was one of the intensifying imposition of managerial control and surveillance. They found the newly imposed managers interfering not only in their employment conditions but in the way they used the public space around their homes, and even in how they organised their very private living arrangements. This repression was not successful in destroying the community's sense of identity, because unlike the isolation imposed on individuals in asylums, in these Welfare Board stations whole family networks were imprisoned together. Kinsfolk could not only support each other but begin the long process of forming networks of resistance and defiance. Yet the lands which the Dhan-gadi had previously regarded as their own independent homes, such as Burnt Bridge and Bellbrook, came increasingly to be experienced as prisons. While older people remembered the independent farming days, younger people who were growing up in the 1950s remember only the repression.[1]

For the Wiradjuri, there was a different experience.[2] They did not face the imposition of additional managers in their south-western region, but rather a relentless push to destroy their remaining non-reserved camping areas and their small unsupervised reserves. Either the Welfare Board expelled and evicted reserve residents from their homes, or it called in local government authorities with bulldozers to smash their camps while they were away working. This was not a return to the dispersals of the 1920s, because the Welfare Board maintained its commitment to the concentration of the Aboriginal population. But rather than herding people onto trucks in the way the Protection Board had conducted concentrations in the 1930s, by the 1950s the Welfare Board was allowing the hostility of white townspeople and the strongly

278

defended residential segregation of the towns to force Kooris to move reluctantly onto the stations. Cowra station had by then a long experience of AWB control. The tightening bonds of Welfare Board supervision were met with more open defiance than on the newer north coast stations, and only served to weld the old and the incoming station residents into a greater sense of solidarity than they might otherwise have had. But access to the long-established and comfortable non-reserved campsites was gone forever, and the Wiradjuri experience of their lands was made ever more insecure.

SEGREGATION AND LAND

The Welfare Board's intention in the late 1940s had been to shift the Aboriginal residents of the camps and small reserves onto the stations but then rapidly disperse them into houses in country towns. Its almost total failure to do this was the main stumbling block to its 'assimilation' program. It had found itself unable to penetrate white rural commitment to residential segregation. The Aboriginal need for housing was acute: in 1949 the Board estimated that 600–700 houses were required simply to meet the current demand. In the following year alone it built 60 houses on the stations. But from 1946 to 1960, only 39 houses were built for Aborigines inside municipal boundaries.

This matter was commonly seen by whites at the time and later as an issue over the right of Aborigines to have the same access as whites to 'decent' housing. This was understood in the material sense of well-built, functioning structures which allowed healthy living but which were also 'decent' in the sense of conforming to European lifestyles and morality.

Yet in reality most of the fights were not over houses but over land, land of the smallest but perhaps the most significant size in Australia's colonised history, the house block. The rural towns simply would not admit Aborigines, and their usual weapon was control over the sale of land. Suddenly no land could be found for acquisition by the Board, or vendors of potentially suitable land would inexplicably take their blocks off the market, as they did at Nambucca Heads in 1958. When the Board did succeed in buying land, the tradesmen who had been engaged to build the houses would be intimidated by their fellow townsmen until they withdrew their tender, as happened in Cowra in 1951, or the Board would be flooded by deputations and petitions from local government councils and white residents.[3]

In the few situations where Aboriginal people's views were recorded at length, it becomes apparent that they saw these struggles not only in terms of access to good-quality houses, which they unquestionably wanted, but as issues about their right to gain secure residential tenure and access to land in the town of their choice, in the wider locality of their choice. The infuriating thing for many Aboriginal people was that they were denied even so small a piece of land as a house block *on their own country*.

For local whites, a form of spatial politics was also central to their concerns and strategies. Their goals in almost every town where a dispute occurred appeared to be fundamentally to exclude Aboriginal people from residential areas. There were at least two dimensions to the desire to quarantine white living areas in country towns. One was the prevalent anxieties about sexual relationships and racial mixture, and so there was a desire to maintain separation of the races in sexually vulnerable situations, such as public schools and residential areas. The other dimension was the overall need to control access to public places by keeping the Aboriginal population defined as 'outsiders'. If they did not sleep within the town boundaries, they could not be said to really belong. The politics of keeping racial control over towns meant that while the colour bar in the public streets or at the local hotel or even at the local school was important, what was really essential was to maintain racial 'purity' in the dormitory or residential areas. Arguments about falling property values were just one expression of this more fundamental matter in local power relations and local identity formations.

The following examples are drawn from only a few areas of the State, but even so their diversity suggests some of the ways in which *land* was an issue, for both whites and Aboriginal participants, in what were also clearly 'civil rights' matters.

Wilcannia, 1948–50

Wilcannia in the late 1940s was a place which demonstrated the effects of Protection Board and Welfare Board pressure, but which also showed the slower changes in the pastoral industry.[4] Some of its Paakantji population had been forced to Menindee station in 1934, where they were held by force with Ngiyampaa people from Carowra Tank until the better employment of the early war years allowed some families to return to Wilcannia. Then, in 1941, some of the Tibooburra Wangkumara who had escaped from the Protection Board at Brewarrina had settled in Wilcannia, where there was no APB presence but where some relatives from the corner country were already living. In the next few years, others of their kin came south from Wanaaring and Tibooburra as the pastoral properties there slowly mechanised.

In 1948 the Welfare Board announced that it was going to move Menindee mission from Paakantji country on the Darling to Wiradjuri lands around Murrin Bridge. The Paakantji people who had remained at Menindee refused to make this move, and many chose to live on the unsupervised camping areas at Wilcannia. This population lived in camps and humpies spread out for many kilometres along the eastern bank of the Darling River opposite the town of Wilcannia, which was built on the higher, western bank to escape flooding. Wiimpatja recall these humpies as poor but as allowing great flexibility in social arrangements, whereby people could camp close to those to whom they were related or with whom they had supportive relationships, and further away from people they didn't get on with. Such living arrangements also allowed people to orient their camps towards the country they came from.

Ted Noffs, then the local minister, wrote to the Sydney press in 1948, protesting at the extremely poor conditions in which the Wilcannia Wiimpatja were living, and demanding some form of government intervention. He argued that a number of the Aboriginal pastoral workers had funds either to rent or to put a deposit on a house to buy it over time, but that no town whites were prepared to rent or sell to Aboriginal families. The Welfare Board was prompted by the bad publicity to step in and offer to build a dozen or so simple houses, but it was in a dilemma about where to build them. A reserve existed opposite the town, near some of the existing camps, but this whole eastern bank was lower and so far more flood-prone than the town side of the river. The white townspeople were appalled at the idea of the Aboriginal population being housed within their town boundaries. Murris appeared divided and the Welfare Board held a meeting to hear Aboriginal opinion. Some had moved up to the redsoil high-ground vacant land known as The Mallee, on the north-western edge of the town, where they argued they would be safe from floods, as well as having space to orient housing as they wished. Some preferred the beautiful tree-shadowed eastern riverbank.

Eventually the eastern bank was voted for. Some Wiimpatja argue that intimidation by the townsfolk had left people with such an awareness of hostility that they voted against the townside site. The Welfare Board built fourteen houses in two tight rows, precluding any of the flexibility in proximity and orientation that had been possible in the camps, and ensuring that the Aboriginal homes would be inundated in each subsequent flood. Both formally and informally, the white township had defended its dormitory area by excluding Aborigines absolutely from the high side of the river. In 1964 when C. D. Rowley visited the town, there was only one Aboriginal family to be found who had managed to rent any dwelling in the town.

Dual occupation breaking down: Walgett and Weilmoringle

Walgett was on the east of the pastoral Western Division, where the impact of both the economy and the Welfare Board had been felt. Some of the Yuwalaraay who had been forced to move to Brewarrina in 1936 had escaped later and moved east to Walgett on the border of their own country because it had then had no AWB presence. By 1941 a manager had been appointed at Gingie Reserve, but many people refused to move there and continued to camp on the Namoi River at Nicholl's Bend in town.

Active dual occupation of these western pastoral lands was becoming far more difficult over these years. The last of the pastoral camps in the area seem to have been closed down as mechanisation and some postwar subdivision further eroded the need for labour. Dungalear camp people remember that all the camp residents had moved into Walgett by the end of the 1940s. The Dungalear Murris did not abandon their land. Many people continued to work on the property through the 1950s while living in Walgett, and children who had not lived on the camps also followed their parents to work there in the 1960s.[5]

Some old people sustained their sense of obligation to take a teaching role: Ivy Green continued to take everyone she could, Murri or white, out to the property to show them her country. She took grandchildren and distant relatives, school groups and, in 1981, she took me along with a Legal Service lawyer and Murri friend, still teaching not long before her death. Even then, the manager on the property was obstructive, treating her with no respect and at first refusing her entry. Patiently adopting a 'silly old woman' role, she badgered him until, reluctantly and with great irritation, he agreed that she could take us onto the campsite. She laughed at him as he walked away, contemptuous that he had been so ignorant as to try to stop her visiting her own land.

Alarmed by the rising Murri population in the mid-1950s, Walgett's white townspeople expressed concerns which were taken up by the tabloid Sydney press. It was alleged that the increasing numbers and public drinking of Aborigines were driving whites out of the town. The fledgeling Aboriginal–Australian Fellowship sent a delegation up to Walgett to investigate, and found a pattern of spatial segregation which was commonly reported during these years: separate church services, separate playgrounds for children at the public school even though it had been desegregated, separate seating in the picture show, but most noticeably, separate living areas with no utilities or services. The Gingie Mission had no road built to cover the 6 blacksoil miles into town, and no water supply other than the river. The Namoi camp at Nicholl's Bend was at least close to town, but it too had no water supply, no sanitation and no electricity. The Shire Council regarded the camp as so far beyond its responsibility that during the 1955 floods it had proposed building a levee which left the camp outside to be inundated. A Murri woman interviewed by the AAF delegates explained her position: 'They won't let us live in the towns and be respectable and I won't live on a Station where you get ordered around'.[6]

The spatial politics of the town segregation were obvious, rigid and entrenched. What was less visible was the struggle over access to pastoral lands that had gone on before Murris were forced into the town camps.

Weilmoringle, the pastoral property where the manager had failed in his attempt to force Murris to leave for Goodooga in 1941, had continued to employ Aboriginal workers from the camp through the 1940s and early 1950s. Then, as the need for labour fell, the property management again began to apply pressure to force the camp residents to leave land they regarded as their home. Weilmoringle Murris told their stories to C. D. Rowley when he visited the camp in 1964, when they were still struggling to gain security of residence on the pastoral land. They described the previous manager's attempt to drive them away during the present drought by refusing them the use of the water tap at the shearing quarters, but they had dug wells in the riverbed and rolled water up to their houses in drums. The current manager had relaxed the pressure somewhat, but there was still no assurance that they would not be forced to move at any time. As one man said: 'the way we are now, I mean, we can't say it's my camp or their camp. The boss will come along and say "Youse'll have to shift to some other place". And that's the finish!'[7] What these families insisted on was that they needed security of residence in their chosen homesite. Another man told Rowley: 'What we're really driving after is a bit of land to build on. We don't need any help from the government if we could only get the bit of ground to start off . . . If we could get a bit of land we can build our own place which we can call our own'.[8]

On many properties, similarly determined struggles had continued until the Murri camp residents had finally been forced to leave. When they moved into the closest town, they brought to the camps there these same desires for security of residence within their own chosen country. But the towns they came into had white residents determined to protect their blocks and their control over the power structures of the town by making sure that Aboriginal people had no claim to secure residence, no claim to really belong.

Coonamble, 1960: Australia's Little Rock

Coonamble, on the southern bank of the Castlereagh River in the central west between Dubbo and Walgett, accorded itself the title of 'Australia's Little Rock' as the town split over whether land within the town was to be made available for Aboriginal people to build houses.[9] This was one of the many clear instances of the argument for whites revolving not around the future and imagined homes themselves, but about access to land in the dormitory areas of the town and the social relations that would then be allowed. The town council had repeatedly refused Welfare Board requests to purchase land within the municipal boundaries to house a few carefully selected families from the reserve across the river, where there were no houses other than those built by Aboriginal people themselves from flattened kerosene tins and bush timber. There was no electricity or water supply at all.

Some local whites formed an 'Aboriginal Welfare Association' to assist Murri families there. They included the Waterford brothers, John and Bede, who came from a family of Irish smallholders long established in the region, with John then a grazier near Quambone and Bede a solicitor and the owner of the *Coonamble Times*. Another was Ron Funnell, a dealer in skins and hides, an alderman on the Municipal Council and an active member of the ALP. As the Welfare Association, they proposed that the Council buy some of the trams being removed from Sydney streets as emergency housing for the reserve residents, but the Council rejected the proposal on the grounds that the ceilings of the trams were 3.25 inches lower than building regulations specified, and so could not be allowed to replace the shacks and humpies in which people were now housed.

Then three blocks of residential land in the middle of the town dormitory area came up for quick sale at £27 in lieu of unpaid rates. Early in 1960, John Waterford quietly bought the land, and then informed the Council it was to be transferred to the Welfare Association and then on to the Board to build houses for three Aboriginal families. At first the Council agreed, then as the implications sank in the town broke into an uproar and 117 residents petitioned the Council demanding that the transfer be blocked. As tensions rose, Aboriginal people disappeared from the streets and kept their children home from school, fearing reprisals. The divisions within the town were revealing. The only other ALP alderman was Frank Fish, who bitterly opposed Funnell and the transfer of land, on the grounds that 'the aboriginal has yet to prove himself fit to live with the white man'. Another councillor insisted he 'would stop at nothing to stop Abos living among white people, [he] would even destroy their houses'. The Australian Workers' Union also weighed in heavily in opposition to an Aboriginal presence in what they argued should remain a white residential area. 'The natives', a union spokesman said, 'should be allowed to live well out of town'. A suggestion of the deeper currents of anxiety were reflected in the argument put up by one prominent white opponent of the land transfer who recounted a scene where a white man was seen to embrace and kiss an Aboriginal woman in a Coonamble street. This, it was implied, would be the outcome of allowing Aboriginal people to live within the white dormitory area. Yet there were also strong defenders of the transfer outside the Welfare Association, in particular the Country Women's Association which insisted that 'our association makes no race, colour or creed distinction'.

The urban press had been well alerted by the coverage given to the conflict in Bede Waterford's *Coonamble Times*, which had dubbed the town 'Australia's Little Rock'. Helen Hambly, Ray Peckham and others piled into Helen's car and visited the town and found Waterford's accounts accurate, and met Mrs Kathleen Boney, who lived in one of the tin huts on the camp and worked as a domestic in town homes including that of Ron Funnell.

Eventually the widespread publicity pushed the Council into holding a public meeting, to which the AAF duly received an invitation. Helen and others returned, bringing Cecil Holmes as a journalist and observer. They dropped in to Kath Boney's as a courtesy before they entered the town, only to find that the Aboriginal townspeople had neither been informed nor invited to the meeting. Most of the men were out working, but Kathleen Boney and five other women from the camp came up to the meeting, sitting silently as the bitter arguments raged, and the meeting divided evenly over a resolution to block the transfer of land. The chairman refused to use his casting vote, and called for another show of hands. Then Kathleen Boney spoke. As Helen Hambly remembered it:

> Then Mrs Boney stood up and, in a very gentle, lovely voice, like a cooing dove, said 'We *do* want to live in town, we *do* want our children to go to school, we *do* want to live in proper houses, and . . .

And this time the Aboriginal women raised their hands in the vote, and pushed the numbers in favour of the land transfer, and a major symbolic victory was won. Cecil Holmes wrote the episode up in *People* for urban audiences, and while he expressed some doubts about how Coonamble would rise to the challenge, he closed on a hopeful note. He referred to the accompanying photograph of Lola Dodds, a beautiful young Murri girl who lived at the camps. She was at high school and studying at home by lamplight for a university entrance. Holmes ended his article hoping that now Lola Dodds would see a better future in Coonamble.

But such victories were shortlived. Helen Hambly remained in contact with the Coonamble community. As she remembered the aftermath of the meeting:

> Anyway, the meeting finished, we came back to town and Mrs. Boney

went back, the women went back to their humpies, and nothing was done. We still had to bring pressure on the Aboriginal Welfare Board to build those houses.

They finally were built, four houses . . . in sight of the humpy where Mrs Boney still lived.

She never got a house. How dare she speak up and want something?

After two years I visited up there and went looking for her and she was in a tent, in the rain and the cold, with all her furniture outside the tent, beside the river. I still don't know if she ever got a house to live in. Mrs Boney dared to ask for something, so no way would she get it.

And Lola Dodds? Helen Hambly remembered her too, with a sadness and bitterness which reflected her growing frustration at the intransigence of rural racism in New South Wales:

And once I began to go to the country, I went back regularly to the same places, but after a while I got that I hesitated to ask how is so-and-so? and where are . . . people and friends I had made. Because so many times the answer was: they died. Young women that I loved, thirty years of age, and you'd say 'where is Yvonne?', 'Where is Gloria?' They were dead. And you know, we talk about the child mortality rate, but the mortality rate for all Aboriginal people! And it's something that's so distressing when you know them and you know the struggle and how they care for each other.

Like Lola Dodds in Coonamble who passed the Leaving, how I don't know, studying in a humpy, and was very ambitious to really better herself, to help her family and her people. The first time I met Lola she was cooking on a, a little fire outside a humpy, and I went back a year later . . . Lola had died. Her mother was ill, she was looking after her mother when I met her. Her mother died and Lola had to look after the family, and then Lola died.

I mean, people can't exist in that climate, badly fed, badly clothed and badly housed.[10]

The struggle over segregation in rural New South Wales continued into the 1960s to be, as Joe Anderson had said in 1933, about land, about rights and finally about survival: 'A hundred and fifty years ago, the black man owned Australia, and now he wants more than the white man's charity. He wants the right to live!'

Lismore, 1957–60

While there was increasing press coverage of the disputes around land and housing in New South Wales over the late 1950s, there were very few in which Aboriginal people were able to record even their demands, let alone any more detailed reflections on what they understood the land in question to mean to them. An important exception is the dispute over land for housing in Lismore from 1958 to 1961, in which both local and State Aboriginal spokespeople gained at least a small platform to make clear the depth of significance around the land issue.

Pastor Frank Roberts Snr had been tenacious in struggling to retain security of residence at Tuncester near Lismore since at least the 1920s. He had used lawyers to try to protect his children's access to the public school in 1928 so the families would not have to return to live under managerial repression on Cabbage Tree Island. In 1937 and 1938 he had written to Bill Ferguson and Jack Patten to expose with careful precision the Protection Board intimidation which had been aimed at forcing his and other Bandjalang families there to move from Tuncester to the concentration station at Stoney Gully near Kyogle (see Chapter 16). Roberts and his community had won this battle, and after the reserve had been reduced in size and renamed Cubawee they were still there. But conditions had deteriorated through the 1940s and 1950s because the Welfare Board had no interest in renovating reserve housing when it still wanted to close the reserve altogether.

In 1957 the Welfare Board tried to acquire a few blocks of land within the town to rehouse some of the Bandjalang of Cubawee, with the intention of forcing the rest to Kyogle. As in so many other towns, the Lismore City Council blocked the sale in 1958, and debate over its decision began to rage. The Board responded by calling Cubawee 'the worst settlement in the state'. There were councillors and citizens who supported Aboriginal access to the town living areas. Those who were in the Lismore Aborigines Welfare Committee did so because they opposed racial inequality and discrimination, but they argued as well that the dilapidated housing and low-lying swampy grounds of Cubawee posed a health risk to both Aborigines and whites, and that the Cubawee residents were all suffering from hook and threadworm infestations.[11]

Bert Groves was then the Aboriginal representative on the Welfare Board, and he effectively used the travel and speaking opportunities this gave him to express the arguments he had been developing since the mid-1950s to oppose 'assimilation'. Some months after the Council blocked the land sale, Groves spoke in Lismore in a debate on the land-for-housing issue. His opponent was a local Church of Christ pastor, A. Caldicott, a member of the Welfare Association who was seen as a moderate supporter of Aboriginal rights. Groves demanded that

> pressure should be brought to bear on the Government to force it to resume land for the aborigines, who were the rightful owners of the land in the first place.
>
> *Pastor Caldicott:* Do you think it is right and proper to resume property belonging to others when suitable land could be obtained by other means?
>
> *Mr Groves: The land belongs to the Aborigines.*[12]

Early in 1959 Roberts gained space in the *Northern Star* for his angry denunciation not only of the Council but also of the Welfare Board and the Welfare Committee. He flatly denied the statements that the Cubawee residents all suffered from hookworm and other health problems, accusing the Welfare Committee of misrepresenting the situation completely. He characterised the attempts to move people away from Cubawee as another shirking of the responsibility to provide decent services to the land which his family and other Bandjalang people had been fighting to keep for decades. 'It is a frightful experience for the aborigines for the authorities to fire a double-barrel gun at us continually . . . We are contented to live and die at Cubawee, which can be renovated.' Roberts insisted that there was no need to bargain with local whites. He pointed out that the government could compulsorily resume any additional land required for Aboriginal housing, irrespective of local government wishes. He summed up the whole dispute with the sentence, 'We have been robbed of our heritage'.[13]

Their unequivocal statements show that Groves and Roberts saw these conflicts as being not only about the simple right for all citizens to equal access to the nation's resources but as about their heritage, which they presented as consisting of prior and continuing rights in land; this they located in the historical context of the repeated attempts to make them move away from their chosen living areas within their country. Like the earlier statements of William Cooper in 1887 and Fred Maynard in 1927, their use of the language of the liberal individual rights of citizenship carried extra meanings about the traditionally sanctioned rights of original owners. This is how Roberts expressed it in 1959: 'We are members of a democratic people and therefore have a perfect right to live in a place suitable for us'.[14] He repeated the demand in 1960: 'We are on the Federal and State electoral rolls and have a right to franchise and, therefore, a perfect right, as members of a democratic people, to live where we wish to live'.[15]

So segregation disputes must be seen as more than demands for access to the material conditions and services of towns on the basis of simple equality with fellow Australian citizens. They were also demands for land, for secure residence within one's 'heritage', in one's 'own country', or at least as near as people could achieve as they faced the constriction of access to pastoral and other lands. The land issue was interwoven in each of the problems which faced Aboriginal people during these years. At the most fundamental level, these disputes were demands by Aboriginal people for recognition of their right to live undisturbed and with security on land of their choice.

288

21
Moving Away

This book has focused on the efforts many Aboriginal people in many communities have made, from the beginnings of the invasion, to stay on or near their land, and to make their residence on their own country more secure. Those efforts were successful to a surprising degree considering the forces aligned against continued Aboriginal presence. There is an extraordinary correlation in many areas in New South Wales between the language affiliation of today's Aboriginal residents and the language recorded as having been spoken there in the earliest days of white presence.[1]

This was not, however, a universal condition. In New South Wales the pressure on Aboriginal people to leave their country and community became acute during the 1950s and 1960s. What are the implications of this for relations to land among those who by force or by choice are no longer living on their own country or have spent a long time away? Has land continued to be an issue in their lives, in their view of themselves and their place in the world, in the way they represent themselves and in the way they relate to others?

Jeremy Beckett has described the way the travel patterns of the rural capitalist economy which took seasonal pastoral workers long distances from their own communities often led to marriages. Men might take up residence in their wives' country or bring their spouse home to live with their own family. This extended the area in which a person might feel secure to travel for work or leisure because there were kin there who would have obligations to be welcoming and supportive.[2]

Occasional enforced moves before the 1936 amendments affected communities like the Walgett people transported to Angledool in 1923, who had walked back home, negating the attempt to separate them from their land. In its most active phase from 1934 to 1939, the 'Dog Act' had shifted people on an unprecedented scale, and while most people eventually returned to somewhere close to their first homes, it took a very long time for some to make this return journey. For those who married at the concentration site, there may have been a choice to stay for good. A more lasting impact on residence in the middle years of the century had been the APB and then AWB policies of removing children from their communities and sending them to employers and disciplinary locations around the State. Although the determination of these abducted children to return to their community ensured that most did so, others married or formed long-term relationships in communities far away from their own.

During the 1950s, however, the hard-won stability of people's residence on significant land began to undergo its greatest change as many Aboriginal people were forced or chose to leave their own countries and move into urban industrial areas. By the mid-1950s, the population of migrating Aboriginal people in Sydney had begun to rise rapidly, alarming inner-city councils and changing the demographic pattern of the State's Aboriginal population forever. Before 1956 most of the 12 400 Aboriginal people in the State were believed to live outside Sydney. From that date the proportions began to shift: by 1967 the Welfare Board could count 15 440 Aboriginal people in rural areas, but admitted that there could be a further 15 000 with whom the Board had no detailed contact, many of whom had moved to Sydney and the other industrial centres of Wollongong and Newcastle.[3]

Given the tenacity with which Aboriginal people in so many areas had clung to the right to stay on their land, it is important to ask how such a process occurred, whether the shift was entirely under duress, and if not then on what grounds such choices were made. The need for jobs was an important pressure on rural Aboriginal people as it was for white workers. The white railway fettlers and pastoral workers were also faced during the mid-1950s with the fact that there were fewer and fewer jobs for them in rural areas, but there were increasing opportunities in factories in the industrial cities on the coast. The white working class abandoned rural areas far more quickly than did Aboriginal workers, and so for a while this eased the job situation. But eventually the pressure of economic need began to draw Aboriginal workers and their families too.

Even more important was Aboriginal frustration with the suffocating racism of country towns. The streets and public places continued to be segregated, and *de facto* curfews still operated in many towns when C. D. Rowley toured rural New South Wales in 1964. It was not only Lake Cargelligo which guarded its 'Whites Only' toilet. Essential services such as medical care and hospitals remained available to Aborigines only on the most limited terms. The AWB was still giving tacit support to the segregation of hospitals into the late 1960s, as Aboriginal women continued to give birth in segregated labour wards, or on hospital verandahs or sheds in the grounds. The Department of Education had promised to desegregate the public schools, but in many this meant an internal segregation in separate 'slow learners' classes and with separate playing areas. Then the attempts by the Board from 1948 to secure 'houses in town' had demonstrated over and over again that even the government could not break open residential segregation.

Many Aboriginal people had become impatient with this failure after a decade. They chose to leave their own country to try living in a large town or one of the coastal industrial cities. Their decisions could be said to be voluntary, but it would be just as true to say they reflected the intolerable conditions of rural New South Wales.

The AWB too had begun to despair of rural change by 1960. Rather than recognise the intransigence of white determination to sustain residential segregation, however, it began to blame Aboriginal people for the discrimination they faced. It was their habits of 'clinging together in artificial groups' and the fact that they were 'content to live in substandard dwellings' which the Board now said were to blame for rural hostility. The Board began to see the only way out as being the relocation of rural Aboriginal populations to the cities, where there was plenty of factory work and where Aboriginal families could be more effectively dispersed among the much larger population. It argued that 'the conditions under which aborigines live in rural surroundings close to the haunts of their ancestors . . . build up a defeatist attitude'.[4]

So from 1960 the Board began to exert the kind of intimidatory pressure its predecessor had used to effect dispersal in the 1910s. It argued that Aboriginal families, and particularly young people, had to be prepared to 'pull up roots' and go to the cities for training and work. In 1962 it stated bluntly that unless people chose to leave for work in the cities, those for whom the Board had no legal responsibility, that is, those who were not 'half-castes and full-bloods', would be forced off the reserves and stations. By 1963 it began to acquire Housing Commission houses in Sydney for Aborigines, and it indicated that any Aboriginal family who wanted a house would have a far greater chance of getting one if they agreed to move to the city. This decision, the Board pointed out ominously, would be 'a test of the determination and ability of Aborigines to fit into the [white] community'.[5] Under these threats, there must have been many Aboriginal decisions to leave rural reserves which were made in the belief that if they did not go their young people would be forced away, or they would all be expelled from the reserve, or the Board would never help them find a house. Such choices cannot be called 'voluntary'.

* * *

However the choice was made, many Aboriginal people moved to the cities from the mid-1950s to the early 1970s. How did they view themselves then in relation to their home country? Did they expect to have any relationship with the country to which they moved? Some answers can be found in the life stories of Aboriginal people caught up in these migrations.

Clive Williams, a Bandjalang man from Coraki, was a highly respected and influential man within his community. As his children reached school age during the later 1950s, he had become more and more concerned about how to get the educational and social resources he wanted for them. He and his wife Ida, a member of the Gumbaynggirr Drew family from Kinchela, had moved off the over-crowded reserve at Box Ridge into a small cottage on the edge of Coraki, where they felt both comfortable and secure, but even here they knew that the available education would never be free from discrimination. Ida and her family had suffered intensely under the Protection Board regime. Their grandfather's fertile family farm at Kinchela had been taken over for its Boys' Home. Then, like so many children on the north coast in the early 1920s, Ida and her brothers and sisters had been seized by the Board and sent to the Homes themselves. Ida had found her way back to her area, but she carried bitter memories: 'When I was young, I went to Cootamundra Girls' Home and I vowed none of my children would ever go there. My two brothers were sent to Kinchela Boys' Home and it wasn't any better than the girls' home. It was horrific'.[6] In the early 1960s, confronting the need to make decisions for the sake of their children, Ida and Clive Williams decided that Clive should go to Sydney to establish himself and then bring the family after him. Clive got work with the Department of Main Roads and found a house in Rozelle to rent. After fifteen months battling loneliness and fatigue, he was able to bring his family down and enrol the children at school.

In 1966 the Commonwealth Department of Territories made *One Man's Road*,[7] a film in which Clive told his story, which at that time fitted well with government policy of 'encouraging' Aboriginal people to leave country areas and come to the cities where there was employment. The film had its limitations. It understated the pain Clive and Ida had felt in deciding to leave country which was so important to them—Ida 'cried for a week to go back to the country'—and there was only passing reference to the racism which was so much a part of north coast life.

The family had not, however, abandoned their affiliation either with their country or their kin. They formed a nucleus for migration, for they were followed by some kinsfolk of their own generation and also by young relations. With their commitment to education, the Williamses offered their tiny home to nephews and nieces who wanted to further their training in the city, allowing them a safe place to stay while they finished high school or tech, and so acting as a supportive channel for young people to escape the parochial racism of the north coast. Gary Williams was one of the young family members who came to Sydney for education and stayed with Clive and Ida in Rozelle in 1963. He learnt later from older Gumbaynggirr men that a number of them had been going out to the sites of Eora rock carvings on the coast since the 1950s, where they would sit quietly on the headlands for a while to try to re-establish a sense of custodial presence, conscious that there was no one there now to look after the land.

Similar processes of chain migration have fostered to this day a situation in which Aboriginal people in Sydney identify themselves with their country of origin, choosing places to live and work where they can relate to kin and homeplace. Clive Williams became an active member of Tranby Co-operative in inner Sydney and contributed to their programs on north coast reserves (see Chapter 22), and he and Ida continued to identify themselves as Bandjalang and Gumbaynggirr people.

There were others who came to Sydney who never saw themselves leaving their home for ever. Isabel Flick and her family left Collarenebri to escape the segregation, the police harassment and the growing unemployment of the north-west. She believed her children must be able to get a better education in the city than in the hostile country towns. Yet her mother, brothers and sisters remained in Collarenebri or nearby, and Isabel always saw her responsibilities as lying there. She made frequent returns to Collarenebri during the 1970s, and by 1978 she had returned, to take up an activist role in demanding improvements in housing and health conditions in that town. Her complex view of this place, within her father's country, has often been expressed not only through her knowledge of stories associated with the land but with her memories of childhood there, strong stories of family warmth but also of contested schooling, of confrontations with store-owners and cinema proprietors, that is, with experiences of making a place for herself, her family and her community.

Her attention has often been focused on a funeral fund, a consequence of the ever-present tragedy of the high death rate among Murris at home and away. Isabel and her family, like others in Collarenebri, have spent many hours maintaining the two cemeteries just outside the town, extraordinary sites where generations of Murri families have tended the decorated graves. These cemeteries hold the old people, and their burial sites mark the community's living places on the outskirts of the town for a hundred years. So for Isabel this is her land in the traditional sense, but intensified with the painful as well as the rich experiences of being a Murri there.

There have been others who have left their country for whom it became clear there was to be no permanent return. Jack Campbell had lived his early childhood on Burnt Bridge, then he and his family had had to flee the Protection Board's Inspector Donaldson after Jack's mother fired a shotgun over his head to protect her children (see Chapter 11). After living in Sydney until his mother's death in 1932, Jack went to live with his father's relations at Wallaga Lake. Then, after a short apprenticeship, he returned to Burnt Bridge during 1937. There he underwent initiation, learning lessons both about Dhan-gadi law and his country there which he was to hold central to his life ever after.

Yet he continued to travel between the north and south coast, as many young men did, and after the war he married Nancy Wellington and settled at Roseby Park, on the coast 20 miles from Nowra. A deeply reflective man, Jack had taken his learning during initiation with the greatest seriousness. He never abandoned his responsibilities to the Dhan-gadi lands and people. He returned there to participate in an initiation during the 1970s, but otherwise he did not take an active role in north coast affairs. With his marriage in the 1950s he recognised that he would be living on country not his own, but he believed that as a responsible man he should help to look after the land on which he and his family lived. For Jack, one could not claim to be a mature and responsible adult unless one took up responsibilities for caring for land and the people who belonged to it.

Jack Campbell's custodianship was nevertheless always undertaken with the proper consultation with his wife and her sister, whom he regarded as the authoritative owners of the country. At no time during his active political career from the 1960s until his death in 1983 did he ever fail to consult or acknowledge his wife and her family. Yet his life's work was to establish security of residence for his wife's community over the reserve at Roseby Park, as well as to contribute more generally to the extension of Aboriginal land all over the State and to the protection of sites of great religious significance on both north and south coasts. In Chapter 1, I have discussed the means within contemporary central and northern Australian communities for renegotiating custodial relations to land where the person expected to fulfil the custodial role cannot do so. Campbell, and no doubt many other men and women in south-eastern Australia since the invasion began, have drawn on such mechanisms. Despite the massive changes brought about by invasion and colonialism, they continue to believe that a central and rightful part of an adult's responsibilities is their obligation to care for the land

and its people, and they try to establish and sustain such responsibilities even when they are no longer living on their own country.

This has not been a choice made only by people of Campbell's generation. Nor has it only been possible to establish or renegotiate relationships with land in beautiful rural settings. There are other, younger people who have had less direct teaching in formal oral tradition or ceremony, yet who have also taken up obligations towards land after they have moved to live on country which is not their own by birth. Judy Chester's family were forced to leave Wellington in the late 1950s because her mother had a serious illness and needed to be close to medical attention. Judy's family lived first in Redfern, then, after her father suffered an injury at work, they moved to the grossly underresourced 'new' suburb of Green Valley south-west of Sydney. In 1967 Judy was a young mother with a small family in what was often described as an urban wasteland. Yet she began to feel it was important to learn about that land.

> I suppose I didn't really feel connected to it until I had the kids. You see my kids were born and reared there and I thought, this is our country, it's where my kids were born.
>
> And then I started getting interested in who lived here before, and how we have to respect the sites and look after that land. Especially when I found out that the whole Gandangara nation was killed off, you know?
>
> I thought, well, there's nobody from that country here to look after it, so we as Aboriginal people have to look after this land for them, and I tried to find out as much as I could about the sites in the area, and about the people, because I thought, this is my kids' country.[8]

This individual conviction that one should assume responsibility for the land on which one was living and on which one's children were born, regardless of its being covered with bitumen and concrete, was not uncommon. In later decades it was to be the basis on which urban land councils were to form. These newcomers who were willing to take up custodial obligations for land needed to negotiate with the owners. There are remaining Gandangara from the south-western areas of Sydney who have continued to be active as custodians. Robyn Williams, of the same age as Judy, is a Gandangara woman whose grandmother was able to pass on directly to her family the stories for the land around what is now Liverpool and Camden. She has acted as a catalyst over the 1960s and 1970s, drawing together Aboriginal newcomers who, like Judy, were interested in taking up custodial roles. In organisations which grew out of Aboriginal women's supportive networks for childcare, such as the St John's Park Aboriginal Women's Group, Robyn, Judy and others researched places and history, and taught themselves and their children more about the land for which they had taken custodianship. When Land Councils were established during the early 1980s, it was informal networks such as these which were given a voice.

For many Aboriginal people, therefore, relating to land continues to be an important way to achieve a sense of maturity and fulfilment of their obligations to themselves, their communities and their children. Moving away has neither severed their sense of relating to their home country, nor has it removed the *idea* that a custodial relationship to land is an important part of an adult's social role.

Yet by no means did all those people who left their own country maintain a sense of identification and engagement with their own land, nor were all able to negotiate relationships with new land and its owners which were satisfactory to everyone. The pressures which demanded migration, the imposed policies or the constriction of opportunities until there was no option but to leave, have left many scars and many questions. What of the people who were taken away as children and have only been able to return to their communities as adults? How do they perceive their relations to land and how do their communities see them? And do those people who chose to leave in the 1950s and 1960s, but who now return after decades in the city, have less authority having been unable to fulfil obligations all those years? And do those who stayed now have greater authority? Such questions are the uneasy backdrop of contemporary land politics in the 1990s, as Aboriginal people are forced to carry the burden of the massive interventions in their relationships to place and community which have taken place over the last century.

22
Reasserting Land Rights, 1957–64

The 1950s saw a rising number of conflicts around segregation in which land issues were present, entwined with other urgent issues. Over the same decade more Aboriginal people than ever before came under intensifying pressure to leave their own country to look for work, education and housing in the coastal cities. Although often poorly recognised by non-Aboriginal supporters and opponents alike, pressure was building for a re-emergence of land issues onto the centre of the political stage.

The 1950s had seen not only a rise in conflict over segregation of town space, but direct assaults on the remaining Aboriginal land base. The coastal areas bore the heaviest losses in this period, as towns expanded and particularly as holiday and leisure use of coastal land became more lucrative. The first hit were the remaining Gumbaynggirr and Dhan-gadi reserves on the mid-coast, many of which had been settled and farmed independently by Kooris from the 1880s. The Buchanans' land at Cow Creek near Nambucca had already been leased to whites in the devastating land loss of the 1920s, so its revocation in 1952 was bitterly resented but did not lead to new dislocation. At Urunga too, at the mouth of the South Bellinger River, the population had already been forcibly transported to Burnt Bridge in 1937, so there were no large-scale movements when the 250 acres of reserve land were revoked in 1954.

Stuart's Island was very different. This large, beautiful island near the mouth of the Nambucca River had been a traditional Gumbaynggirr camping ground and had been lived on continuously by the extended family of Frank Whaddy after it was reserved in his name in 1883. Although some people had moved off when the Welfare Board closed the segregated school on the island, there were still members of these families living there in 1955. They had been pushed into one corner of the island because the local golf club had taken a special lease with the Welfare Board and cleared the rest for a golf course. In that year the Board revoked the reserve and forced the remainder of the residents to leave their homesites and burial ground. In a deeply felt desecration, one of the fairways was built over the graves.[1] Then Euroka Creek, part of the independent farm land at Burnt Bridge, was revoked in 1956, despite the crowding on the new mission and the continuing insistence by the original farming families that the land had been set aside for them by Queen Victoria.[2] These were virtually the last of the independently settled lands in the Gumbaynggirr and Dhan-gadi countries. Although these revocations intensified the bitterness of the landowners, they had suffered their greatest losses in the 1920s, and believed they could do little now to retrieve their most fertile land. They were tragically deceived in this belief, but they were not to learn of this until 1981.

THE BANDJALANG DEFEND THEIR LANDS

The coastal Bandjalang to the north were also coming under intensifying pressure in the mid-1950s. The Cubawee families in Lismore were facing the closure of their reserve site and pressure to live separately in town houses. During 1958 there were repeated calls on the State government to open up Crown land on the far north coast to foster 'a big increase in the tourist trade', and during a major program of harbour dredging and camping area improvement, 180 acres of Aboriginal reserve land at Yamba was revoked to allow better tourist access to the foreshores.[3] Other smaller reserves were revoked over the next couple of years, but the main revocations occurred in the high country of the inland Bandjalang.

After the concentration of the Stoney Gully people on Woodenbong in 1940 (see Chapter 16), there was some respite from land loss, but an increase in Welfare Board presence in the area began with a manager installed at Tabulam in 1946, and one of the first district welfare officers was located at Casino in 1948. Employment relations in this former cattle country were now utterly disrupted. What work Kooris could get gave no guarantees of access to land, as the earlier cattle camps had done, but neither was it at equal wages. Aboriginal protests led finally in 1955 to intervention by the Department of Labour and Industry to enforce the payment of award wages to Aboriginal workers. Hostility between whites and Kooris intensified in this rapidly changing social and economic context, until even the AWB remarked on how tense the atmosphere was around Woodenbong and how prevalent the discrimination. Conditions deteriorated still further in 1958, when corn harvesters were introduced into the new agricultural areas around Tabulam, undercutting the remaining economic base of the Bandjalang there.[4]

Such processes all contributed to growing anxiety, but then the revocation focus began to shift to this inland area. There were 33 reserve revocations from 1957 to 1964, about half of them scattered across the State, but fourteen were in a block from the north coast and eleven of these were from the inland Bandjalang country. Land prices were rising as agriculture and dairying penetrated the beef-producing areas, and mechanisation changed the structure of each of these industries. Reserve lands were eagerly sought after in this climate for development or expansion of neighbouring holdings.

Despite the pressure which the Bandjalang were under in the late 1950s, they also had some unique strengths. They were a language group which had always had a fertile land base, and although the Queensland Native Police had operated in the area, a large population had survived after the invasion violence. The rugged nature of much of their country allowed protection of many significant sites during later years, and dual occupation had allowed a strong knowledge of Bandjalang language and culture to be sustained.

The coastal Bandjalang had had a longer and more difficult exposure to heavy colonisation, although cushioned by the high demands for labour in the subtropical climate with multiple harvests each year and an abundance of natural resources. This had allowed the coastal communities to develop highly sophisticated dealings with whites, as Frank Roberts Snr had demonstrated repeatedly. This was not only a case of the strengths of one individual, for as a lay preacher Roberts had developed a relatively autonomous Christian network between Bandjalang communities across the whole region, and this had allowed communication and discussion on land and segregation issues among both coastal and inland communities, drawing together the inland traditional knowledge and confidence with the coastal people's experience in white politics. In the mid-1950s Frank Roberts Jnr was ordained as a Church of Christ preacher, and his institutional connections were turned to the same work as his father had been carrying on since the 1920s.

The highly politicised Christianity of father and son brought them into contact with the Revd Alf Clint, an Anglican priest whose longest alliances were with socialist trade unionists rather than with the Australian Board of Missions (ABM) who employed him. Clint had grown up in Balmain and been involved with working-class co-operatives all his life. In Australia co-operatives have often been taken up by farming communities and small businesses, and have aimed at conservative social goals.[5] Alf Clint, however, had experienced the co-operative movement as one which offered support and independence to poor working-class communities.[6]

Alf had been a 'Bush Brother', actively supporting striking pastoral workers during the big 1930 strikes around Brewarrina and Bourke, and it was here that he had begun a lifelong interest in Aboriginal communities. Later, while in Papua New Guinea, he began working with villagers there in developing co-operative enterprises, and on his return to Australia he persuaded the ABM in 1951 to adopt co-operatives as a strategy for its work among Aboriginal people. Clint's radical politics alarmed the State government, which made it harder for him to work there from the mid-1950s before finally withdrawing its permission for him to enter Queensland reserves in 1961.

Meanwhile, Clint had been contacting both union and Aboriginal people throughout New South Wales from at least 1953, informing them about co-operatives as a means to economic independence.[7] His confidence in co-operatives arose from his belief that the collective ownership of enterprises, and the communal and egalitarian distribution of work and profits, reflected the traditional social organisation of Aboriginal communities. In fact co-operatives arose in the conditions of nineteenth-century trade unionism in which socialists advocated utopian new forms of collective organisation based on what they nostalgically imagined a pre-industrial, secular community of agrarian workers must have been like, organised around a collective and equal distribution of both labour and profits.

This had little congruence with any Australian indigenous societies, none of which have been organised around a secular notion of 'the community'. Instead, most seem to have organised their social, economic and political life around families and individuals who had their most compelling links not to a secular 'community' but to the land and, through it, to a transcendent, supra-human Law. Clint's reasoning sounded valid to the Left, however, in the economistic terms of 1950s socialism, where an 'economic base' was thought to be essential. His logic was also acceptable in liberal reformist circles, such as those of the Welfare Board, in which it was thought that the most important need was to teach Aboriginal people disciplined and responsible work habits. So for a number of reasons, Alf Clint's ideas appealed strongly to unionists and socialists of the time, and as well drew interest and support for at least a time from the NSW Welfare Board itself.

Western philosophies were of little interest to Aborigines, but the co-operative idea offered something absolutely compelling, something which was not at all apparent to most white supporters of the idea: co-operatives offered a defence against both the intensifying revocation of reserves and the growing pressure to move into 'pepperpotted' houses in towns. A co-operative could allow people to stay on their reserves and within their community. It could give people independence from white managers, because the co-ops would be self-governing. It would allow people economic independence from the Board, and it would

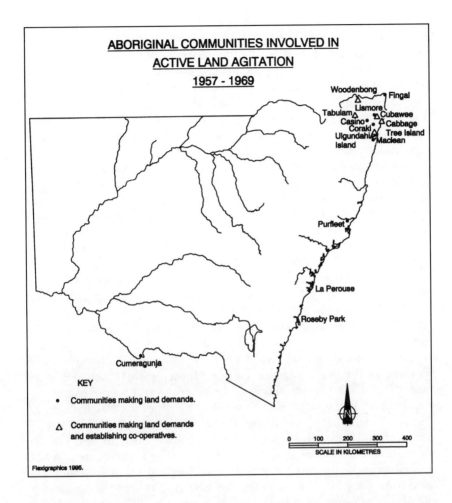

ABORIGINAL COMMUNITIES INVOLVED IN
ACTIVE LAND AGITATION
1957 - 1969

Woodenbong
Fingal
Lismore
Tabulam
Cubawee
Casino
Coraki
Cabbage
Ulgundahi
Tree Island
Island
Maclean

Purfleet

La Perouse

Roseby Park

Cumeragunja

KEY

• Communities making land demands.

△ Communities making land demands
and establishing co-operatives.

0   100   200   300   400
SCALE IN KILOMETRES

Flexigraphics 1995.

provide an unarguable case for remaining on one's land. The Bandjalang took up the idea strongly, as rumours started to circulate that Cabbage Tree Island reserve was to be leased or sold. After discussions in 1958, they supported Alf Clint when he took the proposition to the Welfare Board that co-operative enterprises be started on Cabbage Tree Island, Woodenbong and Tabulam stations.[8]

Cabbage Tree Island became the first New South Wales co-operative, launched officially in August 1960, as a retail store and sugar plantation on 45 acres leased formally from the Welfare Board.[9] In the view of the Board, the enterprise was being run by the ABM; in the opinion of Alf Clint and the Cabbage Tree Island Bandjalang, it was being run by the community, under the direction of Bob Bolt, the chairman of the island Board of Directors. With its rich alluvial soil and its experienced workers, the co-op worked well from the start. Its rapid sucess in gaining the interest and enthusiastic participation of the islanders and its early financial returns sustained the Welfare Board's cautious support, and so it responded positively as the Bandjalang pushed forward. Within a few months they had petitioned the Board to agree to lease land on Ulgundahi Island, Cubawee and Coraki reserves to Bandjalang co-operatives. Early in 1962 further plans had been put before the Board, with a proposal for a co-operative sawmill at Woodenbong and a co-operative farm at Tabulam.

Bandjalang goals had been partly articulated by Frank Roberts Snr in 1959 when he stated that the Cubawee dispute exposed the fundamental problem that 'we have been robbed of our heritage'. He was not alone among the Bandjalang in expressing the conviction that their present goals required recognition of dispossession, restoration of land security and compensation for lands irretrievably lost. Euston Williams and Alex Vesper of Woodenbong were recording the stories of their country with Roland Robinson at the time, demonstrating the deep knowledge they and other landowners there held of the Bandjalang law for the whole region.[10]

Vesper was intensely committed to organising politically to secure Bandjalang tenure over the land which still remained in their possession as reserves. Still deeply troubled by the loss of Stoney Gully, he revealed his sense of personal obligation to Jack Horner, saying, 'I should never have allowed the land at Kyogle to be taken away. I was *responsible* for that land'.[11] In 1959 he was organising meetings at Woodenbong to discuss the land issue, and when he felt too closely observed he moved the meetings from the community hall into the open air and outside the station fenceline so no uninvited Board officers could listen. Yet he wanted to make his wider demands heard beyond his own community. To do this he made contact with the emerging political organisations, the Aboriginal–Australian Fellowship and the Federal Council for Aboriginal Advancement through Roland Robinson. Having organised for fourteen Woodenbong Kooris to become members of the AAF, Vesper attended the third annual Federal Council meeting in Sydney in March 1960.[12] Robinson described Vesper at this time:

> Alex is now seventy years old, a tall, upright, hardworking man with a shock of white hair. He still works at all kinds of bush work—fencing, clearing, and so on. He is deeply religious, both in the tribal sense and in the Christian sense, and will not be parted from an old leather-bound bible which he always has with him.[13]

Faith Bandler has described his presence and impact on the Federal Council meeting, with Aboriginal and white delegates from many areas in Australia, but an agenda which was still dominated by topics like 'Social Services campaign report and Action to be taken against discrimination in employment'.[14] Bandler recalls that Vesper rose to his feet, holding his bible, and demanding attention for a message from the Bandjalang people and their struggles over land. His intervention generated great discussion. It was the first time the issue of land had been raised in such a dramatic way, as a matter that required urgent priority even over matters of civil rights. The Bandjalang had given notice: the public campaign for land rights had been reopened.

Both Vesper and Euston Williams continued to work actively, maintaining contact and coming to Sydney for meetings, encouraging both AAF and FCAA members to see the priority of the land question. Jack Horner remembers Williams and Vesper as spokespeople chosen by their community because of their fluency in English. They presented the principles they derived from elders like Cecil Taylor, who authorised their statements from his knowledge of Law and language. In Horner's view, 'Alex Vesper educated us on land rights in FCAATSI as early as 1960 and in all conferences until 1969'.[15] The issue was being raised in a different way on the mid-north coast, where in 1960 Aboriginal residents at Purfleet had begun a well-coordinated rent strike. Led by Horace Saunders, a fisherman with six children, a total of twenty Koori families faced Welfare Board prosecution and eviction. Their focal protest was that the Board demanded they 'prove their sense of responsibility' by paying rent to live in the appalling slum conditions of the Board's stations. More broadly, their protest opened up the injustice of their lack of control over any of their own land. Eventually, in 1961, even the Board had to admit that what it faced at Purfleet and elsewhere was not financial irresponsibility but widespread civil disobedience, in protest, the Board conceded, 'for dispossessing them of their lands'.[16]

Over these two years, the results of meetings and conferences from the north coast where Aboriginal people were participants now invariably produced resolutions calling for various means to address the land issue. A conference attended by both Aboriginal delegates and whites was called in Casino during May 1961, by the Casino Advancement League. The resolutions called for more encouragement for Aboriginal co-operatives and for a special scheme to acquire land for Aboriginal people, along the lines of the War Service Settlement scheme. Such growing pressure showed in FCAA annual general meetings, where now more resolutions were passed about 'detribalised reserves', calling for an end to revocations, an expansion of the land base and better housing and wages.[17]

The Welfare Board, however, was becoming anxious about the co-operative idea. The Cabbage Tree Island Co-op was doing well but was not likely to produce enough of a profit to lead to any substantial self-sufficiency for the island's population. The Board was only interested in economic outcomes, and so it sought advice from the Forestry Commission about the timber co-op proposed from Woodenbong and from the Department of Agriculture on the farming co-ops of Cubawee, Tabulam and Cabbage Tree Island. The commission assessed the feasibility of the proposals and rejected each in conventional economic terms as being able to support, at most, only a few families, and because they required an input of capital to start them, without a firm guarantee of viability. It refused to allow Woodenbong Kooris access to Crown logs. The Board had no capital and no inclination to help with establishing the enterprises.[18] To the extent that it was interested in Aboriginal economic independence, it was far more interested in the family farm model, which it felt stressed individual nuclear family achievement, rather than the collective approach fostered by co-operative management. It began to encourage individual share-farming with neighbouring white farmers or individual leases on a number of reserves, including Tabulam and later Woodenbong, against the residents' clear preference for collective enterprises.[19]

Despite this retreat by the Welfare Board on co-operatives, the Bandjalang communities became more assertive about their demands. They were encouraged by intense activity on the part of AAF members, who travelled extensively during 1961 and 1962, making new contacts, keeping people informed of events and plans in other areas, and fact-finding to report to unions and interested supporters. Dick Hunter was an extraordinary Aboriginal man from Broome who had travelled as a seaman around the coast and spent a number of years in Sydney, from the mid-1950s, taking an active part in political organisations. With Ray Peckham and Helen Hambly, these three made a series of major trips during this time.

As the three were members of the Communist Party, ASIO was deeply suspicious, reporting that 'they tour Australia on behalf of the CPA'. Hambly's recollection, however, is that the CPA was far more interested in campaigns to challenge legal discrimination than in the information they brought back about deeper Aboriginal issues of cultural difference. Certainly these three activists were energetic in their travels, and were deeply involved in the delegations to Coonamble and the central west during the conflict over housing blocks in 1960. They reported on labour and living conditions from Lake Tyers in Victoria on up the south coast of New South Wales to report to the South Coast TLC in November 1961. Then this group travelled with Charlie Leon, now president of the AAF, and Roland Robinson to the far north coast. But there were other AAF members who were just as energetically trying to learn more about rural conditions by going there. Jack and Jean Horner used their holidays to travel to the Armidale area in one trip and then to the

304

north coast, making contact with the rent-strikers in Purfleet who were facing eviction. Emil and Hannah Witton were among other AAF members who also travelled extensively along the coast, reaching the far south coast with Ken Brindle on one trip and then the far northern Bandjalang communities on the next.[20]

The Welfare Board was increasingly anxious in the face of this activity. The AAF had launched a campaign to have discriminatory clauses of the Aborigines Protection Act repealed, and although it had made the tactical decision to focus on Section 9, which prohibited the sale of alcohol to Aborigines, the Board was well aware that the eventual target was the whole act and the Board itself. So it instructed its managers to implement even more tightly the regulations forbidding entry to reserves and stations to any whites at all, and to any Aboriginal people who were not approved by the manager and the Board. The irony of the Welfare Board's assimilation policy was that while it tried to disperse families to anonymity, it needed ever-increasing control over as yet 'unassimilated' people to hold them within its re-education stations or under the surveillance of the DWOs. This control over access was increasingly an issue. Not only was Helen Hambly refused entry to stations on the south coast, but so too were Dick Hunter and Ray Peckham. Then, in October 1961, Charlie Leon, who was the Aboriginal member of the Welfare Board, was denied access to north coast stations by a manager, a decision later confirmed by the Board itself on the grounds that Leon had not given prior notice of his arrival.[21]

The Bandjalang made their demands even more explicit in the conference Frank Roberts Jnr organised in Casino in September 1962. Over a hundred Aboriginal people attended from sixteen mainly Bandjalang communities in the far north, from both inland and along the coast. Many of the resolutions dealt with land issues. The conference demanded the establishment of experimental farms to train Aborigines in farming methods and farm management and funds to help them buy land for farming. It insisted there be no further revocations of reserves; that Section 8 of the Act be repealed, to end any further Board control over entry and presence on reserve lands; that there be large increases in funding for housing on reserves; and that these lands be available for private ownership to remove them entirely from domination by the Board. Finally, the meeting expressed its sense of regional traditional and historical coherence by insisting that further representation on any administrative bodies be elected from Aboriginal communities on a regional basis.[22]

This focus on land was reflected in a rising emphasis in AAF documents with the issues which so concerned the Bandjalang. A special meeting was held in September 1962 when it had become apparent that the government was going to respond to AAF pressure to repeal the alcohol restriction of Section 9, but would leave intact the rest of its discriminatory laws. There had been disquiet among some AAF members that the focus on Section 9 had been too narrow. Now the meeting resolved to intensify pressure to repeal the whole act and replace it with legislative guarantees that, among other things, Aborigines would have effective representation in the management of reserves and stations. Most particularly, the AAF now demanded that there be no further revocations, and that reserve lands should no longer be leased or sold to whites.[23]

The intensity of Bandjalang pressure about land in the late 1950s and early 1960s arose because they were being threatened in the way the Dhan-gadi and the Gumbaynggirr had been in the 1910s and 1920s. When the Macleay Kooris had been organising political action and trying to gather Aboriginal and white support, the Bandjalang had been protected by the continuation of the cattle industry in the inland and the relatively small white population on the coast. Although they had supported the more southerly organisers of the AAPA, they had not taken any initiating role.

By the 1950s the circumstances had changed dramatically. Stripped of their land, the Dhan-gadi and the Gumbaynggirr focused on protesting AWB control, despite an underlying bitterness over the injustice of their dispossession. It was the Bandjalang who were now in a desperate struggle to protect their remaining land and communities. So it was the Bandjalang who in the 1950s initiated the political demands concerning land: an end to revocation, a restoration of a wider land base, and compensation for land lost irretrievably. The co-operative movement offered them a novel form in which to express these ideas: it allowed them to defend continued occupation of reserve lands and to do so as communities in collective enterprises rather than as individual farmers.

While this power of the co-operatives had been increasingly troubling the Welfare Board, it had escaped the notice of many of the white supporters. These people had been working actively in the AAF to foster co-operatives because they saw them as advancing the goals of equality and civil rights. An ABC team of investigative journalists was perceptive enough to recognise the oppositional role of the co-operatives. 'Four Corners' broadcast a study of the north coast co-ops in September 1963 in which it filmed extensively on Cabbage Tree Island and interviewed both Alf Clint and Bob Bolt, the Bandjalang managing director of the co-op. The report made the point very clearly that the co-ops offered an alternative to the government's assimilation goals and that it was for this reason that Aboriginal people were participating so enthusiastically. Many members of the AAF were taken aback. It seems that this program jolted many into recognising that there might be differing priorities between Aboriginal activists and their white supporters. The AAF newsletter carried this reflective paragraph in September:

> Always a thought-provoking program, *Four Corners* raised some interesting questions on the value of Aboriginal Co-operatives, and how they fit into or conflict with government Assimilation policies. It provided a sharp reminder for some Fellowship members that the word 'assimilation' if narrowly interpreted can lead to the absorption and final disappearance of the group identity of the Aboriginal people.[24]

The Australian Board of Missions, however, was now worried at the politicised nature of the co-operative movement operating in its name, and began to distance itself from Clint. In August the organisation, which was now strongly identified with the old house in Glebe which had been bequeathed to it, took its name to become known as the Tranby Co-operative for Aborigines Ltd.[25]

A GROUNDSWELL OF AWARENESS

The Bandjalang proposals and demands would not have been effective in attracting support among Aboriginal people from other areas if they had not reflected issues which were emerging there as well. There were two regions with quite similar concerns, although for different reasons. In the Western Division, as with the high-land Bandjalang, dual occupation was being finally eroded and so people with a strong history of access to traditional lands were now being forced into towns and confined on reserves or stations. These western areas were to emerge more openly in demands for land during the next decade. On the south coast Kooris were facing escalating urban expansion and tourism even though this was less rapid than in the north, and here they were already mobilising to protect their remaining reserves.

Many of the reserves set aside for Aboriginal people during the 1860s and 1870s on the south coast continued to exist. There were some large Aboriginal living areas, like Roseby Park, which had a complex history in which the land of traditional camping sites had been secured by donation from surrounding white landowners, then with small sections reserved but others occupied by tradition and 'permissive occupancy' rather than formal dedication. Such sites were often on spectacularly beautiful shorelines, lake frontages and headlands. Roseby Park, Wallaga Lake and other reserves further south were potentially enormously lucrative as holiday developments. In 1949 a section of the eastern foreshores of Wallaga Lake Reserve, close to the entrance of the lake, was revoked by the Board and handed over to local whites for holiday cottages. This section of the reserve was not only beautiful but deeply significant to the Koori landowners, as it contained a number of burial sites.[26]

The Welfare Board was by this time, however, interested only in the eventual goal of closing down the reserves, and it refused to repair the housing or infrastructure on this or other reserves which were remote from the coastal towns. By 1955 the Board could report confidently that it expected to be able to house many of the residents of Roseby Park station in Nowra soon, so that 'in the not too distant future it will be possible to close down Roseby Park Station'.[27] By then, this was the home of Jack Campbell, living there with his wife Nancy Wellington and her family. Campbell's experiences at Burnt Bridge had left him with grave concerns about the Board's intentions for reserve lands, and now, after the example of Wallaga Lake, south coast people were only too aware that their land was the target of developers.

The first major conflict arose further north, over Aboriginal people's living areas which were not formally reserved. A number of Wodi-Wodi families had been living near Port Kembla on a rich traditional campsite known as 'Hill 60'.[28] It was an ideal site, situated on a rocky headland which allowed a clear view of the sea for spotting schools of fish, and which sheltered rich shellfish grounds at its base. The centuries of use by Wodi-Wodi people were attested by the great shell middens in the area. A public recreation reserve known as Coomaditchie had been declared on adjacent land in 1929, and both were used as campsites for Aboriginal and white unemployed during the Depression. During the 1950s the area reverted to mainly Aboriginal use, and their affiliation to the site was made clear as early as 1955 when they told a government land inspector that they had no intention of moving. The Welfare Board began to apply more direct pressure to force people to move into housing commission houses planned for the surrounding area, and by March 1957 had begun assisting in evictions of residents.

By 1958, the Hill 60 residents had made a stand. On behalf of ten other Aboriginal families, Jack Tattersall wrote to the Minister of Lands appealing for secure residence so that homes could be built for them on the site. Tattersall described the 'old southern "Jim Crow" attitude against us from a section of the folks with a lighter pigment in their skin', but his main ground for the request was that 'this reserve is the only home we have'. Some of the families facing eviction had members in the Waterside Workers' Federation, and the South Coast Trades and Labour Council became involved. The TLC negotiators stated their understanding of the demands of the Aboriginal people with whom they had been consulting: 'these people, as well as having been robbed of their land, have been gradually losing their culture. We want to help them to preserve some historic Camping, Feasting and Burial Grounds'. In August 1961 they believed they had won an agreement from the government for the setting aside of thirteen building blocks on the Hill 60-Coomaditchie site, with Welfare Board approval for the construction of that number of houses.[29]

The Welfare Board failed to fulfil this promise, like so many others. Within months it decided it had only enough funds to build six houses, expecting that other residents would then be forced to move to Housing Commission flats, because, as it stated, the other families 'did not contain sufficient aboriginal blood to be classified as Aborigines within the meaning of the Act'. The campaign continued with strong support from south coast unions, and in September 1962 a single-acre Aboriginal reserve was declared, and six small houses built. Aboriginal residents hoped to be able to extend their land there, but in 1967 the area immediately behind Coomaditchie was turned over to sand-mining, devastating the environment. Hill 60 has not yet been regained.[30]

By 1961, Roseby Park had come under direct threat. Hunter, Peckham and Hambly travelled along the coast in December with the South Coast TLC delegate Joe Howe, a Port Kembla wharfie, and they were most concerned at the appalling living and working conditions of the many Koori seasonal workers along the coast picking peas and beans. Hambly remembered, however, that the Aboriginal people they consulted at each settlement were insistent that land issues were of great importance to them. Particularly at Roseby Park, she recalled that Jack Campbell and his family had expressed the extreme concerns of the community. Despite her preoccupation with living and labour conditions, she recalls that her attention was redirected during this trip to recognising the importance of land for New South Wales Aboriginal people. She remembered that this was still unfamiliar to the non-Aboriginal supporters in Sydney: 'They [Kooris] told us they wanted their land to grow their own beans and live, and when I came back to Sydney and said that, people said, "Oh, you're making that up, they're not ready for that!" '.[31] A shift in the investigating group's attention was apparent in the report Joe Howe presented to the South Coast TLC later in December:

> At Roseby Park, a road has been surveyed through the property and the people fear that the Aborigines Welfare Board is planning to sell a part of their land. The Aborigine people everwhere are proud of the land where they live and strongly resent the repeated moves by the Board, to sell or lease the land. One of their main needs is to ensure that the last remaining pieces of land that are now Stations or Reserves are kept intact and become the property of the Aborigine people themselves. They ask for support from all people in this struggle to retain these areas of land, that they have for so long regarded as their property.[32]

This message from communities in both fear and hope over their land did increasingly find its way to the metropolitan organising groups. As was often the case, it was the growing Aboriginal pressure which began to push supportive white organisations to change their policies. By January 1962 the CPA policy had changed noticeably to oppose 'assimilation' and to give limited support for land acquisition for 'those driven off reserves'.[33]

Early in 1963 the growing awareness of land demands was reinforced by yet another area. This was Cumeragunja, the now dispersed community which had never forgotten its desire to win its land back. Victorian Aboriginal people appeared to be facing a different situation from those in New South Wales. There had been minimal intervention by the Victorian Aborigines Board for decades, and there were now only four reserves left in the State after the government's effective withdrawal from Aboriginal affairs in the 1880s. Then, after an inquiry in 1956 into Aboriginal living conditions, an Aborigines Welfare Board was set up in 1957 with a brief to pursue an aggressive policy of assimilation by dispersing reserve communities. Lake Tyers, one of the remaining reserves, was a community in constant contact with Aboriginal people on the New South Wales south coast, and they had communicated their fears of reserve revocation. The managerial control at Lake Tyers was brutal, and Dick Hunter made a special visit there during 1962 after a station resident was shot at by the manager because he had not reported his return to his home.[34]

In this climate, the Cumeragunja exiles in Melbourne began to plan a return to their land. All but 200 acres of the 2695-acre reserve had now been leased out or revoked in favour of neighbouring white farmers. But there were about 70 Aboriginal people who still refused to leave, despite the dismantling of all the extensive station buildings except the schoolhouse. In 1960 the Cumeragunja exiles in the Kew branch of the Victorian Aborigines Advancement League (VAAL) launched a Land Committee and began to prepare a detailed plan for reclamation of the remaining 1500 acres of reserve which were leased to whites, then the redevelopment of the farming there.[35] They drew up a detailed set of plans, reminiscent of the many well-thought-out and practical proposals William Cooper had submitted over the years.

This proposal was taken to the NSW government in February 1963, in a delegation which included Kevin Atkinson, from the family of those early petitioners for land, John Atkinson and William Cooper, as well as Pastor Doug Nicholls from VAAL and Charlie Leon and Jack Horner from the AAF. They presented a case to the Board which drew on the community's memory of their history on the reserve:

The land is at present neglected, but it is potentially highly productive.

It was, in fact, farmed very successfully by Aborigines from 1884 to 1903. The leases of the individual blocks were then withdrawn, however, and let to local Indian hawkers . . . There are now twelve Aboriginal families at Cummeroogunja. They comprise approximately 100 people who feel closely identified with their traditional territory. The proposed 1700 acres sheep and wheat farm cannot provide a living for them until irrigation makes more intensive production possible; but even in its early stages of development the farm will raise the standard of living of the people of Cummeroogunja considerably. It will also lift the morale of a people who are losing their confidence in themselves, but who are still keen to improve their lot by their own hard work.[36]

The older-style proposition of family farm blocks was now more appealing to the Welfare Board as its anxieties about co-operatives festered. So it gave guarded support for the idea, and agreed to cancel a 200-acre lease to one of the neighbouring farmers as a sign of goodwill. VAAL members and the Cumeragunja residents began a program of building and improvements on the land to which they did have access, and brought six head of Hereford cattle as the nucleus of a herd to run along with the planned wheat farming. Then they waited while the NSW Board investigated the legalities of indemnifying itself against any problems or financial losses.

The growing pressure from communities in these three areas, the north coast, the south coast and Cumeragunja, had created a groundswell of awareness of land issues in New South Wales and Victoria. The AAF seemed by this time strongly committed to the attempt to campaign around the issue of land ownership and protection. In his address to the AAF's annual conference in February 1963, the president, Charlie Leon, had 'laid stress on the importance of co-operatives', reflecting the strength of the north coast pressure to secure viable enterprises to protect their land.[37]

Then, at its Easter Conference in April 1963, the FCAA learnt that Aboriginal people at Yirrkala in Arnhem Land were facing the loss of a large area of their reserved land. The federal government had excised 140 square miles of reserve land and handed it over to Pechiney Bauxite, the Swiss-controlled company (later Nabalco) which wanted to mine bauxite at Gove. The traditional owners of the land, supported by Edgar Wells, the Methodist missionary there, and the FCAA, submitted a series of petitions on bark to federal Parliament, expressing their determination to protect their land. Their novel form of petition, their confident assertion of ownership and the clear injustice of the government's land grab attracted wide public and union support. In October a federal Select Committee was established to inquire into the land issue and that of royalty payments to the Yirrkala community on the basis of their claim to ownership as well as the dramatic effect the large mining operation would have on them. As the AAF newsletter reported, 'this is the first time Aboriginal people's land rights have been the subject of an official inquiry'.[38] Early in 1964, news came through that the Mapoon communities had been forcibly evicted from their lands on the western coast of Cape York to make way for more bauxite mining at Weipa.[39]

In New South Wales too, the pressure on communities to give up the land they still held appeared to be escalating. In February 1964, the local *Southern News* reported that the Randwick Council Planning Committee had recommended that the Aboriginal population at La Perouse be 'integrated into the adjacent housing commission development' because, it argued, the housing on the reserve was of a poor standard. The La Perouse community had fought one successful battle to stay on their land in 1928, although the cost had been the revocation of the foreshore section of the reserve. Now they were determined to stay. Charlie Leon reported to the AAF that the La Perouse Aborigines are 'strongly opposed to the Randwick Council's proposed plan to move them from the reserve, which they regard as their home'. The AAF accused Randwick Council and land speculators of wanting the reserve land for lucrative development, arguing: 'Let those who wish to leave the reserve and live elsewhere do so, but for those who wish to stay, let the Randwick Council and the Board get together and develop the La Perouse reserve area as a modern housing estate for Aborigines'.[40]

With feeling building in New South Wales, and with the dramatic threat at La Perouse adding local urgency to the interstate issues which had been gaining publicity, Leon delivered a call to the AAF in February 1964 to focus its attention on land: 'In spite of the Fellowship's many achievements in the last eight years, in some ways its work was just beginning. He urged that we concentrate our efforts on winning land rights for Aborigines in the coming year'.[41] Later, in August, the AAF provided some of the main speakers to the National Aborigines Day Rally in Sydney, and Joyce Mercy from the Bandjalang area of Maclean was one who 'laid stress on the need for Aboriginal people to have rights to land ownership': 'Australia is the only country in the world which does not recognise that its indigenous people have a right to land'.[42]

It seems clear then that the early months of 1964 were an intense period of activity and commitment to the land question for New South Wales as well as for the more remote areas of the country. Jack Horner has recalled: 'In the Fellowship, we were convinced by early 1964 that Vesper was dead right and that land was an essential'.[43] Yet the next few years saw major activity in New South Wales represented largely in terms of civil rights and the need for legislative change, with the Freedom Ride in 1965 and then the campaign to include Aboriginal people on the census and allow the federal government to assume control over Aboriginal affairs. Why this occurred, only to be followed by a major reassertion of the land issue onto the State and federal agenda in the early 1970s, will form the problem of Part VI.

Part VI

The Ground on which the Embassy Rose, 1965 to 1972

23
Referendum and Reality

The successful referendum result in 1967 seemed to promise that Aboriginal people would be included in Australian society and civil life as never before. Yet by 1972 New South Wales Aborigines set up a Tent Embassy outside Parliament House in Canberra, symbolising their sense of exclusion not only from the civic life of the nation but from their own land.

By the beginning of 1963, Aboriginal activists and their supporters faced difficult decisions about the most effective way to continue their campaigns. The AAF had gained a degree of success by focusing on State political decisions when it campaigned during the 1962 election campaign to get Section 9 of the Aborigines Protection Act repealed. There had been disquiet among its members, however, as the tactical decision to focus on Section 9 had made alcohol seem the main issue, when for most people it was town segregation and the Welfare Board's control measures that were more important. A number of the AAF members had been extremely active travelling in country areas from 1960 on, and they were in close touch with rural Aboriginal and support groups. The local issues of segregation, colour bars and reserve revocations seemed most urgent to this group.

Charlie Leon had called in early 1964 for land rights to be the focus of AAF activity. There were others, more tied to urban conditions, who were hopeful of the potential long-term impact of legislative change and reorganisation of administrative structures. The urban base of the AAF was more open to direct influence from the large white support organisations, which saw the issues in terms of legislative discrimination. Jessie Street was one such interested and powerful supporter. She had recognised the potential for mobilising white support and for educating the public in a campaign to change the Constitution to allow the federal government to assume administrative control over Aboriginal affairs in all States, as well as to take the important symbolic step of including Aboriginal people in the national census. While her proposal was ambitious and ultimately had an enormous impact, it was nevertheless an abstract idea when she suggested it in 1958; it was hard to explain, and the campaign took enormous resources to conduct. The idea had been introduced at the large public meeting in 1958 which launched the AAF, and a petition to hold a referendum to change the Constitution had been circulated over the next few years. With the partial success of the attempt to reform the NSW Act in 1963, the AAF needed to decide whether to focus its limited energies on an all-out campaign to gain and win a federal referendum or to focus on local conflicts which emphasised land issues.

The choices were difficult. Within a few months the AAF had effectively split. A large section of its Aboriginal membership re-established Bill Ferguson's Aborigines Progressive Association, with a mainly Aboriginal membership, including Bert Groves, Pearl Gibbs and Ray Peckham, supported by a few non-Aboriginal members like Helen Hambly.[1] Their goals were to continue to support rural activism, with frequent country trips. They helped to establish a branch of the APA in Walgett during 1964, and Peckham, Hambly and Dick Hunter continued their country visits.

Many Aborigines continued to be involved in all the organisations operating at the time. Groves and all the APA members had many contacts with the newly developed and carefully anti-communist Foundation for Aboriginal Affairs (FAA), run by Charlie Perkins and Ted Noffs, as well as continuing a relationship with the AAF through 1964.[2] Charlie Leon, Joyce Mercy and others continued to support the AAF, while Ken Brindle, a leading figure in Redfern community politics, worked with both the AAF and the FAA throughout the period. He was, in turn, strongly supported by the AAF and the Council for Civil Liberties in his attempt to free Redfern Aboriginal people from police harassment and violence.[3] The Aboriginal AAF members had all clearly supported rural activism and endorsed land rights as a significant issue, but they decided to direct their efforts towards supporting the referendum campaign.

Despite the demands on activists to make these difficult strategic decisions, the pressure on land in New South Wales did not let up. The revocation process accelerated, with more north coast reserves coming under threat. In 1964 six out of the nine reserves revoked were on the north coast and five of these were on the Bandjalang high country.[4] Lismore City Council had finally agreed to let the Welfare Board build a series of houses just outside the town. This new area, known as Gundurimba Road, certainly offered better housing than the huts at Cubawee, but the Board pushed through the closure and the complete revocation of the old reserve land in 1964, leaving a sense of violation and insecurity among people who had been struggling to save that land for so long. The attempts to use co-operatives to defend community occupation of reserve lands were continuing, but the Welfare Board was by the mid-1960s refusing any longer to assist co-operative farming. It would only support individual leasing of small areas of reserve land or share-cropping with white neighbours. It gave leases to two individuals at Woodenbong reserve, hoping to end the hopes of co-operative farming.

Yet the Cumeragunja community, whose family farm block plan was now regarded favourably by the Board, were kept waiting for the legal clearance necessary to begin farming on the reserve land. They were still waiting in March 1965. The white farmers' leases had been cancelled in April 1964 and the people had raised £5000 to begin the development process, but the Board delayed while the crown solicitor deliberated. Finally the agreement allowing farming to proceed was signed in May 1966.

By the mid-1960s the Board was beginning to acknowledge that its failure to break down rural segregation was the result of white hostility and obstruction.[5] It chose to increase further the pressure on rural Aborigines to leave their communities to settle in industrial cities. At the same time, as the conditions under which Aborigines were living had become more public through Aboriginal and white agitation, the Board made a last attempt to minimise the isolation of some Aboriginal communities and to be seen to be addressing the health and housing crisis. Some large and remote stations were closed and a series of housing settlements were rapidly built on small pieces of reserve land at the edge of towns like Brewarrina, Bourke, Kempsey and Moree from 1964 to 1966. All cheap and jerry-built, this makeshift housing at least allowed the Board to call them 'town settlements' rather than reserves.[6] These white towns had all won their battles to keep Aboriginal families outside municipal boundaries, but the Welfare Board then simply dumped large Aboriginal populations in overcrowded and badly built houses on the very edges of the towns, exacerbating anxieties and tensions.

For Aboriginal people, this often seemed like a further entrapment. For those at Brewarrina, for example, the move to West Brewarrina in 1966 meant the loss of access to hundreds of acres of reserve around the old mission, one of the worst losses of reserve lands in the west. The new 'town settlement' was a slum, poorly built on a treeless hill, and rapidly referred to by all as 'Dodge City'. Fences and locked gates increasingly confronted these Murris as access to pastoral lands closed down too with loss of employment, and their growing sense of frustration was to be expressed in the political cry 'we are landless and landlocked'.[7]

THE FREEDOM RIDE: CIVIL RIGHTS AND LAND

By the end of 1964, the idea had emerged among the Sydney networks to do a bus trip which would attempt to expose the entrenched racism of rural New South Wales. The name 'Freedom Ride' was derived from American civil rights models, and the white students who became involved were most aware of the Gandhian strategies of non-violent non-cooperation which had been adopted so successfully in America by Martin Luther King. But the itinerary and the issues of the New South Wales trip arose from the conditions on the ground, the struggles over public and residential space which had been developing increasing heat over the last two decades. The APA under Groves and Gibbs was heavily involved with Charlie Perkins in formulating an itinerary which focused on the areas of their recent activity, the north-west and the north coast. Ted Noffs also insisted on an interest in Wilcannia, where he had been involved in disputes around land and housing since the 1950s. In January 1965 a flight was chartered by the *Australian*, and Perkins, Noffs and journalist Graeme Williams travelled to towns whose names were becoming bywords for segregation, Nowra, Cowra, Wilcannia, Walgett, Moree and Kempsey, resulting in a series of press articles.

The Freedom Ride departed from Sydney on 13 February 1965, a bus with Charlie Perkins and 29 nervous white students aboard, heading north-west. What began as a tentative exercise firmed into a dramatic series of confrontations with the whites of country towns, particularly in Walgett and Moree. Local Aborigines increasingly took part in the attempts to break the colour bar in hotels, shops and swimming pools, and protected the bus riders from an attempt on their lives as Walgett whites tried to drive their bus off the road. This journey was to have far-reaching impacts, not only by showing the metropolitan public vivid evidence of the crudity and brutality of rural white crowd behaviour, but also by focusing the attention of the students on Australian conditions.

For although the students had arrived with expectations based on overseas events, the campaign in Walgett was fuelled by very local anger at the tightening restrictions of the town. The Murris there had bitter memories, not only of the struggles over schooling and safe residence at Nicholl's Bend, but of the days of Angledool's transportation to Brewarrina, and of the pressure to leave Dungalear and the remaining camps. There were many Aboriginal shearers in the town, well experienced in industrial action. The AWU had usually proved unhelpful, as in Coonamble, but other unions were now interested in offering support. The Waterside Workers had sent a delegation with the APA to Walgett in mid-1964, and they continued an involvement after the Freedom

Ride visit in February 1965. Walgett Murris had formed a branch of the APA, with Harry Hall as spokesperson, a shearer who was a strong supporter of the February bus visit. Early in August, two Murri women and four students tried to force their way into the 'whites only' section of the cinema. They were arrested.

The Sydney base of the APA, with Groves, Peckham and Hambly, had discussions with Perkins, as well as Tranby College, Student Action for Aborigines (SAFA), and some members of the AAF. The result was two delegations from Sydney, a fortnight apart, in mid-August 1965, involving Aboriginal unionists like Ray Peckham from the Builders' Labourers Federation, and Chicka Dickson, Jack Hassan, Bob Perry and others from the Waterside Workers'. Federation.

Helen Hambly has recalled the tension in the streets on the first August visit, as local Aborigines such as Harry Hall, Ted Fields and Mavis Rose gathered at an arranged spot outside the cinema, and then led the way in, demanding to be sold tickets to the 'whites only' section. They succeeded, to the cheers of the Murri crowd. The group was denied service in most other places, however, including the hotel. Whites on the delegation were treated with hostility by the townspeople, but Hambly remembered that, as a white woman travelling with a party of Aboriginal men, she was faced with particular contempt and accusations of promiscuity and betrayal of her 'own people'.[8]

The Welfare Board manager at Gingie Reserve paid great attention to these two delegations and the local political activity they supported. He reported to the Welfare Board that 'communist influence' was suspected, with both Aboriginal people and the white students being assumed to be 'innocent accessories' to 'others with sinister motives'. Yet the manager's report also reveals the very local terms in which the Walgett Murris stated their demands: he described the public meeting during the second delegation visit, in which Walgett Aboriginal people made many heated references 'to white men having taken their lands from the Aborigines'.[9]

LAND ISSUES CONTINUE TO EMERGE

Concerns about land were becoming more frequent in the resolutions and agendas of Federal Council and AAF meetings during 1965. Jack Horner, as well as being the FCAA secretary, had begun working as Alf Clint's secretary at Tranby. In this context of high awareness of the land issue, Horner compiled a record of the Welfare Board's use of reserve land between 1938 and 1964. The results were deeply disturbing. In 1938, around 15 000 acres had still been held as reserve and station; since then, 13 534 acres had been revoked or leased to whites, leaving barely 1500 acres accessible to Aboriginal residents. This was a powerful demonstration that the rising anxiety of Aboriginal people about the continuing loss of reserve land was based on very real and immediate pressures.[10]

At the FCAA annual meeting at Easter, land had risen to second on the agenda, behind equal wages but ahead of discriminatory laws. The federal government had by this time agreed to hold a referendum, but only on the issue of the inclusion of Aborigines in the census. The FCAA and the AAF were determined not to lose the opportunity which now seemed so close, and continued to demand that the Commonwealth have the power to make laws on Aboriginal issues. This again absorbed political energy and resources, but the issues around land continued to be forced to public attention by local Aboriginal activism.

On the south coast, further tourist and residential expansion was threatening the Aboriginal community at Wreck Bay, within the Commonwealth land near Jervis Bay. In January 1965 the residents there became alarmed that the federal government intended to drive them off their scenic reserve by allowing white settlement in three vacant houses from which Kooris had been evicted for failure to pay rent. Most of the Kooris there signed a petition to the government expressing their fears for their land but also for their community, and 'emphasising that they wish to stay together as an Aboriginal Community'. A compromise was eventually reached in which one Aboriginal family was allowed to move back into a vacant house, and the government assured the community that no Aboriginal family would be evicted to make way for a white family.[11] Throughout the year, the conflict at Purfleet over rent and control of the reserve's administration remained high, and by October Kooris were being evicted for non-payment of rent, the strategy now widely recognised as a protest at dispossession as well as at poor-quality housing.[12]

A sense of the rising prominence of land in the public statements of Aboriginal activists during the year can be gained from a debate in March when a team sponsored by Tranby College debated the Bankstown Junior Chamber of Commerce, who defended the proposition that 'the present policy of assimilation was in the best interests of Aborigines and the general community'. Tranby's opposing team included Kath Walker and Doug Nicholls who, as whip, won the debate with the assertion that 'Aborigines are not just another depressed social group, but an ethnic minority, descendants of the original land-holders, with rights to land, to their culture and to a say in their destiny'.[13]

At the end of 1965, a NSW-wide conference was held in Sydney in October organised by Aboriginal members of the AAF and the APA. The conference participants were mostly rural Aborigines, including many from the north coast, with some speakers from Cumeragunja and others from towns such as Walgett and Brewarrina. The outcome was a set of demands with a clear emphasis on land. Each item had a land dimension. The housing item, first in priority in the conference resolutions, demanded houses to be built on reserve lands where people wanted to live. The government was to be called on to consider Aboriginal employment in rural areas in its decentralisation plans, so that pressure would cease being applied to make people move away from the area of their choice. And the fears about reserve revocation were expressed in the item headed Land Rights:

> An injunction to be sought to prevent the Board from alienating any land set aside for the use of Aborigines in New South Wales until the legal position with respect to reserve land is investigated by a committee elected by Aborigines.[14]

In Sydney too, the land issue was becoming more widely publicised as the La Perouse situation worsened. The Welfare Board had begun to demolish some of the older huts on the reserve as they became vacant, and had threatened some families with eviction for non-payment of rent. The Kooris there feared that the Board's intention was to drive them off their land in order to help Randwick Council open the reserve for lucrative white residential development. The Koori response included a proposal for a redevelopment of the whole area to allow better housing for Aborigines, as well as for other residents in nearby areas.[15]

The Welfare Board continued its plans to foster individual use of reserve lands over any collective or co-operative development. Early in 1966 it had approved the rental of portions of Woodenbong Reserve to two individual Kooris in a share-farming arrangement with a white neighbour. Most Koori residents saw this as a clear betrayal by the individual Koori lessees and by the Welfare Board of the residents' long struggle to get collective security over the Williams family's reserve lands. They appealed for help to the Council for Civil Liberties, threatening the Board with legal action. They then sent a deputation to present the Board with a list of demands, including an insistence that 'all future land negotiations be made through the Aborigines Progressive Association of Woodenbong' and the requirement that the white share-farmer be forced to remove his crop. The Board was disturbed by this, reporting that the local 'Aborigines Progress Association, comprising residents of the Station as a whole, had made strong representations to the Board for permission to farm the land as a community project'. Retreating, the Board agreed to allow the community to draw up plans, again, for a collective enterprise.[16]

So the issue of land rights was firmly back at centre stage in New South Wales Aboriginal politics by mid-1966. The NSW government had launched a Joint Parliamentary Committee of Inquiry into Aborigines Welfare which began to take evidence late in 1965. Through 1966 it travelled to many rural areas, including the Bandjalang areas around Woodenbong and Cabbage Tree Island in April, the western towns of Moree, Walgett and Bourke in May, the Gumbaynggirr and Dhan-gadi lands of the Nambucca and Macleay valleys in June, and finally Cumeragunja in July. Few Aboriginal people were called to give evidence in sessions, which were usually held in the local Council Chambers, though the committee did take Aboriginal evidence at some reserves. Charlie Leon spoke before the committee to ask for land both on and off reserved areas, to be handed over to individual Aborigines, while James Morgan and members of the Ballangarry, Buchanan, Duroux and Quinlan families called for land to be used collectively at the hearings on the north coast and at Cumeragunja.[17] Aboriginal people expected that the Joint Committee would take seriously the Aboriginal evidence it was hearing.

Then, in mid-1966, events took a dramatic turn in the Northern Territory. The Gurindji strike reinforced the calls for land rights already being made by New South Wales Aborigines, but it also distracted the attention of white supporters from the forms in which the land issue was raised in the complex politics of the south-east.

NEW ALLIES

Aboriginal pastoral workers had finally been granted equal pay in the Territory under federal industrial awards late in 1965, only to be told that they would have to wait three years for payment to begin to allow the pastoral companies time to adjust to the new cost. By Easter 1966, Aboriginal stock and domestic workers on many Northern Territory properties had begun to strike, and a fund was set up in the eastern States by unionists and other members of the Left affiliated with the FCAA, all of whom could readily appreciate the goals of an industrial campaign for equal wages. But the issues were wider than the simple industrial ones of equality of wages and conditions with which white unionists felt comfortable. By September, the whole Aboriginal workforce of Gurindji people at Wave Hill station had withdrawn altogether from the stockcamp on the station to move to an independent camp on Wattie Creek, from which they announced that they wanted the Vestey's pastoral company to get off their land. Although white Left organisations were at first slow to grasp the fact that the Gurindji had wider aims than industrial equality, Left union and social groups eventually swung into support for the Gurindji.[18]

For Aboriginal people in New South Wales, the Gurindji demands were immediately recognisable. The demand for restoration of their lands echoed the desires which most of them had grown up with. The Wattie Creek camp looked little different from the camps around many New South Wales country towns at the time, and the experiences of exploitative employment were all too familiar, both from the recent pastoral camp days in New South Wales and from the seasonal agricultural work which so many were finding was their only job hope by the mid-1960s. A wave of solidarity and the growth of pan-Aboriginal sentiment was fostered strongly in this period.

For white Australians in the south-east, the parallels between the 'remote' conditions of central Australia and the 'settled' rural lands of New South Wales were much harder to perceive. A great deal of white interest was drawn by the fact that Vestey's was a British company owned by an English lord. This meant that nationalism and anti-monarchism, now strongly manifest in the Australian Left, could be given unrestricted play. The Gurindji could be characterised not only as industrial militants and traditional land rights campaigners but also as Australian nationalists battling against the British aristocracy and capitalist establishment. Yet the rising awareness of the land dimension in the Northern Territory dispute did not necessarily lead to a greater awareness among whites of the land concerns of Aboriginal people in more heavily colonised areas. The Communist Party, after considerable prodding from its member Frank Hardy, had finally concentrated substantial resources in support of the Gurindji, but the party's policy in 1967 still referred only to 'guaranteeing equal rights in employment, education and housing, and full political rights' to Aboriginal people in the south-eastern States.[19]

By the 1960s the right-wing groups which had been such an important political support for Aboriginal groups from the 1920s to the 1940s had taken up a totally oppositional stance on Aboriginal matters. Gone was the interest in a unique Australian cultural identity, drawing on Aboriginal people as well as decorative culture, which had been possible in the right-wing movements of the 1930s and 1940s. Now the Right was dominated by a dislike of what were seen as the activist present-day Aborigines, and right-wing groups increasingly characterised land issues and any recognition of Aboriginal culture as divisive of the goal of Anglo-Saxon uniformity. Other right-wing groups, such as the League of Rights, had become concerned early in the 1950s when Aboriginal and white concerns were expressed about British atomic testing in the Western Desert.

There were, however, new left-wing allies emerging whose cultural interests were often closer to those of the old Right cultural nationalists than to the hard-line egalitarians of the culturally uniform Australian 'old Left'. These new allies were the diverse groupings of young people, who sometimes called themselves 'New Left', but who might just as well associate themselves in Australia with the anarchist, libertarian tradi- tions, or, only a little later in the 1960s, call themselves 'hippies'. It was within this context that I first became aware of the questions around race relations in Australia. These groupings were influenced by the anti-colonial movements in India and Africa, through writers like Franz Fanon as well as Sartre and Camus, and by Native Americans' as well as African Americans' civil rights movements. We were interested in recognising cultural differences, and identified cultural repression as a dimension of European imperialism in its new manifestation of Ameri- can postwar expansion.

These groups also shared the rising anxieties in Western societies about the dangers of postwar technology: nuclear power generation and the growing use of herbicides and pesticides for intensive agriculture in underdeveloped as well as Western economies. Such criticism of modern technology set these emergent groups apart from the mid-century communists who had shared capitalism's faith in technology to fulfil mankind's needs. In fact there was a widespread rejection of both cultural and technological modernism among the New Left groups. This frequently led us to an interest in 'traditional', pre-capitalist cultures which did not appear to emphasise material accumulation or social competition.

The resulting support acknowledged and celebrated Aboriginal tra- ditional values and relations with both kin and land, but over the years it may also have shaped the expression of Aboriginal goals and interests. Earlier Left ideologies of uniform egalitarianism had constrained Aborig- inal activists like Bill Ferguson to expresss his demands most frequently in the language of liberal uniformity. The desires of more recent sup- porters to find traditional and anti-materialist values may also have constrained Aboriginal groups, but this time by insisting that they justify their land demands with more emphasis on 'traditional' spiritual mean- ings for land than on the secular meanings tied to both kin relations and economy which may be just as important to them.

In 1966, 'old' and 'new' Left supporters were each attracted to the Gurindji strike, the one to the industrial aspects and the other to the traditional orientation of the land struggle. So the attention of the white public became increasingly focused on Wattie Creek as the most potent symbol of Aboriginal desire for land. The more circumscribed demands of Kooris and Murris in the south-east for farming and residential land, even their searches for missing title deeds from Queen Victoria, seemed to be on a far smaller and more mundane scale than the broad sweep of the demands for hundreds of square miles which the Gurindji spokesmen could make in their own language. So it was the Northern Territory expressions of these demands which came to stand for all, and to eclipse any awareness among whites of the continuing calls from south-eastern people for justice over land.

RISING EXPECTATIONS AND BITTER REALITIES

The growing interest in the Gurindji strike and other Aboriginal matters had increased the pressure on the federal government to take some action. It had finally agreed to include the issue of the federal control of Aboriginal Affairs in the referendum to be held on 27 May 1967, and the AAF and FCAA now devoted all their attention to the referendum. A large overall 'yes' vote was recorded in all States, which was not only enough to ensure that the two measures were carried but seemed to mark a new and widespread white sympathy with Aboriginal people, a strong desire to welcome them into the community of the nation by making a symbolic gesture of inclusion.

The voting returns could have raised some questions, because the weakest 'yes' votes were consistently recorded in the rural electorates where the Aboriginal population was largest.[20] This suggested strongly that relations on the frontlines of interaction between Aboriginal people and their colonisers continued to be tense. Yet it must have been difficult not to be jubilant. So many years of hard work by the AAF, FCAATSI, VAAL and others seemed to have been rewarded with an unprecedented and complete victory. This was certainly how the AAF recorded the result, with a headline that read 'YES . . . YES . . . YES . . . YES . . . YES . . . YES . . . YES . . . SAID OVER 90% of AUSTRALIAN VOTERS!'[21]

Aboriginal people expected some immediate action. Instead, by September, they were confronted with the bitter reality of a government reluctant to make any change in existing policies. The Prime Minister, Harold Holt, had created a small Office of Aboriginal Affairs, but had invested it with no powers and no funds. The *Sydney Morning Herald* scoffed that his decision 'makes a mockery of the referendum in May'.[22] The Aboriginal support organisations were furious. They saw the government's position summed up in a phrase it used frequently in its announcement of its intention to work 'as we have in the past, in co-operation with the States'. FCAATSI denounced the decision not to set up a ministry, and demanded an urgent inquiry into the conditions of Aboriginal people across the country, emergency grants to the States and to organisations concerned with Aboriginal welfare, and the immediate drafting of legislative prohibition against discrimination. The AAF was equally angered. Faith Bandler accused the federal government of being 'apathetic and petty' and continued bitterly: 'What Mr Holt is in fact doing is giving the power back to the states'.[23]

The appointments to the small Office of Aboriginal Affairs in fact included W. E. H. Stanner and Nugget Coombs, both widely known to regard assimilation as an inappropriate policy, to sympathise with demands for land and to acknowledge the validity of Aboriginal desires to 'maintain a separate and distinct social and racial identity'.[24] But the government itself was quite clearly uninterested in any real or rapid changes, and so activist disappointment was hardly tempered. FCAATSI now began to accelerate its land rights activity.[25] Over the next year its 'Land and Reserves Committee' developed its membership and its dynamism. In 1969 north coast activist Pasepa Close from Fingal was elected to the chair of this national committee, and later Pastor Frank Roberts Jnr took on this role, which he continued to maintain even after FCAATSI itself began to decline in importance during the early 1970s.[26]

In New South Wales, however, the outlook became even more bleak. On 13 September 1967 the report of the NSW Joint Committee was tabled. It was an even greater shock than the federal government's retreat over the referendum. The committee had certainly condemned the Board strongly, but rather than endorsing the Aboriginal criticisms, the report accused the Board of being too slow and hesitant in its assimilation activities. It recommended the dismantling of the Welfare Board and its replacement by a dispersed administration handled by mainstream departments like the Housing Commission and the Education and Health Departments, with co-ordination by a small 'Directorate of Aboriginal Affairs'. If the structure of Aboriginal Affairs in the State was now to be diffused, the policy directions for this new joint administration were starkly clear and simple. The committee recommended a far more aggressive assimilation, in which Aboriginal people were now to be under surveillance from many more authorities which all demanded normative compliance with 'white standards'. The committee was also clear about its view of reserves and the self-contained Aboriginal communities which lived on them:

> The Committee believes that the congregation of Aboriginals on reserves is one of the main factors retarding them from becoming full members of the community . . . Your Committee recommends that every effort be made to encourage Aborigines to leave reserves . . . The Committee is firmly of the opinion that in due course all Aboriginal Reserves should disappear.[27]

The committee was aware that it would meet Aboriginal resistance. The report dismissed any suggestion that Aboriginal communities had traditionally-based cultural practices and values by explaining their

328

differences from whites as the result of the ignorance of an artificially isolated population. These reserve residents 'could and should' be forced out of their sheltered environment. With breathtaking failure to recognise the stresses suffered under poverty and repression, and despite having found 'no evidence' of traditionally-based cultural differences, the committee outlined its recommendations in the following terms:

> To convince people living on reserves that, in their own interest, they should move to centres where employment is available will not be an easy task. These people live in a community of their own where all are on the same standard of living, where few have any great ambition to get on in the world, where worldly goods are shared and, most important of all, where the stresses of modern living are not experienced . . . They are apparently quite content to remain as they are. Because there are no higher levels to which they might aspire, the lowest level becomes the norm . . . The older generation would find it most difficult to leave reserves and settle happily into the city. But the Committee is convinced that many of the younger generation could and should make the move.[28]

The committee advised the government that no further housing should be built on reserves, and that it should divest itself of as many reserves as possible, turning the existing residential portions over to the Housing Commission and leasing the few fertile reserve areas which remained to individual Aboriginal farmers. It acknowledged that good crops were now being harvested at both Cumeragunja and Cabbage Tree Island, but it was scathing about Aboriginal desires to farm land collectively:

> The pattern of living on reserves gives no indication whatsoever that the residents could and would work together for the common good. Nowhere was evidence placed before the Committee that the real interest or purpose of co-operatives was understood or desired by Aborigines.[29]

It also noted that many Aboriginal witnesses had put before it their demand for recognition of dispossession by a process of compensation. It was again dismissive, and its overall conclusion on land, employment and compensation was that 'the only sound solution to the employment problem is to encourage residents of Aboriginal reserves to move to centres where employment is available. This will require intense counselling'.[30]

This report then was in total conflict with every desire expressed by Aboriginal people about land, their reserves and their desire to live in close proximity to their kin and communities. While some of its recommendations were acceptable, such as the dismantling of segregated and discriminatory education and the end of the Welfare Board as such, the Joint Committee recommendations on land and on forced migration to the cities were greeted with alarm and anger.[31] This was yet another government betrayal, and one which struck deeply at the directions which New South Wales Aboriginal communities had been formulating ever more clearly through these middle years of the 1960s.

The rising frustration began to emerge in internal differences, as both conservative and militantly 'nationalist' groups began to voice criticisms of FCAATSI. Some, aligned with Perkins, criticised FCAATSI in 1967 for being too left-wing and politicised. Others were moving towards a cultural radicalism, and expressed concern at the continuing dominance of white members and affiliates in FCAATSI and its adherence to the formal processes of Western organisations rather than adopting the forms and priorities of Aboriginal societies. Yet others were growing impatient with FCAATSI's moderate political style, and were demanding more dramatic and speedy solutions. The issues were complex and, because the attacks came from both Left and Right, confused.

There was, however, a general expectation circulating that leadership of the Aboriginal movement would soon be largely and appropriately in Aboriginal hands. This led the AAF to dissolve itself in July 1969. In September a motion was carried in the VAAL which endorsed the resignation of all non-Aboriginal office-holders. A similar amendment was moved at the 1970 Easter Conference of FCAATSI, but there were many dissenting voices, including those of well-respected Aboriginal leaders such as Frank Roberts Jnr. The outcome for FCAATSI was that while many Aboriginal activists stayed in the Federal Council, others such as Pastor Doug Nicholls and Kath Walker left to form the National Tribal Council. While FCAATSI continued to function to co-ordinate union and other organisational support, its role as a unifying vehicle for Aboriginal demands was past.[32]

Land rights, however, was emphasised by all groups on all sides of these disputes, leaving no doubt that land had re-emerged as a primary demand. In a material sense, people were formulating demands for real areas of land which would offer economic opportunities. In a symbolic sense, land had both a positive and a negative quality. On one hand, Aboriginal relations with land symbolised the rich traditional culture and society of pre-invasion Australia; the hard-fought struggles to retain association with land in the south-east indicated the continuing power of those cultural and social values which led Aboriginal people to try to identify and organise themselves around relations to land. On the other hand, land was symbolic as an absence: the land to which Aboriginal people did not have access or acknowledged ownership was a symbol of invasion and dispossession, and to the extent that much of it was never recoverable, it stood for the great debt white Australia owed to the people on whose land its prosperity was built.

Yet another land crisis had emerged in New South Wales in 1969, and again it was on Bandjalang lands. The unrestricted tourist and residential development of the Queensland Gold Coast had been spreading south towards the New South Wales border for some time, and in 1969 there was an attempt to open up the Fingal Peninsula on the southern head of the Tweed River for speculation. The situation alarmed New South Wales residents, already appalled at the gaudy style of Gold Coast development just across the water at Coolangatta, but the issue which caught press attention was that the sandy, undeveloped and extremely beautiful Fingal Peninsula was the site of an Aboriginal reserve and home to a large and articulate community of both Bandjalang and South Sea Islander background.

Some members of this community owned blocks of land along the beachfront, others had leased or held land by permissive occupancy for over 75 years, while others again lived on the reserve. All were united in opposing the resumption of their land. After hearing about the plans to resume the land, a number of members of the Bandjalang and Islander community had applied to the Department of Lands to have their occupancies and leaseholds converted to freehold. In previous years this had been an accepted practice, particularly on such sandy 'waste' land, but in the new circumstances where ocean frontages were so lucrative, the applicants were refused. A community meeting elected a deputation to travel to Sydney and Canberra to state their case. The delegation members, Pasepa Close, Nolene Lever and Alf Bekue, issued the following statement, leaving no doubt about their analysis of the issues:

> The people of Fingal now know they must fight for their rights and their survival . . . Foreign forces are pressing directly or indirectly to push us off our land and out of our homes. Fingal people are challenged to fight as never before to defend our rights and retain and possess our land. All our intellectual resources are now taxed and challenged, but the word 'defeat' is beyond our concept. Fingal people are now in a battle for our land rights and human rights.[33]

The Fingal delegation succeeded dramatically. Supported by the established Bandjalang networks, including Frank Roberts Jnr and others, they caught the attention of 'Four Corners'. So as well as their interviews with politicians, they gained an extremely sympathetic coverage of their case on ABC television early in April, which appealed not only to supporters of Aboriginal demands but to the chauvinism of New South Wales residents who wanted to avoid the crass commercialism of Queensland-style development along the whole coastline. On 9 April the NSW Minister for Lands agreed that these long-term Bandjalang and Islander residents could convert their tenures, gradually purchasing their land freehold for $900, to be paid off over twenty years. There was guarded congratulations for them in the local press, but also some thinly veiled threats, like that from the Tweed Heads *Daily News* editorial:

> It is time for the Fingal coloured community to face up to the facts of the tourist bombshell about to burst all around them, let's say in 10 years. They are living on some of the Tweed and Gold Coast's most potentially valuable land and nothing they can do can withstand the march of progress.[34]

This ominous warning was not lost on the Bandjalang, nor indeed on any coastal Aboriginal communities, who were all too aware of the loss of their lands over the past three decades to tourist development. The Fingal victory was the first time in close to 80 years that Aboriginal people had been able to force back the tide of encroachment on their lands. It was not to be the last time, but the immediate future did not hold many wins.

As a result of the Joint Committee report, in 1969 the Aborigines Welfare Board was superseded by the Directorate of Aboriginal Welfare, under the directorship of psychologist Ian Mitchell. The Directorate was to be located within the Ministry of Social Welfare and Child Welfare. It was to be advised by a nine-member Aboriginal Advisory Committee, of whom six members were elected, one from each of six regions defined by the government to cover the State. This form of 'representation' did not reflect the structures favoured by Aboriginal people in their own organisations, in which, typically, regional bodies were the most stable form, at which major debates, decisions and negotiations occurred, and which then entered into coalition with other regional organisations. The State-level elected structure of the Advisory Committee isolated regional delegates, and with no formal regional body to instruct them, they tended to act as individuals rather than representatives in the manner expected of them by white politicians. The Aboriginal Advisory Committee did not, in any event, begin meetings until early 1971.

The Housing Commission was to take over all Aboriginal residential management, but the Directorate was to continue co-ordinating the ongoing 'rehousing' of all 'adversely housed' Aboriginal people. Its policy was set entirely within the parameters established by the Joint Committee report. In Mitchell's first annual report, tabled in June 1970, he indicated that the old policy of refusing to build further housing on reserves was to be maintained and those houses built in rural towns would continue to be pepperpotted 'to prevent large congregations of Aboriginal families in any one district'.[35] Great stress was laid on the issue of 'counselling' Aboriginal families on the manner in which they should conduct themselves in a new house within a town.

The Directorate was strongly aware of the desire for land rights and security of tenure among New South Wales Aboriginal people, and suggested that when the Aboriginal Advisory Committee commenced, they would give advice to the government on how to give Aborigines 'title to areas utilised by them'. This form of words was consistent with the Joint Committee's recommendation that only residential areas on reserves be retained, which might be eventually owned by Aboriginal residents on terms similar to those by which other Housing Commission residents could negotiate purchase of government public housing properties.

But this was very different from the demands for land rights which had for so long been articulated by Aborigines in New South Wales. In the closing pages of this 1970 Report, the director tried to reassure Aborigines that there would be no major revocation of reserves without the agreement of the Advisory Committee. But he went on to make this patronising statement under the heading 'Land Rights':

> Although the basis of the Land Rights agitation stems from the traditional culture's spiritual affiliation with the physiography, much of the movement's sympathy, though misrepresented, has its proponents in New South Wales. While some residents of reserves in this State have very strong affiliation with the area, the sense of ownership lacks the intimacy known in the tribal situations.[36]

Early in 1971, the Aboriginal Advisory Committee met for the first time, but the outcomes for State policy were hardly reassuring. The Directorate continued its general refusal to build new housing on reserves, although the unrelenting pressure from Bandjalang people had forced it to agree to the construction of fourteen houses on Woodenbong. Elsewhere, however, the Directorate had begun to demolish vacant and dilapidated huts on reserve lands, just as the old Welfare Board had done.[37] The Advisory Committee was composed of elected representatives from across the State, but as it happened no member from the far north coast, nor, aside from Harry Hall from Walgett, were there any members known for their activism or independence of thought on any issue.

The Directorate Report again insisted that Aboriginal reserves would not be revoked on a large scale, but one of the first votes the Advisory Committee took was to approve the total revocation of the reserve at Kinchela, the site of both successful farming and the notorious Boys' Home.[38] The site was therefore rich with both traditional and historical significance, and its revocation would have been a staggering blow to hopes to retain the last few remaining old reserves. There was an outcry from Aboriginal groups, and a series of approaches to the Directorate delayed the revocation. But the Directorate was still insisting it was going to dispose of the land early in 1972, and it drew mounting and innovative protests.

While the areas of highest Aboriginal population and housing demand were country towns like Moree and Bourke, the areas in which the Directorate was actually instructing the Housing Commission to begin building Aboriginal housing were the urban areas of Sydney and Newcastle: 'Although housing programmes are to some extent governed by the demand in particular areas, more emphasis is being placed on siting houses in towns and cities with greater employment potential'.[39] When families applied for a house, they were told that they were unlikely to get one in a country town without a long delay, but that 'families wishing to move to centres of greater employment potential are given special consideration'.[40]

Such encouragement was not to be the end of the matter, however. In 1971 also, the Directorate announced the beginning of what was to become the 'Aboriginal Family Resettlement Scheme', known throughout the Aboriginal communities of the State as 'Relocation'. This was a structure of intensive support in the destination town for families once they decided to move to an urban industrial area. From 1971 until its demise in 1980, the targets for relocation were the towns with large Aboriginal populations, first Bourke and Brewarrina residents who were directed to Newcastle, to be followed by Murris from Moree and Boggabilla who were sent to Tamworth; then Wilcannia residents were directed to Albury or Cobar and finally Lake Cargelligo and Murrin Bridge Kooris were sent to Wagga.

The program was only supposed to be mobilised once a family had made their own decision to move away from their home area, but Aborigines have reported many examples of pressure being applied to entice community leaders, often those who already had a house and employment, to make the move in order to become the focus of chain migration. Despite the wide suspicion with which the program was viewed, the offers of rapid access to decent housing were powerfully attractive, and in the nine years of its operation over 200 families were 'encouraged' to move, no doubt with the 'intense counselling' advocated by the Joint Committee. Yet there was a constant 25 per cent 'failure' rate in which families returned to their home communities quite soon. Many more returned after 1980 as the program collapsed when a recession demonstrated that the long-term restructuring of Australian industry was leading to drastically reduced numbers of the factory jobs in which most 'relocated' workers had been placed.[41]

The diffusion of Welfare Board powers had its own effects. The intrusion of Housing Commission officers began to be felt by Aboriginal people as yet another means of control over their lives, and the existence of the Aboriginal Advisory Committee offered no compensatory sense of access to decision-making. As the elderly Koori preacher at Woodenbong, Frank Bundock, was to describe it in 1972, 'We're now under three bosses, it's too much for us to bear'.[42]

24

'Hungry For Our Own Ground'

They gave us rations, a little bit of rations when the managers were here, but we are hungry for our own ground.

—Mrs Milli Boyd, Woodenbong, May 1972

There was, by mid-1971, a rising sense of crisis about land in New South Wales. While there was strong recognition and sympathy with Aboriginal attempts to protect land in the Northern Territory and Queensland, there were particular local pressures bringing land issues into urgently sharp focus for New South Wales activists.

It is still often assumed that the main influences on Aboriginal political activists in Sydney during the early 1970s were the African-American civil rights movement and the radical development of the Black Panther urban defence initiatives. Certainly there was intense interest in this area, and a delegation including Sol Bellear from Chinderah, near Fingal, went to America in 1970 and spent some months with Panther groups. The black berets, black leather gloves and sunglasses of the Panthers were conspicuously displayed by Aboriginal activists in the protests against the South African sporting teams in 1971, and there were strong links with the Pacific organisation the Polynesian Panthers, who sent a delegate to Australia in 1972. The Aboriginal Legal Service and Medical Service, formed in Sydney in 1970 and 1971, have often been assumed to draw on some aspects of the urban defence organisations set up in America, but their form and goals were far more influenced by specific local conditions of rapid urbanisation and growing police harassment. After the formation of these services, activists searched the available international precedents for useful strategies. Over this period there were a number of international delegations, including some to China, which Australia at that time did not recognise, and many to consult with Maori activists in New Zealand.

Aboriginal activists had always been more aware of Native American experience than had white Australians. William Cooper, in the mid-1930s, had been widely discussing the US Indian Lands Development Act with other Aboriginal activists and used it to criticise the NSW

335

government for its failure to support Cumeragunja's independent farming potential. In 1969 Aboriginal activists were just as aware of the seizure of Alcatraz by Vine Deloria Jnr as they were of the Panthers' organisations, and *Bury My Heart at Wounded Knee* was as widely read as *Soul on Ice*. Aboriginal activists conceptualised their situation, even in urban areas, in terms of their position as a dispossessed and colonised people. This fundamental concern over the issue of dispossession was expressed strongly in 1970 when a large group of Aboriginal people challenged the official re-enactment of Cook's landing at Botany Bay by holding an alternative ceremony, laying wreaths in the Bay to commemorate the Aboriginal landowners who had died defending their land. Each wreath had the name of a language which was no longer spoken because so many of its people had died.

The early 1970s saw a rising awareness of the issue of racism among white, left-wing and counterculture activists. The war in Vietnam was analysed in terms of the engagement of racism and imperialism, while sporting ties with white South Africa were challenged, with demonstrations against surfing teams in 1970 and then against the Springboks Rugby Tour in 1971, which was also the UN year against racism. In mid-1971 meetings began between Aboriginal activists and white supporters such as Dennis Freney and Meredith Burgmann to plan a major public demonstration of support for Aboriginal people and to voice opposition to racism in Australia. This 'Moratorium for Black Rights' was to take place on National Aborigines Day, 14 July 1972.[1]

By far the most important development in those years, however, was the expansion of the Aboriginal organisational network focused on land. In November 1970 a statewide conference of Aboriginal people had been held in Sydney. Here a Lands and Rights Council was formed which was meant to become involved in every aspect of Aboriginal affairs but to make land its priority. Pastor Frank Roberts Jnr took the main role in organising this council, which followed on from his active interest in the earlier FCAATSI Lands and Reserves Committee. Then, intensifying the focus on land issues, Roberts was again central in setting up the NSW Aboriginal Lands Board in 1971. Both these bodies drew in many of the young Aboriginal activists in Sydney, like Lyn Thompson from the Craigie family in Moree, who became secretary of the Lands Board. Both the Lands and Rights Council and the Lands Board brought together Aboriginal campaigners from all over the State who were committed to the goal of land justice.[2]

For the first time since the brief coalitions of the 1930s, the organisational link was made between the coastal and the western activists. Frank Roberts Jnr used to travel tirelessly to communities all over the State on behalf of the Council and Lands Board, often with

Con O'Clerkin for company. Kaye and Bob Bellear travelled with them on one trip to Brewarrina and Goodooga during the early 1970s. The people they met included Tombo Winters, a shearer and a member of the Fernando family which had suffered intensely at the hands of the Protection Board's child removal policy and then in the enforced move from Angledool to Brewarrina in 1936. Tombo and his family lived at Dodge City, the 'town settlement' where the Welfare Board had forced the Brewarrina station residents to move in 1966. Stephen Gordon met Frank Roberts Jnr there too. He was another Brewarrina shearer and union activist, and the grandson of Henry Hardy, whose memories of the Murri resistance to the Angledool move had been recounted many times to his grandson.

Yet another young community leader contacted in these trips was Julie Whitton, from the Pikampul and Kamilaraay lands on the Macintyre River, whose community at Toomelah were the custodians of Boobera Lagoon, and who had suffered enforced dislocation from Boomi and had then had their new reserve turned into a concentration site with people from Tingha dumped there in 1938. Roberts recorded 25 such conferences and meetings he had attended in rural areas from 1970 to 1973.[3] The Lands and Rights Council and the Lands Board allowed a forum for these communities to plan a concerted campaign to challenge the dislocation and dispossession policies of the NSW government.

In this context of intensifying activity, late in 1971 the long-awaited NT High Court judgment on the Yirrkala people's challenge to the Nabalco bauxite mine at Gove was finally brought down. Mr Justice Blackburn's decision acknowledged that Aboriginal people had had a 'spiritual' link to land but rejected the Aboriginal insistence that this had involved a property relationship, that is, any economic or social relationship to the land. Blackburn argued that there was no capacity within Australian common law or property law to recognise any indigenous rights to land.[4]

This was a severe blow to those Aboriginal activists and their supporters who had believed that the existing law could be used to reclaim land. For the next two decades, until the 1992 Mabo judgment demolished Blackburn's judgment in law and in history, Aboriginal activists believed they needed to influence politicians to create new laws rather than look to the old colonial legal structure to give them justice. Such influence could be exerted creatively, and aside from the conventional lobbying of politicians, Aboriginal activists were unquestionably looking for opportunities to use press coverage to increase public awareness of their demands.

The future did not look completely hopeless, because Coombs and

Stanner in the Office of Aboriginal Affairs had been making it clear that there were political opportunities to make changes. They had conducted an interdepartmental study, also released late in 1971, to provide advice to the federal government. Its report was known to be generally supportive of the Yirrkala people's right to claim royalties, to favour leasehold ownership of reserves in all States and to advocate the 'provision of funds to buy land outside the reserves in the States and the Northern Territory'.[5]

But the McMahon Coalition government rejected the advice from its Office of Aboriginal Affairs. On 25 January 1972, the day before Australia Day, McMahon announced that the Yirrkala people would receive royalties from the bauxite mining, but only at a trivial rate. The government was to allow a weak form of Aboriginal leasehold over some reserve areas in the Northern Territory, but traditional ownership was not to be regarded as the reason for renewed tenure of any reserves; there was to be very little money available to purchase land and there was no reference to any land acquisition outside 'traditional' areas nor to any compensation for dispossession. Mining companies, on the other hand, were to be allowed to mine unimpeded on any Aboriginal reserve land because the strengthening of this industry was 'in the national interest'.[6]

There was a swift reaction from New South Wales Aboriginal people. A great deal of the planning among Aboriginal activists in Sydney in those days was done in the Burton Street house of Lyn and Peter Thompson in East Sydney, and from there a vigil was established outside the NSW Parliament immediately after the statement was released, despite the unseasonal cold and rain. Many of the people there that night were already well experienced in the political strategies of inno- vative symbolic protest: Lyn and her brother Billy Craigie from Moree, Bob Bellear from Chinderah, Gary Williams from Nambucca Heads and Woodenbong, Tony Koorie from Lismore, Allana Doolan from Queens- land, and close white supporters like Bob Bellear's wife Kaye and Lyn Thompson's husband Peter. All of these activists came from communities scarred by the loss of their lands. Their experiences of dispossession or forced migration were recent, within their parents' memories, and often within their own lifetimes. Their outrage arose from a very personal anger over their community's recent losses. As the night deepened, the members of the vigil, 'wet and bedraggled', decided that to make a greater impact they had to take their protest to Canberra, to set up their camp in front of the centre of government. There had been ideas circulating for some months about a symbolic protest, and Kevin Gilbert had suggested that an 'embassy' was one way to achieve this. Without having a plan fully developed, the Sydney group nevertheless agreed they would not be shifted from their Canberra camp until all those years of dispossessions were acknowledged and compensated.[7]

So a small number of young Aboriginal men including Billy Craigie, Tony Koorie and Michael Anderson, whose family was from Angledool, left Sydney later that night in a car organised by Communist Party supporters and driven by *Tribune* photographer Noel Hazard. Equipped with signs drawn in Sydney and a beach umbrella and some plastic picked up from a supporter in Canberra, this group set up their Embassy on the lawns of Parliament house in the early hours of Australia Day, 26 January 1972. Their focus on land was unmistakable. Placards held by the shivering protesters as dawn broke read:

LAND RIGHTS NOW OR ELSE

LEGALLY THIS LAND IS OUR LAND. WE SHALL TAKE IT IF NEED BE

LAND NOW NOT LEASE TOMORROW

The first statement made that day was a demand for land rights: 'The land was taken from us by force . . . we shouldn't have to lease it . . . our spiritual beliefs are connected to the land'. The second insisted that the new Embassy would remain until the government's policy statement was retracted, and land rights were granted.[8]

As the days went by, the beach umbrella was replaced by tents, and the original small group of activists were reinforced with Aboriginal people from Victoria and Queensland. Their tents held some echoes of the Resurrection City which had been set up in Washington in 1969 to protest African-American poverty, and there were other similarly haunting precedents of symbolic protest. But the most immediate and fundamental models for the Embassy were the thousands of camps in which Aboriginal people continued to live all over Australia for the whole time the Embassy stood. As John Newfong said, 'The Mission has come to town'.[9]

The sight of the canvas-and-plastic Embassy on the neat parliamentary lawns was immediately recognised by Aboriginal people around Australia. They responded to its ironic, powerful symbolism with widespread support, despite some concerns about the 'Black Power' label some of its activists embraced, with its connotations of direct action and possible violence. The government's embarrassment grew over the weeks. The permanent 'diplomatic staff' of the Tent Embassy continued to be a small group, limited by the need to finance their support. One of the weapons with which the government sought to undermine them was to accuse them of being only a 'handful of militants' who had no base of support among the majority of Aboriginal people. Yet in reality support was building by the day, and indeed was being heightened by incidents within New South Wales which demonstrated the contempt with which the State government treated Aboriginal people's desire to have a secure home.

THE ROOTS OF THE EMBASSY

Just after the Embassy was erected, Harold Brown and his wife Val Close, with their four children, were evicted from their Woodenbong reserve home by the NSW Housing Commission.[10] Harold Brown, well known in the community as a responsible and reliable worker, had been thrown out of work when wet weather led to stand-downs at the timber mill in which he worked. He and his family lived in one of the new houses on the reserve, the only new housing built on any New South Wales reserve in many years. He had applied for social security and after a prolonged wait his first cheque arrived just as he was called back to work. He was then accused, despite his impeccable record, of having applied for social security under false pretenses. This matter was still in dispute when Brown was again stood down through no fault of his own, but the Department refused to allow him any further support. Now he and his family were in serious financial difficulties and they could no longer pay the rent for their house.

So on 17 February officers of the Housing Commission, the Child Welfare Department and the police arrived to evict the family. The other Bandjalang residents of the reserve took up a collection and offered to pay the $30 dollars which would cover the immediate rental arrears, and this diverted the officials while they conferred about whether they should accept it. They agreed only to postpone the eviction, and returned on 21 February, in a party with four Housing Commission officers, two Welfare officers, four policemen and two white labourers. They insisted that the Browns still owed $100, which they were prepared to reduce to $80. As this represented an impossible sum for the Browns, the eviction went ahead. The white officers removed all the Browns' furniture, piled it onto a truck and took it to the home of a relative 150 yards down the road. All this time, the residents of the reserve stood around in support of the Browns, some jeering at the police and Welfare officers, others silent and fearful, seeing their own fate before them. The reserve community then met and passed a formal motion:

> We the residents of Muli Muli Village Woodenbong, refuse to pay any futher rent for the houses we occupy on the reserve until Mr and Mrs Brown are re-instated in the house they have occupied at Woodenbong for the last twelve months.

Their case was taken up by the Richmond/Tweed TLC, and by other supportive organisations including the Sydney networks organising the Moratorium for Black Rights, and suddenly the Browns were informed that their rental arrears had all been paid by an 'anonymous donor'. The Browns demanded complete restitution, including the return of their furniture, but the Housing Commission was refusing to admit its errors. Just as suddenly, the Browns were told that the 'anonymous donor' had withdrawn the offer.

The reserve residents maintained their refusal to pay rents until the Browns' case had been resolved with justice, and they widened their demands to take up their long-standing desire for secure tenure over their land and support for their proposal to farm the land co-operatively. In response, the Housing Commission and the Department of Child Welfare and Social Welfare together drew out the old and powerful weapon which had been used so often in the past against Aboriginal people trying to stand up for themselves. First, eviction notices were served on many other Muli Muli reserve families, and then 'the Child Welfare Department threatened to declare the children of these evicted families wards-of-the-state and remove them from their families'.[11]

When the Minister for Social Welfare and Child Welfare and Aboriginal Affairs, Mr John Waddy, made an official visit to Woodenbong in mid-April to open a community hall, he was greeted with tense hostility. His Welfare officers had already deepened the people's anger by insensitively covering a monument the community had erected to Doc Williams, the family patriarch and community founder, with plastic sheeting, so as not to detract from the Minister's own foundation plaque. When Waddy did arrive his unease was obvious: he was accompanied by ten armed police officers, an unprecedented show of strength in this small rural village.

The NSW Aboriginal Lands Board held a major conference late in April, where country delegates met and discussed the urgent land problems facing them. With Frank Roberts Jnr again prominent, and Lyn Thompson in her role as organising secretary, there were delegates from Woodenbong, Brewarrina, Boggabilla, Moree, Purfleet, Roseby Park, Wallaga Lake and many other communities where land had been central to political demands for decades. The western delegates explained for the coastal community representatives the land issues which were important for them. Not only did they want to protect significant sites like the Narran Lakes, but also the sites of massacres like Hospital Creek and the burial grounds of their old people. Then they demanded the right to access to the large tracts of land just taken from them, the old mission lands at Brewarrina, where whites could lease land for 99 years but Murris could gain at most a five-year lease over their own country.

The conference demonstrated that despite the differences in their histories, there were many common concerns between the western and coastal representatives, like those from Toomelah, Purfleet and Woodenbong, from communities all still in dispute with the State government about having to pay rent for substandard housing on what they knew to be their own land. And the burning issue continued to be the government's plans to dispose of Aboriginal reserve land, and, most urgently, the sale of Kinchela. The Lands Board elected a deputation to see Mr Waddy on the third day of the conference, but the deputation was curtly refused an interview. The conference unanimously passed a motion calling for Waddy's immediate dismissal.[12]

With the sale of Kinchela looming, the Lands Board activists felt they needed to take more dramatic action. Lyn Thompson and Kaye Bellear went to Waddy's house one evening shortly after the Lands Board conference. They set up an L. J. Hooker sign on his front lawn, having repainted the name to 'L. J. Koorie' in an ironic reversal to point up his role as a real estate agent putting Aboriginal land on the market. Then Lyn and Kaye challenged Waddy to his face, knocking on his door and walking straight into his living room as so many Welfare officers had done to so many Aboriginal families. With Waddy flustered and trying to ring the police to demand the trespassers be removed, Lyn and Kaye insisted he tell them how he would feel if his home were to be sold from under his feet. They were still demanding his answer as the police led them away.[13]

Peter Tobin was a white Australian who had just completed his law degree and already had a long history of involvement in support of Aboriginal struggles. His family had lost many members in the Holocaust in Germany, and both his commitment to socialism and his opposition to racism had led to his involvement in Abschol, for whom he had conducted a number of survey trips to Walgett in the late 1960s to assess the degree of legal discrimination Murris faced in the west. He had already been asked by some elderly Aboriginal people to locate the title deeds of land they believed had rightfully belonged to their ancestors. Tobin was aware that whites were generally ignorant of the pervasive concerns with land which underlay so much of the politics of rural Aboriginal communities. As a strategy to counter the criticism being made of the Embassy that it did not reflect 'grassroots' concerns, he raised with Aboriginal activists the idea of a trip to rural areas. Together they devised an itinerary which would allow them to record the views of ordinary members of Aboriginal communities, and at the same time address Aboriginal desires to document their former landholdings to allow them to assess just what their situation was.

In May 1972 Peter Tobin, Gary Williams, Billy Craigie and Lincoln Wood, a younger Koori from western Sydney, set out for the north coast.

They stopped first at Purfleet outside Taree and then at many communities further north, including Greenhills at Kempsey, Burnt Bridge, South West Rocks, Bellwood at Nambucca Heads, where the Stuart's Island families had settled after their island was taken from them, then on to Cabbage Tree Island and Fingal. Then they spent long days in the Grafton Lands Department office, examining in great detail the hundreds of parish maps covering the Land District from many different periods, some of which held the pencilled traces of Aboriginal reserves and permissive occupancies now revoked. They dreamed maps for weeks afterwards. Their work has still not been equalled for its care and thoroughness.[14]

From the coastal areas around Grafton, the team headed inland to Woodenbong, the country of Gary Williams' father's family. After a long stay there, they drove across the mountains to Toomelah on the Macintyre, then to Moree, in Billy Craigie's home country. After returning to Sydney they carried out more interviews and made another trip to Wallaga Lake. At each place they talked to the respected and responsible older members of the communities, and completed 50 questionnaires in interviews with family heads. They found intense interest wherever they went, and, as had happened to Pearl Gibbs and Bill Ferguson in the 1930s, they were repeatedly given instructions to search for the deeds for land which so many people were deeply convinced had been handed over to their grandparents by Queen Victoria. The people who spoke to this research team showed that they still held the old understandings of what these reserves were: a recognition of traditional land ownership, compensation for dispossession and a promise from the English Crown of inalienable security of tenure.[15]

The time at Woodenbong was the most intense experience of the trip. The rent strike was at its height, and the community was tense with determination, but also with anxiety about whether their children would be at risk, and whether they would lose not only their houses but their treasured land. Alex Vesper was there, the long-time campaigner who had first demanded that the FCAA conference in 1960 give land and compensation priority in its discussions. So too were Frank Bundock, the elderly lay preacher, and Gordon and Euston Williams. Their father Doc Williams had been the principal Gidhabal custodian of the land at Muli Muli in 1908 when, as part of Tooloom cattle station, it had been 'set aside for the use of Aborigines' as Woodenbong reserve. Along with the group of senior Bandjalang men and women who lived at Muli Muli, Pastor Frank Roberts Jnr was also there at the time of the team's visit.

The longest surviving interview transcript is the powerful testimony of Mrs Milli Boyd, the granddaughter of Doc Williams and niece of

343

Gordon and Euston. She spoke in her fluent Gidhabal, a dialect of Bandjalang, as well as in English, expressing her passionate determination to defend Muli Muli.

Milli Boyd described how her grandfather, on his deathbed, commanded his kin to *ya:na*, which means 'Stand still on this block', and to 'keep on sitting down here', an instruction delivered in the future continuous tense. This direction has been solemnly upheld by Doc Williams' descendants, who, Mrs Boyd explained, might leave Woodenbong for a time but always returned and continued their association with the land. Many, like herself, intended to stay living ('sitting down') on Muli Muli until their death. When Peter asked Mrs Boyd whom she understood to own the land, she responded:

> Well, they [the Protection Board] gave us rations, a little bit of rations when the manager was here, but we still want this ground. We are hungry for our own ground. This is my ground . . .
>
> This ground is very precious to us, it's like serving God . . .
>
> We got a small run, Stan and Gordon [her uncles] have described the tribal boundaries in some book . . . My old father told me goanna. Doc Williams was goanna . . . [the land] is shaped like a goanna . . .

> *How much of the goanna run did different individual people own?*

> The very same. We all owned it together with my aunties and old Gordon's family, the one gift from God, that's what the old people say.

> *Where did these gifts and the right to own this land come from?*

> Wherever Doc came from, his grandfather born, right back to first generation. My great-great-grandfather he was born here. That gift for that birth still here, that goes by the birth of the people, of the first generation. The right to own this land came from the first generation from Doc Williams, before Doc Williams, here before Tooloom station.
>
> Muli Muli is very precious to the Williamses because our grandfather died here. Herbert Charles' mother died here, she wouldn't go anywhere else to die, so did my father die here . . .

Mrs Boyd explained that all Doc Williams' descendants, who were Gidhabal speakers, were regarded as custodians of the land. Those who had married into the extended Williams family, members of the Boyd, Charles and Roberts families, were also regarded as legitimate residents of the land. These were the people, Mrs Boyd said, who were the landowners.

Her understanding of the nature of their landholding title was that it was perpetual and inalienable:

> We should never say to another Aborigine, sell that ground at Muli Muli. When he said '*Ya:na*, live here, this is our ground', he gave us this ground. Therefore, he didn't give us this ground to split it up into bits,

he just meant it for us, the [extended] Williams family . . . *'Ya:na*, stand still on this block!'

The run [Gidhabal or goanna dialect area] must always belong to us, even the oldest son couldn't get rid of the land. Land not to be touched. The oldest son couldn't just do what he liked . . .

Mrs Boyd explained her feeling for the land in terms not only of the experiences she had had growing up and raising her family on Muli Muli, nor only as the revered burial site of her relatives, but as a place surrounded by mountains and other landforms of great religious significance:

What sort of meaning do the sacred sites have for you?

Strong meaning for me inside. Important, my secret ground the old burial ground where the old full-bloods lie, like old Dickie Williams, the Doc's uncle. Williams found this place, Williams died here, Williams remain.

Relationship between Williams and the sacred mountain strong. Only one Gidhabal mountain, called Gidabal B'larni, the Tower. Bulls Head Mountain is like a god to us. Closely tied up from our hearts to our minds. Even if I'm tired, I'd come back here and then in the morning I'd be all right.

When asked how she would feel if she were forced to leave by the Housing Commission over the rent strike, or if she lost the reserve land altogether, Mrs Boyd replied:

We still say it's ours. It's still a Williams town, I said it and I'll keep on saying it. This is my ground, because when they said you move out, I'll move out but I'll remain in this ground. If I've got to go over the hill and stay in them old cars, I'm going to walk on that bit of ground my grandfather walks on. This block of land is mine, it'll be mine until I die.

I'd weep for this place, it's my ground. I'll weep for this land because my aunties died here . . .

We should have this land, this is our land. We're hungry for our land.

Alex Vesper told the research team how he and others had made approaches to claim the Muli Muli land in the 1930s, by right of adverse possession since Kooris had lived on it for generations. Vesper, Gordon and Euston Williams and the other men of high standing along with younger members of the extended Williams family like Val Close and Harold Brown, made statements which endorsed Mrs Boyd's testimony.

There were several explanations given of why reserves had been created, which reflected the varying reasons for reserves in different regions, with the pastoral area around Woodenbong having had no early farming reserves in the way the coast had done, and with the more recent experiences of repressive managerial control very evident in people's explanations. Brown and Close, for example, who were still struggling to regain their home after the Housing Commission eviction, said that 'Aborigines used to be free, roaming, hunting and so on, but they were given little blocks of land to stop making a nuisance of themselves. Also for cheap labour'. Gordon Williams could recount the detailed history of the local reserves, many of which had been revoked as the Protection and Welfare Boards tried to 'centralise' Aboriginal residents of the region at Woodenbong. He remembered reserves as areas given to the Kooris by the old station-owners who had 'stood by' the Kooris.

Yet others, like Pastor Frank Bundock, saw the reserves as recognition of prior rights and as compensation, however inadequate: the reserves were 'a tiny bit of restitution, giving back what was taken, yet we don't own it'. Bitter as he was over the loss of Stoney Gully, Alex Vesper saw reserves as an attempt to 'stop Aborigines advancing'. His view of the future was endorsed by the other community residents interviewed:

> While Aborigines should be granted title to reserves that is not sufficient compensation. We want 1000 acres per person. We're the rightful owners of the whole of Australia. The whites are just invaders. The people here are descended from the original tribe. We've inherited this land and anyhow we've been fighting for it over the last fifteen or twenty years. Whites are entitled to inherit, but blacks can't. We're free. White men don't tell us what to do. Blacks should be self-dependent.

Each of these elderly or middle-aged community members explained their desire for their land by reference both to their historical experience, including the deaths and burials of their loved ones, and to their awareness of and reverence for the spiritual meanings of their country. Their statements echo those of Milli Boyd but they also resonate with the meanings for land which had been made public by Aboriginal people across the State over the last 200 years:

> Burial grounds are sacred. Each tribe has its sacred mountain, Woodenbong people have the Bulls Heads and Stoney Gully people have Mount Lindsay. These matters are very serious and people who have gone to such places without any right have died.

> We have real rights to this land. The mountains have been handed down from generation to generation, the people have looked to the mountains to guide them, and on those mountains live spirits, creative beings which are a part of this land, but in our ways this is secret. We were first here before the white man, this is valuable land and we have full rights to it so we should cultivate it. This land was granted to our forefather. When a European dies he hands his property to his relations. This place was willed to us. Our ancestors cleared this land and we're going to live off it. Once tribal rights were claimed through the family, the same thing is

done by the British with capital. We have a tradition of tribal rights not of individual inheritance to land.

This is our homeland, *Yugaja*.

At Wallaga Lake, the community members interviewed showed similarly strong knowledge of the traditional Law for that area, and just as detailed a knowledge of the history of land dealings over the generations of colonialism: pastoral station-owners had encouraged Koori camping to ensure an accessible labour force and are remembered to have handed over small portions of their pastoral leases or freeholds to become the permanent homes of Aboriginal landowners.

> Give us a lump of land each which can be called our home. To deprive us of this land would be a terrible thing, like taking away my birthright.

> This land was never the white man's property but belonged to the Wallaga tribe. We hope it's owned by the people of Wallaga Lake. We're going to fight for our piece of ground. We're proud of this place, it's the home of our old ancestors, a place where they've left things for the younger generation to learn and treasure like the sacred tree, corroboree grounds and burial grounds. Reserves were drawn up here for Aborigines to live on so we should be able to live and work here. We want to have homes here, a community garden, a caravan park, an orange grove, a boomerang factory, to make this a model reserve. So this place can be independent and we can support ourselves. So we can be equal to whites. Everybody is dedicated to here.

The research team had stopped at Burnt Bridge, one of the few remaining Macleay reserves where the families who had been farming the land since the 1870s had had to battle dispossession so many times and with such tenacity. The traces of that history of the valley can be glimpsed in these brief comments recorded in 1972.

> Some people living at Burnt Bridge and South Kempsey are descended from the original tribe in the area and these include the family names of Mosely, Richie and Quinlan. The old people say that Queen Victoria granted 1000 acres to old Johnny Mosely.

> Reserves are land set aside for Aborigines, therefore it should belong to them. It's our own ground, a village for Kooris. This reserve belongs to all the Kooris in Kempsey who originally came from here.

> This place is home, it is everything. I'm here because I belong here. There's nowhere to go after here, once people are arseholed out of Commission homes in town. At present we have no rights over this land legally but we have moral rights. We come from here so I reckon we should have every right to this land. This land is a part of me. My great-grandparents came from Burnt Bridge.

If this reserve were taken from us or moved we'd fight for it. They'd carry me out in a box. It wouldn't be fair, it would be like hunting us right out of Australia. We have every right in the world to be living here. It's up to Aboriginal people to decide where they want to live or whether they want to stay here, not the government. Aborigines should have land rights everywhere because Australia belongs to us.

We're entitled to this reserve and to the prime land taken from us. They left us the useless land. We're entitled to our homeland. Get a couple of thousand ships and ship 'em all out!

At Purfleet the Koori residents expressed their sense of historical experiences being entwined with the knowledge of traditional custodianship. These speakers had a feeling of personal identification with land which has direct echoes of the pre-invasion practice of identifying and orienting oneself in relation to the land to which one belonged:

This reserve is the black fellows', though Welfare owns it. We're here because our parents came from here, we were reared up here and went to school here. We identify with it. This land means everything, it means survival, it's the only home we know. It belonged to my forefathers and I'll fight for it.

At South West Rocks also these ideas were clear:

We'll never leave this place. We've been born and bred here. I want something that really belongs to me. I don't know what the legal position is but this is an Aboriginal reserve and I've been taught to live here as long as I want. Burial grounds and sacred sites are scattered around South West Rocks. It's home, it's everything.

The way these people talked about their land in 1972 opened out the simple demand for land rights into the many-dimensioned meanings we have seen present at different times throughout the history of colonial occupation in New South Wales. Even where the details of traditional Law and stories were no longer known, there was a very clear awareness of traditional knowledge, of stories bedded into the land, and of religious meanings and kinship relationships which flowed from these stories. There were similar echoes of traditional meanings for land in the way in which people associated and identified themselves with land, and oriented their relationships with each other in terms of that association. There were further meanings, however, which arose from the memories of the intense experiences of violent and repressive colonisation, the memories of massacres and dispossessions, both long past and very recent. Then there were the many 'everyday' memories, the experiences of lifetimes passed on the one site, often under Board control. Some of these memories were shot through with bitterness at the repression, while others were memories of the warmth as well as the tensions of community life. These had been inscribed into the knowledge of traditional meanings for these sites, and so had deepened in intensity.

The burial sites of revered and loved ancestors were a focal point for both the 'traditional' and the colonial meanings, and people in virtually all of the places where meanings were recorded explained their feelings for land in terms of their desire to stay close to the graves of their old people, to feel close to the memories of those old people and to be able to protect them, to be the custodians of their grandmothers' and grandfathers' graves, as these were a testimony to the long association and the intense personal commitment between the families and the land.

These stories, these meanings for land, were the authority for the Embassy, and the basis for the activism around land in the 1970s.

THE EMBASSY DESTROYED AND REBUILT

In Sydney, the preparations for the 'Black Moratorium' continued. It had been first planned as a protest against racial inequality and repression, a turning inward by white anti-apartheid opponents to challenge the discrimination in their own country. The strong Aboriginal control over the planning process through the 'Black Caucus', then the establishment of the Embassy and the powerful expression of grassroots desires for land justice which had been made on the Abschol trip shifted the focus of the coming demonstration to land. The aims of the Black Moratorium, finalised over April and May by the Black Caucus, and announced early in June, were unequivocally directed to land as the primary goal. These demands were:

1 Absolute ownership, including mineral and forestry rights, of all reserves and traditional areas to be vested in the Black communities associated with those areas.
2 Full compensation for all land seized since 1770.
3 The right and power of Black communities to control their own lives and their land.
4 Support for all Black struggles, including those for health, employment, housing, education and an end to all discriminatory legislation.[16]

The strongest impact of the Abschol transcripts had been made by Milli Boyd's striking metaphor of hunger, land and power. She had responded to a question about who owned Muli Muli reserve by first describing the APB managers' distribution of rations, meeting one type of hunger but at the same time demanding subservience and creating dependence. But these rations had not met a deeper hunger for the

Bandjalang, their desire to protect and hold onto their land: 'They gave us rations, a little bit of rations when the manager was here, but we still want this ground. We are hungry for our own ground'.

Her words were chosen to represent the theme of the coming demonstration. They were linked with a central Australian word meaning 'land' which had been transcribed by New South Wales activist Pat Eatock on a recent trip to Alice Springs. The intention was to suggest the unity of purpose to achieve land rights across the continent, from the most heavily colonised regions to the most remote areas. So '*Ningla a-na*: Hungry for our land' became the rallying call for the thousands of Aboriginal and non-Aboriginal Australians, along with Maori and Tongan supporters, who marched through the streets on National Aborigines Day, 14 July 1972. Marches were held around Australia, including Wollongong, where Pastor Roberts Jnr marched alongside Jack Campbell, Ted Thomas and Percy Mumbulla, and was followed by Merv Nixon and the powerful ranks of the South Coast Trades and Labor Council.[17]

The images of massed support for Aboriginal land demands alarmed the Minister for the Interior, Country Party member Ralph Hunt. The Black Moratorium added to the government's impatience with the Embassy on its front lawns, and Hunt hastened passage of an ordinance which would make penalties for camping in a public place far more severe. A copy of the draft ordinance was handed to the Embassy protesters on 17 July, and they began to prepare to defend the camp. Early on the 20th, Pat Eatock discovered the police asking for the first copies of the finalised ordinance, and she was able to rally support from a number of white students and others standing by to help in the Embassy's defence. By mid-morning 70 Aboriginal protesters and supporters were surrounding the tents.

The police moved in, with extraordinary brutality, demolishing the tents, injuring some demonstrators and arresting many others, all in front of the television cameras of the national and international media. The broadcast that night of these images of ugly and unnecessary violence shocked white Australia. This extraordinarily inept strategy on the part of the government was exacerbated when Hunt spoke on national television about the handful of 'unrepresentative militants' who 'stirred up trouble' and of the 'thousands of Aborigines who had disassociated themselves'. Given the widespread Aboriginal empathy and support for the Embassy, strongly expressed throughout previous months and demonstrated so powerfully in the Abschol survey in New South Wales, such untruths only served to galvanise Aboriginal determination to re-establish the tents.

Two hundred Aborigines and supporters set the tents up again on 23 July, only to be surrounded by 360 police who had been held in reserve behind the Parliament building. Again scenes of brutal violence ensued as police broke through the circles of protesters who had linked arms around the tents. A number of activists were inside the tents, including Bob Bellear, Bob Pringle, the Builders' Labourers official, and Tiga Bayles, and they were attacked as the police tried to destroy the canvas structures altogether. The battle again resulted in hospitalisations and many arrests. The violence was so intense that there was a general belief that it had only been good luck that serious injuries were avoided. Again, the struggle had been filmed and was shown on national television.[18] Then the networks of collaborative organisation set up by the Black Caucus of the Black Moratorium committee mobilised an extraordinary journey by more than 2000 Aboriginal and non-Aboriginal suppporters who travelled to Canberra to re-erect the tents on the following Sunday, 30 July. Despite high tension, the demonstration was managed tightly by Aboriginal marshals, and the government retreated, allowing a symbolic restoration of the Embassy.

The Embassy had flung onto the public stage the powerful idea of land rights. Land had been the underlying current for so long in Aboriginal politics, but it had not until then reached the wider public debate. Now there was a flurry of political responses. In New South Wales the State government failed to sack Mr Waddy, but late in 1972 it renamed the Aboriginal Advisory Committee as the NSW Aboriginal Lands Trust, and announced that there would be 'land rights' for the State's 30 000 Aboriginal citizens. What it meant was that the title to all the remaining reserves would continue to be held by the Minister, on behalf of the Lands Trust, and Aboriginal people could apply to the Trust for a lease over their own land.

Gough Whitlam had committed the federal Labor Party to land rights when he visited the Tent Embassy. With the ALP election victory in December 1972, Whitlam honoured his promise by moving rapidly to set up an inquiry into the most effective method of granting land rights. The issue rapidly became caught in a bitter conflict over the rights of the States, which continued to hold all legal responsibility for land transactions, and so the federal Land Rights Bill could only ever address land matters in the Northern Territory, Canberra and Jervis Bay.

Yet in spite of the severe limitations of both the State and federal responses to the land demands Aboriginal people were making, the nature of those government responses had changed dramatically. Nineteen seventy-two was the year of the Embassy but, perhaps more importantly, it was the year that Milli Boyd's testimony was recorded and brought to a wider public. There could be no return to the pretence that land justice was not a central issue for Aboriginal people and therefore for all Australians.

Epilogue
'Back to Where the Story Started': Kurnell 1988

Land has been a constant thread running through the actions, statements and demands of Aboriginal people in New South Wales from the
earliest days of invasion. From the first public Aboriginal political
demands in the mid-nineteenth century in this State, land was present
as a central goal. Land is not a new demand, picked up by political
activists from ideas formulated in remote 'traditional' areas.

It has often been a material demand, for particular traditional
hunting and camping lands, to gain a farm in agricultural areas and to
defend it, then to try to regain it, or to try to retain access to particular
country in pastoral areas. But there have invariably been deeper motives
expressed than the material goal of economic independence, important
though this has been. My question has been about how far Aboriginal
people have continued to try to use land for social and cultural purposes:
as a way of identifying themselves; to negotiate their relationship with
members of their own communities; to assert their political standing as
a means of dealing with the intense pressures and demands of colonialism; as a way to develop a survival lifestyle which is grounded, literally,
in traditional meanings, but which is responsive to the rapidly changing
historical contexts of the new economic and social order.

The significance of land and place for Aboriginal people in New
South Wales by the time of the Embassy was still strongly tied to
awareness of 'traditional' meanings. This can be seen explicitly in the
Woodenbong and Wallaga Lake testimonies, as well as those from other
places on the coast surveyed during 1972. This has also been the case
in areas like the far west, for example, in such situations as the 1983
Wiimpatja insistence that they, not the National Parks and Wildlife
Service, should be the rightful custodians and interpreters of
Mootawingee, north of Broken Hill. There continues to be strong
emphasis placed on sites of intense religious meaning, the sacred and
significant places whether mountains, beaches, rocks, trees or caves, sites
of art and religious focus. The archaeological remains of campsites are

also important in their evidence of free use of the land and its resources by its owners.

But the meanings Aboriginal people see in land are no longer only those which derive directly from pre-invasion times and knowledge. Drawing on the social and cultural processes of their traditional knowledge, and on their values and expectations, Aboriginal people have woven other threads of significance into the fabric of meaning. These new threads have arisen from the intense, traumatic or enriching experiences of colonial times.

So Woodenbong is now important for its original meaning of a place in traditional Gidhabal land, but also for its symbolic 'standing for' the wider lands as they became inaccessible and, furthermore, for its association with the experiences of community life under the increasingly repressive Protection and Welfare Board regimes. These are 'historical' significances, meanings derived from both the dramatic and the mundane elements of life lived out on one small fragment of Gidhabal people's land. Some of these memories are of intense pain and humiliation, relating to the experience of colonisation. But many are of the rich web of community relations which continued from before or were created by the pressures and tensions of station life. So it is with stations across the State, among those who were residents of Brewarrina, Terry Hie Hie, Menindee and all the others.

The campsites from which Aboriginal people worked on pastoral properties also have this multilayered significance. They are often readily identifiable as the traditional land of the residents, but, under dual occupation, they were also sites that show evidence of engagement in the new economy. So they speak of continuing custodianship of people's own lands but also of both the exploitation and the achievement of work in pastoral industries. Whether access to such places has been lost, at least temporarily, as it has at Dungalear, or whether, like Weilmoringle, Aboriginal people have secured their residence there, these sites remain in the imagination of generations of people.

The independent farming reserves were just as significant, with their meaning intensified because they were not only people's own land, but were land they had won back, believed secure, then farmed or lived on successfully by anyone's criteria, acquiring memories and associations, only to find their tenure challenged and lost against their intense resistance. Both the richness of associations and the intensity of the conviction that these lands had been formally and legally acknowledged as Aboriginal explains the tenacious focus many older people maintained on the demand to protect and restore 'the old reserve' lands. This determinedly narrow focus often frustrated white allies of the 1970s. We often assumed that people should broaden their vision to include the whole of their traditional lands, rather than to continue to concentrate on these fragments, which were seen by whites and some young Aboriginal activists as either the scraps of a paternalistic coloniser or as sites of unrelieved repression and misery. Yet for older people, with a direct experience of independent control, and for those younger family members who listened to them, these small reserve lands well deserved the attention they received.

Beyond the threads of meaning, the stories, memories and knowledge that held people emotionally in relationships with particular places, Aboriginal people have used land to identify themselves when travelling or in migration, to define themselves as people from a particular country, and as people with a responsible relationship to particular lands. The issue of diaspora has not been explored in Australia and I have barely touched on its complexities in these last few chapters. There has been heavy pressure on Aboriginal people to justify their demand for land by proving detailed traditional knowledge or long-term and unbroken association. So there has been little opportunity to acknowledge the profound impact of policy and economy in moving people away from their land, particularly in the last three decades. Yet there can be no easy assumption that those who move or are moved away have severed their relationship to their homelands. Many have continued to mobilise ideas of land, and of responsibility for their old or new lands, to locate themselves in the social and political world of their new community and in its relations with wider Australia. The determination to take up responsibilities for land, and to ensure that the land where one is living has custodians, are powerful social processes generated from the values and practices of traditional Australia, but continuing to be meaningful for Aboriginal people in the late twentieth century.

In traditional society people negotiate their political standing and social relations and responsibilities through the conduct of the obligations of custodianship for the land. So in Australia under colonialism, land has usually been one demand among many. It has been a dimension of Aboriginal demands for a justice which guarantees equality as citizens of the modern Australian state, but at the same time acknowledges traditional ways of understanding the world. The land issue has over time taken precedence or been shifted to the position of a long-term goal depending on the urgency of other matters, but it has seldom been absent. It was often not recognised by observers, however, because a desire for land was not expected or not of interest to white allies. There have been many situations when Aboriginal participants have known that the conflicts they were involved in were long-standing struggles over land, about where they could walk, where they could live, where they could feel safe. These conflicts have appeared to whites, however, observing them in press reports or seeing only their final .open confrontations, as disputes over equality.

Yet the wider Australian discourses on land and on Aboriginal affairs have consistently affected the choices Aboriginal spokespeople made about how they would frame their demands if they wished to gain support or to be heard. The interests and the goals of white allies, of both Right and Left, have opened possibilities for expressing some demands or have shut them off. This has been all the more so because land continues to be an important issue in white politics, economics and sentiment, with an ambivalence which still includes for non-Aboriginal Australians all the elements of land as a threatening presence, a prized commodity or a precious but fragile responsibility.

The land movement has always been a dynamic process, and this did not cease with the Embassy. The pattern continued by which different regions emerged as the leaders of the movement depending on where the pressures on access to land were intensifying. By the mid-1970s, the north-west and far western communities were coming under greatest pressure. Reserve land had been lost by revocation, and jobs had evaporated as the pastoral industry finally collapsed in that area. The government continued to refuse to house Aboriginal people on reserve lands or even in the towns of their choice. Murris attempted to challenge this pressure to move away, as well as the residential segregation of the towns themselves, by setting up housing companies funded through the new federal Labor government after 1972. Aboriginal assertions of rights to residential land in the towns, alongside their establishment of defensive organisations like the Legal Service, were met with increasing police repression and heightened tension on the streets of these country towns. Nevertheless, the housing companies for the first time had hard cash to purchase land or houses at just the time that whites in many far western towns were leaving for better employment prospects. It was the Aboriginal Housing Companies which finally began to force cracks in the walls of white residential segregation in the western towns.

Facing loss of access to land and this growing social and economic pressure, western communities began to voice their concerns about land. So it was that a coalition on Land Rights emerged through the mid-1970s, strengthening the links between western and coastal activists which had been established in the Land and Rights Council set up by Frank Roberts. The western spokespeople were the heirs of the Angledool and Tibooburra communities, whose access to their lands was now closed down altogether. The coalition which formed the independent political body, the NSW Aboriginal Land Council in 1977, included not only Jack Campbell, Ted Thomas and Kevin Cook, long active in land and union matters, and the veteran Frank Roberts Jnr, with other north coast representatives, but spokespeople too from Collarenebri, Toomelah, Walgett and Brewarrina, and soon after, from Wilcannia and Menindee. So it was another coalition of regional spokespeople who took the challenge up to the Wran Labor government to recognise formally Aboriginal people's rights to land in legislation and in financial terms.

The Land Rights Act which was finally achieved in 1983 was, like all pieces of legislation, a compromise which reflected the intensity of the struggle between Aboriginal groups and their opponents, outside and inside the ALP government.[1] The legislation offered no mineral rights, and only very little protection over heritage sites and material. The Minister for Lands reflected a conservative bureaucracy as well as representing a conservative rural constituency. He intervened when the Bill was before Parliament to amend it in a manner which completely emasculated the mechanism by which Aboriginal people could claim land. Yet there were also strengths. The Act recognised the long-voiced Aboriginal demand that their land be held communally and inalienably, and all land gained by claim or purchase was to be protected in this way.

The Land Councils which were to be established under the new law recognised the long-established reality that Aboriginal people organised most effectively at regional level, rather than with a centralised 'State-level' executive body. The new three-tiered structure not only gave a strong role to Local Land Councils, but allowed them to participate in powerful Regional Land Councils, which could give a consolidated voice to regional opinion. Just as important, there was a well-funded mechanism for the purchase of land, a necessary component of any just system because so much Aboriginal land in New South Wales had been alienated by sale or lease, and was not therefore available for any claim process.

Aboriginal celebrations at what was undoubtedly a successful stage in the long campaign towards land justice were severely tempered by an accompanying piece of legislation. The Wran government announced that it would only pass the Aboriginal Land Rights Act on the condition that Aboriginal people did not oppose a parallel law, the Retrospective Validation of Revocations Act. In a sad and frustrating irony, Aboriginal people found out what the government and its legal officers had learnt in 1979. A legal ambiguity had been created in 1913, whereby the Crown land of Aboriginal reserves had been vested in the Protection and Welfare Boards until 1969, not in the Lands Department. This invalidated all revocations of Aboriginal reserves in that period.

This meant that the many losses of Aboriginal farms and homes, the dispossession of around 25 000 acres of 'old reserves' by 1969, against which Aboriginal people had fought such tenacious and heart-breaking struggles, had all been not only morally indefensible but also technically illegal. In reality, in 1983, the freehold title over many of those old reserves was invalid and Aboriginal people, as the beneficiaries of the now defunct Directorate of Aboriginal Affairs, could have successfully reclaimed their land. The Wran government was not prepared to take such a step. So while it claimed to be generously handing over permanent title in the Land Rights Act to 6000 acres of remaining reserve lands to the resident Aboriginal communities, it was, at the same time, removing any Aboriginal hopes of regaining 25 000 acres of 'old reserve' lands. These were the lands which held such deep and intense significance for so many people, the very reserves which they have so firmly believed were granted to them by Queen Victoria in recognition of their traditional ownership.

The Act has therefore been regarded with deep ambivalence among Aboriginal communities. There have been some triumphant successes where Regional Land Councils were able to pool the smaller amounts of land purchase money which came to Local Land Councils, and so make collective decisions on strategic land purchases. Often they have had to do this anonymously, to avoid continuing white hostility to Aboriginal land ownership. With such strategies, large properties such as Weinteriga on the Darling between Wilcannia and Menindee have been restored to Aboriginal custodianship.

There are other aspects of Aboriginal people's concerns around land which are not well met by the Act, however. In particular, Aboriginal desires to regain ownership and management over important sacred sites have had to be advanced by other means. So western Aboriginal people have blockaded the spectacular scenic and art site at Mootawingee to force government to recognise their interests in it. They have still not succeeded in achieving adequate recognition of their custodial responsibilities although they are now in firm control of the interpretation of the site to visitors. In the north, Aboriginal people at Toomelah and Moree have found that the Act gives no protection to Boobera Lagoon, a site about which there is abundant and rich oral tradition detailing its significance to all the Murris of the region, yet which is being physically destroyed by the use of speedboats and the drainage of water to irrigate surrounding cotton crops. The Land Rights Act has never provided the weapons to defend these dimensions of Aboriginal interest in land, and Aboriginal communities continue to take up such struggles by the long-established means of political lobbying and direct action.

As well, there have been grave pressures on the operation of the Act itself since 1983. There was little training offered to Aboriginal people who were suddenly expected to undertake major land research, organise purchases and then successfully take on economic management of land

and enterprises. There have been great constraints on the type of land use considered legitimate by the succeeding conservative governments, and in a number of bureaucratic strategies, Aboriginal attempts to secure land for anything other than conventional profit-making agriculture have been obstructed. So desires to use land for broader cultural or social purposes, or to rest it from production to try to regenerate its native ecology, have been constantly frustrated.

The election of a Liberal-Country Party conservative government in mid-1988 led to a concerted assault on behalf of this goverment's white rural power base. Unsuccessful attempts were made to seize the funds allocated for Aboriginal land purchase, and when this was found to be simply illegal, the government implemented a policy of dismembering those elements of the Land Council structure which allowed a strong Aboriginal voice. The Regional Land Councils were this government's main target, and with an amending Act in 1990, these mid-level councils were stripped of any financial or political powers. The conservative government since then has fostered an approach from the increasingly centralised NSW Aboriginal Land Council which emphasises individual ownership; land seen as investment; profit-making enterprises to the exclusion of cultural or social land uses; and, most recently, an alteration to the nature of Aboriginal landholding which allows land to be sold for profit or otherwise alienated, in order to meet the demands of banks which refused to lend any development finance on land they could not mortgage.

These shifts over the early 1990s have caused concern and, in many areas, disillusionment with the formal government-administered mechanisms to regain and protect land. Yet Aboriginal interest in land continues to be widespread and frequently expressed. With the Meriam/Mabo decision of the Australian High Court in 1992 which recognised that Aboriginal people had held, and in some cases continued to hold, title over their land, there was a great rush of genuine hope and excitement among Aboriginal people throughout New South Wales, a hope that this might offer a real path towards land justice at last. There is now a new, more sympathetic Labor government in New South Wales, and the question of how Native Title legislation might be interpreted in this State is wide open. It is not clear how this will develop. Yet there have been powerful indications that however imperfect government responses may continue to be to Aboriginal demands, those demands will not fade.

Anyone who doubted that relations between land and people remain at the centre of Aboriginal politics and symbolism need only to have been there that night on the hillside at Kurnell.

On 26 January 1988, thousands of Aboriginal people from all over

Australia marched in Sydney to celebrate their victory in surviving a long and violent invasion over 200 years. The hosts were Murris, Kooris and Wiimpatjas, the Aboriginal people of New South Wales, who had suffered the longest and most intense impacts of colonisation.

The event commemorated on that date was the founding of the colony by Phillip and the First Fleet at Farm Cove in Sydney Harbour, but the Aboriginal organisers chose another site for the climax of their business that day. They said their work was about restoration and new beginnings, so they would go to the place where the story of the invasion had really begun, to Kurnell, the landing site of James Cook in 1770 on the southern side of Botany Bay.

At sunset, as white Australia celebrated with fireworks, the Aboriginal people of Australia began to restore the links which had been ruptured by the invasion. At the invitation of New South Wales Aboriginal people, the men and women from commmunities where traditional ceremonial life has been maintained began to dance and sing the stories which begin in their lands but travel across the country towards the east. As Central Land Council chairman Wenten Rubuntja explained it:

> When the English people found our country and Aboriginal people, they put their cities and their culture all over our country. But underneath this, all the time, Aboriginal culture and laws stay alive.
>
> In Central Australia . . . our culture, our laws and the song in the land has a voice—the Walpiri voice, the Arrernte, the Luritja, the Pitjantjatjara, Gurindji—many voices . . .
>
> The Aboriginal people living along the coast where the white people took over first, they might not know their language any more, but the emu story and the snake story goes all over Australia . . . When they see us dance we can celebrate that we all belong to the songs that go across the whole of this country.[2]

Many Aboriginal people and their white guests spent that night on the slope above the water at Kurnell. It was an unseasonally cold clear night, with the water of Botany Bay reflecting the bright moon above, the still glow of the oil refinery and the eerily silent lights of planes landing and taking off beyond hearing range. The trappings of white Australia were not denied, but had been made powerless by distance and the intensity of the ceremonies which began with the dusk. All through that night, the dance fires burned. Young and old, men and women, defiantly, joyously, danced the stories for the country.

At sunrise, exhausted but elated, the dancers ceased, and Aboriginal people from Sydney and the south-east spoke to us about what had happened on that land and what it meant to them. Then, quietly, Aboriginal leaders from across the country shepherded people into lines to walk through the smoke of smouldering green branches, a ritual cleansing and protection which can be used for many purposes. On that morning, it was said to be to release people from the sadness of so many past deaths and pain and to protect us all there from the powerful forces now able to move again in the land.

Most saw that dawn through tears, Aboriginal and non-Aboriginal people there both profoundly moved by the power of the night and the ritual of care and protection.

The custodianship of the land had been made again a public thing.

Notes

The following abbreviations have been used in the Notes and Bibliography. See also the Abbreviations list on p. xv.

ADB   *Australian Dictionary of Biography*
AHA   Australian Historical Association
AIAS   Australian Institute for Aboriginal Studies
AIATSIS   Australian Institute for Aboriginal and Torres Strait Islander Studies
ANU   Australian National University, Canberra
APBM   Aboriginal Protection Board Minutes
APBR   Aboriginal Protection Board Report(s)
AWBR   Aborigines Welfare Board Report(s)
CC   Chief Commissioner
CCL   Commissioner for Crown Lands
CLD   Crown Lands Department
Col. Sec. Colonial Secretary
CSIL   Colonial Secretary's In-Letters (later Chief Secretary's In-Letters)
CUP   Cambridge University Press
DEIL   Department of Education In-Letters
DT   *Daily Telegraph*
GD   Governor's Despatches
HRA   *Historical Records of Australia*
HRNSW   *Historical Records of New South Wales*
JRAHS   *Journal of the Royal Australian Historical Society*
JRSNSW   *Journal of the Royal Society of New South Wales*
JPP   Joint Parliamentary Papers of the NSW Parliament
ME   Minutes of Evidence
ML   Mitchell Library, Sydney
MCM   Municipal Council Minutes
MP   Member of Parliament
MUP   Melbourne University Press, Melbourne
NGG   *NSW Government Gazette(s)*
NPD   *New South Wales Parliamentary Debates*
OUP   Oxford University Press
PDCF   NSW Premier's Department Correspondence Files
PSF   Public School Files

SA   NSW State Archives
SC   Select Committee
SMH   *Sydney Morning Herald*
SCTLC   South Coast Trades and Labor Council
SUP   Sydney University Press, Sydney
UNE   University of New England
UNSWP   University of New South Wales Press, Sydney
UQP   University of Queensland Press, Brisbane
VPLA   Votes and Proceedings of the NSW Legislative Assembly
VPLC   Votes and Proceedings of the NSW Legislative Council
VN   *Voice of the North*
WW   *Workers' Weekly*

Chapter 1 Land and Meanings

1   Rose 1988; Rowse 1993:104–27.
2   Hercus 1980.
3   Cited in Knudtson and Suzuki 1992:134.
4   Vansina 1985.
5   Hamilton 1994; Thelen 1989.
6   Sahlins 1985.
7   Rose 1984; Mackinolty and Wainburranga 1988:355–60.
8   Rose 1992:207.
9   Rose 1991; Bell 1983; Kolig 1980, 1983.
10 AHA Conference, 1982. Transcript, lecture given to Aboriginal History class, Macquarie University, 1987. Tape and transcript in my possession.
11 Knudtson and Suzuki 1992:131, paraphrasing Strehlow.
12 Rose 1992:115.
13 Maddock 1983:28.
14 Williams 1986:77, Fig. 17.
15 Meggitt 1972:127–32.
16 Rose 1992:117, 119.
17 Ibid.:110.
18 Myers 1986:129, 128.
19 Ibid.:148.
20 Reynolds 1987, 1992.
21 Bell 1983; Hamilton 1980, 1982; Williams 1986.
22 Brock 1989.
23 Meggitt 1972:120; Rose 1992:106.
24 Myers 1986:129.
25 Rose 1992:107–8.
26 Myers 1982; Rose 1992:227.
27 See Peterson 1983:135–9; Myers 1982:187–9. The detailed relationships between 'owners' and 'managers' of land, which have recently been well reported in NT land claims, have not been discussed here because the corresponding detail is not available for the south-east.
28 Myers 1986:151; Payne 1989:41–2.
29 Stanner 1956 (1987:235).

30 Bell 1983:73–7; Palmer 1983.
31 Allen 1972.
32 Mathews 1903.
33 Mulvaney 1976:88; Allen 1972.
34 Webb 1984.
35 McBryde 1984; Hercus 1980.
36 This should not be confused with the later use of the word in Ch. 5.
37 Lourandos, Ross and Hercus 1989.
38 Elkin 1975:210–13; Poiner 1980:51.
39 Toyne and Vachon 1945.
40 Liston 1988; Reynolds 1987.
41 CCL Fry to CC, Clarence River, 20.11.1848, 48/13475. CSIL Special Bundle, Aboriginal Reserves. SA 4/1141/2.
42 48/14196. CSIL Special Bundle, Aboriginal Reserves, SA 4/1141/2
43 Gammage 1983.
44 Barwick 1984:105.
45 Donaldson 1984.
46 Barwick 1984:106–8; note to Curr 1886:87.
47 Langloh Parker 1905:12.
48 Mathews 1894:108–15.
49 Bride 1969:429–34, citing letter from Thomas.
50 Mathews 1896b:305.
51 Mathews 1896a:152.
52 Donaldson 1984:23.
53 Mathews and Everitt 1900:279.
54 Langloh Parker 1905, 1953.
55 Berndt and Berndt 1988.

Chapter 2 Invasion and Land: 'a system of terrorism'

1 Butlin 1983, 1993; Campbell 1985.
2 Langloh Parker 1905:39
3 NSW SC on the Condition of the Aborigines, 1845; Mahroot's evidence, 8.9.1845:1–5.
4 Curthoys 1982; *SMH* 4.4.1928; Members of the Aboriginal Community 1988. See Ch. 12.
5 CCL's Reports, 1852, 1853, 1854; GD 74, 75.
6 Revd Fyshe Palmer to Dr John Disney, June 1795, reproduced in Brook and Kohen 1991:15; Wilmot 1987.
7 Palmer to Disney, June 1795.
8 Brook and Kohen 1991:228–60.
9 Governor King to incoming Governor Phillip Bligh, 1807, *HRNSW*, vol. 5:513; Brook and Kohen 1991:16–18.
10 Governor Macquarie's Journal, ML A773, 10.4.1816:239.
11 Brook and Kohen 1991:21–33.
12 CCL's report, 1852, 1853, 1854; Morris 1989.
13 Pearson 1984.
14 Gammage 1983.

15 Webb 1984.
16 Barwick 1991; Fels 1986.
17 See Millis 1992; also Reece 1974; Aveling et al. 1987; Elder 1988; Morris 1992.
18 CCL Bligh to CC, Report for 1847 (Jan. 1848), cited in CCL R. Bligh to CC, 8.1.1849; CCL Letters Sent, Gwydir, 1849 to 1852, SA 2/7634.
19 Bligh to CC, 8.1.1849.
20 Ibid.
21 Bligh to CC, 8.1.1849, 49/1; 28.1.1851, 51/8.
22 Interview T37. *Gulay* is a Yuwalaraay-Kamilaraay word for a netted string bag made by women of this area.
23 Reece 1982.
24 Interview T27.
25 Cited in Grimshaw et al. 1994:22, from Bradley 1969.
26 CCL Bingham, Murrumbidgee, 48/14196. CSIL 4/1141/2.

Chapter 3 Land and White Desire: Nostalgia and Imagination

1   The following discussion is informed by the range of primary documents cited, and by Waterson 1968; Williams 1975; Bolton 1981; Carter 1987; Powell 1988; Dovers 1992; Frawley 1992; Hall 1992.
2   Phillip 1789:122–3.
3   Williams 1975:61, citing Reeves 1902 (1969:193).
4   See Powell 1977, 1988; Williams 1975.
5   Howitt 1972:57, cited in Hall 1992:80.
6   This argument was seen frequently in Macquarie's writings, for example. See discussion in King 1957:20–1.
7   Reynolds 1987, 1992.
8   Speech at meeting to protest 'Squatting regulations 1844', cited in King 1957:59.
9   British Secretary of State to NSW Governor, 1831, *HRA* 16:116.
10 CCL Fry to CC/Col. Sec., 20.11.1848. SA 48/13475.
11 Gipps, *HRA* 22:667.
12 Milne, CCL, SA, 1860, cited in Williams 1975:69.
13 Lang 1833.
14 Thompson 1986, 1993.
15 Williams 1975:74.
16 Davidson and Wells 1988; Robinson 1988; Richards 1991.
17 Briggs 1962.
18 See Ch. 6 for examples of such competition on the south coast and at Corranderrk in Victoria.

Chapter 4 Recognising Native Title, 1838–52

1   Macquarie, 4.5.1816, *HRA* 9:142–4. See discussion in Brook and Kohen 1991:33.
2   Surveyor-General to Col. Sec., 27.11.1848, 48/523, CSIL Special Bundle, Aboriginal Reserves, SA 4/1141/2; Bridges 1966, 1970.

3 Brooke and Kohen 1991.
4 Chairman Windeyer to Mahroot, of Botany Bay, 8.9.1845:3; NSW SC on the Condition of the Aborigines, 1845, ME, Govt Printer, October 1845.
5 See Reynolds 1992.
6 For a compelling discussion see ibid.:103–24.
7 Land and Emigration Commissioners to James Stephen, *HRA* 20:740.
8 Act 36, for regulating the sale of waste land belonging to the Crown in the Australian Colonies, S.3, 5/6th Victoriae, 22.6.1842.
9 See Millis 1992:716; Gipps to Stanley, 17.1.1844, *HRA* 23:343.
10 Gordon Gairdner, senior official in charge of Australian affairs, Internal Colonial Office Memo, CO 201/400, cited in Reynolds 1992:147.
11 Robinson to Grey, quoted by Earl Grey in his dispatch to Governor Charles Fitzroy, 11.2.1848. CSIL Special Bundle, Aboriginal Reserves, 1849, SA 4/1141/2.
12 Grey to Fitzroy, 11.2.1848.
13 Ibid.
14 Ibid.
15 Ibid.
16 Clark 1963:94.
17 CCL Mayne to Chief Commissioner, 1.6.1848. Discussed in Executive Council Meeting, 18.7.1848:374–5. CSIL 4/1523, Reel 2438.
18 Reynolds 1987, 1992; Bridges 1966; Millis 1992.
19 Executive Council Minutes, 18.7.1848. CSIL, SA 4/1523 (MF Reel 2438).
20 NGG 26.4.1850:685–6.
21 T. Mitchell, Surveyor-General to Col. Sec., 27.11.1848, 48/523. CSIL Special Bundle, Aboriginal Reserves, SA 4/1141/2.
22 These fisheries were interdicted to whites in 1842: *Government Gazette* 1842:587. The Yuwalaraay version of the story of the fisheries was recorded in Langloh Parker 1905:8, 102. R. H. Mathews spelt the name 'Ngunnhu', but his habit was to use 'unn' to represent the sound now spelt 'an', like the 'a' in 'above' and the 'u' in 'cup'.
23 Richard Bligh, CCL Gwydir, 27.10.1848, 48/12590. CSIL Special Bundle, Aboriginal Reserves, SA 4/1141/2.
24 T. Mitchell to Col. Sec., 27.11.1848. CSIL In-Letters, Special Bundle, Aboriginal Reserves, 4/1141/2.
25 Minute 4/50, 29.1.1850, Executive Council Minutes 1850. SA 4/1526:30–1.
26 Circular to all CCLs, from the Chief CCL, NSW, 16.2.1850. CCL Gwydir, Letters Received, SA 2/7627.
27 Gordon Gairdner, Colonial Office Memo, CO 201/400.
28 Surveyor A. W. Mullen's Report to Western Lands Board on Brewarrina Fisheries, including survey map, 9.2.1906. Western Lands Board Special Bundles, SA 7/7593.
29 Quotation is from Commissioner for New England, Annual Report for 1853, 12.1.1854, GD 75. See in passim all CCL reports cited in this chapter, 1849–59, for similar, although not always so explicit, statements.
30 Ibid., then see specific instructions from Surveyor Mitchell to CCL Bligh, Gwydir, 3.9.1850. CCL Gwydir, Letters Received, SA 2/7627.

31 R. Bligh, CCL Gwydir, to Chief CCL, 28.1.1851. CCL Letters Sent, Gwydir A, 1849–52. SA 2/7634.

32 Chairman Windeyer to Mahroot, of Botany Bay, 8.9.1845:3, NSW SC on the Condition of the Aborigines, 1845, ME, Govt Printer, October 1845.

Chapter 5 Dual Occupation

1 Hardy 1969, 1976.

2 CCL's reports, 1852, esp. for Albert, Bligh, Gwydir and Macleay Districts, GD vol. 74.

3 Bligh to Chief CCL, 24.1.1853, GD vol. 74.

4 CCL Macleay River to CC, 6.2.1853, GD vol. 74.

5 Ibid., CCL's report for Albert, 1852.

6 1.1.1853; CCL Bligh for Gwydir also discusses Aboriginal women's labour as domestic servants as being 'of the most essential importance', 24.1.1853, GD vol. 74.

7 W. R. Bligh, Acting Commissioner, New England District, 12.1.1854, GD vol. 75.

8 Berndt and Berndt 1987; McGrath 1987.

9 CCL New England to Chief CCL, 12.1.1854 54/11 (Annual Report for 1853), GD vol. 75:103–4.

10 See CCL Lockhart, Albert district, 1853, GD vol. 74.

11 *Bourke Historical Journal* 7:165–80; ABPR 1899, 1908; APBM 19.6.1913, 19.3.1914, 14.5.1914.

12 Bridges 1966:266–8; Troy 1993 24–7 and throughout.

13 Mathews 1894:114.

14 Curthoys 1973:166–8.

15 Goodall 1982a:48–54.

16 Wolpe 1975, first taken up in relation to Australia by Hartwig (1978), then applied to specific regional situations by Dawn May in 1994 (pastoral Queensland), Jeremy Beckett in 1977 (Torres Strait Islands) and myself in 1982 (north-west NSW [Goodall 1982a]).

17 *Bourke Historical Journal* 7:169.

18 Berndt and Berndt 1987.

19 Rosser 1985; Mathews 1977; Interviews T5, T6, T45 about north-west properties, C62 about Yancannia; Goodall 1982a.

20 Pastoral property records, Bangate, Dungalear and Gingie Stations, analysed in Goodall 1982a.

21 McGrath 1987; Goodall 1982a.

22 Goodall 1982a. For NT comparisons see Rose 1991, 1992; McGrath 1987.

23 Langloh Parker 1905:93.

24 Ibid.:12–13.

25 Ibid.; R. H. Mathews, see Chapter 1.

26 Langloh Parker 1905; Robinson 1958, 1965.

27 See discussion in Williams 1975:75.

28 The following description of land use change from 1860 to the 1880s is mainly taken from King 1957; Jeans 1972; Buxton 1974; Williams 1975; Powell 1988.

29 Buxton 1974:180.
30 Jeans 1972:214–15.
31 Jeans 1972: 240.

Chapter 6 Aboriginal Land Demands

1 Surveyor-General's maps, SA no. 6009, 'Darling River No. 4', 28.2.1851.
2 Thompson 1993.
3 *Report of the Protector*, 1883:3–8, VPLC; Curthoys 1982:49–51.
4 See, for example, John Atkinson to J. M. Chanter MP, 4.11.1887, CSIL Box 1/2667, 87/12756; F. L. Wortley, an African-American member of a community of 35 Murris at Borah Creek, near Narrabri, asking if it was true that 'blacks of the Colony' were 'allowed land from the Crown'. 12.2.1890, 90/4626, SA 5/5978.
5 See Barwick 1972:21.
6 Attwood 1986:97.
7 Barwick: 1972:47. The spelling of Cumeragunja I am using is that used by Jack Patten in 1938; it is consistent with current Aboriginal spelling (Koori Information Centre, pers. comm.) and gives a fair indication of pronunciation to an English speaker.
8 Fels 1986:255–6.
9 Barwick 1972:47–9.
10 *Riverine Herald* November 1886, see Barwick 1972:49.
11 Atkinson to Chanter, 4.11.1887; Cooper to Chanter, 16.11.1887. CSIL Box 1/2667, 87/12756.
12 Atkinson to Chanter, 4.11.1887.
13 Brennan 1907:213–14.
14 Correspondence beginning in 1872, unfortunately not conserving the original Aboriginal requests or the representations on their behalf, but all Lands Dept responses appended in Lands Dept files: 77/9843 and APB Register of Reserves, Folio 1.
15 Ibid., Folio 53.
16 Ibid., Folio 68.
17 Ibid., Folio 92.
18 Report of the Protector, 1883:11. NSW VPLC.
19 Ibid.:11–25.
20 APB Register of Reserves, Folio 30.
21 Fr Considine, Burragorang Parish, to Cardinal Moran, St Mary's, 9.11.1908. Catholic Archives, St Mary's Cathedral.
22 *SMH* 12.12.1890.
23 APB Register of Reserves, Folio 68. Report of Protector, 1883:20.
24 APB Register of Reserves, Folios 69, 70, 71.
25 Report of Protector, 1883:23.
26 APB Register of Reserves, Folios 60, 61, 65, 73.
27 Ibid., Folio 20.
28 Ibid., Folios 80, 186; APBR 1893.
29 APB Register of Reserves, Folio 41.
30 Ibid., Folio 60.

31 Cooper to Chanter, 16.11.1887.
32 My emphasis. Internal report, Undersecretary for Lands to Principal Under-secretary, Treasury, 3.7.1886. CSIL Box 1/2594, 86/6915.
33 APBR 1883–84:4.
34 APB Register of Reserves; *NGGs.*
35 Curthoys 1982:31–56.
36 The Report of the Protector (31.12.1882) shows results of surveys from each police district. The distribution of poverty is clearly related to changing land use. Employment and self-sufficiency is reported to be high in those areas where the pastoral industry remained stable. Where land use had intensified rapidly, Aboriginal impoverishment was high. A useful analysis of these results has been conducted by Johnston (1970:76).
37 Compiled from APB Register of Reserves; Reports of Protector, 1882, 1883; APB Reports and Minutes, 1884 onwards; *NGGs.*

Chapter 7 The Aborigines Protection Board

1   Barwick 1972:17.
2   Reports of Protector, 31.12.1882:2–3, 14.8.1882:2.
3   APB, First Report, 26.3.1884:2.
4   Alexander Stuart: Minute of Col. Sec., 26.2.1883:1–3, VPLA.
5   APB, First Report, 26.3.1884:2.
6   Ibid.:3.
7   Buxton 1974; Waterson 1968.
8   *NGG* 17.6.1885:3802.
9   APBR 1885–1935; VPLA; JPP.
10 Compiled from APB Register of Reserves, APB Reports and Minutes, 1885–94.
11 Reports of Protector, 1882; APBR 1884 onwards.
12 F. L. Wortley to Attorney-General, 8.2.1890. CSIL Box 5/5978, letter no. 90/4626.
13 APB Register of Reserves, Folios 90, 115, 155.
14 Goodall 1982a:156, 161.
15 APB Register of Reserves, Folio 95.
16 Ibid., Folios 147, 148 (Walhallow), 163, 164 (the Mole), 165, 166 (Wingadee), 168 (Kunopia), 201 (Terry Hie Hie).
17 Ibid., Folios 95, 98. APBR 1895. Interviews T35, T39, T41.
18 APB Register of Reserves, Folios 141, 143; APBR 1903:8.
19 Compiled from Register of Reserves; APB Reports and Minutes; *NGGs.*
20 Jenkin 1979:129–31.

Chapter 8 The Aboriginal Experience of Regained Lands

1   APBR 1910, Appendix B.
2   Interviews C44, T51, C61 (re Burnt Bridge), and T64 (re Bellbrook).
3   APB Register of Reserves, Folio 170, 175; Barwick 1972:52.
4   APB Register of Reserves, Folios 141, 143,160; APBR 1894:2.
5   APB Register of Reserves, Folios 30, 56; Catholic Archives, Burragorang

Parish; Interviews C44, T51, C61; Family history reconstruction by Gloria Ardler, La Perouse Family History Group; APBM 4.12.1918; 19.6.1924.
6   CSIL Box 1/2594, letter 86/6915.
7   SC on APB, ME:45.
8   APB Register of Reserves, Folio 241; APBR 1899:5; J. J. Moloney to NSW Premier B. S. Stevens, 1.7.1937. PDCF A37/193.
9   Snr Sergeant Hogan, Taree, to Sub-Inspector Edwards, Kempsey, 29.11.1908. CSIL Box 5/6990, letter 08/943.
10 J. Hull to NSW Premier, 13.8.1937. PCDF A37/193.
11 APBR 1899:5.
12 Interviews C44, T51, C61; Morris 1989.
13 William Cooper, 1887; *Macleay Argus* 7.4.1925, reporting the vocal presence, at meetings to defend land tenure, of the senior Dhan-gadi men who were both farmers and the knowledgeable men who were A. P. Elkin's informants on traditional culture in the 1930s: Morris 1989: 67–71.
14 Brennan 1907:212.
15 Reynolds 1988:153–4.
16 Goodall 1987.
17 See for example Joe Anderson as 'King Burraga' in *Cinesound News Review* 100, 1933, in which he states that Aboriginal people had 'kings in their own right, long before the white man came to Australia'.

Chapter 9 Escalating Pressures

1   Rusden 1883, vol. 2:513.
2   Collier 1911:37.
3   Roberts 1924. Roberts's later work, published in 1935, included a number of references to 'the natives' in the main text, and a brief additional section, 'The Aborigines', which thoroughly supported the pastoral side of the conflict, pronouncing that 'It was quite useless to treat [the Aborigines] fairly, because they were completely amoral and usually incapable of sincere and prolonged gratitude' (1975:331).
4   *Cooper v. Stuart*, 14 App. Cas, at p. 291.
5   The *Cooper v. Stuart* appeal judgment was cited and upheld in the case of *Milirrpum v. Nabalco Pty Ltd* in the NT Supreme Court in 1971, and in later cases following on from its arguments, notably *Coe v. Commonwealth, 1975*. It was overturned in the Australian High Court full bench ruling in 1982, *Mabo v. Queensland, 1988*.
6   Peterson 1985.
7   Maynard 1985.
8   Ibid.; Topliss 1985; McBryde 1985.
9   Healy 1978:51.
10 Smith 1980.
11 In a preface to *Poems of the late Adam Lindsay Gordon*, 1880.
12 Smith 1980:22.
13 Grishin 1992.
14 Topliss 1985.
15 1871, cited in Powell 1976:71.

16 Hall 1992: 88–93.
17 Ibid.:90; Frawley 1992.
18 Powell 1988:34–5.
19 Kinchela Aboriginal School file, DEIL.
20 Fletcher 1989:40.
21 Goodall 1982a:ch. 4.
22 Fletcher 1989:ch 2, 3.
23 Burnt Bridge Aboriginal School file, DEIL.
24 APBR 1903:8, 1906:9; G. E. Ardill to APB, Inspection Report, 6.6.1911. CSIL Box 7121.
25 John Mosely, George Davis and others to Dept Public Instruction, 9 April, 1900. Burnt Bridge Public School file, DEIL.
26 APB Reports show both sudden increases in ration issues and population rises on most reserves.
27 APB Register of Reserves, Folio 74.

Chapter 10 Land, Children and Power

1 CLD Reports, 1906:1–2; 1907:1; 1908:6.
2 File 07/229, CSIL 5/6944.
3 *Wingham Chronicle*, 18.11.1908. File 08/943, CSIL 5/6990.
4 J. Ridgeway to T. Garvin, 13.7.1908. File 08/943, CSIL 5/6990.
5 Snr Sgt Hogan, Taree, to Sub-Inspector Edwards, Kempsey, 29.11.1908. File 08/943, CSIL 5/6990.
6 Referred to in F. Mündt, Manager, Roseby Park APB Station, to Premier, (received) 15.7.1907. File 07/124, CSIL 5/6990.
7 Ibid., and APB Minute to Chief Secretary: 'The Condition of the Aborigines', 9.7.1907. File 08/246, CSIL 5/7030.
8 Barwick 1972. I made similar assumptions in Goodall 1982a:73–5.
9 APBR, 1906:3 1908:8.
10 APB Minute to Chief Secretary: The Condition of the Aborigines, 9.7.1907, and Treasury Minute, commenting on same meeting between Premier and APB, 20.7.1907. Both in File 08/246, CSIL 5/7030.
11 Smith 1975:140. Tabulation of official Aboriginal population figures derived from annual police census records of the Aboriginal population in each police district, for NSW, 1826–1973.
12 Quiggin 1988; Sir Charles Mackellar, Report of Royal Commission into the Treatment of Neglected and Delinquent Children, VPLA 2–6, 91–6, 1913.
13 *NPD* 57:1967, 27.1.1915.
14 APBR 1906 to 1922–23.
15 R. T. Donaldson to W. H. Wood, Chief Secretary, 3.1.1908. File 08/246, CSIL 5/7030.
16 *NPD* 57:1951, 27.1.1915; 56:1353, 24.11.1914.
17 Donaldson to Wood, 3.1.1908.
18 *NPD* 56:1353. 24.11.1914.
19 APBR 1910 to 1915.
20 APBR 1910:6, and similarly strongly worded statements in all earlier reports since 1903.

21 APBR 1911, Appendix J, 'Receipts and Expenditure', and equivalent appendices in all later reports; APBR 1912:2–3.
22 APBR 1910, cf. p. 4 with pp. 5, 8, 9, 11, and similar discrepancies in APBR 1911:2 and later.
23 Transcript of this meeting in CSIL Box 7204, 13/121, 13.5.1912.
24 *SMH* leader, 14.5.1912; *DT* 14.5.1912, 25.5.1912.
25 APBR 1915:1. Aboriginal recollections of Donaldson are widespread, and are repeated frequently among all the interviews conducted for this research, e.g. T35.
26 APBM 15.3.1915, 6.4.1916, 2.3.1921.

Chapter 11 Dispossessions

1 Jeans 1972:220–1. APBR 1912:8, 1906 to 1915.
2 *NPD* 36:4547, 15.12.1909; APBR 1908:7–8. The managers were empowered to initiate trespass charges under Sections 131 and 133 of the Crown Lands Act (APBR 1906:2).
3 J. T. Jenkins to APB, Inspection Report, 28.5.1912. CSIL Box 7121.
4 T. Garvin to APB, Inspection Report, 9.6.1912. CSIL Box 7121.
5 APB Records of Wards; Clark 1966; Conversation with Naomi Mayers, member of the Cumeragunja Briggs family; Interview C33.
6 APBR 1909:6, 9; 1911:3, 7, 9; APB Out-Letters 11.8.1914; *Leonard Kerr v. APB*.
7 APBR 1913:4–5; APBM 4.9.1913.
8 APB Out-Letters 14.6.1915, New Regulations 28(A) and (B).
9 APBM 24.5.1917, 23.8.1917, 21.6.1917, 26.7.1917.
10 Ibid. 11.10.1917, 9.5.1918, 13.6.1918, 11.9.1918, 5.11.1918, 14.11.1918.
11 Population figures from APBRs for Cumeragunja: 1908: 394, 1909: 286, 1912: 243; 1915: 230.
12 APBM 14.5.1919, 25.6.1919.
13 APBM 12.1.1921.
14 APBM 17.8.1921, 19.8.1921, 21.10.1921, 7.12.1921.
15 APBM 7.12.1921; 2.3.1922.
16 APBM 2.9.1927.
17 APBM 2.9.1927; Barwick (1963) demonstrates that this was still the case at least in the early 1960s.
18 Barwick 1972:57, 62; APBR 1921–22, 1925–26, 1926–27. William Cooper to B. S. Stevens, NSW Premier, 31.3.1937 and 9.5.1937, PDCF A36/1028; Public Service Board Report into APB, 1938:46; SC on APB, ME, 1938:74, 15.2.1937.
19 APBM 4.2.1927.
20 Interview T48.
21 APB to Undersecretary, Dept Education, 5.10.1917. Walgett PSF, DEIL.
22 H. Clements to Chief Inspector, 5.12.1917, Walgett PSF, DEIL.
23 Interview T41; APB Records of Wards, no. 114. ·
24 Secretary, AWU, to Director of Education, 28.6.1923, enclosing letter from Walgett Branch of ALP; Inspector H. N. Barlex, to Chief Inspector, 7.8.1923; H. Tindall, Headmaster, to Regional Inspector Barlex, 28.7.1923;

Undersecretary, Dept Education, to APB, 23.8.1923. Walgett PSF, DEIL. Interviews T35, T36, T37, T39, T41, T45.

25 Interview T39.

26 *Our Aim* (Journal of the Aborigines Inland Mission) 17(4), 20.12.1923:10.

27 Interviews T36, T37, T41, T45.

28 *Our Aim* 21(6), 23.2.1925:4.

29 Interview T41.

30 APB to Undersecretary, Dept Education, 10.10.1928; Regional Inspector to Chief Inspector, 10.11.1928. Walgett PSF, DEIL.

31 APB Records of Wards records the movement of families to Pilliga; conversations with the late Bill Reid Snr, born on Cuttabri and then living on Pilliga; Lands Dept Annual Reports document the loss of reserves by region; APB Reports and Minutes together provide most records of reserve revocation and leasing, and others are recorded in the *NGGs* for the period.

32 APBM 6.7.1923, 22.5.1924, 22.2.1926; Moree MCM 11.4.1923, 14.5.1923, 11.2.1924, 10.3.1924, 28.4.1924, 22.2.1926.

33 APBRs 1911–21, Appendices for 'Income from Aboriginal stations and reserves', being the income from sale stores which sold to Aboriginal residents, and 'Sundries', which covered income from leasing.

34 These figures derived from detailed examination of APB Reports and Minutes, NSW Lands Dept Annual Reports and *NGGs* for the period.

35 APB Register of Reserves, Folio 73; APBM 18.6.1914, 3.9.1914; Interview C61.

36 APBM 1.10.1914, 14.10.1914, 4.2.1915, 25.2.1915, 4.3.1915, 18.3.1915.

37 APBM 22.4.1915, 20.5.1915, 10.6.1915, 27.5.1915, 7.10.1915, 28.10.1915, 16.11.1915.

38 APB Register of Reserves, Folio 62; APBR 1915:6–8; APBM 18.11.1915, 25.11.1915.

39 SC of APB, ME, 1937:45, APBM 14.5.1919, 14.7.1920.

40 Interview C61.

41 APBM 1.11.1917, 31.1.1918, 3.4.1918, 30.5.1918, 13.6.1918, 2.10.1918.

42 APBM 11.9.1918, 27.8.1919, 27.6.1924, 21.11.1924.

43 APBM 13.10.1920.

44 APBM 23.8.1917, 31.1.1918, 21.3.1918, 30.10.1918, 1.11.1917, 24.4.1925; James Yarrie to *Abo Call*, June 1938.

45 APB Register of Reserves, Folios 41, 43; Miller 1985:107–43.

46 Miller 1985:142.

47 APBRs 1920–21:3, 8; 1925–26.

48 APBM 6.7.1934, 4.12.1935, 5.2.1936, 4.3.1936, 7.4.1937.

49 G. E. Ardill to APB, Inspection Report, 6.6.1911. CSIL Box 7121; J. Barrie to George Nesbitt MLA, 13.11.1917. CSIL 17/117, Box 7483; APBM 23.9.1915.

50 APBM 7.12.1916, 20.7.1922; Police Inspector A. Lewis to APB, 6.11.1917. CSIL 17/120, Box 7483.

51 APBM 14.5.1919, 4.6.1919, 31.5.1922, 20.7.1922, 13.9.1922, 27.8.1926, 29.1.1928; South Lismore PSF 1928, DEIL.

52 APBM 14.5.1919, 25.5.1923, 24.8.1923, 8.2.1924, 23.1.1925, 24.4.1925.

53 APB Out-Letters 18.9.1922, 16.7.1923; APBM 13.9.1922, 25.5.1923.

54 APBM 1.8.1918, 21.11.1924.

55 Interview T51. The account of the shooting incident and subsequent move to Salt Pan Creek is drawn from this interview.

56 Fr Considine to Cardinal Moran, 9.11.1908; Fr O'Reilly to Archbishop, 17.8.1916; J. Smith to Archbishop, 9.7.1918. Burragorang Parish file, St Mary's Archives.

57 St Mary's Cathedral, Internal notes on Mrs Longbottom and Mrs Shepherd's visit, 5.6.1909. Burragorang Parish file, St Mary's Archives.

58 APBM 19.6.1924. APB Annual Reports 1917, 1918; APBM 4.12.1918, 19.6.1924; Interviews T51, C61; Gloria Ardler, La Perouse Family History group, pers. comm.

59 *NGG* 25.2.1916, 16.2.1914, 7.9.1917, 18.2.1916, 27.1.1922, 4.9.1925; APBM 17.9.1919, 13.6.1918.

60 APBM 1.8.1918, 12.3.1919, 31.5.1922, 14.4.1924, 19.6.1925; Bateman's Bay P & C Association to Minister for Education, June 1925, Bateman's Bay PSF, DEIL.

61 Huskisson PSF, 1921–25, DEIL; APBM 23.1.1925, 4.9.1925.

62 B. E. Fitzpatrick to Dept Education, 28.7.1925, 14.8.1925; to Dept Labour and Industry, 28.2.1926; to Minister for Justice, 22.9.1926; Ethel Cannan to Minister for Education, 27.7.1925, 17.8.1925, 10.6.1926; Mrs A. Hamilton to J. A. Perkins MLA, 31.8.1925; to Premier, 14.4.1926. Bateman's Bay PSF, DEIL.

63 Jane Duren to King George V, 14.6.1926. Other Koori protesters: Mrs H. Stewart to Minister for Education, 6.11.1925, 25.1.1926, 22.3.1926; Mrs Les Stewart to Minister for Education, 7.3.1927, 30.3.1927; Mrs Agnes Davis to Minister for Education, 28.7.1926. Bateman's Bay PSF, DEIL.

64 Internal departmental memo, 16.3.1927; Child Welfare Inspector Robertson to Dept Education, 27.4.1927; Regional Inspector of Schools West to Chief Inspector, 18.8.1927; APB to Dept Education, 30.12.1925; Bateman's Bay PSF, DEIL; *NGG* 16.9.1927.

Chapter 12 Fighting Back: Aboriginal Political Organisation

1 APBM 28.1.1915; 4.2.1915; 11.2.1915, 11.2.1915, 15.4.1915. No copies of the *Grafton Argus* survive from this period. The reference to the article, which clearly indicates its sympathy with Kooris whose children were 'being interfered with', is in APBM 4.2.1915.

2 This story was told to Barry Morris (1989:117).

3 APBM 17.9.1919, 15.10.1919.

4 APB Register of Reserves, Folio 92.

5 Ibid., Folio 65.

6 *VN* 10.11.1922:5.

7 APBM 14.2.1923; *VN* 12.6.1925; Mrs Olive Mundine, interviewed 1.9.1987, 27.2.1988; *Uplift* February 1941:20–2; Paisley 1995.

8 APBM, 14.2.1923, 23.1.1925, 25.4.1925, 21.7.1925.

9 *NPD* 56:1353, 24.11.1924; 96:1265, 20.8.1924; 96:1454, 26.8.1924; *SMH*

29.10.1924, 30.10.1924, 9.1.1925, 10.1.1925, 11.2.1925; *Sun* 27.12.1924 (editorial); APBR 1923–24:2.

10   Interviews T64, C65.

11   *VN* 10.8.1925:13.

12   APBM 6.3.1925, 25.4.1925; Interviews T64, C65.

13   *VN* 12.6.1925:13, 10.8.1925.

14   Ibid.

15   *Macleay Chronicle* October 1925.

16   *VN* 10.8.1925:13.

17   APBM 23.1.1925, 6.3.1925, 19.6.1925, 4.9.1925, 23.10.1925; *VN* 10.8.1925:13; 12.6.1925:13.

18   *VN* 12.10.1925:5.

19   *Macleay Argus* April 1925, cited in Morris 1989:119.

20   *Macleay Chronicle* October 1925.

21   *VN* 10.8.1925:13, 10.2.1927:5; J. J. Moloney, Secretary, ASP, Dalley Branch, to J. T. Lang, Premier. PDCF A27/915.

22   Griffiths 1996.

23   White 1993:116–19, 142–3.

24   *VN* 10.11.1922:5; *SMH* 18.5.1927, 20.5.1927, 18.1.1928, 13.2.1928, 19.9.1928, 5.2.1930; *Adelaide Register* 29.12.1921; *Herald* 4.5.1925; *Argus* 11.7.1926.

25   *VN* 10.11.1926 (Elkin); *SMH* 14.3.1928, 12.10.1928, 30.8.1929 (Radcliffe-Brown).

26   Paisley 1995:129–202.

27   See e.g. Revd F. W. Burton, in *The Australian Geographer* 1(1) August 1928:67.

28   *VN* 12.2.1924, 10.7.1924; Wise 1985; Goodall 1982b.

29   *VN* 10.11.1927:6.

30   ANA to J. T. Lang, Premier, 31.7.1925. PDCF A27/915; APBM 4.9.1925, 23.10.1925, 22.1.1926.

31   APBM 22.1.1926.

32   *SMH* 15.11.1927.

33   Interview T51. Ted Thomas also spent time at the Salt Pan Camp and corroborates Jack's recollections on this tape. The description of the camp and its residents is drawn from this interview with the two men.

34   The text of the petition for a Native State and a statement of aims of the initiating Committee were printed in *VN* 10.5.1926:16, 10.6.1926:13, 11.10.1926:11; see also *SMH* 9.3.1927, 7.5.1927, 15.11.1927.

35   *SMH* 22.11.1927; 5.4.1927; Mrs E. McKenzie-Hatton to Premier, 9.2.1927, 27.5.1927. PDCF A27/915.

36   The following discussion and quotations are consistent with each of the three sources for the AAPA platform: APBM 4.2.1927; *VN* 10.5.1927:6; AAPA petition to Premier, received 10.6.1927. PDCF A27/915.

37   APB to Premier 2.9.1927. PDCF A27/915.

38   Frederick G. Maynard, President, AAPA, to Premier, 3.10.1927. PDCF A27/915.

39 This and the following quotations from APB to Premier, 3.11.1927. PDCF A27/915.

40 Attached papers to APB to Premier, 3.11.1927. PDCF A27/915; APB Records of Wards, no. 655; F. G. Maynard to K— B—, 14.10.1927. PDCF A27/915. All following quotations are from this letter.

41 The following account is taken from *Evening News* 16.11.1927; *SMH* 15.11.1927.

42 *SMH* 22.11.1927.

43 *SMH* 15.11.1927.

44 *Evening News* 16.11.1927.

45 Sources are the family history research of Fred Maynard's family; interviews with Mrs Olive Mundine; *Uplift* February 1941.

46 APBM 27.8.1926; *SMH* 1.2.1928, 28.3.1928.

47 *SMH* 4.4.1928.

48 *SMH* 14.3.1928.

49 *SMH* 28.8.1929.

50 APBM 31.7.1920; APBRs 1929–30:2; 1930–31:2.

51 *SMH* 12.6.1931; Interview T51. *Truth* in particular used Anderson as a comic stereotype. *Cinesound Review,* no. 100, 1933: 'Australian Royalty Pleads for His People: King Burraga, Chief of Aboriginal Thirroul Tribe, to petition King for Blacks' Representation in Parliament'. (Caption). The following quotations from Joe Anderson are all from the dialogue of this film, recorded within Interview T51.

Chapter 13 Land as Prison: Moree, 1927–33

1 The following discussion is based on examination of the Moree MCM, APBM, and the reports of the Aborigines' Inland Mission missionary, Mr Haines, published in *Our Aim*. Marie Reay conducted fieldwork in Moree in 1948, and her observations of the bitterness left as a result of this battle over residential space are consistent with the material in the above sources. The discussions about the swimming pool segregation are found in Moree MCM 5.6.1921, 15.6.1925, 25.9.1925, 8.3.1926, 19.4.1927, 11.7.1927, 18.8.1930, 15.6.1925 to 30.5.1927. The use of 'nigger' in Moree MCM is found in the entry for 22.2.1926.

2 The families listed as 'expelled' from Terry Hie Hie by the APB circular 7.1.1915, for example, are also listed in Moree MCM as being prosecuted for failing to move in 1928.

3 APBM 2.2.1921, 18.1.1923, 6.7.1923, 22.5.1924, 22.2.1926, 4.2.1927; Moree MCM 10.2.1921, 9.2.1922, 13.11.1922, 11.4.1923, 14.5.1923, 11.2.1924, 10.3.1924, 28.4.1924, 24.8.1925, 22.2.1926, 7.3.1927.

4 Moree MCM 23.1.1928, 2.4.1928, 16.4.1928, 28.5.1928, 6.8.1928, 3.9.1928, 29.10.1928, 12.11.1928, 10.12.1928; *Our Aim* 21(9) 22.5.1928:10, 21(11) 23.7.1928:8–9, 21(12) 23.8.1928:2, 22(5) 26.1.1929.

5 Moree MCM 7.1.1929, 21.1.1929, 18.2.1929, 15.4.1929, 10.6.1929, 24.6.1929, 30.2.1930, 18.8.1930, 16.3.1931, 25.5.1931, 20.7.1931, 5.12.1932, 16.1.1933; APBM 12.5.1932, 14.10.1932, 9.3.1933, 21.7.1933;

Our Aim 22(11) 22.7.1929, 24(5) 25.1.1930; Aboriginal Census Returns, Moree Police Patrol, 1931.

6 Moree MCM 5.12.1932, 6.6.1933, 19.6.1933, 9.10.1933, 12.2.1934; Town Clerk to Minister for Education, 15.3.1924, Moree PSF, DEIL; *Our Aim* 28 24.3.1934.

7 M. Kinnear, Teacher, Aboriginal special school, Moree, to C. C. Chambers. Inspector, Dept Education, 26.2.1934; C. R. Thomas, Undersecretary, Dept Education, to Undersecretary, Child Welfare Dept, 23.4.1934, Both in Moree PSF, DEIL.

8 Child Welfare Dept Inspector's Report (unsigned) to Dept Education, re Moree situation, 27.9.1934. Moree PSF, DEIL.

9 Reay and Sidlington 1948:182.

10 The methods of asserting and sustaining control over Aboriginal people in 'normal' situations in rural NSW at the time are discussed at length in Goodall 1982a:160–9.

11 Interviews T24, T22; Jimmie Barker, Transcripts, AIATSIS, F Tapes 94B, 117; Interviews T1, T51 (re Kempsey).

12 Reay and Sidlington 1948:301; Interview T41.

13 Notes on conversations with Murris in Walgett, field trip with Karen Flick, October 1995.

Chapter 14 The Depression Crises and Cumeragunja

1 Powell 1988:ch. 5.

2 Analysis of wages books: Bangate, Yeranbah, Gingie and Dungalear sheep properties 1917–40. Proportions of Aboriginal workers rose compared to white workers on all these properties over the Depression years. Bangate, Yeranbah, Dungalear: UNE Archives; Gingie held by Pye family, owners of the property.

3 *NPD* 124:316, 9.12.1930; 124:1057, 4.2.1931. APBM 6.2.1931.

4 Goodall 1982a:258–60.

5 The requirement to have done 'a white man's work' was issued as an instruction to police in 1931. See Instruction to Police, 13.7.1931, cited in Office of Director of Government Food Relief to Dept Education, 28.9.1937, in Brewarrina PSF. The instruction to force Aboriginal people to go to the nearest APB station to receive even Aboriginal rations is referred to in an internal memo, unsigned, Dept Education, citing information received from Dept Labour and Industry, July 1937. Collarenebri PSF, DEIL.

6 See Goodall 1982a:253–86.

7 *NPD* 124:316, 9.12.1930; 124:1057, 4.2.1931.

8 Kelly 1936:34.

9 Interview T39.

10 Kelly 1936:50; SC on APB, ME:104, 121; Kelly 1937; *Abo Call* August 1938:2.

11 Nadia Wheatley, pers. comm.; Plater 1993:84; Interview T53.

12 Undated and unsourced newspaper article pasted into newspaper clippings, collection of Pearl Gibbs.

13 *WW* 1.7.1932.

14 Interviews T57, T58.

15 *SMH* 10.7.1935, 12.9.1935; Dubbo MCM 2.7.1935; ABPM 1.7.1936.

16 Aboriginal union and Labor Party membership information is drawn from interviews conducted during 1970s and 1980s for this study. Only one north-western Murri, Val Mingo, was a member of the ALP in Brewarrina, which he found 'very slow' to take up issues concerning Aboriginal people (Interviews T3, T4). See SC on APB, ME:68 for Ferguson's views on missionaries: APBM for Duncan Ferguson's activities at Pooncarie, 1.11.1929, 17.12.1929.

17 APBM 4.2.1927.

18 W. Cooper to J. M. Chanter MP, 4.11.1887. CSIL Box 1/2667.

19 D. Barwick, 'William Cooper', entry in *ADB* 8:107–8.

20 Horner 1974:47. Correspondence between Burdeu and APNR in Elkin Papers. SU Archives.

21 Interview with Margaret Tucker, recorded Alec Morgan, September 1980:37–8.

22 A. P. Burdeu to R. Swan, Sec, APNR 14.3.1941, Elkin Papers, in which Burdeu writes of his long campaign 'to combat subversive tendencies'. SU Archives.

23 AAL Annual Report 1936. PDCF A36/1028.

24 *Labor Call* 20.9.1934.

25 *Herald* 23.1.1935, 24.1.1935.

26 AAL Annual Report 1936; *Native Voice* 1(1) April 1940:3–4; APBM 13.4.1934, 13.3.1935; Paisley 1995:65–6.

27 Horner 1974:47.

28 AAL Annual Report 1936.

29 W. Cooper to B. S. Stevens, NSW Premier, 15.11.1936, 19.2.1936, 9.5.1936, 15.11.1936. PDCF A36/1028; AAL Annual Report 1936.

30 Cooper to Stevens 19.2.1936.

31 Ibid. 15.11.1936.

32 Ibid. 15.11.1936, 19.2.1936; AAL Annual Report 1936.

33 Cooper to Stevens, 19.2.1936; 15.11.1936.

34 Ibid. 7.6.1937.

35 Ibid. 15.11.1936; Berkhoffer 1979:176–86.

36 Cooper to Stevens, 19.2.1936, 9.5.1936, 15.11.1936, 31.3.1937, 9.5.1937, 7.6.1937.

37 Ibid. 15.11.1936.

38 Ibid. 31.3.1937; Secretary, APB to Undersecretary, Premier's Dept, 24.3.1936. PDCF A36/404.

39 Cooper to Stevens, 31.3.1937.

40 Chief Secretary to Premier, 13.4.1937; Cooper to Stevens, 9.5.1937; Chief Secretary to Premier, 19.5.1937. All in PDCF A36/1028.

41 Cooper to Stevens, 7.6.1937; SC on APB, ME:79.

42 Cooper to Stevens 19.2.1936, 15.11.1936, 31.3.1937. All interviews with ex-residents of Brewarrina station confirm that Danvers was well liked. Cooper to Stevens 19.2.1936, 15.11.1936, 31.3.1937; J. G. Danvers to Secretary, APB, 14.3.1936. PDCF A36/1028.

43 SC on APB, ME:83.

44 APB Records of Wards, no. 704; APBM 6.7.1934, 4.12.1935, 5.2.1936, 4.3.1936, 7.4.1937.

Chapter 15 The 'Dog Act' in the West: Menindee and Brewarrina

1 See *Annual Census of Aborigines, 1927 to 1937* and associated papers relating to NSW, Commonwealth Bureau of Census and Statistics; Goodall 1982a:258–60.

2 See Goodall 1982a:276, Ch. 6.

3 Ibid.:276.

4 See Lang's Question in *NPD* re Collarenebri 1938, reprinted in *Abo Call* 5.8.1938:3.

5 APBR 1931–32:2; my emphasis.

6 APBR 1934–35:2, and see all ABP Reports during the 1930s.

7 Goodall 1982a, 1982b. Sources include Elkin's papers and the PDCF for the later 1930s.

8 APBM 13.4.1934, 12.6.1935; *NPD* 149:4844, 23.6.1936.

9 The evidence about the diagnosis, effects and extent of eye infections is drawn from APBM 5.2.1936, 4.3.1936, 3.6.1936, 7.10.1936; Interview 18; correspondence by Inspector J. N. Harrison and Dr A. E. Machin in Brewarrina PSF, and Inspector N. W. Drummond in Boomi PSF, all in DEIL. The late Professor Fred C. Hollows reviewed this evidence in 1980 and concluded that the diagnosis of gonoccocal opthalmia was unlikely and unreliable. The Board's actions to force this issue to the forefront of parliamentary debate during 1936 is demonstrated in APBM 3.6.1936; SC on APB, ME:1; *NPD* 149:4749–50, 18.6.1936; 149:4837–60, 23.6.1936; 149:5277–80, 2.7.1936. The most vocal parliamentary proponents of the eye disease argument to support the confinement powers were the Chief Secretary, Captain Chaffey, and APB members H. J. Bate and G. E. Ardill Jnr.

10 APBM 13.4.1934, 12.6.1935, 5.2.1936, 4.3.1936; Dubbo, Brewarrina, Talbragar, Walgett MCM, 1933–37.

11 King 1957:177–9; Western Lands Amendment Acts 1932 and 1934.

12 Dubbo, Moree, Brewarrina, Talbragar, Walgett MCM, 1923–37.

13 These general dates for ceremonial activity are drawn from the contemporary work of R. H. Mathews, and later A. P. Elkin and Caroline Kelly (for the north coast); Jeremy Beckett's research into George Dutton's life; Interviews T27, T30, T35; and photographic evidence of ceremonies in MacIntyre River border areas in *At Work and Play* collection, ML.

14 See interviews I conducted from 1976 to 1980 with Aboriginal men and women who had grown up in camps on their traditional country in north-western and far western NSW. In particular, T3, T5, T6, C13, T16, T27, T28, T30, T35, T36, T37, T39, T40, T45, T50.

15 This account is drawn from Horner 1974 and Hardy 1976, who drew in part on oral sources but also from SC on APB, ME:59–62, 103–8; press sources like *Smith's Weekly* 10.9.1938, *DT* 19.7.1938, and *NPD* 151:776–7,

9.9.1937; 156:1425, 31.8.1938. Conditions on Menindee confirmed by Will Webster, Interview C59.

16 APBM 3.4.1936.

17 Mathews (1977) and interviews conducted for this study.

18 Annual Aboriginal Census, Police Patrol returns, Brewarrina, 1927, 1928, 1931, 1934. Brewarrina MCM 26.11.1934.

19 *WW* 24.9.1931, 2.9.1932, 24.6.1932, 15.3.1935.

20 Annual Aboriginal Census, Police Patrol returns, Quambone, 1927, 1928, 1931, 1934, 1937. See APBM for lack of any alternative local stimuli.

21 Interview T74.

22 SC on APB, ME:4; Interviews T18, T21, T57, T58; notes on conversation with Emily Sullivan, Brewarrina, 26.1.1977; *Dubbo Dispatch* 28.6.1937.

23 Brewarrina MCM 28.10.1935, 16.12.1935.

24 Reay and Sidlington 1948:301; Jimmie Barker, Transcripts of interviews held in AIATSIS, Filed Tapes 94B, 117; Interviews T22, T23, T41, T1, T51.

25 Annual Aboriginal Census, Police Patrol returns, New Angledool, 1927, 1928, 1931, 1934, 1937; APBM 5.2.1936, 4.3.1936.

26 Interviews T5, T6, T18, T50, T52; APBM 4.3.1936.

27 Interview T72.

28 Minister for Education to Chief Secretary, 21.4.1936, passing on white Angledool residents' protest. Brewarrina PSF, DEIL; Interviews T5, T6, T18; conversation in August 1976 with P. Prentice, (white) resident of Angledool, 1936.

29 Revd H. Perkins, Presbyterian minister, Collarenebri, to Minister for Education, 10.9.1936; 25.11.1936; H. Maclean, teacher, Collarenebri, to Regional Inspector, 16.12.1936; 16.8.1938; Revd H. F. Peak to APB, 2.12.1938. All in Collarenebri PSF, DEIL. Interview T48.

30 APBM 12.6.1935, 18.5.1937, 6.7.1938, 3.8.1938.

31 Interview T71.

32 Interview T6. Henry uses the older form of Collarenebri.

33 Interview T5O.

34 Interview T6.

35 Interviews T6, T20, T48.

36 This description is drawn from Interviews T5, T6, T50, T17, T18, T20, C63 and SC on APB, ME:37; Annual Aboriginal Census, Police Patrol return, New Angledool, 1937.

37 The following description and quotations are drawn from Interview T18.

38 Interview T20.

39 Interviews T18, T5O. Extract from Report by Board members E. B. Harkness and G. A. Mitchell, Inspection of Brewarrina station, August 9–14 1936 in SC on APB, ME:34.

40 Interview T18.

41 Interviews T5, T6; Bangate Cash Books 1936, 1937, 1938; Mathews 1977:157–9; SC on APB, ME:34; APBM 7.10.1936.

42 Interviews T3, T5, T6, T17, T18, T50.

43 Interview T6.

44 Interview T17. The gradual movement of Angledool Murris off the station was confirmed by all Murris interviewed.

45 Annual Aboriginal Census, Police Patrol return, New Angledool, 1938, 'Comments'. Those who moved back towards Walgett, Collarenebri and Lightning Ridge include many members of the Fernando, Dixon, Trapman, Thurston, Rose and Walford families. Those who moved into the town camp include the Winters and Hardy families.

46 Brewarrina MCM 9.3.1936, 20.4.1936; D. H. Drummond, Minister for Education, to Dept Education, 30.4.1936, after personal representations had been made to him by aldermen and other citizens of Brewarrina. Brewarrina PSF, DEIL.

47 Inspector J. N. Harrison to Chief Inspector, 29.5.1936, 5.9.1936. Brewarrina PSF, DEIL.

48 Chief Secretary to Minister for Education, 7.5.1936; Secretary, APB, to Director of Education, 27.8.1936; B. C. Harkness (commenting as member of APB) to Minister for Education, 4.1.1937. All in Brewarrina PSF, DEIL; APBM 17.7.1936.

49 M. Davidson MLA to Acting Minister for Education, 11.8.1936, passing on petition. Brewarrina PSF, DEIL.

50 Interviews T18, T22, T24.

51 Interviews T7, T19.

52 D. H. Drummond, annotation on B. C. Harkness's letter, 4.1.1937. Brewarrina PSF, DEIL. For a detailed discussion of the Education Dept's confusion over the 1935–39 period, as it moved slowly towards at least a nominal reversal of its policy of segregation on demand by white parents, see Fletcher 1989.

53 APBM 17.7.1936; Secretary, APB, to Director of Education, 27.8.1936. Brewarrina PSF, DEIL.

54 J. N. Harrison to Chief Inspector, 27.1.1937. Brewarrina PSF, DEIL; Brewarrina MCM 8.3.1937, 5.4.1937.

55 Mathews 1977:159; SC on APB, ME:23, 54, 57, 121; *Dubbo Dispatch* 28.6.1937; Interviews T3, T6, T18, T24, T50.

56 Brewarrina MCM 13.9.1937, 25.10.1937, 24.1.1938; D. H. Drummond, 7.1.1938, annotation to memo by Director of Education; Departmental recommendation, 14.2.1938; Dr Donnellan to Chief Medical Officer, 30.3.1938; E. Williams, Undersecretary for Education, Departmental memo, 23.5.1938. All in Brewarrina PSF, DEIL.

57 SC on APB, ME:53–7, 121; Interviews T25, T54, T55. Pearl Gibbs speeches: *SMH* 12.2.1938, *DT* 12.2.1938, *Woman Today* April 1938, May 1938.

58 Annual Aboriginal Census, Police patrol returns, Tibooburra, 1927, 1928, 1931, 1934, 1937; Interview T28; Interviews conducted with Lorna Dixon (née Ebsworth) by Janet Mathews, Field Tape numbers FT 194 (18.4.1975) and FT 198 (19.4.1975), held by AIATSIS; Beckett 1978:1.

59 J. L. Rowett, for residents of Tibooburra, to Minister for Education, 13.12.1937. Tibooburra PSF, DEIL.

60 C. H. Sankey, teacher, Tibooburra, to R. B. Wilson, Inspector, Child Welfare

Dept, 10.12.1937; C. H. Sankey to Inspector of Schools, J. J Pollock, 25.1.1938. Tibooburra PSF, DEIL.

61 J. L. Rowett, for residents of Tibooburra, to R. B. Wilson, 9.12.1937; R. B. Wilson, Inspector, Child Welfare Dept, 'Report on Tibooburra District', 5.1.1938. Tibooburra PSF, DEIL.

62 C. Wood, Secretary, Child Welfare Dept, to Undersecretary, Dept Education, 19.1.1938; B. C. Harkness to Head Teacher, Tibooburra, 28.1.1938; A. C. Pettit to Undersecretary, Dept Education, 29.3.1938; Menindee P & C Association to Chief Inspector of Schools, telegram, 19.3.1938; R. T. Thomas, Headmaster, Menindee public school, to Chief Inspector, 30.3.1938. All in Tibooburra PSF, DEIL.

63 Interview T28; Lorna Dixon FT 194; Beckett 1978:20–1.

64 Interview T60.

65 Interview T28. Eadie's account is consistent with that of Lorna Dixon FT 194.

66 Lorna Dixon FT 198.

67 Interview T28.

68 Interviews T18, T28. FT 194, 198; Dr W. J. Ferguson to Director-General of Public Health, 29.4.1938. Tibooburra PSF, DEIL.

69 Record number 143, Tindale Archives, recording interviews with residents of Brewarrina station; Beckett 1978.

70 Brewarrina MCM 23.5.1938, 6.6.1938.

71 Annual Aboriginal Census, Police Patrol returns, Brewarrina, 1937, 1938; APBM 25.5.1938, 6.7.1938.

72 Beckett 1965, 1978; Interviews T28, T27, T30; Lorna Dixon FT 194, 198.

73 APBM 4.5.1938.

74 Interviews T3, T6, T18, T20, T24, T25, T50; *Dubbo Despatch* 24.2.1939, 12.4.1939; *DT* 30.1.1939.

Chapter 16 The 'Dog Act' on the Coast: Burnt Bridge, 1934–38

1 APBM 4.11.1936.

2 APBM 6.10.1937, 1.12.1937; Tuncurry Progress Association to Premier, 1937. PDCF A37/2380; APBM 12.7.1939.

3 Ibid. 6.7.1934, 12.9.1934.

4 Ibid. 27.1.1931, 3.7.1931, 21.1.1932, 12.5.1932; SC on APB, ME:55.

5 Ibid. Dates are from APBM.

6 APBM 2.10.1935, 4.3.1936.

7 *Abo Call* July 1938:2; AWBR 1939–40:3.

8 F. Roberts to J. T. Patten, 1.8.1938, included in Collarenebri PSF, DEIL; *Abo Call* August 1938:2.

9 *Nowra Leader* 20.9.1935, 15.11.1935; APBM 5.2.1936.

10 *SMH* 14.6.1929.

11 J. J. Moloney to B. S. Stevens, Premier, 10.6.1937; G. C. Golan for Premier to Moloney, ASP, 28.9.1937. PDCF A37/193.

12 APBM 5.8.1936, 4.11.1936, 10.5.1939, 20.12.1939; Kelly 1937; *Abo Call* June 1938:2; Chris Davis to J. A. Lyons, Prime Minister, 21.1.1937; Moloney to Stevens, 1.7.1937. PDCF A37/193.

13 Davis to Lyons, 21.1.1937; Lyons to Stevens 27.1.1937; Premier's Dept to

Chief Secretary's Dept, 2.2.1937, 18.3.1937; Chief Secretary's Dept to Premier's Dept, 19.2.1937, 18.5.1937; Chief Secretary's Dept to APB, for 'urgent advice', 24.3.1937. PDCF A37/193.

14 Percy Mosely to J. J. Moloney, 1.7.1937; L. J. Rose, Private Secretary to Premier, B. S. Stevens, 26.8.1937, notes on meeting between Rose and Mosely. PDCF A37/193. Previous communication is obvious from Mosely to Moloney, 1.7.1937.

15 See Kelly 1937 for description of conditions at the station and the exclusion of Kooris from food and work relief. Kelly also raised these issues during questioning of APB officials during SC hearings. See APBM 3.3.1937, 7.4.1937, for APB awareness of problems with water supply and need for connection to town supply. *Abo Call* July 1938:2. Connection with town supply had not occurred by this date.

16 Mosely to Moloney, 1.7.1937. PDCF.

17 Ibid., 1.7.1937, 2.7.1937. PDCF A37/193; *Macleay Chronicle* 1.7.1937, 7.7.1937; *SMH* 3.7.1937.

18 Mosely to Moloney, cited in Moloney to Stevens, 6.7.1937. PDCF A37/193.

19 Interview C61.

20 Moloney to Stevens, 13.8.1937.

21 J. Hull to Stevens, 13.8.1937. PDCF A37/193. References to *Macleay Chronicle* and *Wingham Chronicle* 23.7.1937.

22 Sawtell was a member of the AWU and the ALP, knew individuals in or associated with the CPA, was active in the Theosophical Society, and was associated with moderate nationalists such as those in the ANA and also with the ultra-nationalist Australia First group. See Horner 1974:39, 105–6.

23 Interview C56; Horner 1974:39; *Abo Call* July 1938:2.

24 Muirden 1968:5–48.

25 Sawtell to Stevens, 2.8.1937, 11.8.1937, 25.8.1937, 4.10.1937. PDCF A37/193. These letters incidentally reveal Sawtell's basic paternalism towards Aborigines, perhaps providing a clue to the reasons for his eventual, and bitterly resented, defection to the side of the government, after gaining a position on the AWB. His subsequent vicious denunciations and ridicule of Aboriginal claims for full citizen's rights were exemplified in the exchange between Sawtell and a member of the Aboriginal political movement in *Dubbo Despatch* 3.4.1953, 20.4.1953. See J. B. Steele to B. S. Stevens, 2.8.1937 and Notice for Theosophical Society meeting, 2.10.1937, at which Sawtell was scheduled to speak on this topic. PDCF A37/193.

26 Sawtell to Stevens, 25.8.1937; L. J. Rose, Private Secretary, to Premier, B. S. Stevens; Undersecretary, Chief Secretary's Dept, for APB to Premier's Dept, 20.9.1937. All in PDCF A37/193.

27 *Abo Call* July 1938:2.

28 Rose to Stevens, 22.10.1937; Elkin to APB, 5.10.1937; Elkin to Stevens, 20.10.1937; Chief Secretary Gollan's notes after interview with Kelly on Burnt Bridge, 18.11.1937. All in PDCF A37/193.

29 SC on APB, ME:45. This letter is referred to as relating to Euroka Creek, on which the two original Burnt Bridge reserves were sited.

30 APBM 14.6.1939, 10.4.1940, 26.6.1940.

Chapter 17 'The Big Fight': Land in Aboriginal Politics, 1937–38

1 Interviews T54, T55.
2 This evaluation of Bill Ferguson's leadership and of the western movement is based on analysis of the extensive press coverage of the Aboriginal movement in the late 1930s; on the archival records held in the NSW Premier's Dept (see PDCF, esp. A37/193, A38/1716, A38/956, A40/200); on detailed local interviews and analysis of the western and north-western regions; on the thorough and detailed biography of Ferguson by Jack Horner (1974); and on interviews I conducted during the late 1970s and early 1980s with Ferguson's son, Duncan, at Brewarrina and his colleague, Pearl Gibbs, in Dubbo.
3 *WW* 24.9.1931, 24.6.1932, 2.9.1932, 15.3.1935.
4 *Sun* 7.10.1937; *DT* 8.10.1937, 11.10.1937, 15.10.1937; *Labor Daily* 13.10.1937, 15.10.1937; *Common Cause* 6.11.1937.
5 *WW* 25.1.1938, 1.2.1938.
6 Goodall 1982a, 1982b; Paisley 1995.
7 'Anthropology in Australia, 1939', *Oceania* 10(1) 1939:27.
8 See SC on APB, ME 2.12.1937:62; PDCF B38/1716.
9 *Abo Call* July:1.
10 *Abo Call* April:2.
11 Stephensen: Papers, ML MS 1284 Box Y2146; *Publicist* 1938–41; *Abo Call* 1938; Horner 1974; Muirden 1968.
12 'Symptoms of Decadence: The Serious Condition of the Australian Body Politic', *Publicist* 1.10.1941.
13 *Publicist* 1.9.1937:5, 1.8.1939:10.
14 Script for 2SM broadcasts made by Stephensen, 29.8.1938, discussing itinerary of his 'recent' trip. P. R. Stephensen papers, ML MSS 1284, Box Y2146.
15 SC on APB, ME, 1938:68–70.
16 W. Ferguson for APA to Premier Stevens, 10.1.1938. PDCF A37/193; *DT* 25.1.1938; *Abo Call* April:1.
17 *Dubbo Despatch* 30.1.1939, 13.4.1939.
18 Ibid.; Bill Reid, Secretary, APA to Stevens, 12.4.1939. PCDF B38/1716.
19 *Abo Call* July:3, August:3, September:1.
20 See *Abo Call* July and August. Details of the organisation of the trip and the car from Violet Shay, whose partner was the owner of the car, from Interview C56.
21 The new policy was announced in *Abo Call* June:1, and its reception in July:1–2. Lang's questions, see *NPD* 155:741, 3.8.1938; 155:849, 5.8.1938; 155:1173, 19.8.1938; 155:1281, 24.8.1938; Patten to Stevens, 13.7.1938; Stevens to Patten, 20.7.1938. PDCF B38/1716.
22 *Abo Call* June:2.
23 Ibid., July:2.
24 Page 1, both editions.
25 Patten to D. H. Drummond, 2.8.1938, Collarenebri PSF, DEIL. Patten to Stevens, 2.8.1938. PDCF B38/1716.

26   *SMH* 11.2.1938, enclosed in Memo, Premier's Dept to Chief Secretary's Dept, 19.12.1938. PDCF A37/931.

Chapter 18 The Cumeragunja Strike, 1939

1   Cooper to Stevens, 1.1.1938. PDCF A38/931.
2   *Argus* 18.1.1938, 20.1.1938, 9.2.1939, 21.1.1938; *SMH* 9.2.1939.
3   Chief Secretary to Premier, 9.2.1938; J. L. Rose, for Premier, to W. Cooper, 5.3.1938; Cooper to Stevens, 31.3.1938. PDCF A38/931.
4   Cooper to Stevens, 23.5.1938 (four letters).
5   J. L. Rose, for Premier, to Cooper, 19.7.1938; Premier's Dept to Chief Secretary's Dept, 27.7.1938, 15.11.1938. PDCF A38/931.
6   Cooper to APB, 28.11.1938; to Stevens, 20.2.1939. PDCF A38/931.
7   Cooper to Stevens, 20.2.1939.
8   Ibid.
9   Ibid., 1.1.1938.
10   *SMH* 6.2.1939, 9.2.1939; *DT* 7.2.1939, 10.2.1939; *Age* 7.2.1939; *Argus* 6.2.1939, 7.2.1939.
11   J. T. Patten to Stevens, Urgent Telegram, 3.2.1939; Cooper to Stevens, 20.2.1939; H. Hargreaves to W. Gale, 5.2.1939. All in PDCF A38/931.
12   National Secretary, ARU, to Stevens, 21.9.1939 and considerable correspondence from various support groups, including the newly formed Aborigines Assistance Committee (19.8.1939), which had a white membership but Aboriginal organisers from the AAL. PDCF A38/931.
13   *Age* 12.4.1939, 1.6.1939, 12.10.1939; *Herald* 18.5.1939, 24.7.1939, 12.10.1939.
14   *Daily News* 7.2.1939. Patten took a libel action and called Thompson as a witness. Thompson refused to appear. The action failed.
15   *Dubbo Despatch* 10.2.1939.
16   *DT* 10.2.1939 and rest of NSW press. The article in *WW* 28.2.1939 appears to have been written in Melbourne.
17   Correspondence dated 18.5.1939 and 27.3.1939 to Premier, NSW, from these groups, respectively. PDCF A38/931.
18   The government reassured all correspondents that their plans were now being made with the full involvement of anthropological expertise. See all replies to correspondence, PDCF A38/931.
19   Annotation by Stevens, 26.6.1939. PDCF A38/931.
20   Undersecretary to Premier, and Stevens's reply, 1.7.1939. PDCF A38/931.
21   Secretary, APB to Chief Secretary, 6.4.1939. PDCF A38/931; APBM 8.2.1939, 8.3.1939.
22   Cooper to Stevens, 25.4.1939. PDCF A38/931; *Herald* 18.5.1939; *Argus* 29.4.1939.
23   *NPD* 158:4332, 2.5.1939; *Sun* 12.5.1939; *Herald* 27.6.1939; *Age* 28.7.1939.
24   *Herald* 11.10.1939; *Age* 12.10.1939.
25   APBM 8.11.1939, 10.12.1939, 17.1.1940, 12.2.1940, 13.3.1940.
26   Lipscombe to Undersecretary of the Chief Secretary's Dept, 19.12.1939. PDCF A40/200.
27   *Aborigines Protection (Amendment) Act, 1940* (No. 12). The 1936 amendments

were further perpetuated, intact, by the *Aborigines Protection (Amendment) Act, 1943* (No. 13).

28 *Native Voice* 1(1) April 1940:8 (AAL journal edited by Cooper); *Northwestern Watchman*, 11.1.1940.

29 *Dubbo Liberal*, 2.1.1940.

30 Interview T16.

31 Weilmoringle Pastoral Records, 1938–48. Noel Butlin Archives, ANU.

32 Interview T28.

33 AWBM 19.11.1940. Annual Census of Aborigines, Bourke Police Patrol return, 1941 (including Wanaaring); Lorna Dixon Interviews FT 914, 198. Interviews T27, T30.

Chapter 19 Shifting Boundaries

1   AWBR 1947:3, 4, 5; 1950:7; 1951:4; 1952:8.

2   AWBR 1952.

3   AWBR 1945ff. cover Aboriginal employment in some detail. See, for example, discussion of mechanisation in 1957:6, 1958:7; Bandler and Fox 1983:133; *Sun* 3.5.1956.

4   Sanders 1985, 1986.

5   AWBM 21.1.1941; AWBR 1947:3, 4; 1948:2.

6   AWBR 1948:2, 1949:4, 1953:5, 1954:3, 1958:4, 1961:6, 12, 1963:11.

7   South Australian Nunga popular song, 1970s: 'For the white man makes it prison, most everywhere we go.'

8   AWBR 1944:8, 1952:11, 1960:6, 9, 1961:11.

9   AWBR 1952:10, 11, 1960:9.

10 AWBR 1956:11.

11 AWBR 1951:7.

12 AWBR 1951:4.

13 AWBR 1950:6, 1951:4, 1958:5, 1959:5, 1967:10.

14 Goodall 1982a; AWBR 1963:5.

15 AWBR 1951:4, and most later reports for similar statements, e.g. 1963:5.

16 Tom Evans, A Family History of Murrin Bridge Reserve, 1992, manuscript in my possession, based on correspondence between the Lake Cargelligo Progress Association and the AWB, recorded in AWB Minute Books. SA 8/2949.

17 Elliot 1979:xvii–lix; Healy 1978:154–80; Willis 1993.

18 'Clever man', in Ngiyampaa and Bandjalang respectively, the Aboriginal English term for a highly initiated man who has become powerful in restorative medicine but also in the exercise of retributive justice by 'sorcery'.

19 AWBR 1957:3, 1959:7.

20 See Woolmington 1991 for an account of an 'Assimilation Committee' in Armidale, 1955–56.

21 Bandler and Fox 1983:75–9; Horner 1987:33.

Chapter 20 Spatial Politics: Surveillance, Segregation and Land

1 Morris 1989; AWBR 1951:7; Foley 1988:201.
2 Read 1988:chs 4–6.
3 AWBR 1949:4, 1950:6, 1960:3, 4.
4 This account is drawn from Rowley 1971; George 1975:69–71; Memmott 1991:80–5.
5 Bob Morgan, pers. comm., August 1994.
6 Bandler and Fox 1983:61–70; J. Horner, FCAATSI Report to World Council of Churches, 1972.
7 Rowley 1971:291.
8 Ibid.:189.
9 This account is drawn from Cecil Holmes: 'A Town Finds its Conscience', *People* 26.10.1960; AAF Newsletters, June 1960, July 1960, February 1962; R. Funnell, introduction to commemorative article, *Coonamble Times*, 000; Interviews T66, T67, T68; Jack Waterford (John's son), pers. comm.
10 Interview T66; See AAF Newsletter, February 1962, for Mrs Boney's trip to Sydney to report inaction on housing.
11 *Northern Star* 15.7.1958, and other clippings collected by Frank Roberts Jnr in 'Blue Wren' Scrapbook, held by Roberts family. Jack Horner (pers. comm.) dates this meeting between July and Groves's retirement in October 1958.
12 'Aborigines Not Ready For Assimilation', *Northern Star* n.d., 1959 or 1960, in 'Blue Wren' Scrapbook.
13 Letter to Editor, *Northern Star* 9.2.1959.
14 Ibid., 9.2.1959.
15 Ibid., 23.6.1960.

Chapter 21 Moving away

1 See Read 1988:xvii for a graphic example of the correlation in Wiradjuri country, and Goodall 1982a for similar evidence in the north-western region.
2 Beckett 1965.
3 AWBR 1956; then NSW Joint Committee into Aborigines Welfare, 1967:7 for 1967 estimate.
4 AWBR 1960:9.
5 AWBR 1960:9, 1961:12, 1962:4, 10, 1963:7.
6 Statement to Royal Commission into Aboriginal Deaths in Custody, 22.5.1990.
7 Completed and first shown on Channel ATN 7 in Sydney in August 1967. National Film and Sound Archive.
8 Interview T70.

Chapter 22 Reasserting Land Rights, 1957–64

1 Stuart's Island Tribal Elders Descendants Land Claim, researched by David Morrissey, on behalf of Mrs Jessie Williams, Mrs Phoebe Mumbler, and others, January 1982.

2   NSW Crown Solicitors' Office to Dept Youth and Community Services, 12.2.1979, ref. 78/4630:6. Copy in my possession.

3   *Daily Examiner* 5.2.1958, 19.11.1958, 26.11.1958; NSW Crown Solicitors' Office to Dept Youth and Community Services, 12.2.1979, ref. 78/4630.

4   AWBR 1947:4, 1956:7, 1958:8.

5   Lewis 1984.

6   See Loos and Keast 1992.

7   South Coast TLC Minutes, 27.5.1953 and after, plus discussion paper by Terry Fox.

8   AWB Report 1959:8; Jack Horner, pers. comm.

9   *Richmond River Express* 4.3.1960, 10.8.1960, 15.8.1960; AWBR 1960:8.

10 See Robinson 1965.

11 Jack Horner, notes taken during 1960 conference, in Horner's possession.

12 Correspondence between Vesper and Horner, 30.1.1960, 19.2.1960, 20.2.1960, 22.2.1960. FCAATSI Papers, ML MS 2999; ML1716/75, Box Y603.

13 Robinson 1965:70.

14 FCAA agenda, third annual conference, 1960. FCAATSI Papers.

15 AAF Newsletter, March, April 1961. Jack Horner, pers. comm.

16 B. Fowler, 'Aborigines and the Welfare Board', Letter to Editor, *SMH* 6.9.1960; AWBR 1961:5.

17 AAF Newsletter, June 1961, May 1962.

18 AWBR 1962:11, 12.

19 AWBR 1963:12–13, 1965:10, 1966:9–10.

20 ASIO, 'Aborigines: Summary of Communist Party of Australia Policy and Action', November 1962, Appendices B:9 and C; Interviews T66, T67, T68; AAF Newsletters, September 1961, October 1961; Joe Howe, Helen Hambly, Dick Hunter, Ray Peckham: 'Survey into living and social conditions of Aboriginal people from Wollongong to the Victorian Border: Report to South coast Labour Council', 6.12.1961, SCTLC Archives.

21 AAF Newsletter, October 1961, May 1962.

22 Ibid., October 1962.

23 Ibid., September 1962.

24 Ibid., September 1963.

25 Ibid., August 1962; Loos and Keast 1992.

26 'Yuin Tribe Wallaga Lake Land Claim', June 1978, researched by Terry Fox on Behalf of Ted Thomas and the Wallaga Lake Community, in Land Claims in NSW. Reprinted by the NSW Aboriginal Land Council in 1981.

27 AWBR 1955:8.

28 This account is drawn from the research report of Terry Fox for the SCTLC (*c.*1984), after detailed review of the Council's minutes, 1938–70, and based on extensive interviews and archival research into coastal Aboriginal land.

29 SCTLC Minutes 27.7.1961. Report of letter by J. Howe to *Mercury*, regarding Hill 60; 9.8.1961, report of deputation to NSW Minister for Justice and AWB.

30 SCTLC Minutes 29.11.1961, 10.1.1962, 8.2.1962.

31 Interviews T66, T68, and esp. T67.

32 Joe Howe *et al.*, Survey into Living and Social Conditions of Aboriginal People from Wollongong to the Victorian Border, 6 December to 12 December, 1961. SCTLC Archives.
33 ASIO Report, November 1962:38. Australian Archives.
34 Interviews T66, T67, T68.
35 VAAL 1985:63–8.
36 Leaflet associated with the 1963–66 Cumeragunja files of AAF, held by Faith Bandler.
37 AAF Newsletter, March 1963.
38 Ibid., April 1963, October 1963.
39 Ibid., January 1964.
40 *Southern News* 25.2.1964; AAF Newsletter, March 1964, May 1964; *Sun* 8.5.1964.
41 AAF Newsletter, March 1964, AGM on 19.2.1964.
42 Ibid., August 1964:1.
43 Jack Horner, pers. comm.

Chapter 23 Referendum and Reality

1 AAF Newsletter, February 1964.
2 Ibid.
3 This included the killing of Patrick Wedge and then Brindle's own bashing by police as he tried to support the families in their search for a real inquiry into Wedge's death.
4 *NGGs*; AWB Reports for these years.
5 AWBR 1967:10.
6 AWBR 1964–68.
7 Phil Ayers, Vocational Officer, Brewarrina, 1971–77, pers. comm.
8 Interview T68; Read 1990:114–15.
9 Cited from SAFA archives, recording the second delegation's events, ibid.
10 Horner 1965. Roneoed report presented to AAF and FCAA meetings, compiled from AWB Reports, copy in my possession.
11 AAF Newsletter, January 1965.
12 Ibid., November 1965.
13 Ibid., March 1965.
14 Ibid., October and November 1965; Jack Horner, forthcoming.
15 AAF Newsletter, November 1965, February 1966, August 1967.
16 Ibid., August 1966, September 1967; AWBR 1967:13.
17 AAF Newsletter, March 1967; Joint Committee Report 13.9.1967, Proceedings:41–60.
18 AAF Newsletter, September 1966.
19 21st National CPA Congress; *Tribune* 19.4.1967.
20 Bennett 1985.
21 AAF Newsletter, June 1967.
22 Editorial, 9.9.1967.
23 AAF Newsletter, September 1967.
24 Coombs 1978:8.
25 AAF Newsletter, September 1967.

26 *Daily News* 9.4.1969.
27 Report of the Joint Committee of the Legislative Council and the Legislative Assembly on the Aborigines Welfare Board, 13.9.1967:20
28 Ibid.:19.
29 Ibid.:8, 21.
30 Ibid.
31 AAF Newsletter, October 1967.
32 This account is drawn from AAF Newsletters, 1968 and 1969, Bandler 1989, Read 1990.
33 *Daily News* (Gold Coast, Tweed and Brunswick) 3.4.1969.
34 *Daily News* 'What Future for Fingal Group?', editorial, 10.5.1969.
35 Annual Report, Directorate of Aboriginal Welfare, June 1970:9.
36 Ibid.:18.
37 Ibid., June 1971:6.
38 Ibid.
39 Ibid.:26, Table F, compared with p. 24, Table D.
40 Ibid.:7, 8.
41 Ibid.:19; Mitchell and Cawte 1977; Eckermann et al. 1984; McLeod 1982; Eaglehawk and Crow leaflet, 'Relocation', 1975, copy in my possession.
42 Tobin 1972:7.

Chapter 24 'Hungry For Our Own Ground'

1   Freney 1991.
2   This account is drawn from a series of interviews with Peter Thompson, Gary Williams, Kaye and Bob Bellear which I conducted in June, 1995; from the research of Terry Fox in relation to south coast Aboriginal politics in the early 1970s; from various roneoed pamphlets and reports from meetings of the NSW Aboriginal Lands Board, in April 1972; and from a report of the NSW Aboriginal Land And Rights Committee, written by Frank Roberts Jnr in December 1973.
3   Frank Roberts Jnr, Report of the NSW Aboriginal Land And Rights Committee, December 1973.
4   Robinson 1993:80–7.
5   Coombs 1978:172.
6   Ibid.:9.
7   This account of the Embassy relies on the recollections of Gary Williams, Peter Thompson, Kay and Bob Bellear, and the ephemeral papers, leaflets, etc, produced during the campaign to organise the Black Moratorium and then to support the Embassy.
8   *Canberra Times* 27.1.1972, 28.1.1972, cited in Robinson 1972:97.
9   Read 1990:129.
10 This account is drawn from a detailed report to inform unions and other supporters, issued by the committee organising the Black Moratorium in Sydney, written initially in April 1972, with an addendum on 30 May.
11 Summary of a report of the NSW Aboriginal Lands Board Conference, 22–24 April 1972, Sydney. Roneoed copy in my possession.

12 Ibid.; recollections and photographs of the meeting from Peter Thompson and Terry Fox.
13 This account based on the recollections of Kaye Bellear and Peter Thompson.
14 Tobin 1972.
15 Ibid. The original notes and the questionnaires have not yet been located.
16 Progress report of the Black Moratorium Committee, announcing next meeting 17 April 1972; aims taken from pamphlet announcing meeting of teachers in support of Moratorium, 26 June, with Lyn Thompson and Gary Foley speaking; National U Broadsheet promoting attendance at the Black Moratorium, authorised by Lyn Thompson for the Black Moratorium Committee.
17 Terry Fox, Working with South Coast Aborigines, Report compiled to present to the Bishop in the Catholic Diocese of Wollongong. Copy in my possession.
18 This event was filmed by Alessandro Cavadini and his powerful footage is included in the film *Ningla A-na*.

Epilogue 'Back to Where the Story Started': Kurnell 1988

1 The only published account of the NSW Land Rights Act in its early stages is Wilkie 1985. For later developments, see my unpublished 1990 report 'Land Rights in NSW' for Tranby Co-operative College, reviewing the implementation of the Land Rights Act to that date.
2 *Land Rights News* 2(6) January 1988.

Bibliography

PRIMARY SOURCES

1) Official Printed Sources

Commonwealth of Australia
Commonwealth Arbitration Report, 31, 1932
Initial Conference of Commonwealth and State Aboriginal Authorities, April 1937, National Library, Canberra

New South Wales
New South Wales Select Committee on the Condition of the Aborigines, Minutes of Evidence, 1845, Govt Printers, October 1845

NSW Government Gazettes, 1840 to 1969
Report of the Protector of Aborigines, 1882
NSW Parliamentary Debates, 1905–1969
Alexander Stuart: Minute of the Colonial Secretary, 26.2.1883:1–3, printed in VPLA, NSW, 1883
Report and Recommendations of the Royal Commission into The Treatment of Neglected and Delinquent Children, Sir Charles Mackellar, 1913, VPLA, NSW
Aborigines Protection Board Reports, 1884 to 1938–39
Aborigines Welfare Board Reports, 1939–40 to 1968–69
Directorate of Aboriginal Welfare Reports, 1970 to 1975
Aboriginal Lands Trust Reports, 1974 to 1977
Crown Lands Department Reports, 1905–6 to 1944–45
Western Lands Department Reports, 1905–6 to 1944–45
Select Committee on Administration of Aborigines Protection Board, Minutes of Evidence, 1937–38, 1940, JPP
NSW Arbitration Report, 26, 1927
Aborigines Protection: Report and Recommendations of the Public Service Board of NSW Board 1938, printed 1940, JPP
NSW Joint Parliamentary Committee into Aborigines Welfare, 1967, JPP
Historical Records of Australia, Series I
Historical Records of New South Wales

2) *Official Manuscript Sources*

Commonwealth Manuscript Sources

Police Annual Aboriginal Census *Annual Census of Aborigines, 1927 to 1937*, papers relating to NSW, Commonwealth Bureau of Census and Statistics

NSW Manuscript Sources

Governor's Despatches, 1842, vol. 63; 1853, 1854, vols 70–5. ML CY1949, CY1950

Commissioners of Crown Lands

Gwydir: Letters Sent from 1849, 2/7634; Letters Received, 2/7627. SA (Commissioners for Crown Lands Reports are in Governor's Despatches, vols. 70–5. ML CY1949, CY1950. Further reports in CSIL)

Colonial/Chief Secretary's Correspondence: In-Letters (CSIL)

Material relating to Aborigines was analysed from the following locations in this archive. The incoming letters to the APB can only be readily traced until 1921, after which there was a change in indexing system.

Special Bundle Aborigines Reserves, 1848–51, 4/1141.2
Executive Council Minutes, 1848–50, 18/7/1848:374–5 CSIL 4/1523, 4/1526, Reel 2438

CSIL Main Series

1886, 1/2594;
1887, 1/2667, 1/2645;
1890, 5/5978, 5/6004;
1907, 5/6990;
1907, 5/6944;
1907–08, 5/7030;
1908, 5/6990;
1910, Box 7073;
1911, Box 7121;
1912, Box 7165;
1913, Box 7204;
1914, Box 7260;

1915, Box 7324;
1916, Box 7392;
1917, Box 7483;
1918, Box 7956;
1919, Box 8018;
1920, Box 8099;
1921, Box 8205;
1936, 12/7354;
1937, 12/7545;
1938, 12/7565;
1939, 12/7583, 12/7588

Lands Department

Surveyor-General's maps: no. 6009, 'Darling River No. 4', 28.2.1851
Applications for land and reservation of land: 77/9843, 78/2157, SA 2/1138; 78/4240, SA 7/6404

Aborigines Welfare Board

This archive includes the remaining records of the Aborigines Protection Board along with those of the Aborigines Welfare Board.

APB Minute Books, 1890–1901, 1905–6, 1911–38: 4/7108–27.
APB Out-Letters: 1914–27, 4/7128
APB Records of Wards, *c.*1912 to 1928, 4/8553–54
APB Index to Ward Registers, 1912 to *c.*1936, 4/8555–56

APB Register of Reserves, 1861–1904, 2/8349
APB/AWB Photographs, *c.*1924 to *c.*1961, 4/8566–78
AWB Minute Books, 1940–68, 8/2949

Premier's Department Correspondence Files
A27/915, relating to the AAPA
A37/193, relating to A. P. Elkin and C. Kelly. See Secondary Sources
A37/2380, Tuncurry (file destroyed 1960, contents described in PDCF index)
62/1515. All files relating to Aborigines from 1936 to 1962 were 'aggregated'
into this file during deliberations arising from AAF pressure to reform the
Aborigines Welfare Act in 1961–62. Particularly useful files include:
    William Cooper's Correspondence: A36/404, A36/1028
    Burnt Bridge Correspondence, APA campaign, related non-Aboriginal
        correspondence, inter-departmental comment, 1937–42: A37/193,
        B38/956, A40/200
    Cumeragunja Strike: A38/931, B/38/1716

Department of Public Instruction/Education Files
The files of public, provisional and 'special' Aboriginal (segregated) schools are
held in the NSW State Archives Office in alphabetical order according to school
name. Correspondence relating to all years has been collected into a single file
under the school name. The following school files contain substantial material
relating to Aboriginal students and local race relations.

Balranald public
Bateman's Bay public
Bomaderry public
Boomi public
Brewarrina public
Brewarrina Aboriginal
Burnt Bridge Aboriginal
Caroona public
Collarenebri public
Darlington Point public
Dungalear proposed provisional
Euraba Aboriginal
Gulargumbone public
Goondabluie and Mogil proposed
    provisional
Huskisson public

Kempsey public
Kinchela Aboriginal
Lismore South public
Moree public
Pilliga public
Pooncarie Aboriginal
St Joseph's (Burragorang) provisional
Singleton public
Tibooburra public
Toomelah Aboriginal
Tweed Heads public
Walgett public
Walhallow Aboriginal
Woolbrook public
Yass public

Department of Youth and Community Services
NSW Crown Solicitor's Office to Dept Youth and Community Services,
    12.2.1979, ref. 78/4630:6. Copy in my possession

3) *Other Contemporary Sources*

a) Aboriginal-authored: published, manuscript and other media
Australian Aboriginal League Annual Report 1936. PDCF A36/1028

Joe Anderson, as 'King Burraga' in *Cinesound News Review*, no. 100, 1933
The Australian Abo Call, 1938, edited by Jack Patten for the APA
Native Voice, 1940, edited by William Cooper for the AAL
Dept Territories, *One Man's Road*, 1967, National Film and Sound Archive
Stuart's Island Tribal Elders Descendants Land Claim, 1982
Frank Roberts Jnr, Report of the NSW Aboriginal Land And Rights Committee, December 1973. Copy in my possession
'Yuin Tribe Wallaga Lake Land Claim', June 1978, in *Land Claims in NSW*, reprinted by the NSW Aboriginal Land Council in 1981
Lyn Thompson, 'Summary of a report of the NSW Aboriginal Lands Board Conference', 22–24 April 1972, Sydney. Copy in my possession

b) Local Government
The following records were consulted in the relevant local government chambers.

Brewarrina Municipal Council
Dubbo Municipal Council
Moree Municipal Council
Talbragar Shire Council
Walgett Shire Council

c) Pastoral industry
The following north-western Pastoral Property records, including cash books, ledgers, wages records, store accounts and station diaries, contain substantial evidence of continued Aboriginal residence and pastoral and domestic labour.

Angledool, 1904 to 1940, Butlin Archives, ANU
Bangate, 1897 to 1940, UNE Archives
Dungalear, 1910 to 1938, UNE Archives
Gingie, 1863 to 1940s. 1863–81, ML; 1900 to 1940s, held at Gingie Property, via Walgett
Yeranbah, 1897 to 1924, UNE Archives
Weilmoringle, 1938 to 1950, Butlin Archives, ANU

d) Newspapers, journals and other media

Adelaide Register	*Dubbo Liberal*
The Age	*Evening News*
Argus	*Herald*, Melbourne
Australian Aborigines Advocate, 1900–29, became *United Aborigines Messenger* 1929 onwards. Organ of the Australian Aborigines Mission	*Illawarra Mercury*
	Labor Call
	Labor Daily (later *Daily News*)
	Land Rights News
Australian Geographer	*Macleay Argus*
Canberra Times	*Macleay Chronicle*
Common Cause	*Man*
Coonamble Times	*Moree Gwydir Examiner and General Advertiser*
Daily Examiner, Grafton	
Daily News, Murwillumbah	*Northern Star*, Lismore
Daily Telegraph	*Northwestern Watchman*, Coonabarabran
Dubbo Dispatch	*Nowra Leader*

Our Aim, 1923 to 1939, organ of the
    Aborigines Inland Mission
People
Pix
The Protector, organ of the Association
    for the Protection of Native Races
The Publicist
Richmond River Express
Riverine Herald
Smith's Weekly

Southern News
Sun
Sydney Morning Herald
Truth
Uplift, organ of the Aboriginal Uplift
    Society, Victoria
Voice of the North, Newcastle
Wingham Chronicle
Woman Today
Workers' Weekly

e) Manuscripts
Governor Lachlan Macquarie's Journal. ML A773
Burragorang Parish file. Catholic Archives, St Mary's Cathedral
Norman Tindale Archives, notes, photos, genealogies, interviews, from 1938 field
    trips, NSW. ML
Elkin Papers. Archive unit, Fisher Library, University of Sydney
P. R. Stephensen papers. ML MS 1284, Box Y2146
Pearl Gibbs, press clippings albums and collection, viewed when in her posses-
    sion, Dubbo, 1981
Frank Roberts, Jnr, scrapbooks, in Roberts family's possession
South Coast Trades and Labour Council, Minutes and Correspondence, 1938
    to 1970. Archives Unit, Library of the University of Wollongong. Aboriginal
    material collated by Terry Fox
FCAATSI Papers, 1957 to 1973. ML MSS 2999; ML1716/75, Box Y599 to
    Y604
Australian Security and Intelligence Office, 'Aborigines: Summary of Communist
    Party of Australia Policy and Action', November 1962, Appendices B:9 and
    C. Australian Archives Office
Aboriginal–Australian Fellowship, Newsletter, full series from May 1960 to
    October, 1969. Faith Bandler's personal archive
Joe Howe et al. (1961) 'Survey into living and social conditions of Aboriginal
    people from Wollongong to the Victorian Border: Report to South coast
    Labour Council' for the Aborigines Advancement League. SCTLC Archives,
    University of Wollongong
'Yuin Tribe Wallaga Lake Land Claim', June 1978, in Land Claims in NSW.
    Reprinted by NSW Aboriginal Land Council, 1981
Cumeragunja files, 1963–66. AAF Papers, held by Faith Bandler
Black Moratorium: various reports, pamphlets and organising material, 1971 and
    1972. Copies in my possession
Terry Fox (1990) 'Working with South Coast Aborigines'. Report compiled to
    present to the Bishop in the Catholic Diocese of Wollongong. Copy in my
    possession

f) Films and photographic collections
At Work and Play collection, ML
Alessandro Cavadini (1972) Ningla A-na

4) Interviews

a) Interviews conducted by other interviewers

Jimmie Barker, interviewed by Janet Mathews. Transcripts of interviews held in AIATSIS, Filed Tapes 94B, 117

Interviews conducted with Lorna Dixon (née Ebsworth) by Janet Mathews, Field Tape numbers FT 194 (18.4.1975) and FT 198, (19.4.1975)

Margaret Tucker, interviewed by Alec Morgan, Melbourne, September, 1980

b) Interviews conducted by Heather Goodall, 1977 to 1995

'T' indicates taperecorded interview

'C' indicates interview during which notes were taken, or written down shortly afterwards.

The location and date of the interview is shown. Copies of the tape recordings (and transcripts where possible) have been lodged with the Australian Institute for Aboriginal and Torres Strait Islander Studies and the NSW State Library Oral History Archive.

T1 Bert Marr, Purfleet, 12.2.76

C2 Ella Simon, Purfleet, February, 1976

T3 Val Mingo, Brewarrina, 29.7.76

T4 Dora Sullivan, Margaret Parker, Evelyn Hardy, Brewarrina, 29.7.76 (fragment: tape damaged)

T5 Henry Hardy, Brewarrina, 29.7.76

T6 Henry Hardy, Brewarrina, 2.8.76

T7 Margaret Parker, Brewarrina, 2.8.76

C8 Marnie Kelly, Brewarrina, 3.8.76

T9 Henry Hardy, Brewarrina, 3.8.76

C10 Henry Hardy, Brewarrina, 5.8.76

T11 Dora Sullivan, Brewarrina, 19.1.77

C12 Mick Collis, Brewarrina, 21.1.77

C13 Robin Campbell, Brewarrina, 21.1.77

T14 Greta Coleman, Brewarrina, 22.1.77

T15 May Cubby, Brewarrina, 22.1.77

T16 Jack Orcher, Brewarrina, 22.1.77

T17 Billy Moore, Brewarrina, 22.1.77

T18 Jack and Donnas Barker, Brewarrina, 23.1.77

T19 Margaret Parker, Brewarrina, 24.1.77

T20 Frieda (Bunny) Hardy, Brewarrina, 24.1.77

T21 Roy Barker, Brewarrina, 24.1.77

T22 Ray McHughes, Brewarrina, 25.1.77

C23 Bert and Eadie Gordon, Brewarrina, 25.1.77

T24 Val Mingo, Brewarrina, 26.1.77

T25 Hazel Clark, Bourke, 28.1.77

T26 Violet Wilson, Bourke, 28.1.77

T27 Wilpi (George Harrison), Bourke, 13.4.77

T28 Eadie Edwards, Bourke, 18.4.77

C29 Isadore Phillips, Bourke, 18.4.77

T30 Wilpi (George Harrison), Bourke, 19.4.77

C31 Evelyn Crawford Snr, Brewarrina, 29.6.77

C32 Agnes Murray, Brewarrina, June, 1977

C33 Duncan Ferguson, Brewarrina, 1.7.77

C34 George Rose Snr, Walgett, 20.7.77

T35 Arthur Dodd, Walgett, 21.7.77

T36 Essena Sullivan, Walgett, 21.7.77

T37 Ivy Green, Walgett, 26.7.77

C38 Jim Fernando, Walgett, 27.7.77

T39 Arthur Dodd, Walgett, 28.7.77

T40 Kathleen Dodd, Walgett, 28.7.77

T41 Don and Melva Nicholls, Walgett, 3.8.77

T42 Susan Dennis, Walgett, 4.8.77

C43 Isabel Flick, Collarenebri, 17.9.77

C44 Jack Campbell, Glebe, September, 1977

T45 Reg Murray, Annandale, 22.2.78

C46 Henry Hardy, Brewarrina, 28.8.78

C47 Duncan Ferguson, Brewarrina, 29.8.78

T48 Isabel Flick, Glebe, 30.11.78

C49 Hannah Duncan (née McGrady), Glebe, 7.2.77

T50 Henry Hardy, Brewarrina, 20.9.80

T51 Jack Campbell, Ted Thomas, Kevin Cook, Glebe, 24.9.80

C52 Mona Fernando, Wee Waa, 1.2.81

T53 Kylie Tennant, Sydney, 9.2.81

T54 Pearl Gibbs, Dubbo, audio recording, 7, 8.3.81

T55 Pearl Gibbs, Dubbo, film recording, 6, 7, 8.3.81

C56 Violet Shay and Florence Caldwell, Alexandria, 23.3.81.

T57 Jack Booth, Dubbo, audio recording, Dubbo, 21.5.81

T58 Jack Booth, Dubbo, film recording, Dubbo, 23.5.81

C59 Tartu (Will Webster), Glebe, 30.3.82

T60 Billy Moore, Brewarrina, 14.9.81

C61 Jack Campbell, Orient Point, 14.7.82

C62 Dorrie Hunter and Alice Bugmy, Wilcannia, 1978, re Kidman stations, 1940s

C63 Peter Prentice, conversation, Brewarrina, August 1976

T64 Reuben Kelly and Olive Mundine, Sydney, 1.9.87

C65 Olive Mundine, Sydney, 27.2.88

T66 Helen Hambly, East Sydney, 15.8.89

T67 Helen Hambly, East Sydney, 22.8.89

T68 Helen Hambly, East Sydney, 10.10.89

T69 Kevin Cook, Glebe, 18.2.92

T70 Judy Chester, Glebe, 13.3.92

C71 Rose (Weatherall) Flick, Thallon, 27.6.94

T72 Donnas Barker, Dubbo, July, 1994

T73 Rose (Weatherall) Flick, Thallon, 8.10.95

T74 Roy and June Barker, Lightning Ridge, 10.10.95

T75 Albert Walford, Lightning Ridge, 12.10.95

Unrecorded conversations during 1977–79 with Les McGrady, Vicky Archibald, Kathy Drew and Ida Williams (née Drew), all ex-apprentices.

5) *Secondary Sources*

Allen, Harry (1974) 'The Bagundji of the Darling Basin: cereal gatherers in an uncertain environment', *World Archaeology* 5(3):309–22

Attwood, Bain (1986) 'Off the Mission Stations: Aborigines in Gippsland, 1860–1890', *Aboriginal History* 10(2):131–50

Aveling, Marian et al., eds (1987) *Australians: An Historical Library, 1838*, Fairfax, Syme & Weldon Associates, Sydney

Bradley, W. (1969) *A Voyage to New South Wales*, Trustees of Public Library of NSW and Ure Smith, Sydney

Bandler, Faith, and L. Fox (1983) *The Time was Ripe*, Alternative Publishing Co. Co-operative Ltd, Sydney

Barwick, Diane (1963) A Little More than Kin: Regional Affiliation and Group Identity among Aboriginal Migrants in Melbourne. PhD thesis, ANU

——(1971) 'Changes in the Aboriginal Population of Victoria, 1863–1966', in D. J. Mulvaney and J. Golson, eds, *Aboriginal Man and Environment in Australia*, ANU Press, Canberra, pp. 288–315

——(1972) 'Coranderrk and Cumeroogunga: Pioneers and Policy', in S. Epstein and D. Penny, eds, *Opportunity and Response: Case Studies in Economic Development*, Hurst & Co., London, pp. 10–68

——(1984) 'Mapping the Past: an atlas of Victorian clans, 1835–1904', *Aboriginal History* 8:100–31

Beckett, Jeremy (1965) 'Kinship, Mobility and Community Among Part-Aborigines in Rural Australia', *International Journal of Comparative Sociology* 6(1):7–23

——(1977) 'The Torres Strait Islanders and the Pearling Industry: a case of internal colonialism', *Aboriginal History* 1(1):77–104

——(1978) in 'George Dutton's Country', *Aboriginal History* 2(1):2–31

Bell, Diane (1983) *Daughters of the Dreaming*, McPhee Gribble and Allen & Unwin, Melbourne and Sydney

Bennett, Scott (1985) 'The 1967 Referendum', *Australian Aboriginal Studies* 2:26–31

Berkhoffer, Robert J. (1979) *The White Man's Indian: Images of the American Indian from Columbus to the Present*, Vintage Books, New York

Berndt, R., and C. Berndt, eds (1980) *Aborigines of the West*, University of Western Australia Press, Perth

——(1988) *The Speaking Land: Myth and Story in Aboriginal Australia*, Penguin, Melbourne

——(1987) *End of an Era: Aboriginal Labour in the Northern Territory*, Report of survey, 1946–1948, AIAS, Canberra

Bolton, Geoffrey (1981) *Spoils and Spoilers: Australians Make Their Environment, 1788–1980*, Allen & Unwin, Sydney

Brennan, Martin (1907) *Reminiscences of the Gold Fields*, William Brooks & Co., Sydney

Bride, T. F. (1898) *Letters from Victorian Pioneers*, Government Printer, Melbourne. Republished Heinemann 1969

Bridges, Barry (1966) Aboriginal and White Relations in New South Wales, 1788–1855. MA thesis, University of Sydney

——(1970) 'Aborigines and the Land Question', *JRAHS* 56(2):92–110

Briggs, A., ed. (1962) *Chartist Studies*, London

Brock, Peggy, ed. (1989) *Women, Rites and Sites: Aboriginal Women's Cultural Knowledge*, Allen & Unwin, Sydney

Brook, J., and L. L. Kohen (1991) *The Parramatta Native Institution and the Black Town: a History*, UNSWP

Burgmann, V. and J. Lee, eds (1988a) *A Most Valuable Acquisition*, vol. 1 of *A People's History of Australia since 1788*, McPhee Gribble/Penguin, Melbourne

——(1988b) *Staining the Wattle*, McPhee Gribble/Penguin, Melbourne

Butlin, Noel E. (1983) *Our Original Aggression*, Allen & Unwin, Sydney

——(1993) *Economics and the Dreamtime: A Hypothetical History*, CUP, Cambridge

Buxton, G. L. (1974) '1870–1890', in Crowley 1974:165–215

Campbell, Judy (1985) 'Small pox in Aboriginal Australia, the early 1830s', *Historical Studies* 21(84):536–56

Carter, Paul (1987) *The Road to Botany Bay*, Faber & Faber, London

Clark, C. M. (1966) *A Short History of Australia*, Penguin, Melbourne

Clark, M. T. (1966) *Pastor Doug: The Story of Sir Douglas Nicholls, Aboriginal Leader*, Lansdowne Press, Melbourne

Collier, James (1911) *The Pastoral Age in Australasia*, Whitcombe & Tombs, Melbourne

Coombs, H. C. (1978) *Kulinma*, ANU Press, Canberra

Crowley, F. K., ed. (1974) *A New History of Australia*, Heinemann, Melbourne

Curthoys, Ann (1982) 'Good Christians and Useful Workers', in Sydney Labour History Group, *What Rough Beast? The State and Social Order in Australian History*, Allen & Unwin, Sydney, pp. 31–56

——(1973) Race and Ethnicity: a study of the response of British colonists to Aborigines, Chinese and non-British Europeans in New South Wales, 1856–1881. PhD thesis, Macquarie University

Darian-Smith, K., and P. Hamilton, eds (1994) *Memory and History in Twentieth-Century Australia*, OUP, Melbourne

Davidson, A., and A. Wells (1988) 'Carving up the country' in Burgmann and Lee 1988a: 42–56

Donaldson, I., and T. Donaldson, eds (1985) *Seeing the First Australians*, Allen & Unwin, Sydney

Donaldson, Tamsin (1984) 'What's in a name? an etymological view of land, language and social identification from central western New South Wales', *Aboriginal History* 8(1):21–44

Dovers, Stephen (1992) 'A history of natural resource use in rural Australia: practicalities and ideologies', in Geoffrey Lawrence, Frank Vanclay and Brian Furze, eds, *Agriculture, Environment and Society: Contemporary Issues for Australia*, Macmillan, Melbourne

Eckermann, A.-K., B. Watts and P. Dizon (1984) *From Here to There: A Comparative Study of Aboriginal Rural-Urban Resettlement, Queensland and NSW*, Cwlth Dept Aboriginal Affairs

Edwards, W. H., ed. (1972) *Traditional Aboriginal Society: a Reader*, Macmillan, Melbourne

Elder, B. (1988) *Blood on the Wattle*, Child & Associates Publishing, Sydney

Elkin, A. P. (1975) 'R. H. Mathews: his contribution to Aboriginal studies', *Oceania* 46(2) Pt I:1–24, Pt II:126–52, Pt III:206–35

Elliot, Brian, ed. (1979) *The Jindyworobaks*, UQP

Fels, Marie Hansen (1986) Good Men and True: The Aboriginal Police of the Port Phillip District, 1837–1853. PhD thesis, University of Melbourne

Fesl, Eve Mumewa (1995) 'How the English Language is used to put us down, deny us rights or is employed as a political tool against us', Griffith University. Revised version, typescript in my possession

Fison, L., and A. W. Howitt (1880) *Kamilaroi and Kurnai*, George Robertson, Melbourne. Facsimile published by Aboriginal Studies Press, Canberra, 1991

Fletcher, J. J. (1989) *Clean, Clad and Courteous: A History of Aboriginal Education in New South Wales*, J. Fletcher Desktop Publisher, Sydney

Foley, Gary (1988) 'Teaching Whites a Lesson', in Burgmann and Lee 1988b:198–207

Frawley, Kevin (1992) 'A "Green" Vision: The Evolution of Australian Environmentalism', in Kay Anderson and Fay Gale, eds, *Inventing Places*, Longman Cheshire, Melbourne, pp. 215–234

Freney, Denis (1991) *A Map of Days: Life on the Left*, Heinemann, Melbourne

Gammage, Bill (1983) 'The Wiradjuri Wars, 1838–1840', *Push from the Bush* 16:3–17

George, Ken (1975) 'The Bakandji Project', *Architecture in Australia* December:69–72

Goodall, Heather (1982a) A History of Aboriginal Communities, 1909–1939. PhD thesis, University of Sydney

——(1982b) An Intelligent Parasite: A. P. Elkin and white perceptions of Aboriginal history. Paper delivered to AHA conference, Sydney

——(1987) 'Aboriginal History and the Politics of Information Control', *Journal of the Oral History Association of Australia* 9:17–33

——(1988) 'Cryin' Out For Land Rights', in Burgmann and Lee 1988b:181–97

——(1990) 'Saving the Children: gender and the colonisation of Aboriginal children in New South Wales, 1788–1990', *Aboriginal Law Bulletin* 2(44):6–11

Griffiths, Tom (1996) *Hunters and Collectors: The Antiquarian Imagination in Australia*, CUP, Melbourne

Grimshaw, M. et al. (1994) *Creating a Nation: 1788 to 1990*, McPhee Gribble, Melbourne

Grishin, Sasha (1992) 'T. S. Gill: Defining a Landscape', *Voices* 2(4):18–33

Hall, C. M. (1992) *Wasteland to World Heritage: Preserving Australia's Wilderness*, MUP

Hamilton, A. (1980) 'Dual Social System', *Oceania* 51(1):4–19

——(1982) 'Descended from father, belonging to country', in E. B. Leacock and R. B. Lee, eds, *Politics and History in Band Societies*, CUP, Cambridge, pp. 85–108

Hamilton, P (1994) 'The Knife-Edge: Debates about Memory and History', in Darian-Smith and Hamilton 1994:9–32

Hardy, Bobbi (1969) *West of the Darling*, Jacaranda Press, Milton, NSW

——(1976) *Lament for the Bakandji*, Rigby, Adelaide

Hartwig, Mervyn (1978) 'Capitalism and Aborigines: The Theory of Internal Colonialism and its rivals' in T. E. Wheelwright and K. Buckley, eds, *Essays in the Political Economy of Australian Capitalism*, vol. 3, Australian & New Zealand Book Co., Sydney

Healy, J. J. (1978) *Literature and the Aborigine in Australia*, UQP

Heathcote, R. L. (1972) 'Pastoral Australia', in Jeans 1972:259–399

Hercus, Luise A. (1980) "How we danced the Mudlunga': memories of 1901 and 1902', *Aboriginal History* 4(1):5–32

Holder, F. W. (1892) *Our Pastoral Industry*, Thomas & Co., Adelaide

Horner, J. (1974) *Vote Ferguson for Aboriginal Freedom*, Australian & New Zealand Book Co., Sydney

——(1987) 'From Sydney to Tingha: Early days in the Aboriginal-Australian Fellowship', *Aboriginal History* 11(1):33–40

——(forthcoming) *Hearing the Other Side: A History of the Federal Council for the Advancement of Aborigines and Torres Strait Islanders*, AIATSIS

Howitt, W. (1972) *Land Labour and Gold*, SUP. First published 1855, facsimile edn

Irving, T. (1974) '1850–1870', in Crowley 1974:124–64

Jeans, D. N. (1972a) *An Historical Geography of New South Wales to 1901*, Reed Education, Sydney

——, ed. (1972) *Space and Society: Australia, a Geography*, vol. 2, SUP

Jenkin, Graham (1979) *Conquest of the Ngarrindjeri: the Story of the Lower Murray Lakes Tribes*, Rigby, Adelaide

Johnston, S. L. (1970) The New South Wales Government Policy Towards Aborigines, 1880 to 1909. MA thesis, University of Sydney

Kelly, C. (1936) Study of a Small Native Community living near a Country Town. Typescript report in Elkin Papers, Sydney University Archives

——(1937) Anthropological Survey at Burnt Bridge, August–September. PDCF A37/193

King, C. J. (1957) *An Outline of Closer Settlement in New South Wales*, Part I, NSW Dept Agriculture

Knudtson, P., and D. Suzuki (1992) *Wisdom of the Elders*, Allen & Unwin, Sydney

Kolig, E. (1980) 'Captain Cook in the Western Kimberley', in Berndt and Berndt 1980:274–84

——(1983) 'Noah's Ark Revisited: on the myth–land connection in traditional Aboriginal thought', *Oceania* 53:118–32

Lang, J. D. (1833) *Emigration: considered chiefly in reference to the practicability and expediency of importing and settling throughout the territory of New South Wales, a numerous, industrious and virtuous agricultural population*, E. S. Hall, Sydney

Langloh Parker, K. (1905) *The Euahlayi Tribe: A Study of Aboriginal Life in Australia*, Archibald Constable, London

——(1953) *Australian Legendary Tales*, Angus & Robinson, Sydney

Lansbury, Coral (1970) *Arcady in Australia: The Evocation of Australia in Nineteenth Century English Literature*, MUP

Lewis, Gary (1984) ' "Million Farms" Campaign, NSW, 1919–25', *Labour History* 47:55–72

Liston, Carol (1988) 'The Dharawal and the Gandangara in colonial Campbelltown, 1788–1830', *Aboriginal History* 12(1):49–62

Loos, Noel, and Robyn Keast (1992) 'The Radical Promise: The Aboriginal

Christian Cooperative Movement', *Australian Historical Studies* 25(99):286–301

Lourandos, Harry, Annie Ross and Luise Hercus (1989) 'Three linguistic studies from far southwestern New South Wales', *Aboriginal History* 13(1):44–62

Mackinolty, C., and P. Wainburranga (1988) 'Too Many Captain Cooks', in Swain and Rose 1988:355–60

Maddock, Ken (1983) *Our Land is Your Land*, Penguin, Melbourne

Mathews, J., ed. (1977) *The Two Worlds of Jimmie Barker*, AIAS, Canberra

Mathews, R. H. (1894) 'Aboriginal Bora held at Gundabloui in 1894', *JRSNSW* 28:98–129

——(1896a) 'The Bora of the Kamilaroi Tribes', *Proceedings of the Royal Society of Victoria* 9:137–73

——(1896b) 'The Burbung of the Wiradthuri Tribes', *Journal of the Anthropological Institute* 25:295–318

——(1900) 'Marriage and Descent among the Australian Aborigines', *JRSNSW* 34:120–35

——(1903) 'The Aboriginal Fisheries at Brewarrina', *JRSNSW* 37:146–56

——and M. M. Everitt (1900) 'The Organisation, Language and Initiation of the Aborigines of the South East Coast of New South Wales', *JRSNSW* 34:262–80

Maynard, Margaret (1985) 'Projections of Melancholy', in Donaldson and Donaldson 1985:92–109

May, Dawn (1994) *Aboriginal Labour and the Cattle Industry: Queensland from White Settlement to the Present*, CUP, Cambridge

McBryde, Isabel (1984) 'Exchange in south-eastern Australia: an ethnohistorical perspective', *Aboriginal History* 8(2):132–53

——(1985) 'Thomas Dick's Photographic Vision', in Donaldson and Donaldson 1985

McGrath, Ann (1987) *Born in the Cattle*, Allen & Unwin, Sydney

McLeod, I., and B. Reid Jnr (1982) *Shade and Shelter*, Jacaranda Press, Brisbane

Meggitt, M. J. (1972) 'Understanding Australian Aboriginal Society: Kinship Systems or Cultural Categories?'. First published in P. Reinign, ed., *Kinship Studies in the Morgan Centennial Year*, Washington, republished in Edwards 1987:127–32

Members of the Aboriginal Community (1988) *La Perouse: The Place, The People and the Sea*, AIAS, Canberra

Memmott, Paul (1991) *Humpy, House and Tin Shed: Aboriginal Settlement History on the Darling River*, Faculty of Architecture, University of Sydney

Miller, J. (1985) *Koori: Will to Win*, Angus & Robertson, Sydney

Millis, Roger (1992) *Waterloo Creek: The Australia Day Massacre, 1838*, McPhee Gribble, Melbourne

Mitchell, I., and J. Cawte (1977) 'The Aboriginal Family Voluntary Resettlement Scheme: an approach to Aboriginal adaptation', *ANZ Journal of Psychiatry* 11:29

Morris, Barry (1989) *Domesticating Resistance: The Dhan-Gadi Aborigines and the Australian State*, Berg, Oxford

——(1992) 'Frontier Colonialism as a Culture of Terror', in B. Attwood and J.

Arnold, *Power, Knowledge and Aborigines*. Special issue *Journal of Australian Studies*, La Trobe University Press, Melbourne, pp. 72–87

Muirden, Bruce (1968) *The Puzzled Patriots: The Story of the Australia First Movement*, MUP

Mulvaney, D. J. (1976) ' "The Chain of Connection": the material evidence', in Peterson 1976:72–94

Myers, Fred (1976) To Have and To Hold: A Study of Persistence and Change in Pintubi Social Life, PhD, Bryn Mawr, Pa.

——(1972) 'Always Ask: Resource Use and Land Ownership', in Williams and Hunn 1982:173–96

——(1986) *Pintupi Country, Pintupi Self*, Smithsonian Institute and AIAS, Washington and Canberra

Paisley, Fiona (1995) Ideas Have Wings: White Women Challenge Aboriginal Policy, 1920–1937, PhD, La Trobe University

Palmer, Kingsley (1983) 'Migration and Rights to Land in the Pilbara', in Peterson and Langton 1983, 172–9

Payne, Helen (1989) 'Rites for sites or sites for rites?', in Brock 1989:41–59

Pearson, Michael (1984) 'Bathurst Plains and Beyond: European colonisation and Aboriginal resistance', *Aboriginal History* 8(1):63–79

Peterson, N., ed. (1976) *Tribes and Boundaries in Australia*, AIAS, Canberra

——(1983) 'Rights, Residence and Process in Aboriginal Territorial Organisation', in Peterson and Langton 1983:134–48

——(1985) 'The Popular Image', in Donaldson and Donaldson 1985:164–80

——and M. Langton, eds (1983) *Aborigines, Land and Land Rights*, AIAS, Canberra

Phillip, A. (1789) *The Voyage of Governor Arthur Phillip to Botany Bay*, London

Plater, D., ed. (1993) *Other Boundaries: Inner-city Aboriginal Stories*, Leichhardt Municipal Council, Sydney

Poiner, G. (1980) 'Aboriginal Social Organisation', in C. Haigh and W. Goldstein, eds, *The Aborigines of New South Wales*. Occasional publication in NSW National Parks and Wildlife Service series *Parks and Wildlife* 2(5):50–2

Powell, J. M. (1976) *Conservation and Resource Management in Australia: 1788–1914. Guardians, Improvers and Profit: An Introductory Survey*, OUP, Melbourne

——(1977) *Mirrors of the New World: Images and Image-Makers in the Settlement Process*, Dawson & Sone, Folkestone, UK

——(1988) *An Historical Geography of Modern Australia: The Restive Fringe*, CUP, Cambridge

Quiggin, P. (1988) *No Rising Generations: Women and Fertility in Late Nineteenth Century Australia*, Australian Government Publishing Service, Canberra

Read, Peter, ed. (1984) *Down There With Me on Cowra Mission*, Pergamon Press, Sydney

——(1988) *A Hundred Years' War: The Wiradjuri People and the State*, ANU Press and Pergamon, Canberra and Sydney

——(1990a) *Charles Perkins: A Biography*, Viking, Melbourne

——(1990b) 'Cheeky, Insolent and Anti-White: the split in the Federal Council for the Advancement of Aboriginal and Torres Strait Islanders, Easter 1970', *Australian Journal of Politics and History* 36(1):73–83

Reay, Marie, and Grace Sidlington (1948) 'Class and Status in a Mixed Blood Community', *Oceania* 18(3):179–207

Reece, R. H. W. (1974) *Aborigines and Colonists: Aborigines and Colonial Society in New South Wales in the 1830s and 1840s*, SUP

——(1982) Aboriginal Community History: A Cautionary Tale. Paper presented at AHA conference, Sydney

Reynolds, Henry (1992) *Law of the Land*, 2nd edn, Penguin, Melbourne

Richards, E., ed. (1991) *Poor Australian Immigrants in the Nineteenth Century*, vol. 2, Research School of Social Sciences, ANU Press, Canberra

Roberts, S. H. (1984) *The History of Australian Land Settlement, 1788–1920*, MUP. Originally published 1924

——(1975) *The Squatting Age in Australia, 1835–1847*, MUP. Originally published 1935

Robinson, P. (1988) *The Women of Botany Bay: A Reinterpretation of the Role of Women in the Origins of Australian Society*, Macquarie Library, Sydney

Robinson, Roland (1958) *Black-feller, White-feller*, Angus & Robertson, Sydney

——(1965) *The Man who sold his Dreaming*, Currawong Publishing Co., Sydney

Robinson, Scott (1993) The Aboriginal Embassy, 1972. MA thesis, ANU

Rose, D. B. (1984) 'The Captain Cook Saga', *Australian Aboriginal Studies* 2:24–39

——(1988) 'Exploring an Aboriginal Land Ethic', *Meanjin* 3:378–87

——(1991) *Hidden Histories*, Aboriginal Studies Press, Canberra

——(1992) *Dingo Makes Us Human*, CUP, Cambridge

Rosser, Bill (1985) *Dreamtime Nightmares*, AIAS, Canberra

Rowley, C. D. (1971) *Outcasts in White Australia*, ANU Press, Canberra

Rowse, Tim (1993) *After Mabo: Interpreting Indigenous Traditions*, MUP

Rusden, G. W. (1883) *History of Australia*, 3 vols, Chapman & Hall, London

Sahlins, Marshall (1987) *Islands of History*, University of Chicago Press, Chicago

Sanders, N. (1985) 'Selling Woomera: Weapons Testing and Nuclear Defence in the 50s and 60s', *Intervention* 18:6–39

Sanders, N. (1986) 'The Hot Rock in the Cold War: Uranium in the 1950s', in A. Curthoys and J. Merritt, eds, *Better Dead than Red: Australia's First Cold War*, vol. 2, Allen & Unwin, Sydney, pp. 155–69

Smith, Bernard (1980) 'The Spectre of Trugannni'. The 1980 Boyer Lectures, ABC

Smith, Len (1975) The Aboriginal Population of Australia. PhD thesis, University of NSW

Stanner, W. E. H. (1956) 'The Dreaming', in T. A. G. Hungerford, ed., *Australian Signposts*. F. W. Cheshire, Melbourne. Republished in Edwards 1987:225–36

Swain, T. (1993) *A Place for Strangers: Towards a History of Australian Aboriginal Being*, CUP, Cambridge

——and D. B. Rose, eds (1988) *Aboriginal Australians and Christian Missions*, Australian Association for the Study of Religions, Adelaide

Thelen, David (1989) 'Memory and American History', *American Journal of History* :1119–24

Thompson, E. P. (1986) *The Making of the English Working Class*, Penguin, London

——(1993) *Customs in Common*, Penguin, London

Thompson, Peter (1993) *Boobera Lagoon: Environmental Audit: Aboriginal Cultural Heritage*. Report to NSW Dept Conservation and Land Management, Western Heritage Group

Tobin, Peter (1972) *Aboriginal Land Rights in NSW: Demands, Law and Policy*, Abschol, Sydney

Topliss, Helen (1985) 'Tom Roberts' Aboriginal Portraits', in Donaldson and Donaldson 1985:110–36

Toyne, P. and D. Vachon (1984) *Growing Up the Country*, Penguin, Melbourne

Troy, J. (1993) *King Plates: A History of Aboriginal Gorgets*, Aboriginal Studies Press, Canberra

Victorian Aboriginal Advancement League (1985) *Victims or Victors? The Story of the Victorian Aborigines Advancement League*, Hyland House, Melbourne

Vansina, Jan (1985) *Oral Tradition as History*, James Currey, London

Waterson, Duncan (1968) *Squatter, Selector and Storekeeper: a History of the Darling Downs*, SUP

Webb, Stephen (1984) 'Intensification, population and social change in south-eastern Australia: the skeletal evidence', *Aboriginal History* 8(2):154–72

White, Richard (1981) *Inventing Australia: Images and Identity 1688–1980*, Allen & Unwin, Sydney

Wilkie, Meredith (1985) *Aboriginal Land Rights in NSW*, Alternative Publishing Co-operative Ltd, Sydney

Williams, M. (1975) 'More and Smaller is Better: Australian Rural Settlement 1788–1914', in J. M. Powell and M. Williams, eds, *Australian Space, Australian Time: Geographical Perspectives*, OUP, Melbourne

Williams, N. (1986) *The Yolngu and their Land: A System of Land Tenure and the Fight for its Recognition*, AIAS, Canberra

——and E. Hunn, eds (1982) *Resource Managers: North American and Australian Hunter Gatherers*, AIAS, Canberra

Willis, Anne-Marie (1993) *Illusions of Identity*, Hale & Iremonger, Sydney

Wilmot, E. (1987) *Pemulwuy: The Rainbow Warrior*, Weldon, Sydney

Wise, T. (1985) *The Self-Made Anthropologist*, Allen & Unwin, Sydney

Wolpe, Harold (1975) 'The Theory of Internal Colonialism: the South African case', in I. Oxaal, T. Barnett and D. Booth, eds, *Beyond the Sociology of Development*, Routledge & Kegan Paul, London, pp. 229–52

Woolmington, Jo (1991) 'The "Assimilation" years in a Country Town', *Aboriginal History* 15(1):25–37

Index